The City in South Asi

The macro-region of South Asia – including Bangladesh, India, Nepal, Pakistan, and Sri Lanka – today supports one of the world's greatest concentrations of cities, but as James Heitzman argues in the first comprehensive treatment of urban South Asia spanning 50 centuries, this has been the case for at least 5,000 years.

The book begins with the origins of the Harappan or 'Indus Valley' Civilization and moves through a discussion of the 'second' urbanization beginning in the Ganga River basin before exploring the colonial city until 1947, the post-Independence city and the explosive growth of today.

Four themes run through the entire work: the economic bases of urbanization, the built environment, the fabric of daily life, and multi-city networks. With case studies in each chapter focusing on specific cities and numerous maps, photographs, and tables, this book provides the basis for a detailed understanding of dozens of sites as well as regional growth processes extending over centuries.

With a strong emphasis on the production of space and periodic excursions into literature, art and architecture, religion and public culture, this interdisciplinary study is a valuable text for students and scholars interested in comparative history, urban studies, and the social sciences.

James Heitzman is the author of *Gifts of Power: Lordship in an Early Indian State* and *Network City: Planning the Information Society in Bangalore*. He currently divides his time between Davis, California and Bangalore, India, where he is co-founder of Nagara, a trust devoted to urban affairs.

Asia's Transformations
Edited by Mark Selden
Binghamton and Cornell Universities, USA

The books in this series explore the political, social, economic and cultural consequences of Asia's transformations in the twentieth and twenty-first centuries. The series emphasizes the tumultuous interplay of local, national, regional and global forces as Asia bids to become the hub of the world economy. While focusing on the contemporary, it also looks back to analyse the antecedents of Asia's contested rise.

This series comprises several strands:

Asia's Transformations aims to address the needs of students and teachers, and the titles will be published in hardback and paperback. Titles include:

Debating Human Rights
Critical essays from the United States and Asia
Edited by Peter Van Ness

Hong Kong's History
State and society under colonial rule
Edited by Tak-Wing Ngo

Japan's Comfort Women
Sexual slavery and prostitution during World War II and the US occupation
Yuki Tanaka

Opium, Empire and the Global Political Economy
Carl A. Trocki

Chinese Society
Change, conflict and resistance
Edited by Elizabeth J. Perry and Mark Selden

Mao's Children in the New China
Voices from the Red Guard generation
Yarong Jiang and David Ashley

Remaking the Chinese State
Strategies, society and security
Edited by Chien-min Chao and Bruce J. Dickson

Korean Society
Civil society, democracy and the state
Edited by Charles K. Armstrong

The Making of Modern Korea
Adrian Buzo

The Resurgence of East Asia
500, 150 and 50 Year perspectives
Edited by Giovanni Arrighi, Takeshi Hamashita and Mark Selden

Chinese Society, second edition
Change, conflict and resistance
Edited by Elizabeth J. Perry and Mark Selden

Ethnicity in Asia
Edited by Colin Mackerras

The Battle for Asia
From decolonization to globalization
Mark T. Berger

State and Society in 21st Century China
Edited by Peter Hays Gries and Stanley Rosen

Japan's Quiet Transformation
Social change and civil society in the 21st century
Jeff Kingston

Confronting the Bush Doctrine
Critical views from the Asia-Pacific
Edited by Mel Gurtov and Peter Van Ness

China in War and Revolution, 1895–1949
Peter Zarrow

The Future of US–Korean Relations
The imbalance of power
Edited by John Feffer

Working in China
Ethnographies of labor and workplace transformations
Edited by Ching Kwan Lee

Asia's Great Cities
Each volume aims to capture the heartbeat of the contemporary city from multiple perspectives emblematic of the authors own deep familiarity with the distinctive faces of the city, its history, society, culture, politics and economics, and its evolving position in national, regional and global frameworks. While most volumes emphasize urban developments since the Second World War, some pay close attention to the legacy of the longue durée in shaping the contemporary. Thematic and comparative volumes address such themes as urbanization, economic and financial linkages, architecture and space, wealth and power, gendered relationships, planning and anarchy, and ethnographies in national and regional perspective. Titles include:

Asia.com is a series which focuses on the ways in which new information and communication technologies are influencing politics, society and culture in Asia. Titles include:

Literature and Society is a series that seeks to demonstrate the ways in which Asian Literature is influenced by the politics, society and culture in which it is produced. Titles include:

Routledge Studies in Asia's Transformations is a forum for innovative new research intended for a high-level specialist readership, and the titles will be available in hardback only. Titles include:

* Now available in paperback

Critical Asian Scholarship is a series intended to showcase the most important individual contributions to scholarship in Asian Studies. Each of the volumes presents a leading Asian scholar addressing themes that are central to his or her most significant and lasting contribution to Asian studies. The series is committed to the rich variety of research and writing on Asia, and is not restricted to any particular discipline, theoretical approach or geographical expertise.

The City in South Asia

James Heitzman

Routledge
Taylor & Francis Group

LONDON AND NEW YORK

First published 2008
by Routledge
2 Park Square, Milton Park, Abingdon, Oxon OX14 4RN

Simultaneously published in the USA and Canada
by Routledge
270 Madison Ave, New York, NY 10016

*Routledge is an imprint of the Taylor & Francis Group,
an informa business*

Transferred to Digital Printing 2009

© 2008 Edited by James Heitzman

Typeset in Times New Roman by Keyword Group Ltd

British Library Cataloguing in Publication Data
A catalogue record for this book is available
from the British Library

Library of Congress Cataloging-in-Publication Data
Heitzman, James, 1950–
    The City in South Asia / James Heitzman.
        p. cm.
    Includes bibliographical references.
    ISBN 978-0-415-34355-8 (hardback) – ISBN 978-0-203-48328-2
    (ebook) 1. Cities and towns–South Asia–History 2. City planning–South
    Asia–History. 3. Vernacular architecture–South Asia–History. 4. South
    Asia–History. I. Title.
    HT147.S64H45 2008
    307.760954–dc22   2007036824

ISBN13: 978-0-415-34355-8 (hbk)
ISBN13: 978-0-415-57426-6 (pbk)

ISBN10: 0-415-34355-0 (hbk)
ISBN10: 0-415-57426-9 (pbk)

Contents

Illustrations

Tables

Figures

Maps

Acknowledgements

This book is primarily the result of a library project, but it would have been impossible even to contemplate it without the numerous periods of fieldwork and site exploration that I have carried out during the last 25 years. I offer my thanks to all the informants and colleagues who have helped me to understand the dozens of places I have visited, and then inserted in this work. I also offer thanks to the many scholars who have critiqued my research efforts over the years and thus moved me toward this book, especially B. D. Chattopadhyaya, Christoph Emmerich, and V. Geetha, who viewed earlier drafts of chapters. Gregory Possehl provided an early version of the map of Harappan sites. John M. Fritz provided me with a digital copy of the Survey of India sheet for the Hampi area. Sunil Sharma provided valuable insights on the genre of Urdu poetry called 'The City's Misfortune,' or *shahr ashob*. Linda Matheson helped me locate materials on the ready-made garment industry of Bangladesh. I owe a series of small debts to the staff at the interlibrary loan office at the University of California-Davis, who provided much of the logistical support for accessing relevant literature and maps.

Thanks to the following individuals and institutions for giving permission to include in this book their textual and graphic materials. Balan Nambiar provided the cover photograph of his sculpture entitled *Poetry in Architecture*. Niels Gutschow gave me a copy of the aerial photograph of Bhaktapur that appeared in his 1982 book, *Stadtraum und Ritual der newarischen Städte im Kathmandu-Tal*. Vandana Sinha of the Center for Art and Archaeology Photo Archives, American Institute of Indian Studies, Gurgeon, provided a high-resolution image of a sculpture from Sanchi. Columbia University Press allowed reproduction of lines from R. Parthasarathy's 1993 translation of *The Cilappatikaram of Ilanko Atikal*. Oxford University Press allowed reproduction of lines from Vatsyayana Mallanaga's *Kamasutra*, translated by Wendy Doniger and Sudhir Kakar (2002). Shamsur Rahman Faruqi and Frances W. Pritchett allowed the inclusion of verses they translated from an eighteenth-century *shahr ashob* poem (http://www.columbia.edu/itc/mealac/pritchett/00fwp/published/txt_nazir_carnival.html). The British Library provided a reproduction of Sir Charles D'Oyly's drawing of Clive Street that appeared in his *Views of Calcutta and its Environs* (1848). Joanne Kirkpatrick sent a digital file for a photograph from her 2003 CD book, *Transports of Delight: The Riksha Arts of Bangladesh*.

I must acknowledge the patience and support given by audiences at Jawaharlal Nehru University, the University of Heidelberg, and the University of California-Berkeley, who heard me discuss early phases of this project. Additional venues for my presentations on parts of this book included: the Southern Center for International Studies in Atlanta; the Institute of Urban Regional Development Studies at East China Normal University in Shanghai; the Institute for Social and Economic Change in Bangalore; the 2004 Annual South Asia Conference at the University of Wisconsin-Madison; and the 2007 Small Cities Conference organized at Ball State University in Muncie, Indiana.

I am very grateful to the series editor, Mark Selden, and my editor at Routledge, Stephanie Rogers, for their confidence in this project and their support during its final phase, which lasted longer than expected. I owe my greatest debt to Smriti Srinivas, my comrade in urban exploration, who has provided pointed criticism of this entire book and contributed ideas that made it more readable.

Preface

Two episodes led to the production of this book. The first occurred in the late 1990s, when I was teaching in the History Department at Georgia State University and was planning a course syllabus on global urbanization for the World History Program. It was not difficult to locate source material pertaining to cities in the ancient 'Western' world, in Sumer or Greece or Rome, for example, and written for general audiences. Following Paul Wheatley's publication of *The Pivot of the Four Quarters* in 1971, there were lots of interesting things to read about ancient East Asia as well. The study of early Mesoamerica always revolved around the urban question, with innumerable archaeological studies and interesting maps. If one was interested in 'medieval' urbanization, there was no shortage of materials about the European city and indeed cities from most world areas, and as for 'modern' cities, the literature was gargantuan. But in all these fields South Asia seemed poorly represented in the literature that was readily accessible to students. I found numerous pieces dealing with specific issues or places, but they would require a large effort of contextualization before they were digestible to those not already familiar with the geography and languages of South Asia.

The second episode occurred in 2003 when I was actually preparing a course on South Asian urbanization for the History Department at the University of California-Davis, and I began accessing web sites connected with 'global cities,' a field that had evolved in part from the theorization of world cities by John Friedmann and Goetz Wolff (1982) and, later, by Saskia Sassen (1991) and others. The global cities approach, a critical analysis of urban hierarchies under the conditions of late capitalism, had lots to say about Europe, the United States and Japan, but quite literally left a blank between Istanbul and Singapore. The approach, however fruitful, was not capable of addressing all aspects of contemporary urbanization; its lacunae loomed large to someone who spent a lot of time in South Asia and was witnessing an explosion of urban construction and demographic growth that rested on deep historical roots. I came to believe that the quandary here resembled that facing my students. Professional scholars were not getting access to relevant materials that they could build into urban theory; they had no window through which they could synthesize materials from the South Asian macro-region.

The causes lie, in part, in the colonial and post-colonial treatment of the city within South Asia. The British perception that the empire they inherited in the nineteenth century exhibited characteristics of social breakdown supported the thesis of urban stagnation that accompanied, implicitly or explicitly, colonial-period understandings of urban history. The (urban-based) nationalist concentration on the mobilization of the masses, fueled by Mohandas K. Gandhi's fascination with an anarchist, decentralized rural future, intersected after Independence with planning initiatives of the nation-state and a transnational field of development that aimed primarily at the rural environment – even as cities were expanding quickly. Under these circumstances, although administrators and researchers expended much effort on urban issues, their published output was often laden with the language of particular locations or managerial problems and framed within alternative social science disciplines. It was, for example, only in 1979 that the Urban History Association of India began as an independent organization, following a seminar on 'Urban History in India' at Guru Nanak Dev University in Amritsar. And it was only in the early 1990s, as liberalization took hold in India, that questions of the urban future began to take center stage in public discourse. Until now we have not seen a synthetic treatment of the vast sweep of South Asian urbanization – a desideratum for the consolidation of an intellectual field.

Thus it was that I resolved to address the needs of readers outside South Asia and also the scholars within South Asia who were rapidly consolidating the multi-disciplinary field of urban studies by creating this volume, which the editors at Routledge have included within their series on Great Asian Cities. This book is designed to provide for experts and non-experts an accessible but scholarly survey of a macro-region that today, as throughout history, is home to one-fifth of the world's population and includes one of the world's great concentrations of urban sites. I acknowledge immediately that the task may seem impossible, given the 8,000 years and multiple regions that this work must address, and I must acknowledge as well the many attempts during recent decades to present synthetic – but ultimately partial – perspectives within this field. My ambitions here are as follows: whereas my colleagues have produced studies on periods of several hundred or even several thousand years, this book covers the complete chronological range; whereas previous volumes have compiled anthologies of case studies by multiple scholars in an attempt to retain disciplinary integrity and also provide breadth, this book distills those efforts into a single voice; and whereas most scholarship on South Asia since 1947 divides urban studies according to national boundaries, this book treats the entire macro-region throughout. As is always the case in projects of this type, the result may seem inadequate at precisely those points where the reader is most familiar with the subject, but I beg a consideration of the work as a comprehensive treatment, before one dismisses the forest for the trees. In any case, as I have often said to my students, our intellectual task is to create the conditions for the abolition of our work, and I hope that this attempt at a comprehensive viewpoint may spur my colleagues on to more exciting synthetic projects in the future.

For the present, the goal is to provide for students and professionals alike the missing window to a field, complete with bibliographic tools that may allow backward chaining for those interested in particular issues.

My willingness to chart this gigantic terrain, or indeed my ability to begin, stems from the peculiarities of my career, which prevented immersion in a specific chronotope and reinforced a trans-disciplinary inclination. At an early stage I was interested in the political economy of ancient Buddhism, when my penchant for spatial analysis first came into play, and I became a lifelong student of 'second urbanization' archaeology in South Asia (Heitzman 1980, 2007). Later I worked on the epigraphy of South Indian cities within the context of state formation and religious institutions (Heitzman 1997, 2001a, 2001b, 2004; Heitzman and Rajagopal 2004). Involvement with Information Studies brought me to the study of contemporary Bangalore, the 'Silicon Valley' of India, and the relationship between regional development, cities, and globalization (Heitzman 2004; Heitzman and Srinivas 2005; Walcott and Heitzman 2006). Through these efforts I not only avoided the pleasures and pitfalls of a single department, but managed through my comparative drive to strangely qualify myself as that most dangerous of historians, the scholar of multiple periods.

Four interrelated themes run through this book:

1   The economic bases of urbanization: for older periods, the interactions between the environment and production or exchange allowing the concentration of population at specific sites; for more recent periods, the articulation of industrialization and capital flows with the social and physical organization of urban space.
2   The planning of the built environment: the relationship between models of social organization or architectural norms and the physical organization of settlements; the agencies responsible for effecting urban design or directing the allocation of space.
3   Living in the city: The occupational, class, caste, gender, and cultural bases for the differentiation of urban populations; the relationships between socio-cultural complexes and issues of urban management.
4   Multi-city networks: The processes producing regional and multi-regional interaction spaces and the roles of individual cities within those spaces, leading toward an understanding of globalization.

Each chapter presents several case studies that exemplify one or more of these themes and demonstrate the interaction between actors and changes in the built environment over time. The chapters march along mostly in chronological order, although the organizing principle of Chapter Two departs a bit from this framework. The chapters are modular, in the sense that each could stand on its own, but they also follow thematic threads through multiple periods. Within this framework I have attempted to balance tales of the largest sites with perspectives on multi-layered secondary cities and towns. The strategy has allowed the presentation of continuous histories for a number of major and some smaller places, but I must apologize if many deserving cities have necessarily received less attention.

On a bibliographic note, unless employing an older source for relevant graphics or empirical data, I have generally referred to source material with publication dates after 1980, expecting that those interested in specific questions will find earlier relevant materials in the sources sections of later works. I have also attempted to insert within this book's bibliography, as often as possible, titles that provide the broadest views of sub-disciplines. These limitations, along with the obviously personalized quality of this research, produce a large bibliography that is in no sense comprehensive or complete, and which never presents the full range of the work carried out by the scholars listed there. The mammoth effort of compiling a comprehensive bibliography on South Asian urbanization awaits another's hand.

I have made an effort to include on the maps in each chapter all of the cities mentioned in that chapter's text. I have often referred to current provinces or states of the contemporary nations in South Asia when contextualizing those cities within regions, even when such a reference would be, in a strict sense, anachronistic. The reader who is unfamiliar with the modern provinces and states may benefit from consulting readily available maps on the Internet.

1 The ancient heritage

In 1982 I attended a scholarly conference in the city of Madurai where historians delivered professional papers on the study of early South India. One of the papers concerned Lemuria, described as a continent that once existed south of Kanyakumari, the southernmost point in India, but which sank beneath the sea in prehistoric times. Although this concept seemed a bit far-fetched to me, there was no difference between the audience's public reception of this paper and that accorded to the other presentations at this conference; everyone treated it as just another problem in the 'normal science' of the historical discipline. Subsequent exposures to Lemuria revealed that the idea surfaced among nineteenth-century geologists attempting to explain global distribution of paleo-species through hypothetical land bridges, then enjoyed a brief currency among early ethnographers interested in the original homeland of *homo sapiens*, and finally became transformed during the twentieth century into a primordial land whose inhabitants could be accessed through spiritualist channeling. In Tamil Nadu, however, the existence of this lost world has achieved the status of official history. As the continent of Kumarikantam, it has appeared in the curriculums of state-run Tamil-language schools, served as the subject matter of comments in the state legislature and a film funded by the state government, and generated a substantial body of literature that has described and mapped it in great detail. Sumati Ramaswami, in her study entitled *The Lost Land of Lemuria* (2004), contextualizes the survival of this fabulous land, inaccessible now because of oceanic catastrophe, as an exercise in the modern productivity of loss, a re-enchantment of a disenchanted reality, an attempt by subaltern groups to reclaim center stage within an altered construction of the past.

As a land of hunters and gatherers living in a state of nature or as a bounteous land of farms, fields and mountains, Kumarikantam would conjure the sensibility of nostalgia typical of lost utopias. But it is much more: it is the source of urban life. Passing references in the two-thousand-year-old Tamil Sangam literature and later commentaries describe the compilation of the earliest Tamil literary corpus in the Madurai we know today but mention also that two earlier compilations had occurred in cities named 'southern' Madurai (Tenmadurai) and Kapatapuram, which disappeared under the sea. Heroic efforts of the Pandyan kings preserved some of the advanced knowledge produced in these early metropolises, these centers of trade and industry, and transmitted fragments of language and culture to posterity in historical times. Kumarikantam is not simply the homeland of the entire human race but the heartland of cities and thus civilization, which retained a tenuous hold in Tamil Nadu while spreading throughout the world. The 'scientific' character of these assertions receives support from regular references to the (now discarded) geology of sunken continents, more recently supplemented by global warming and the example of the 2004 tsunami, and archaeological discoveries of submerged structures just offshore at the sites of Pumpuhar and Mahabalipuram (the latter revealed by the tsunami). If only more scientific research were devoted to underwater exploration off the southern coast of India we would discover more clues to the lost continent and thus prove the validity of the textual references in early Tamil literature! In this sense the Kumarikantam phenomenon resembles the lost continent of Atlantis – site of another super-urbanized and now-lost civilization – and, closer to home, the lost port of Dwaraka, the home of Krishna according to North Indian Sanskrit texts, where recent discoveries of underwater structures have stimulated paroxysms of cultural pride.

The more prosaic treatment of early urbanization in South Asia presented in this chapter traces permanent settlements going back about 8,000 years and brings the story of the city up to about 1,000 years ago. The early phases of the discussion here will please, I am afraid, only professional archaeologists and historians who describe urbanization as a phenomenon appearing about 2,500 BCE and known only through its physical remains located primarily in Pakistan and northwestern India. The chapter then examines a 'second' urbanization that became consolidated by about 500 BCE and became the basis for all subsequent urban forms in the subcontinent. This second urbanization peaked just after the beginning of the Common Era and, although attenuated in some regions by the fifth century, became the foundation for a reorganized urban system connected with the growth of regional kingdoms and an expansion of Indian Ocean trade. By the tenth century, at the latest, this system underwent a significant amplification and slowly evolved into the substratum of today's gigantic urban configurations. The chronological framework presented here will hopefully inform those interested in evaluating the historicity of lost cities in South Asia, whether they lie under the sea or, like Ayodhya, on the land.

Archaeology, literature, and early cities

The discerning traveler through the northern plains of South Asia may notice the periodic appearance of mounds amid cultivated fields or near (sometimes under) villages and towns and, in a moment of reflection, ask why these anomalous features of higher elevation should exist within a region of relatively low relief. In many cases, these hillocks are the result of human activity; they are what archaeologists in the Arabic-speaking world call *tells*, consisting of the accumulated debris of many human generations living on one site, pulling down the decaying walls of old mud-brick homes, mixing them with accumulated debris and building new houses above them. They are the remains of central places – villages, towns, and cities – that were important to people in the more distant past.

Few appreciate the antiquity of the agrarian and urban settlements represented by these mute mounds which people today plough and plant with crops, pillage for soil and bricks, or tread when they cross their doorsteps. Even the first modern historians of South Asia, while cognizant of the archaeological material lying near at hand, subordinated physical culture to textual analysis. During the nineteenth century, when British scholars oversaw the assembly of the historical disciplines, the model for archaeological reconstruction was to begin with references in textual sources and then correlate them with information gleaned through ground surveys and excavations. The most important chronological baselines were the ministries of Gautama, who established Buddhism, and his immediate predecessor, Mahavira, who promoted Jainism; information gleaned from the texts associated with their religious traditions suggested that these men lived around the middle of the first millennium BCE. The first Director of the Archaeological Survey of India, Alexander Cunningham (1814–93), enjoyed considerable success in following references from such textual materials, or from travel accounts such as that of the seventh-century Chinese monk, Xuan Zang, in order to identify specific mounds with places appearing in literary sources. The early results of this research clearly indicated that a society of considerable urban complexity and sophistication existed in what are today northern India, Pakistan, and Bangladesh about 2,500 years ago.

The Vedas, which were originally hymns recited by sacrificial priests during fire sacrifices and which were transmitted in purely oral form almost unchanged for many generations, provide an alternative avenue for understanding the early history of South Asia. Comparative linguistics in the nineteenth century suggested that the Vedic corpus that has come down to us in written format may date back to a period between 1,500 and 1,000 BCE. The world presented in the Vedas, located mostly in the Punjab region of India and Pakistan, is distinctly non-urban, although the hymns contain references to impermanent strongholds of mud, stone and timber stormed during military conflicts (Rau 1973). Various bodies of texts viewed as appendages of the Vedas, such as the early Upanishads composed in the early-first millennium BCE, measure wealth in cattle and do little to change our vision of northern India as a complex but non-urbanized world of village farming communities and forest.

The Epics called the *Mahabharata* and the *Ramayana* – the former (like Homer's *Iliad*) describing a great internal war between two coalitions of aristocratic warriors, the latter (like Homer's *Odyssey*) describing the exile and adventures of a warrior prince – provide deep insights into the culture and social organization of northern India and Pakistan as far back as the late-second millennium. We must exercise caution, however, in our analysis of these tales transmitted orally for hundreds of years, full of interpolations and anachronisms, and without archaeological evidence to corroborate their standardized presentation of cities (Lal 2002). The main characters in the Epics pursue power, glory, honor and pleasure rather than the control of more mundane resources gathered from the agrarian economy or commerce. The heroes value portable, disposable wealth: prestige goods made from metals or other rare items obtained through extractive activities; the skilled services of attached laborers and dependent women; animals such as elephants or, more typically, cattle. The problems of administration typically lie deep in the background, except for the Santi Parvan of the *Mahabharata*, where the dying Bhishma, resting on a bed of arrows, dictates a managerial treatise that is obviously a later insertion. The religious rituals supported by the warrior (*kshatriya*) elite, enacted by *brahmana* ritual specialists, do not occur within permanent structures dedicated to deities but take the archaic form of sacrifices performed within temporary, consecrated enclosures. Political organization, described by historian Romila Thapar (1984) as lineage rather than state and by George Erdosy (1995: 99) as 'simple chiefdoms,' revolves around specific named centers. When the Pandava heroes of the *Mahabharata* break off from the main lineage of the Kurus to found their own kingdom, they establish their capital at Indraprastha, described in glowing terms as a shining metropolis. Yet when their rivals invite the Pandavas back to the original capital, Hastinapura, for a gambling festival, the gaming takes place in a more standard venue – an ornately decorated, temporary pillared hall assembled from wood, textiles, and other perishable materials. And everywhere we find the nearby forest, the site of so many royal adventures and the regular destination of exiles. When Rama, the hero of the *Ramayana*, departs from his capital of Ayodhya (portrayed as another metropolis by the bard Valmiki) he and his companions quickly find themselves in the forest and they remain there during wanderings through central and southern India except for sojourns in the hermitages of ascetics, the rude fortifications of various animal kingdoms, or the fantastic capital of the demonic enemy, Ravana. The heroes and the sages of the epics live in a society exhibiting technological sophistication, occupational specialization and status differentiation, but we might question the scale of urbanization in a world where the omnipresent wilderness, the struggle between legitimate settlement and untamed nature remain primary narrative devices.

Basing their analysis primarily on textual corpuses and associated archaeological surveys, scholars at the beginning of the twentieth century viewed the urban history of South Asia as beginning around the time of the Buddha preceded by a gestation period of indeterminate length shading into a semi-nomadic mode of subsistence during the second millennium BCE. But this perception was about to change.

The first urbanization: Harappan civilization

Explorations in what is now Pakistan during the late-nineteenth century conducted by scholars around early Buddhist monuments or by construction crews obtaining building materials yielded stone seals featuring animal motifs and an unrecognized script. The first structured excavations during the 1920s at Harappa and then at Mohenjo-daro yielded artifacts that resembled items uncovered during contemporary excavations in Iraq (old Sumer) dated to the third millennium BCE.

These discoveries stimulated the growth of an entirely new field in South Asian archaeology dedicated to the study of what came to be known as the Harappan (after one of its most important sites), Indus Valley, or Sindhu-Sarasvati Civilization (after the two major rivers along which its sites clustered). The nomenclature of civilization applied to this extensive archaeological complex derives not only from its literate or proto-literate character but also from the indisputably urban character of its major sites.

Excavations during the 1970s and 1980s at Mehrgarh in Baluchistan provided convincing proof that the rise of agriculture and village life, evolving into more complicated forms of urbanization, was not the result of diffusion from the west but originated in the creativity of South Asian peoples (Jarrige *et al.* 1995). Mehrgarh lies at the foot of the Bolan Pass, along an ancient trade route allowing travel to the highlands of Afghanistan and Iran and also to the plains of southern Pakistan, with relatively easy access to a variety of ecological niches. Archaeologists discovered here a continuous record of habitation dating back to a pre-ceramic culture in the early-seventh millennium BCE which makes this site contemporaneous with Çatal Hüyük in Turkey (Mellaart 1967) and Jericho in Palestine (Kenyon 1970), several of the world's oldest known settlements. At that point the inhabitants of Mehrgarh were already constructing permanent structures of mud bricks including houses and storage facilities designed to preserve barley, gathered by semi-nomadic groups using flint sickles and relying on hunting for part of their subsistence. The subsequent story of this site includes the evolution of increasingly sophisticated ceramic technologies, domesticated animals and more permanent settlement structures. By the late-fifth millennium the inhabitants utilized copper, manufactured wheel-thrown pots, and produced artistically fired beads. By the fourth-third millennium BCE, permanent settlements and cultivation, possibly with irrigation facilities, had replaced traces of seasonal habitation. Wheat and grapes were important crops. Traces of large-scale pottery production suggest the presence of a multi-site marketing system. Large numbers of terracotta human forms appear in and around house sites. Extensive terracing and large retaining walls indicate a movement toward monumental public architecture. Trans-regional trade seems to have been important at Mehrgarh even from its earliest phases (revealed by the presence of shell ornaments coming from the ocean, 500 kilometers distant). The later phases of occupation link directly with nearby sites such as Nausharo yielding Harappan artifacts, thus providing a sequence from the very beginnings of settled life through the first urban urbanization in South Asia.

Archaeologists have identified hundreds of sites where pre-Harappan village farming communities developed the complete range of technologies (including traces of monumental walls) that would give rise to Harappan urbanization. In addition to Mehrgarh four such artifact assemblages have been identified, each associated with their primary sites: Amri and Nal; Kot Diji; Damb Sadaat; Sothi and Siswal (see Map 1). Investigators now describe a pre-Harappan period beginning in the late-fourth millennium BCE, when changes were occurring within multiple cultures that prepared the ground for the complexity of the mature Harappan

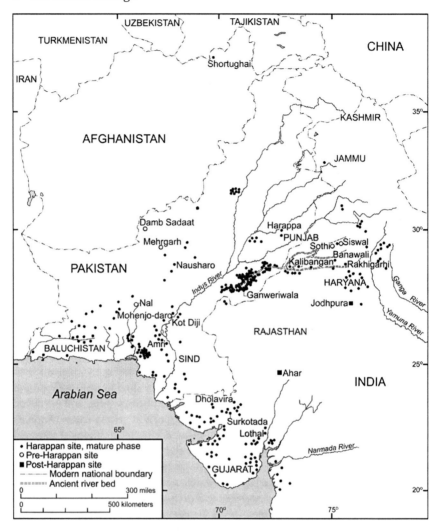

Map 1 Sites of the mature Harappan phase, ca. 2600–1900 BCE. Adapted from Possehl 2002.

phase between 2600 and 1900 BCE. The transition to the mature phase seems to have occurred rapidly, perhaps within only a few generations (Possehl 1999; 2002: 50–3).

More than 1,000 sites display the cultural characteristics that we associate with the mature Harappan Civilization. They exist in all parts of Pakistan south of Kashmir, in Gujarat, Haryana, Jammu, Punjab, and Rajasthan in northwestern India, and even along the Amu Darya in northern Afghanistan. Most of the locations remain small, constituting village sites; if the average size of settlements during the early Harappan phase was 4.51 hectares, it increased to only 7.25 hectares during the mature phase (Possehl 1999: 555). The largest sites, however, are quite big. They include Mohenjo-daro (with a city core of about 100 hectares, and suburbs possibly covering more than 200 hectares) in Sind; Harappa (more than 150 hectares) in the center of Pakistani Punjab; Dholavira (between 60 and 100 hectares) in Gujarat; Ganweriwala (82 hectares) in Pakistani Punjab near the border with Rajasthan; and Rakhigarhi (between 80 and 105 hectares) in Haryana (Smith 2006: 109).

The region called Cholistan, lying in the southeastern part of Pakistan's Punjab province, is among the most thoroughly explored regions of the Harappan civilization. Today this is an arid ecosystem, a northwestern extension of India's Thar Desert, but ground surveys and aerial photography reveal that a major river system once flowed here. Between 3,500 and 1,300 BCE there was enough water to support a flourishing complex of village farming communities evolving into a four-tier hierarchy of settlement sizes. During the first centuries of occupation, nomadic occupation roughly balanced the number of more permanent agricultural settlements. By the time of the early Harappan phase (3100–2500) permanent settlements comprised 92 percent of all extant sites while nomadic campsites had shrunk to only 7.5 percent. After 2500, during the mature phase, out of 174 identified sites (most of them small villages) 45 percent were purely industrial locations for the production of bricks, pottery or metal objects while 19 percent of habitation sites also included kilns for commodity production. During this phase Ganweriwala, the pinnacle of the settlement hierarchy, became two closely associated mounds, today rising to a maximum height of 8.5 meters above the plain. After 1900 there was a dramatic drop-off in the number of sites and purely industrial zones, suggesting that the settlement complex was collapsing with the disappearance of the river system (Mughal 1997). The Vedic hymns preserve several references to the existence and subsequent disappearance of the Sarasvati River, corroborating a theory of radical transformation in this ecosystem by about 1300. The Cholistan surveys reveal, therefore, a complete sequence: the rise of village farming communities; the elaboration of more complex settlement hierarchies; and occupational specialization leading to urban growth and subsequent decline.

Mohenjo-daro, perhaps the most important archaeological site in South Asia, excavated repeatedly since the 1920s (Marshall 1931), provides a detailed view of a primate city during the mature Harappan phase, including monumental constructions within a 'high' town or 'citadel' to the west, and habitation areas in a separate 'low' town of greater extent to the east. The northeastern portion of the citadel mound rises 13 meters above the plain and is the location of a Buddhist monastery dating from the early-first millennium CE that was constructed on the more ancient tell. Earlier British scholarship, never far from a military interpretive framework, described massive brickwork visible on the edges of the citadel as the remains of fortification walls (Wheeler 1968: 29–31, 40, 72–7). Hundreds of soundings on the mound have indicated, however, that its height is not part of a fortification scheme, nor is it simply the result of accumulated debris, but is a planned feature; before occupation occurred, a mobilized workforce had constructed massive retaining walls for a giant foundation that raised the bases of buildings 5 meters above a plain flooded regularly by the nearby Indus. The citadel mound has yielded the most impressive architectural remains – all constructed of mud or burnt bricks – found in any mature phase settlement. These include the Great Bath, perhaps the most photographed of all Harappan monuments: a watertight pool measuring 12 meters north-south and 7 meters east-west, capable of retaining 140 cubic meters of water. Water came from a well in a room on the east and outflow went through a drain consisting of a 1.8-meter-high drain roofed with a corbelled vault. The water was accessible by a stairway on the north side of the bath. Brick colonnades that probably supported a wooden superstructure, including screens or window frames, surrounded the bath. A public street enclosed the entire complex. The 'granary' to its west consisted of a foundation measuring 27 meters north to south and 50 meters east to west divided into 27 brick plinths, in nine rows north to south and three rows east to west separated by passageways, that once supported wooden pillars or beams. An 'assembly hall' or market in the southern part of the citadel mound featured 20 brick foundations arranged in four rows of five each. More public buildings seem to lie under the Buddhist monastery.

On the eastern mound or 'low' town, which also may have rested in part on a massive artificial foundation (Dales 1965: 148; Jansen 1978), the most extensive horizontal excavations of any Harappan site have revealed the plans of contiguous habitation blocks. Several boulevards running roughly north-south (including a wide thoroughfare named 'First Street' by the excavators) provided a means of walking directly through the entire settlement. Smaller, parallel lanes ran north-south for shorter distances, intersected by other smaller lanes running east-west – a generally cardinal orientation. Obvious differences in house sizes and layouts betoken distinct gradations in class or status. In the northeastern habitation block a large, coherent complex of rooms demonstrates an unusual sturdiness of construction, perhaps evidence of a major public building, while another complex was labeled a 'palace' by the excavator (Mackay 1938: 41–70, 148–51).

Building interiors were invisible from the street, but entrance to a household compound would present the visitor in some cases with a courtyard surrounded by rooms, or in other cases with a simple cooking and sleeping area in one or several rooms. The remarkable preservation of house walls suggests that windows, if present, existed high on the walls; examples of artworks showing windows indicate that wood may have been the primary component in window construction and ornamentation (Kenoyer 1998: 57–8). Roofs, undoubtedly flat, were probably constructed of wooden beams (spans seldom greater than 4 meters) and mud plaster. Some remains of stairways at this and other sites demonstrate that people had access to their roofs. There is clear evidence of delineated bathing areas within homes, especially some of the larger units; outside, carefully constructed brick drains running through public space intersected with pipes coming from homes to draw sewage out of the city and into sumps that could be dismantled for periodic cleaning (Jansen 1993). Water supply for the entire city came from an estimated 700 wells. With the possible exception of the elaborate drainage systems, the plan of the residential area at Mohenjo-daro and the hypothetical reconstruction of house architecture demonstrate close similarities to housing types still used in this part of the subcontinent.

The plan of Harappa, where excavations started slightly earlier than at Mohenjo-daro, includes an alignment of two main mounds (excluding the area of the modern village, which lies above another section of archaeological remains) on massive retaining walls and basements pierced on at least one side by a gate. At Harappa one finds another 'granary,' or two blocks of parallel brick basements that seem to have supported a wooden superstructure covering an area of 46 by 17 meters. At the site of Kalibangan along the bank of the former Ghaggar River, once again we find two distinct mounds: a heavily fortified section in the west measuring 120 by 240 meters, containing possible ceremonial platforms; and a separate, fortified area to the east measuring 240 by 360 meters encompassing habitation areas. If Harappan urbanization up to this point seems to demonstrate a standard plan, juxtaposing high-status public space in the west with a lower-status but differentiated population living in the east, town planning from other sites produces a more variegated pattern. At Dholavira, for example, a larger enclosing wall with bastion-flanked gateways encompassed a 'lower' town and a walled 'middle' town in turn flanked by a smaller, fortified 'castle' and adjoining 'bailey.' At the smaller sites of Banawali and Surkotada, a single outer fortification surrounded two subsidiary divisions separated by bastioned walls with gates. It appears, then, that the Harappans were concerned about issues of security and mobilized labor resources to establish spatial segregation within their settlements, but the architectural alignment varied widely from one site to the next. There were shared concerns, but not standard templates, in the careful planning of their towns (Chakrabarti 2004).

The economy of the mature Harappan phase rested on agriculture and animal husbandry. A crop package of wheat, barley, lentils, peas, chick peas, and flax was well developed by the late-third millennium BCE. Several species of millets that originated in Africa (sorghum or *jowar*, finger millet or *ragi*, pearl millet or *bajra*) seem to have reached South Asia by the early-second millennium BCE. Other millets and fruits, the Bactrian camel and the horse arrived from Central Asia. At most sites, a substantial proportion of the population must have made their livelihood raising sheep, goats, and cattle, or interacted with nomadic or semi-nomadic groups specializing in the care of animals (Weber and Belcher 2003).

The site of Lothal in Gujarat provides some clues concerning the organization of trade routes that made possible the movement of goods at the regional level or between South Asia and points west. This small center (4.8 hectares) seems to have served as a warehousing or trans-shipment point complete with an artificial harbor and quay. A seal found here came from Dilmun, the name used in Sumerian records for the area around Bahrain in the Persian Gulf. Sumerian sources describe trade with Dilmun but also mention Meluhha, a term denoting the Harappan cultural region. It seems that commercial groups from Meluhha settled down in Mesopotamia for extended periods during the late-third millennium.

Archaeological work in Oman and between Dubai and Abu Dhabi has found further evidence of Harappan traders on site and the direct borrowing of Harappan ceramic, metallurgical, and seal-cutting technologies around 2300 BCE. Meanwhile, on land routes, Shortugai in northern Afghanistan appears to have been a purely colonial project allowing Harappans access to the only known sources of lapis lazuli. The high level of artistry evident in the processing of luxury and functional items made from metal (gold, silver, copper-bronze, lead, electrum), semi-precious stones, and sea shells, often found hundreds of kilometers from the points of origin for their raw materials, testifies to the vibrancy of a manufacturing sector closely tied to wide-ranging commercial networks (Allchin, and Allchin 1997: 167–76; Tosi 1991). The large site of Dholavira, located on a rather unproductive island in the present Rann of Kutch, is best conceived as an entrepot linking traders to the regional economy of early Gujarat (Bisht 1989; Chitalwala 1993; Dhavalikar 1993). Terracotta models of ox-carts and graphic representations of riverboats, very similar to designs still in use, indicate control over the transportation of bulk goods.

During the mature Harappan phase a widespread standardization of technology, craft production, and administration occurred throughout the Harappan sphere of exchange. The concentration on water control and bathing in household construction (including intramural drains, vertical pipes, and chutes through walls to streets) and public drainage systems remained a defining feature of their urban planning. In regions where bricks were the main building material, builders almost universally applied size dimensions of 1:2:4. Widely distributed motifs appearing on pottery seem to have accompanied mass production for extended markets. The presence of a graduated series of weights, following in their lower denominations a binary system of 1, 2, 4, 8, 16, 32, etc., foreshadows a measuring system that enjoyed a very long history in South Asia and proves that a single means for conducting commercial transactions existed in multiple sites. Most important is the evolution of stamps decorated with geometric forms from the pre- and early Harappan phases into beautifully crafted seals that displayed detailed pictographs and a completely original script during the mature phase. Although 90 percent of the known 3,000 inscriptions come from Mohenjo-daro and Harappa (Allchin and Allchin 1997: 191–2), seals and clay seal impressions from many Harappan sites and from abroad demonstrate their widespread usefulness as commercial certificates. In some cases, the presence of obviously mythological or ritual scenes suggests that some seals had institutional or administrative uses. The remains of a signboard from Dholavira and a small collection of longer or cylindrical seals feature enough characters to suggest that the Harappan script was a functional representation of natural language, although part of it may have been an iconic system presenting logos, brands, or directional markers similar to highway signs today. In any case, the nature of the literary evidence consisting almost entirely of very short examples of script found on seals and impressions (perhaps in most cases representing the names of persons, organizations, or places) has frustrated attempts at decipherment. The combination of script and other types of standardization points toward a high degree of administrative control strongly suggestive of a state, or a grouping of city states, with clearly expansionist tendencies during the late-third millennium.

We can glimpse the daily lifestyles of the Harappans through the many personal artifacts they have left behind. Figurines of women and 'mother goddesses,' more common than male figurines, often display elaborate headdresses and hair ornaments, some common to many sites, others more limited in scope and perhaps indicating differences in status or ethnicity. Some women wore turbans or head bands, others tied their hair in a double bun at the back or displayed long braids. Necklaces, chokers, and belts accompanied short skirts. Adult women wore anklets of steatite and bangles on their left arms; the presence of truncated cylindrical stone amulets, worn around the neck, may indicate married status. Men with high-status demeanors, like the so-called 'priest-king' of Mohenjo-daro, wore full-body robes draped over the shoulder with woven or printed designs. Men, like women, pulled their long hair into a double bun behind the head and tied it with microbead hair ornaments. Long braids, bangles, and skirts were common to men as well as women. Images of children include small terracotta images perhaps used in votive rites. Other images represent children playing with toys. We have quite a few examples of their toys in the form of terracotta tops and clay marbles, miniature cooking vessels and furniture, and numerous figurines of domesticated animals (bovines, sheep, goats, ducks, rabbits, a fighting dog with projecting collar, a begging dog with collar, bears with collars, or performing monkeys) and wild animals such as elephants, rhinoceroses, and tigers that seem to have lived in Pakistan during the third millennium. The unsophisticated clay disks of various sizes found in many locations resemble the pieces used in a game called *pittu* today, in which one player throws a ball to knock down a pile and another player must stack the disks in sequence by size before chasing everyone else in a game of tag. Adults indulged in more complex games using cubical dice exactly like today's versions or gaming boards that required the movement of game pieces or tokens (Kenoyer 1998: 122–67).

Presented with an urban society demonstrating such sophistication and expansive energy, we must wonder why Harappan culture failed to expand further or develop even more complex forms. The archaeological record reveals a major shift around 1900 BCE (when long-distance contacts with Mesopotamia seem to have ceased) away from larger urban sites and toward smaller settlements. The strong centralizing tendencies of the mature Harappan, represented by the writing system, standardized weights, and common ceramic styles, disappeared. In this 'localization era' (Kenoyer 1991: 370–2) a variety of artistic styles asserted themselves. Earlier catastrophic explanations for the end of urbanization that proposed human conquest or widespread geo-morphological change have given way to more nuanced regional perspectives. A hydrological explanation for Cholistan's eclipse is convincing but the simultaneous extinction of sites in Sind and Pakistani Punjab must stem primarily from socio-economic causes. The late Harappan phase also witnessed an increase in Indian settlements, indicating the possibility of major movements of population. An earlier survey in Haryana and Punjab revealed up to 160 mature-phase sites and 149 later sites; a more recent survey in Haryana alone revealed 71 mature-phase and 275 later locations, plus 130 in Uttar Pradesh (Francfort 1985: 61–2; Allchin and Allchin 1997: 214–15).

What was the urban legacy of the Harappan accomplishment? Some scholars have tried to push the chronology of the northeastern sites into the late-second millennium, when they (almost) intersect with archaeological materials tied to a second urbanization (Shaffer 1993). Others have traced possible paths of cultural influence emanating from Harappan sites in Gujarat toward central India. Once again the regional picture presents a variety of patterns. In zones directly adjoining the Harappan interaction space, such as eastern Rajasthan where copper and tin exploitation occurred very early, distinct assemblages represented by the large village sites of Jodhpura and Ahar indicate that a parallel growth of chalcolithic, non-urban cultures was occurring during mature and late Harappan times. Moving into Central India, we find a village-based Malwa culture, and moving south into Maharashtra we encounter Malwa characteristics giving way to a later Jorwe culture, in villages thriving during the second millennium BCE. Simultaneous expansion of 'neolithic-chalcolithic' sites was occurring in a zone stretching from western Uttar Pradesh, where a village-based culture using 'ochre-colored' pottery evinces late Harappan characteristics, through a series of cultural assemblages stretching all the way to Bengal (Chakrabarti 1999: 205–61). One must consider these cultures as distinctly non-urban, although they laid the groundwork for agrarian regimes that would support early historical cities. Thus, while we must acknowledge that the Harappan settlements bequeathed a physical culture, resource base, and cultural styles that became standard for many later village farming communities and towns in South Asia, we must also accept evidence for the complete disappearance of urbanization for perhaps a millennium following the disintegration of the Harappan complex. Along with the 'collapse' of classic Maya civilization in Mesoamerica, this phenomenon remains one of the world's great archaeological conundrums, and as in the Maya case explanations range from the social (shifts in political hierarchies) to the technological (the advent of iron in the late-second millennium being a prerequisite for the exploitation of eastern and southern jungles) to the ecological (tectonic shifts and alteration of river courses combined with over-exploitation of environmental niches).

The second urbanization

The preconditions for a second urbanization in South Asia, also known as early historical urbanization, began during the early part of the first millennium BCE when iron-using village farming communities began to appear within the Yamuna-Ganga river system east of the older Harappan site distribution. Continuities with earlier village cultures indicate that they were, in part, the most recent manifestation of agrarian economies emerging directly from local and regional conditions of production and exchange. They manifested, nonetheless, a novel cultural assemblage characterized, in part, by a pottery known to archaeologists as the Painted Grey Ware (early to mid-first millennium BCE). We know of several dozen settlements yielding this pottery that supported relatively large populations living in dense, contiguous spaces – places that we can describe as cities or towns – by 600 BCE at the latest. Fortifications characterized the largest of these sites. The earliest fortifications often began with a ditch or moat and the heaping of excavated earth or mud into bunds that were perhaps surmounted by wooden palisades. Later, mud brick or burnt brick revetments were added to the outer walls of some forts, along with battlements at regular intervals and multiple gateways, strengthened by brick-built bastions and guard houses. The elaboration of more complicated fortifications accompanied the appearance of a pottery known as the Northern Black Polished Ware (mid- to late-first millennium BCE) and punch-marked coinages issued by a variety of independent political units that culminated in the metal currency issued under the Mauryan Empire (third-second centuries BCE). Textual materials (e.g. sections of the Epics) during this period project a coherent body of religious practice and philosophical inquiry, plus an expanding role for the state (Thapar 2002: 139–46). An understanding of this second urbanization is crucial for an analysis of all subsequent change in South Asia, for since that time we may witness an uninterrupted sequence of economic development, state formation, and cultural expansion affecting the entire subcontinent as well as Central, East and Southeast Asia.

One of the most impressive early historical cities in northern India is Kausambi (see Map 2), known from multiple literary sources as the capital of the Vatsa region. The location of the city on a bluff along the Yamuna River, about 45 kilometers from its juncture with the Ganga River, is one key to its strategic importance as a commercial hub. As George Erdosy has suggested (1988: 53–4), the site lay within a range of cultivable but inferior soils, the last major agrarian region on the southern edge of the interfluvial zone, but within striking distance of mineral extraction regions to the south. The primary excavator of Kausambi (Sharma 1969: 22) claimed that permanent occupation of the site began in the twelfth century BCE, with an initial mud fortification dating back to the eleventh century, but later investigators have more conservatively dated the first walls to either the seventh or fifth century BCE (Erdosy 1988: 55–61; Chakrabarti 1995: 196–7). Today the site features a mound averaging more than 10 meters in height, formed from the detritus of centuries of occupation, appearing as a plateau that dominates the surrounding countryside. A wall 6.4 kilometers in length still encompasses the entire site. Individual towers are more than 22 meters high, providing exceptional views of remains of the city's moat and a separate ring of mounds about 1.5 kilometers away. An inner citadel or palace, built before the occurrence of Northern Black Polished Ware, lay in the southeastern sector of the settlement. Excavations uncovered a vast trove of artifacts and artwork, now located in the Allahabad Museum, bringing the intensive habitation of the city up to at least the fourth century CE.

The dozens of smaller tells located throughout Allahabad District have been the object of an intensive surface survey by Erdosy (1988) who evaluated their size at different time periods based on the visibility of type artifacts in order to describe a four-tiered size ranking of settlements between 600 and 350 BCE, evolving into

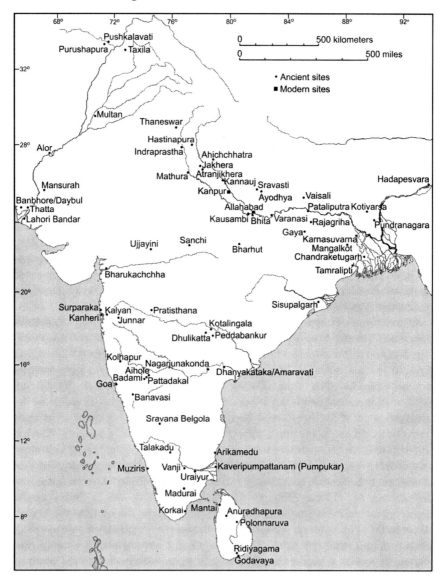

Map 2 Urban sites, ca. 1000 BCE–1000 CE.

a five-tiered ranking by 100 BCE. At that time, although Kausambi exceeded the next largest site by a factor of nine, the number of the city's suburbs and fairly large intermediate-sized (6–50 hectare) sites in its vicinity was at its peak. Among the mid-sized neighbors was Bhita, a fortified town perhaps originally occupied in the fourth century BCE. As one of the only early historical sites in South Asia that has undergone extensive horizontal excavation, Bhita is important for revealing a main thoroughfare stretching west from its southeastern gateway with flanking rows of shops backed by habitation areas (Marshall 1915).

The settlement pattern in Allahabad District stands in contrast to the situation in Kanpur District to the west, in the heart of the Yamuna-Ganga basin, where Makkhan Lal (1984) identified dozens of village farming communities that flourished between 200 BCE and 300 CE, but only seven sites sized between 6 and 11.25 hectares. Further to the northwest we have Ahichchhatra, known to literary sources as the archaic capital of the Panchala region, where a mound between 10 and 20 meters deep lies behind a defensive wall about 5.6 kilometers in length. Ahichchhatra seems to have constituted the linchpin of a separate regional hierarchy of sites that may have included Atranjikhera 80 kilometers away (a site 50 hectares in area with a mud rampart dating from ca. 500 BCE) and Jakhera, 15 kilometers from Atranjikhera (a site 8 hectares in area with a mud rampart dating from the eighth-sixth centuries BCE). These examples suggest that the patterns of urbanization varied according to developments within the 16 major regions (*mahajanapada*) mentioned repeatedly in early literary sources and represented by early coinage (Chakravarti 2000).

Monastic orders and early cities

The sacred scriptures of monks preserved in the Pali language and committed to writing later in Sri Lanka comprise an important body of texts that purport to describe the society in and around north Indian cities between ca. 500 and 400 BCE. They include the disciplinary rules of the monastic order established by the Buddha, or accounts of the Buddha's interactions with a wide range of persons in carefully delineated settings, and present embedded detail that seems to have entered collective memory at a very early stage in the order's history. In a typical dialogue the Buddha travels to the outskirts of a settlement along with a band of his disciples, installs himself in a grove or in an abode provided by a local layperson, and then engages in religious discussion with many types of visitors. Five cities are of particular importance to his ministry. The Buddha delivers his first discourse and revisits Sarnath, a suburb located several kilometers west of early Varanasi (Baranas) – the latter identified archaeologically with Rajghat (See Chapter 2). The Buddha visits Kausambi. He visits Sravasti (Savatthi) and Vaisali (Vesali) – extensive ruins today – where he comments on the strategic options for ruling aristocratic assemblies that struggle for survival against the waxing power of neighboring kingdoms. He spends time on the Vulture's Peak at Rajagriha (Rajagaha, the King's house), the early capital of the region called Magadha, close to the sylvan location at Gaya where he first achieved enlightenment; even today one may climb the peak and observe the remains of the stone walls constructed on the surrounding hills that provided security for the parricide king of a nascent empire. Although, according to K. T. S. Sarao (1990: 179–82), these five cities comprise about 65 percent of all place references in the early Pali scriptures, they exist within a more extensive matrix of at least 132 settlements known to the early monastic community.

Ever since Richard Fick (1920) demonstrated the potential for social and economic analysis offered by these accounts, scholars have combed the early Pali scriptures for insights into social organization. Narendra K. Wagle's effort (1995) identified vocabulary within the Pali scriptures defining a settlement hierarchy including the village (*gama*); the multi-group village/town or city ward (*nigama*); city/fortress (*nagara*); and metropolitan city (*mahanagara*). In the latter one could experience the hustle and bustle of crowds and the frivolity of sensual pursuits but also the influence of the commercial heads of households (*setthi gahapati*) who commanded great wealth. Through the scriptures we meet Anathapindada living in Sravasti, who is the first example of the wealthy merchant who supports world renunciation (Fiser 2001). We are introduced to Ambapali the courtesan, living in Vaisali, who was a great benefactress for the order – the first example in South Asian literature of an important occupational category for women allowing access to wealth and influence. We eventually encounter persons making a living in the full range of activities necessary for the maintenance of a complicated urban environment: service workers; artisans; professionals (physicians, writers, accountants, money-changers; entertainers; military and bureaucratic officials of the state; traders ranging from caravan personnel to shopkeepers.

Scriptures describing the Buddha's death include detailed discussions of his body's cremation and the distribution of relics from the funeral pyre to various constituencies among the laity who, imitating pre-established practice, constructed monuments called *stupa* or *dagaba* (or *chaitya/chetiya*) in memory of the great teacher. It is likely that these early monuments were large mounds of earth, which explains why few have survived. Later a new style of expressing political legitimacy through monumental architecture channeled public resources to the construction of stupas in brick and stone. Donation inscriptions confirm that funding came not only from political leaderships but also from mercantile and artisan communities operating within an urban milieu, often involved in inter-city trade.

The many donations at early monumental sites that are attributed to female donors always mention that the women were the wives, daughters, sisters, or disciples of other persons, usually men, who were the recipients of the merit earned by religious giving. Just as gifts were vehicles for the expression of familial devotion, they served as the sign of female concern for the well-being of dominant males – but in fact women were controlling the sometimes large resources being transferred. The order of nuns at an early stage became a path of personal but also social liberation and produced the world's first collection of female devotional poetry (Murcott 1992).

The earliest sculptures preserved on the monuments of monastic institutions also allow us to visualize complete, three-dimensional recreations of urban buildings which often correspond to descriptions in Pali literature. Fortified gateways are a recurring graphic theme appearing on gateways in Sanchi, Mathura, and Amaravati (Coomaraswamy 2002). Gateways at the main stupa at Sanchi (see Figure 1) allude to Gautama's great departure as he rejects worldly pursuits. In the parade

Figure 1 Urban procession portrayed at Sanchi, northern gateway, west pillar, second–first century BCE. Reproduced by permission of the American Institute of Indian Studies.

of departure we see cavalry with careful delineation of gear, details of male and female dress and ornaments among the various spectators, and pictures of various structures in the city. The procession emerges from a city gate that is part of outer fortifications, with lower sections of the fort walls pierced only by small windows and with superstructures consisting of railed platforms supporting barrel-vaulted roofs with pillars. Beyond the wall and gateway bastion the artists have created a three-dimensional effect allowing us to look into the city where spectators stare from the upper stories of mansions with railings.

The concentration of monastic sites along trade routes along the coast and through the Western Ghats in Maharashtra, where free-standing structures became translated into caves, is a clear indication of the dependence of monastic architecture on the support of commercial groups who contributed one-third of all gifts recorded there. Eighty cave sites with 1,200 rock-cut monasteries, with the largest concentrations at Kanheri and Junnar, allow a vision of architectural styles that characterized the earliest urban environments and became encapsulated within monastic sites as a mnemonic corpus denoting cosmopolitanism. Chaitya halls at cave complexes still preserve carefully the details of internal construction for vaulted roofs of urban mansions through careful reproductions of arched roof beams, in some cases (unnecessarily) in wood that has survived for at least 1,500 years. The multiple roofs of the city, each with its light-yielding window, became a motif on many cave monuments as well, and became a standard feature of later temples (Mitra 1971; Dehejia 1972; Ray 2003: 263).

For the heads of households living permanently in village-and-city networks the monastic communities that we label Buddhism and Jainism projected a vision of diligence privileging simplicity of lifestyle, the restriction of consumption, and the value of hard work. For monks and nuns, they established a controlled social order of equals on the outskirts of settled life and an idealized hunting-and-gathering lifestyle that ultimately depended on the sharing of wealth by those households (Chakravarti 1987: 177–81). The strong relationship between societies immersed in material gain and faiths of renunciation, formalized through ritual donation and transfer of merit, has evoked explanatory frameworks that sometimes privilege the ethical and universal qualities of the religious message and at other times privilege their appeal to the downtrodden or their symbiosis with social elites in a world undergoing massive economic development manifested by growing urbanization. The monastic orders may have played important roles as 'mediators' among an array of social groups that were undergoing 'assimilation' to more complicated institutional environments (Bailey and Mabbett 2003). The expansion and intensive institutionalization of the monastic orders, instead of the host of alternative faiths, undoubtedly rested on the charismatic activities of their founders and the strong organizational forms they constructed but also depended on the simple coincidence that they developed in precisely the region where the first imperial force in South Asian history originated.

Cities and early empire

The multi-regional struggle for supreme power, intensifying even in the Buddha's time, culminated in the triumph of the Magadha kingdom, consolidated by Chandragupta Maurya in the late-fourth century and leading under his grandson Ashoka (ca. 269–232) to an empire stretching from Afghanistan to Bengal and from Nepal to Karnataka. The capital of Magadha – effectively the capital of the subcontinent – had already shifted to an open port on the south bank of the Ganga River called Pataliputra (originally Pataligama, today the city of Patna). The Greek ambassador Megasthenes, who visited Pataliputra around 300 BCE, left an account of the city that describes the capital as a parallelogram 80 stadia (14.8 kilometers) in length and 15 stadia (2.8 kilometers) in width, surrounded by a huge ditch and a wall with 570 towers and 64 gates (McCrindle 1877: 68, 205).

What seems at first to be an exaggerated guess by a foreign visitor in fact resembles the modern configuration of Patna and receives confirmation from archaeological discoveries of palisade sections in brick and timber that conform to Megasthenes' specifications. Pataliputra would have been, therefore, the largest urban center South Asia had ever seen, with a population that could have been five to ten times that of Kausambi.

The Mauryan accomplishment would have been impossible without a road network, already growing for a number of centuries, linking all regions of the subcontinent. One of the most important routes, described in ancient sources as the 'northern path' (*uttarapatha*), ran all the way from Bengal to the Khyber Pass in what is today Afghanistan. In the neighborhood of Kausambi (later Allahabad) the route could pursue a course paralleling either the Yamuna or Ganga River before coming to a major junction near Indraprastha/Hastinapura (later Delhi) and then following one of several alternative courses across Punjab. Subsidiary roads linked the northern path to urban sites throughout the Yamuna-Ganga basin. Separate routes ran (1) along the Indus River; (2) from one or more cities along the western Yamuna River (e.g. Mathura) toward Rajasthan and Gujarat; and (3) from Bengal along the eastern coast to Orissa. Another important route described in ancient sources as the 'southern path' (*dakshinapatha*) ran from cities along the Yamuna River through the Avanti/Malwa region with its important ancient centers at Ujjayini (Ujjain) or Vidisa/Sanchi, then over the Narmada River toward peninsula India. There it intersected with cross-peninsular routes linking the deltas of the Andhra country in the east to passes crossing the Western Ghats and leading to the west coast. Extensions of the southern path went through Karnataka (where a number of Mauryan inscriptions have been found) or along the eastern coast to the far south. As we will see, the basic configuration of major routes would remain a permanent feature of the South Asian landscape; individual cities and network segments would wax or wane over the centuries depending on changes in the larger political and economic environment (Deloche 1993: 90–3).

The political and economic unification effected under the Mauryan Empire necessarily exerted an impact on the pattern of urbanization in its regional components. Ujjayini had stood behind a fortified rampart 5.6 kilometers in length since perhaps the seventh century BCE, but now, according to Ashoka's inscriptions, it served as a provincial capital under the Mauryas. In the east the city of Pundranagara (modern Mahasthan in Bangladesh) seems to have become a another provincial capital under the Mauryas, within the region known as Varendra; today one finds a rectangular fortified enclosure 5.6 kilometers in length, rising 5 meters above the plain with corner bastions about 11 meters in height (Chakrabarti 1992: 44–51). In Orissa, where Ashoka's conquests had caused massive loss of life, we find the site of one of his inscriptions in close proximity to the site of Sisupalgarh where a pre-existing settlement became enclosed within a fortification wall planned with geometric precision during the early-second century BCE. The plan of the defenses, an almost perfect square with a periphery measuring 4.8 kilometers, included clay ramparts 7.6 meters in height and 33.5 meters wide at their base, with two gateways on each wall at regular intervals (Chakrabarti 1995: 223–5, 240–2).

The plan at Sisupalgarh resembles closely the descriptions of fortified administrative centers presented by the *Arthasastra* (Treatise on Power) attributed to Kautilya, the prime minister who supposedly engineered the rise of Chandragupta Maurya to supreme authority. If this attribution is accurate we may have in the *Arthasastra* (or sections of it) a specifically Mauryan viewpoint on the relationship between the state and urbanization that became implemented in one of their outlying provinces. A perusal of this document reveals that the relentlessly statist concerns of the author(s) provide an important and even privileged position for cities, but ultimately subordinate questions of urbanization to the problems of managing a region (*janapada*) and its resources amid the intense competition of a multi-state, non-imperial system.

The *Arthasastra* states that 'all power comes from the countryside' (7.14.19). Its understanding of political control rests on a settlement hierarchy with a sub-district headquarters for every ten villages; a district headquarters for 200 villages; a divisional headquarters for 400 villages; and a provincial headquarters for 800 villages. On the periphery of the kingdom, and separated from the village-based economy by forests serving as the source of elephants and other forms of extractive resources, the prince establishes frontier fortresses that define the boundary with the forest buffer zones of neighboring realms (2.1.4–6). Market towns and ports serve as nodes for trade, which stands along with agriculture, animal husbandry, and mining as the source for taxation. The fortified capital, the site of the royal palace, stands at the center of the kingdom. The text spends considerable effort defining the ideal construction of its moats, walls and bastions; its quadrilateral ground plan with six gateways on each side; the layout of the palace at the heart of the city; and the housing pattern of the four main status groups (*varna*) in different neighborhoods (1.20, 2.3, 2.4). In practice, the security role of the capital with its many bureaucrats stands alongside, and intersects with, its role as a commercial center. The bureaucracy, including its special categories for urban administrators (2.36), rests on a multi-faceted artisan and industrial base coordinated by city-based 'guilds' (*sreni*) of occupational specialists linked through overland caravan routes and boat traffic on rivers. While describing how the ruler may extract support from the industrial/trading economy the text provides a sample list of non-government jobs: 16 occupations in food service and personal service; 15 types of entertainer; 13 craft producers; 12 different jobs in transportation and warehousing; five kinds of jewelers and their assistants; and professionals including physicians, midwifes, accountants and clerks. The difficulties involved in regulating all these groups along with the ramified military and administrative staff of the state in crowded cityscapes appear in the sections on house building regulations (3.8.3, 3.8.14) and on regulations for fire prevention (2.36.15). Hygiene laws include prohibitions against those perennial problems: throwing dirt or dead bodies onto the streets, and urinating or defecating in public spaces (Kautilya 1992; *Kautilya's Arthasastra* 1915).

By the second century BCE a distinctive pattern of spatial organization characterized urban centers in South Asia manifested through the intersection of long-term security strategies, religious belief and political sophistication. Fortifications enclosed the main habitation zones, commercial hub, and administrative seat. Fortification construction originally of mud or mud-brick cores had become more elaborate, with brick or stone facing for walls, along with gateways or bastions added later. In a society with great differences in occupational specialization, status and wealth, most citizens inhabited humble homes of mud, brick or thatch, which have typically disappeared from our view except for their basements. Even the mansions of the more well-to-do have typically disappeared because, aside from a stone or brick foundation or first story, their upper stories most likely were of wood which was more commonly available from the extensive forest cover. Outside the built-up area of the city and its fortifications stood the sacred precincts of the monastic orders with their distinctive and standardized architectural features. In the absence of extensive, solid evidence for the architecture of non-monastic institutions we must assume that what we would later term temples were not a major target of patronage for the elites funding public architecture; if such temples existed, they remained more humble structures that have eluded archaeology.

The second urbanization in peninsular India

The most durable feature of human settlements in peninsular India, during the initial phases of the second urbanization, was the presence of 'megalithic' cultures characterized by the production of stone (mostly funerary) monuments yielding characteristic grave goods such as iron weapons and black-and-red ware. Several thousand megalithic sites lie scattered from Maharashtra to the southern tip of India and into Sri Lanka, within a time frame stretching from ca. 1300 BCE to 300 CE, in a non-urban context. In most cases, the appearance of village farming communities or urban sites in peninsular India that exhibit the type artifacts of the second urbanization took place during or after the third century BCE, reflecting either a diffusion of a north-central Indian political economy associated with the Mauryan expansion (overlying or juxtaposed with a separate megalithic pattern) or the intersection of indigenous urbanization with that expansion. At a political level, these developments occurred under the aegis of the Satavahana polity (ca. 100 BCE–200 CE) that apparently arose in the old region of Mulaka, with its capital at Pratisthana (Paithan), but later established its base in the Krishna-Godavari delta at Dhanyakataka (Dharanikota). Commerce linked the east and west coasts and, through Ujjayini, the Yamuna-Ganga river system (Parasher 1992; Thapar 2002: 234–44).

Under the Satavahana hegemony monastic institutions, ranging from the cave sites of the Western Ghats to the major stupa at Amaravati, became the signature monuments of social and economic power and the sign of a settlement's importance within a hierarchy of city sizes and functions betokening economic specialization. Two inscriptions from Amaravati allow a vision of the importance of women in this process. In the first, a nun who is also a householder (*gahapati*), along with other women and their relatives, donates to the order; in the second, a female ascetic along with her daughter (also a nun) and her granddaughter are the donors (Burgess

1887: 55, 90–1). We can see here the construction of entirely female lineages of devotion that were vehicles for merit-making benefiting their families but also constituted independent spheres of activity through which resources flowed. Half of the donations at Amaravati and nearby Jaggeyapeta that record the gender of donors indicate that women were transferring, and thus controlling, wealth.

An example of the interconnections between monastic sites and small cities comes from the Asmaka or Assaka region located along the Godavari River, where we find a hierarchy of central places:

1   Kotalingala, at the confluence of the Godavari and Paddavaga Rivers, is a mound 50 hectares in extent, delineated by mud fortifications with traces of bastions at the corners and gates at cardinal points, yielding evidence even of pre-Satavahana coinage. Nearby, on opposite banks of the Godavari, are the small, contemporary ruins of Vemnurru (three to four hectares in area) with evidence of small-scale ironworking, and Karnamamidi with evidence of early pottery and bricks.
2   The mound at Dhulikatta, a site strategically located in an area of fertile black soil, is 18 hectares in extent with ramparts showing the base of a brick fort wall and gateways at cardinal points. Structures include a 'palace complex,' many granaries, and a stupa with monastery located about one kilometer from the walls. There is evidence of small-scale ironworking.
3   Peddabankur, about 10 kilometers to the east, displays no fortifications around a site measuring about 30 hectares with three main enclosures. There is evidence of small-scale ironworking and also a 'mint' yielding several thousand Satavahana coins with terracotta molds and die-struck pieces in pots. Another small mound exists at Chinnabankur about 4 kilometers to the north.

The first two sites conform to a picture of administrative-cum-military centers, while the third looks more like a commercial or production center. All sites rest on a combination of agrarian and artisan production linked to trade routes running to Vidarbha and to the coast. Widespread microliths at all these sites, and the presence of nearby megalithic sites, indicate the coexistence of several modes of production and subsistence (Sarkar 1987; Parasher 1991).

In the southernmost part of peninsular India, where Ashoka's inscriptions had noted the presence of independent Chola, Pandya, and Chera (Keralaputra) dynasties, a body of Tamil-language texts known collectively as the Sangam literature point to the growth of important central places associated with trade and with the seats of chiefly lineages. The earliest manifestations of public architecture in this region are not Buddhist but Jain, represented by dozens of cave sites associated with short donation inscriptions. We can discern by the first century CE the social lineaments of an emerging urban culture in three main locations: Madurai, the inland capital of the Pandyas on the Vaikai River, closely associated with the port of Korkai on the east coast; Uraiyur, the capital of the Cholas near the head of the Kaveri River delta, associated with the coastal port of Kaveripattanam

(Pumpuhar) to its east; and Vanji, capital of the early Cheras, located farther west and more closely aligned with the hill country.

The peak of the second urbanization

The early historical intersection of regional urbanization and trans-regional trade peaked throughout South Asia during the first three centuries of the Common Era. Two giant, interacting complexes underpinned this revolution: the Indian Ocean trading system and what we may call the 'Kushana effect.'

At strategic locations along the coasts of the Arabian Sea and the Bay of Bengal a series of trade emporia provided markets for regionally variable raw materials and finished goods and afforded new opportunities for profit to seaborne traders from all coastal regions in South Asia as well as merchants from the west. From the Greek side the first-century trading manual, entitled *The Periplus of the Erythraean Sea,* provides details of itineraries, ports-of-call, and the regional availability of goods in Sind, the western coast of India, Tamil Nadu and Sri Lanka. Many finds of Roman artwork and over 70 coin hoards dating from ca. 50 BCE to 300 CE indicate that peninsular India, in particular, was participating in extensive trade with the Mediterranean through the Red Sea. Situated near the mouths of navigable rivers or adjacent to protected anchorages, linked to regional sources of raw materials or settlements specializing in the production of high-value, low-bulk commodities, most coastal emporiums were nodes for the transfer of goods and few attracted large populations (Turner 1989; Begley and de Puma 1991; Cimino 1994; Thapar 1997).

The main port in Gujarat was Bharukachchha (Bhrigukachchha), known as Barygaza to the Greeks and Romans and Broach today, located about a day's sailing up the estuary of the Narmada River. Further to the south were the distant precursors of Mumbai: the ports of Suraparaka/Supparaka (modern Sopara) located on an island with backwater harbor, and Kalyana (see Map 19) located near a protected anchorage on the bend of the Ulhas River – the latter site described as the 'largest settlement on the west coast' during this period – close to the monastic cave sites at Kanheri (Ray 1986: 63–4; Hebalkar 2001: 109–15). The main port along the Kerala coast was known to the Greeks as Muziris or Musiris, identified at times with Cranganore (Kodunallur), a site on the estuary of the Periyar River with access to north-south inland waterways (Deloche 1994, 2: 89–90; Rajan 1996). In Sri Lanka, perhaps the most significant port was Mantai, also known as Mahatittha (Pali), Mantottam (Tamil) or Matota (Sinhala), located near the mouth of the Malwatu Oya and thus serving as the primary port for Anuradhapura (Carswell 1991). Numerous literary references to Tamralipti (modern Tamluk), originally on the seacoast but now about 50 kilometers from the ocean, portray it as the leading port in the deltaic region of Bengal, but a cluster of at least 28 sites on the rivers Rupnarayan, Hughli and Haldi were also trading sites between at least 200 BCE and 300 CE. A separate cluster of villages existed around the port of Chandraketugarh on the Vidyadhari River, once an important tributary of the Bhagirathi (Sengupta 1996: 118; Chattopadhyaya 2003: 77–80).

One of the best studied ports is Arikamedu in Tamil Nadu, known to the Greeks as Poduke and today also called Virampatnam, lying on the bank of the Ariyankuppam River where its final northward bend provides a safe anchorage just before it joins the Bay of Bengal. Several warehouse and production clusters survive in a mound stretching about 500 meters along the river; there are few indications of habitation zones near the port facilities, although several dozen megalithic sites exist within a diameter of 10 kilometers. Finds of Roman amphorae and other ceramics and artworks of Mediterranean origin indicate the direct import of wine, olive oil, and fish sauce peaking between 50 BCE and 50 CE. Scholars have traced the growth of a glass bead industry at Arikamedu that supplied a market reaching China and Japan by the third century at the latest (Begley 1996; Francis 2002: 27–50).

Another example from the southeastern coast of Sri Lanka is Godavaya, located at the mouth of the Valave Ganga. Here we have a stupa/vihara complex on a rocky elevation next to the sea, with a protected harbor to its east and a lagoon on the west where the river reaches the ocean. This area is the site of ancient inscriptions, with a pottery sequence beginning in the first century BCE. Habitation sites stretched over one kilometer to the north along the banks of the Valave Ganga, along with several additional monasteries. 12 kilometers from the navigable river's mouth is the archaeological site of Ridiyagama with a settlement completely under water today but yielding thousands of ceramic fragments (Weisshaar 2001: 291–356). This configuration exemplifies a pattern that we have already encountered at a number of sites: the pairing of a seaport town with an inland administrative-cum-commercial center accessing an agrarian hinterland and/or mined resources.

The second phenomenon contributing to the peak of early historical urbanization was the 'Kushana effect' caused by the first-century consolidation of an empire stretching from modern Kazakhstan to northern India. The establishment for several centuries of a single political authority that mediated contacts between the Parthian and Han empires enabled the smooth functioning of the Silk Route which gave access to the Bactrian oasis cities of Bukhara (Buxoro) and Tashkent and to the Chinese-controlled towns of Kashi, Hotan, Dunhuang, and finally the capital, Xian (See Map 10). On this overland complement to the Indian Ocean trading network the multi-cultural coinage of the Kushana kings became an important medium of exchange, not only within the zone up to the middle-Yamuna-Ganga basin where their authority was more direct but throughout northern India. A preliminary survey of sites yielding 'Kushana antiquities' conducted over 20 years ago identified 68 places in Punjab, 73 in Rajasthan, 82 in Jammu and Kashmir, and 171 in Uttar Pradesh (Prasad 1984: 180–6). Another survey has identified 357 find spots for their coinage in addition to 260 find spots for coins of the Satavahana kings and related rulers (Sharma 2001: 136). In many of the older urban sites of the second urbanization the depth of the 'Kushana period' remains is often the deepest and richest in artifacts. The Kushana effect reached as far as Bengal, where we may contrast the provincial role of Pundranagara (Mahasthan) with the apparently sub-provincial or district centrality of Bangarh, with a rampart and moat about

1.7 kilometers in length, yielding evidence of its greatest prosperity before 300 (Chattopadhyaya 2003: 75). Through their extensive lists of jobs practiced in the city, textual references testify to the expansion of occupational specialization (Thakur 1981: 94–181).

The city that experienced perhaps the greatest positive impact from this amplification of commercial growth was Mathura, the old capital of the Surasena region. In the third century BCE a massive mud wall encompassing almost 4 square kilometers had existed in this environment with relatively low agricultural potential, suggesting that trade flowing through multiple routes was playing an important role in the local economy. When Mathura became the eastern base for the Kushana kings it was also emerging as the hub of a ramified pattern of land-based trade routes ultimately connected to oceanic routes. The many references to the city in the literature of Buddhism and Jainism, along with the numerous archaeological remains of monasteries, indicate the importance of the city to commercial patrons (Srinivasan 1989). In addition, Mathura has yielded abundant statuary evidence for the worship of a variety of deities, including an 'explosion' in the representations of Vaishnava images, especially depictions of Vasudeva-Krishna (Singh 2004: 388–9).

In peninsular India, with the eclipse of the Satavahanas, a number of successor polities appeared to found their own regional capitals. Among these was the seat of the third-century Ikshvaku kings at Vijayapuri, later called Nagarjunakonda, along the Krishna River (a site flooded by recent dam construction). Here a well-preserved complex of public buildings included a fortified citadel, palaces, Buddhist monuments and early examples of temple construction. Inscriptions indicate that women associated with the royal family constituted 75 percent of the donors to Buddhist institutions; men constructed temples and performed Vedic sacrifices. Analysis of the extensive artwork preserved here, a variant of a distinctive Andhra school best exemplified at Amaravati, allows a reconstruction of palace interiors, elite and everyday dress and adornment, and even furniture styles (Sarkar and Misra 1972; Krishna Murthy 1977).

Case studies in the second urbanization: Taxila and Anuradhapura

It is hard to imagine an urban center in South Asia that displays a more obvious dependence on geographical location than Taxila, or Takshasila (See Map 3). It lay within a fertile plain measuring about 18 × 8 kilometers, blessed with moderate rainfall augmented by the Haro River and its tributaries and by a series of natural springs. It was well positioned for commercial contacts along the 'northern path' – toward Kashmir and Central Asian trade routes in the north and toward the Indus River route in the south. Taxila long played the role of the eastern capital, in the region known as Gandhara, alongside the region's western capital Pushkaravati or Charsadda, which attracted traders along the northern bank of the Khyber River until its eclipse by the city of Purushapura (later Peshawar) established by the second century CE (Deloche 1993, 1: 31–2). Literary sources

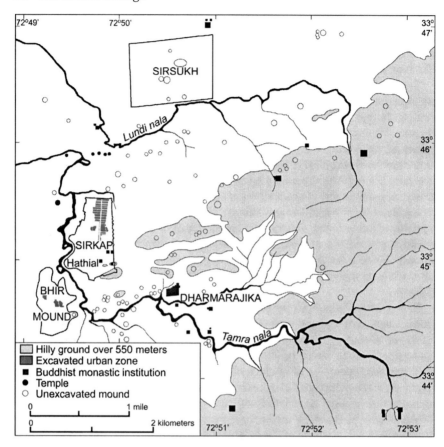

Map 3 Plan of ancient Taxila (Takshasila). Adapted from Marshall 1951: Figure 1.

including the *Mahabharata* and other early texts repeatedly mention the role of the Gandhara people, and Taxila in particular, during events taking place during the late-second or first millenniums BCE; Alexander the Great was in Taxila during his South Asian campaign in 326 BCE; and even the great Mauryan ruler, Ashoka, is supposed to have served as viceroy in Taxila before becoming emperor around 274 BCE. It was the key to political and economic history linking South Asia to the West and to Central Asia for at least a thousand years.

A spur of hills juts into the valley from the east, dividing it into a flatter northern section more suitable for agriculture and a more rugged southern section featuring ravines and knolls watered by the Tamra Nala. The spur ends in the west at a ridge called Hathial lying alongside a northerly turn of the Tamra Nala. Archaeological excavations in the late-twentieth century have revealed occupation at Hathial in small settlements during the fourth and third millenniums BCE, with assemblages reminiscent of Kot Diji. It seems likely that small-scale occupation continued at this well-watered, defensible, and strategic location into early historical times (Dani 1986: 18–35; Allchin 1993).

Extensive horizontal excavations at Taxila have aimed to clarify the relationships between Greek culture and the urban phase of settlement there (Marshall 1951). They reveal that the urban phase at Taxila began during the fifth century BCE with the establishment of a site known today as Bhir Mound, on the western side of the Tamra Nala, now a 50-hectare deposit up to 6 meters in depth. Surrounded by a mud-brick defensive wall, this settlement included densely packed buildings constructed from rubble masonry, coated with mud plaster and sometimes whitewashed. Blocks included a diverse array of dwellings (including a design featuring central open courtyard with side rooms) and shops organized around a series of public squares. Inhabitants used pits or bins located in public spaces for solid waste disposal and soak pits located within house sites for sewage disposal. Surface drains of solid stone or masonry conveyed rainwater from open courtyards into the streets. The most striking building plan is a hall measuring about 17 × 6 meters with three square piers running down its center that once supported wooden pillars and, undoubtedly, wooden roof timbers.

Gandhara came under the control of Greek rulers originating in northern Afghanistan, the successors to the easternmost section of the empire conquered by Alexander the Great, during the second century BCE. A new planned city, known today as Sirkap, rose on the eastern side of the Tamra Nala including the heights of Hathial as well as the flatter zone to its north eventually encompassing 75 hectares. A stone wall varying in thickness between 5 and 7 meters, approximately 5.6 kilometers in length and probably varying between 6 and 8 meters in height, protected the new city. On the northern and eastern walls, a series of square bastions about 7 meters wide projected outward. Coming through the northern gate, one passed by the defensive wall's inner guardrooms and walked due south along a wide main street intersected at right angles by a regular series of smaller lanes; this is Greek urban design around a regular series of parallelograms, a geometry oriented toward a view from above. The constructions on either side include, apparently, shops and personal homes, public buildings, and Buddhist shrines. Among the latter are a number of quadrangular courtyards surrounding stupas and a major compound, measuring 70 meters east to west and 42 meters from north to south, for an apsidal chaitya hall. A massive array of excavated pottery, metal utensils, and approximately 8,000 coins provides a detailed picture of daily life, including views of the well-provisioned kitchen, and a market economy with links stretching from Central Asia to northern India.

Sirkap remained the main portion of Taxila, with Bhir Mound as its suburb, until about 80 CE when the Kushana kings supervised the construction of an entirely new city to the northeast. This heavily fortified site, known as Sirsukh, encompassed 140 hectares and remained the main focus of an expanded Taxila until at least the fifth century, but archaeologists have not conducted major excavations there.

The religious institutions located in the environs of Taxila have bequeathed to us a rich trove of art and architecture. Most unusual are two temples at Jandial north of Sirkap and individual temples at Mohra Maliaran and Tamra displaying designs typical of Greek religious architecture and undoubtedly dedicated to Greek deities – although their sites indicate that they were used for worship well into the Common Era under the aegis of cosmopolitan Kushana rulers. All other religious sites appear to be Buddhist. While the citizenry showed reverence to the Buddha at stupa/chaitya sites within the city, the monastic communities resided outside the city walls in quadrilateral assembly halls associated with their own stupas. The most important Buddhist site in the valley is the Dharmarajika Stupa located southeast of Sirkap; this was supposedly the site of an early stupa construction by Ashoka, although the extant size of the monument (diameter 61 meters, height 14 meters) and its extensions of berm, steps, surrounding chaityas and monasteries are all later additions. In fact, it is likely that most of the Buddhist monastic establishments still extant outside the cities are foundations of the second to fifth centuries, when Sirsukh was in its prime (Dar 1993: 114). Several monastic sites located on Hathial were founded, probably, after the replacement of Sirkap as the main population center. Excavations at all these sites have retrieved iconography and epigraphy that allows a reconstruction of Buddhist doctrinal evolution at the interface with Greek and Central Asian cultural influences, leading to the manifestation of an influential Gandharan artistic tradition.

At the other end of the South Asian world the site of Anuradhapura lies in northern Sri Lanka on a generally flat plain interspersed with rocky hills. This is the 'dry zone' that receives relatively little rainfall from the southwest monsoon, but does experience sometimes-torrential downpours during the northeast monsoon between October and February. The limited availability of rainwater has prompted agriculturalists here, as in many places throughout peninsular India, to construct extensive systems of artificial lakes (often called tanks, after the Portuguese term *tanque*) in order to conserve precious runoff and make it available for irrigated cultivation. Surrounded by hundreds of villages drawing water from small neighboring tanks, Anuradhapura became a primate city and the effective capital of Sri Lanka for about 1,500 years. A detailed history of the city exists in the form of oral chronicles maintained by generations of Buddhist monks, notably the *Mahavamsa* (The Great Lineage), written in Pali during the fifth century CE but purporting to record events 1,000 years earlier. This text, the bedrock for the early history of Sri Lanka, presents a model of the close relationship between the rulers of the city-state and the Buddhist order – a model that has become a potent political force in the creation of modern nationalism.

The earliest settlement of iron-using cultivators at what became Anuradhapura lay on the western bank of the Malwatu Oya (see Map 4). Today this is a small stream but in the early-first millennium BCE, before flood control systems were in place, it must have flooded annually and provided adequate water for limited cultivation and household purposes. The *Mahavamsa* states that king Pandukabhaya, the founder of the city, deepened a natural pond west of the settlement in order to create a tank that today is the Basavakkulam, establishing the infrastructure to support a much larger population in the area that became known

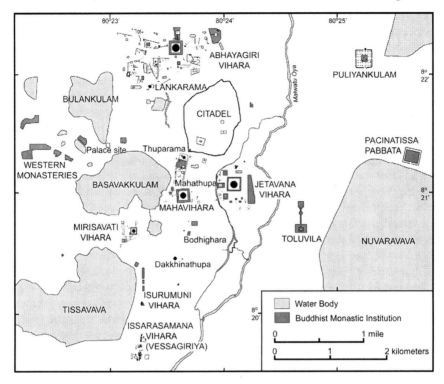

Map 4 Plan of ancient Anuradhapura. Adapted from Survey of Sri Lanka sheet; Sensviratna 1994.

as the Citadel. Excavations in the Citadel, today an extensive mound about 10 meters higher than its surroundings, reveal a major transformation during the period between about 360 and 190 BCE, including the consolidation of a rampart enclosing a area of ca. 100 hectares with a roughly quadrilateral plan and the establishment of cardinally oriented city streets. Coins become common during this period, and the Northern Black Polished Ware appeared. Other indications of long-distance trade include semi-precious stones from the hills; imported iron; seashells; lapis lazuli; carnelian; and Rouletted Ware (a type ceramic widely distributed around the Bay of Bengal). Subsequent periods yield bricks and limestone blocks, varieties of coinage, glass, and pottery styles with Hellenistic affinities (Coningham and Allchin 1995; Coningham 1999).

Providing a narrative that parallels the archaeological data the *Mahavamsa* states that Mahinda, the son of the Mauryan emperor Ashoka, came to Sri Lanka as a missionary spreading the message of Buddhism. Mahinda met King Devanampiy-atissa of Anuradhapura while the latter was hunting in the hills of Mihintale about 19 kilometers east of his capital. The king embraced the message of the missionary monk and introduced Buddhism to his kingdom. Mahinda is said to have transported to Anuradhapura a sprig from the tree under which the Buddha had attained enlightenment (enshrined in the Bodhighara); the Buddha's right collarbone (enclosed in the island's first stupa, the Thuparama); and relics from one of the stupas raised after his cremation (enclosed later in the Mahathupa or Ruvanvalisaya). The king set up the Mahavihara (the Great Monastery) in parklands south of the Citadel and enlarged a second tank known as the Tissavava to provide water. Eventually three large monastic institutions, each focused on a giant stupa, surrounded the city: the original Mahavihara to the south, the Abhayagiri Vihara (founded during the first century CE) in the north and the Jetavana Vihara (founded in the third century) in the southeast. Additional water came from the Nuvaravava, constructed in the first century BCE and augmented during the subsequent millennium by flood control works constructed south of the city. The *Mahavamsa* describes the repeated endowment of monastic complexes by the kings of Anuradhapura, some of them augmenting the scale of the three main monasteries and others standing as independent institutions (e.g. the Vessagiriya, Mirisavatti, and Lankarama Viharas). Following Anuradha Seneviratna (1994: 82), the Archaeological Survey Department, and tour guides at the site, one may conceptualize the urbanization resulting from these efforts as a series of concentric zones. The Citadel constituted the political and commercial core surrounded by a zone of suburban monastic complexes and then a 'village and tank' zone providing resources for the city. On the outer rim, an idealized 'forest and hermitage' zone included a separate grouping of 'mountain' monasteries dedicated to communities of recluse monks during the late-first millennium, e.g. Puliyankulam, Pacinatissa Pabbata, Toluvila, and the 'western' monasteries. Although the overall pattern of urbanization reflects a model originating during the early historical period, the greater part of the present remains reflects renovations and constructions during the ninth and tenth centuries (Bandaranayake 1974).

Encrusted with miraculous events, full of ethnographic detail and vignettes of personal life, the *Mahavamsa* and other chronicles are mostly concerned with political intrigue at the capital and the ramifications for monastic orders often at loggerheads over doctrinal issues. The recurring themes of these texts, teaching the vanity of worldly involvement, include unsavory political and military struggles pitting aristocratic 'clans' against each other and against the kings; rival claimants to the throne battling each other in civil wars; and attacks by royal mercenary troops or invaders from south India. The story lasted until the late-tenth century, when the kings abandoned the city and relocated to a new capital at Polonnaruva. It is a story in which Buddhism's rise accompanied and legitimized the political aspirations of agrarian lords building a regional state (Gunawardana 1989). The close connection between public policy and monasteries has allowed one scholar to analyze the changing patterns of Buddhist architecture in terms of state power: a period of greater royal control until the fourth century produced 'monocentric' plans oriented around a single sacred space such as a large stupa, while a period witnessing greater centripetal forces until the eleventh century produced the 'polycentric' plans with multiple monastic units still visible at Anuradhapura (Bandaranayake 1989).

The second urbanization in literature

During the peak of the second urbanization a variety of conventions evolved in Sanskrit literature to describe the physical wonders of the city as a backdrop to the main characters. In sections of the Epics, for example, these conventions provide depth to the behaviors of the political and military (*kshatriya*) elite. A limited group of texts, however, acknowledge the actions of kings and courtiers but highlight characters from what we might call the upper 'middle' classes, typically merchants, and delineate their relationships with the monastic communities and the artisan or working classes. The most elaborate source of this second type is the *Cilappatikaram* (1993), or the Tale of the Ankle Bracelet, a composition in Tamil that comes to us probably from the sixth century but preserves aspects of a world from perhaps five centuries earlier. The poetics expressed here, typical of early Sangam literature, presuppose five ecological zones each manifesting unique physical features, plants and animals, human activities and emotional states; this framework allows a detailed vision of settlements and detailed descriptions of daily life. In the *Cilappatikaram* two cities, Madurai and Pumpuhar, receive the most attention.

The central part of the tale takes place at Madurai, where the hero, Kovalan, meets his doom after a thieving royal goldsmith denounces him to the foolish Pandyan king who then orders an unjust execution. The text presents the layout of a city that corresponds to the typical fortified administrative center combined with a mercantile-artisan quarter. Lying on the southern bank of the river, the city includes a port with rocking boats, but Kovalan avoids the port area and crosses to the groves of the outer suburbs inhabited only by 'those who practiced dharma,' i.e. Jain and Buddhist mendicants (Canto 13: 228–50). He later heads to the city through a surrounding thorny forest, crosses a moat and passes through a tunnel in the bush made for elephants before encountering a fortress gate guarded by Ionian (*yavana*) mercenaries. He enters, and the text here projects a truly cinematographic quality:

> In a blaze, the city snapped open before him
> Like the yawning treasure-chest of thousand-eyed Indra.
> In the streets where flags spluttered in the west wind,
> Courtesans with their handsome lovers strolled
> Toward the park with its tall marutam trees
> On the banks of the ever-flowing Vaikai,
> And on the white sand dunes sprinkled with flowers,
> They played in boats with high cabins,
> In canoes, and climbed on to bright rafts,
> Eager to sport in water
> > *The Cilappatikaram of Ilanko Atikal: An Epic of*
> > *South India* (1993) Translated by
> > R. Parthasarathy (14: 81–90). Reproduced by
> > permission of Columbia University Press

Kovalan passes the two rows of elegant mansions lining the courtesans' street. He walks through the marketplace and we encounter with him a wide range of occupational specialists and luxury retail shops. He passes through streets dedicated to goldsmiths, cloth wholesalers, and merchants of grain or spices. Open spaces of city groves offer contrast to scenes of urban density (14: 180–252). Meanwhile, Kovalan's faithful wife, Kannaki, stays safely with humble cowherds, whose simple cottages, homely food, and ritual dances are portrayed in detail (15: 223–5). Clearly the areas encompassed by the fortifications included a wide range of land uses and protected local agriculturalists and pastoralists. One could travel within several minutes from neighborhoods that resembled villages to neighborhoods crowded with multistoried buildings inhabited by the wealthiest merchants.

The first part of the epic takes place in Pumpukar, the hometown of Kovalan and Kannaki, where they have grown up as the children of wealthy Jain merchant families. Although Pumpukar possesses royal palaces of the Chola kings, it is not a political seat; it is, instead, a prime example of a coastal trading emporium. The city consists of two parts – fort surrounded by the homes of security personnel and a commercial center teeming with merchants, hawkers, vendors and artisans – separated by an open ground. The waterfront is open, piled high with bales of merchandize brought across the sea by foreigners, including 'Yavanas whose profits never shrunk,' maintaining homes near the harbor. In the city reside merchants, brahmanas, wealthy landlords and their tenants, professionals, and entertainers. Craftspeople live in the suburbs (5: 8–72).

A series of dramatic moments in the epic allow us to move with the main characters through different parts of Pumpuhar. Perhaps the most detailed sections deal with the world of the courtesan Matavi who seduces Kovalan and cohabits with him for a long period during which he runs through his family fortune. The luxuries of her pleasure house serve as the backdrop for high-level musical and dance performances in which the courtesan excels. Later, Matavi and Kovalan travel through the marketplace down the city's main thoroughfare to the row of streets near the sea. They sit in a seaside grove near the mouth of the Kaveri River, contemplating the many boats drawn up on the shore, and compose love songs featuring decidedly subaltern characters. Kovalan's concerns a beautiful girl selling fish by the shore, swatting away flies, who nonetheless captures the heart; Matavi's concerns a girl seduced and abandoned by a stranger from across the sea (6: 146–97; 7). Finally, rejecting his dalliance, Kovalan reunites with his wife and sets off to seek his fortune (and his end) in Madurai, allowing us to move from the center of the city into the countryside. Within Pumpukar the couple visits the temple of the reclining Vishnu, then seven Buddhist institutions and then a Jain shrine before jostling with the crowd on the way to the royal park. Crossing a high road they reach the bathing steps at the mouth of the Kaveri and head west through flowery groves on its north bank aiming at the suburban monastery of Kavunti, a Jain nun and their close confidante (10: 11–47). These generic descriptions allow us to see the idealized coastal emporium as contemporaries may have perceived it.

A companion text to the *Cilappatikaram* exists in Sanskrit affording a vision of the lifestyle and mentality of the well-to-do urbanite in northern India around the year 300. It is the *Kamasutra* (Treatise on Love) by Vatsyayana Mallanaga (1992) probably composed in Pataliputra. The text is justly famous for its descriptions of the mechanics of love-making and techniques for seducing other men's women but these sections lie embedded within descriptions of more conventional patterns of behavior that characterize the middle class. The main character of this book is the *nagaraka*, the 'man-about-town' or the 'bourgeois,' who appears early in the narrative living in a two-bedroom apartment with attached garden dedicated to artistic appreciation and sensual pleasure. With his sidekicks and other bourgeois associates, our hero spends his considerable fortune at musical performances, salons, and picnics, where intellectual discussions about society and the arts form standard fare (1.4.1–39). Where he obtains his income is never stated but through a process of elimination one can guess his economic position and status. He is not a brahmana. He is not a member of the government administration or a royal family, for the sexual aggressions of government personnel, or 'men of power,' receive separate treatment (5.5.1–37). Men living in villages may want to imitate the behavior of the man-about-town but clearly move in a separate, more limited world. Males living in the city but pursuing manual or artisan occupations, including elephant drivers (at the bottom of the status heap), masseurs (associated with homosexuality), jewelers and actors (whose wives are easy prey for the voluptuary) form separate – and despised – class and status groups (5.1.51–6). Women who work as house servants or as water carriers belong with the peasantry in the category of persons one may exploit without applying the rules of courtship etiquette (2.10.22–5). It is most likely, then, that the man-about-town belongs to a mercantile or *rentier* class that draws its substantial income from the management of commercial interests or real estate within the city or in the countryside. This class comprises a highly visible element in urban life: factional, competing for position and favors from the administration, divorced as much as possible from the day-to-day affairs of the business office and patronizing artists or religious foundations. The hero of the *Kamasutra* is a North Indian, brahmanical version of Kovalan, whose sexual adventures drive the early action in the South Indian story.

The purpose of the *Kamasutra*, which is buttressed by numerous quotes from previous authors, is to enhance the success of its urbane and overtly masculinist, heterosexual protagonist at the expense of all women and to the exclusion of men who cannot afford the playboy lifestyle. Reading the text against the grain, however, gives access to a more textured understanding of gender relations and Vatsyayana supports this type of reading with regular statements advocating an 'anything goes' approach. Homosexual behavior by both sexes is the target of negative comments and yet seems to be a common feature of life among 'lower' orders, in more distant regions, and even among the bourgeois. Sections of the text that deal with women and their motivations, if designed to prevent the cuckolding of the discerning male, display nonetheless a keen perception of motivations and strategies within a social hierarchy that publicly privileges men but offers opportunities for female agency. The courtesan, the subject of the entirety of Book Six, pursues an individualist agenda aimed at extracting maximum wealth from her liaisons occurring within the context of cultivated conversation and artistic expression and amid sumptuous surroundings. One need shift the focus only slightly, however, to see in the strategies of the courtesan the sexual politics in every home; the ways of getting rid of an unwanted man, for example, present familiar signs of any decaying relationship (6.3.37–46). But in practice the courtesan is not the main female in the life of the man-about-town, who seems to be married to at least one woman and maintains a householder's life that parallels the affairs at his apartment. The discussion concerning relationships with virgins, which ultimately becomes rather sordid, occurs within the framework of solid, conventional understandings of the well-to-do marriage:

> In a woman who is of the same class, who has not been with another man before, and who has been taken in accordance with the texts, a man finds religion, power, sons, connections, the growth of his faction, and straightforward sexual pleasure. Therefore he should cultivate a virgin of noble stock whose mother and father are living and who is at least three years younger than he. She should come from a family that is respectable, wealthy, well connected, and rich in relatives who get along well with one another. Her mother and father should come from powerful factions.
>
> Vatsyayana Mallananaga *Kamasutra* (3.1.1–2). Translated by Wendy Doniger and Sudhir Kakar. Reproduced by permission of the Oxford University Press.

In a similar vein, the discussion of wives includes advice on managing the polygynous household and the royal harem and eventually moves into advice for the man-about-town on seducing wives, but begins with an extended description of daily life for the single wife who runs a household. In addition to always looking good for her husband and pleasing her in-laws, 'she keeps the house clean and heart-warming to look at, with well-polished surfaces, all sorts of floral arrangements, and smooth and shiny floors' (4.1.2). A closer look at this ideal housewife reveals that she supervises a staff of servants; manages all purchases and accounts; plants gardens; administers fields, cattle, and transportation; and 'prepares the daily portions of income and expenditures,' while controlling her husband's wardrobe. These skills presuppose an extended period of women's education and a division of labor according authority to women of this class.

The first millennium

The Gupta kings (ca. 350–600) recreated a northern empire stretching from Pakistan to Bangladesh and even sent a military campaign down the eastern coast of peninsular India, but theirs was the last polity that used Pataliputra as the capital of South Asia. Archaeology suggests that the Gupta period witnessed a major transition in settlement patterns with widespread abandonment or demographic contraction at dozens of urban sites. With several regional exceptions coinage seems to have declined as a medium of exchange. Non-religious literary sources continued to describe multi-city interactions and an urban culture but many of these references were stereotypical representations of anachronistic features. Accompanying these phenomena was a steady increase in epigraphic sources recording land grants to religious institutions, and a pronounced localization of political authority (Sharma 1987; 2001: 119–64; Thakur 1981: 260–329; Thakur and Jha 1994).

In order to interpret urbanization during and after the Gupta period we must appreciate macro-level changes that were producing new patterns of interaction. The augmentation of land-grant source material, preserved on copper plates or stone, indicates a steady expansion of the agrarian economy throughout the subcontinent, along with state formation on the periphery of the imperial heartland of north-central India, throughout peninsular India and in central or southern Sri Lanka. These are precisely the prerequisites for central-place formation encountered during the preliminary phases of early historical urbanization and they produced an expanded configuration of marketing and administrative nodes. Simultaneously, Afro-Eurasian commercial opportunities expanded dramatically. As testified by the regular visits of Chinese Buddhist pilgrims, South Asian connectivity with the overland Silk Road remained operational, if temporarily disrupted within segments by political or military events. Within the western sector of Indian Ocean, trade connections to the Mediterranean through the Red Sea until the seventh century involved the intermediation of the empire of Axum, while trade through the Persian Gulf apparently increased under the aegis of the Sasanians who may have controlled ports even in southern Pakistan (Whitehouse 1996). Then, in the seventh century, the Arab conquests united southwest Asia while the Tang, based in Xian, created a unified empire in China, forming two interconnected realms of secure commerce. There was a rapid increase in Arab involvement in Indian Ocean shipping down the east coast of Africa, along the western coast of India and through Sri Lanka. By the late-eighth century, as Baghdad became one of the world's great cities and Basra its oceanic port, direct routes were available from the Persian Gulf to China, although most voyages were segmented and involved South Asian intermediaries (Chaudhury 1985: 49–51). It was precisely during this period that South Asian interactions with Southeast Asia were peaking manifested in a wholesale transfer of cultural and institutional forms (Ray, H.P 1995: 160–5). One might imagine, therefore, that changes in the agrarian economy, greater political complexity and the amplification of the scale of Indian Ocean commerce would result in South Asian urban growth.

In the plains of northern India, where a post-Kushana abandonment of many settlements is most pronounced, there was in fact considerable continuity in settlement until the end of the sixth century at many older sites and we may be witnessing a reallocation of central place responsibilities rather than a general decline (Roy 2000; Thapar 2002: 298, 456). The testimonies of Chinese pilgrims that many north Indian cities lay in ruins also include references to chains of functioning commercial nodes that provided access to western and eastern coastal emporiums and to the Silk Road in the northwest well into the seventh century (Liu 1988: 33–4).

John S. Deyell's painstaking work on coinage demonstrates that the volume of silver-copper coins in north-central India in the ninth and tenth centuries, under the domination of the Gurjara-Pratihara dynasty, compared favorably with the volume of money from earlier and later periods. Simultaneously, in a swath of territory from northwest India to Afghanistan, the coinage of the Shahi kings whose economy relied on caravan trade displayed a remarkable continuity in silver content that made it a valuable commodity as far away as the Baltic Sea. This situation has parallels in Gujarat, which in Deyell's view 'has seldom been without a reliable, stable, silver coinage in the last two millennia' (Deyell 1990: 238–40). Turning to epigraphy, if the steadily increasing corpus of inscriptional material concentrates primarily on land transfers, some documents describe towns and commercial networks. B. D. Chattopadhyaya (1994: 89–119, 130–182), working on inscriptions from Rajasthan, the upper and middle Ganga River valley, and Malwa, describes the expansion of 'centers of exchange' or 'nodal points' (*hatta* or *mandapika*) and associated residential areas, often serving as the seats of local ruling lineages. Mercantile and artisan guilds (*sreni*) were responsible for temple construction at these 'rural market centers' that 'could and did emerge in the context of a land grant economy' (p. 149). A detailed survey of long-term trends in Rajasthan sees the eighth century as a watershed in the growth of central places, as evidenced by the formation of 'Rajput' political seats featuring extensive temple construction. The handful of prominent settlements in this region may have included populations of between 30,000 and 40,000, with smaller headquarters housing perhaps 10,000 persons (Jain 1972: 467–8).

We encounter the most impressive concentration of population in Kannauj, or Kanyakubja, which replaced Pataliputra as the premier city in northern India during the late-first millennium. Early literature attests the existence of a settlement here at the dawn of the second urbanization and archaeological finds include portions of ornamental gateways characteristic of early Buddhist monastic institutions. The location shot into prominence by the seventh century when its strategic significance made it the capital of an empire assembled by Harshavardhana (606–47), whose family had its ancestral seat further west in Sthanvisvara (Thaneswar). The Chinese pilgrim Xuan Zang, who visited during Harsha's reign, describes Kannauj as follows:

> The capital, which had the Ganges on its west [sic] side, was above twenty li [5.6 kilometers] in length by four or five li [1.2 kilometers] in breadth; it was very strongly defended and had lofty structures everywhere; there were beautiful gardens and tanks of clear water, and in it rarities from strange lands were collected. The inhabitants were well off and there were families of great wealth; fruit and flowers were abundant, and sowing and reaping had their seasons. The people had a refined appearance and dressed in glossy silk attire; they were given to learning and the arts, and were clear and suggestive in discourse; they were equally divided between orthodoxy and heterodoxy.

There were above 100 Buddhist monasteries with more than 10,000 Brethren who were students of both the 'Vehicles.' There were more than 200 Deva-Temples and the non-Buddhists [religious specialists] were several thousands in number

(Watters 1904–5: 341).

Xuan Zang describes the return of the king to his capital after a successful campaign along the eastern Ganga River and his encampment in temporary quarters in a garden west of the Ganga River. Nearby, east of a great monastery and associated rest house, stands a tower 30 meters tall which contains a statue of the Buddha of the same height as the king and an altar with a place for washing this statue. After a 20-day period during which brahmanas and monks are fed the king leads a parade, accompanied by music from his encampment, to the tower along with a caparisoned elephant on which is a three-foot statue of the Buddha. The king washes his small image in scented water at the altar and bears it to the tower where he offers it silken garments with precious stones. A feast follows, at which monks presumably are fed, and then men of learning discuss intellectual issues in the king's presence before he retires in state to his quarters (Beall 1884: 217–19). These rituals exemplify the manner in which the conqueror confirms dominion over the earth through identification with a personal Buddha and publicly identifies that image with a location of power within the city. The strategic significance thus confirmed during Harsha's reign made this city a crucial token in subsequent struggles for empire in northern India. The Rashtrakutas from peninsular India targeted Kannauj during their northern campaigns in the ninth and tenth centuries. The Gurjara-Pratiharas relocated from Sind or Rajasthan and established their capital in Kannauj in 815. The city was still an important administrative center during the thirteenth century.

When Alexander Cunningham (1924: 430–7) visited Kannauj the population of 16,000 lived in the north end of the old city in an area including the 'citadel' (*qila*). It exhibited a triangular plan about 1.2 kilometers on each side with a mound on the northeast rising at least 20 meters high protected by the old bed of the Ganga; a mound on the northwest rising at least 13 meters protected by a dry stream bed; and a mound on the south at least 10 meters high fronted by a ditch that had become one of the city's main roads. Inhabitants testified that the boundaries of the city had once stretched almost 5 kilometers north to south. Looking at extant fortification ruins Cunningham corroborated this local testimony and suggested the existence of at least three gates to the old city, with a separate mound called Rajgir, the 'House of the King,' lying about 5 kilometers to the southeast.

With a group of colleagues I happened to visit Kannauj in 2002 after the Census of India tallied a population of 71,530. Driving through the undulating relief of the city, which was in fact the top of a giant mound of ruins, one could see a number of older brick walls still visible in road cuts and other places where the citizens had chopped into the mound. In the northeastern portion of the city one could stand on a cliff about 20 meters high that corresponds to the old fortification wall. The view from there included a fine panorama of the mound to the north, where

Figure 2 View of the mound at Kannauj.

local cultivators had been busy destroying sections of the mound in order to create terraces about 4 meters tall (see Figure 2). They were discarding the excess dirt (and artifacts) from these excavations but showed us a small pile of stone pillars and lintels that they had saved. In the walls of the lowest terrace we could touch the brick walls of earlier constructions and found a fragment of imitation Chinese pottery. The lack of historical preservation is symptomatic of a process occurring at thousands of sites in South Asia under the pressure of more recent demographic growth and urban expansion, but in the case of Kannauj it is resulting in the erasure of one of the most important early cities.

In what is today Pakistan, Arabic sources and archaeology provide detailed observations on cities during the late-first millennium. Within the Indus River delta, connectivity with the Indian Ocean trading system had concentrated, since at least the first century, at the port of Banbhore linked to an interior administrative and production center that Arabic writers called Brahmanabad. When Arab conquistadors ostensibly working for the Ummayad caliphate overran Sind in 711–12 they took the deltaic centers and then appropriated the interior cities of Multan and Alor (Aror), already established as political seats, as the centers for their new administration. The Arab rulers of Sind introduced to South Asian cities a new model for urban planning that included the mosque (*masjid*) as an important architectural focus and opened a new dialogue with architectural forms elaborated in western Asia and the Mediterranean world.

Between 730 and 732 a new capital rose adjacent to Brahmanabad that the new rulers called Mansurah. Archaeologists have estimated that this city measured 275 hectares with an L-shaped plan. Fortification walls consisted of burnt bricks with a mud and mud brick core and featured regular semi-circular bastions. A gateway opened on the Indus River to the east. Wide roads met each other at right angles throughout the city. Three roads intersected in an open plaza near a large public building and a grand mosque measuring 76.2 by 45.7 meters stood in the middle of the eastern section of the city. The southeastern part of the settlement had workshops for semi-precious stones, kilns, glass and terracotta. Meanwhile, Banbhore became a city called Daybul covering 22.3 hectares in a roughly quadrangular plan located on the bank of a navigable creek linked to the Arabian Sea and to the Indus River. An inner fortification wall separated the site into two roughly equal zones; outside the northern city wall was an industrial area for cloth dying. Changes in the course of the lower Indus River eventually caused the decline of Daybul and its replacement by a port called Lahori Bandar during the eleventh century. Mansurah, also isolated from the shifting river, was abandoned by the twelfth century in favor of a new provincial capital at Thatta. But during the entire period of Arab rule these sites were embedded in a larger framework of urban sites. Based on a map drawn in 967, André Wink has identified 24 contemporary towns in Sind and 17 or 18 in southern Baluchistan (Wink 1990: 175–89, 201–6; Mughal 1992; Kervran 1999).

In Bengal, a number of archaeological sites such as Bangarh and Mangalkot exhibit a continuity of settlement extending from the peak of early historical urbanization into the Pala period (eighth–eleventh centuries). The continuously occupied site of Karnasuvarna (modern Rajbadidanga) even achieved prominence in the seventh century as the administrative seat of the conqueror Sasanka who attempted to control north-central India (Chattopadhyaya 2003: 85–9). At Pundranagara (Mahasthan) habitation apparently continued through the Gupta period and expanded under the rule of the Pala kings when the site reached its greatest complexity. Its fortified city has yielded evidence for a relatively high level of habitation and activity. Outside the walls, 31 additional mounds indicate the sites of religious monuments and associated settlements. The area stretching about 6 kilometers to the northwest, already the locale for Buddhist monastic establishments, received additional constructions during this period. A new extension of constructions extending about 4 kilometers southwest of the city demonstrates different characteristics that indicate autonomous communities with their own tanks and ceremonial centers (Ahmad 1971; Alam and Salles 2001). Evidence for similar levels of urban expansion by at least the eighth century, closely associated with major religious monuments, exists in multiple locations in Bangladesh and West Bengal (Chakrabarti 1992; Thakur 2000). In addition, the primarily agricultural economy of lowland Assam produced its first known urban site by the ninth century when the Salastambha rulers constructed a capital and military camp at Hadapesvara (modern Tezpur) on the site of a pre-existing market center; the succeeding Pala kings retained this site as a ceremonial center and established links with other market-towns where they constructed forts, described as *nagara* by the eleventh century (Momin 1991).

In an epigraphic study of urbanization in Karnataka between 600 and 1200 Om Prakash Prasad (1989) finds references to 11 towns in the seventh century; 10 in the eighth; 12 in the ninth; and 19 in the tenth. Out of this total of 52 places only nine appear in just one century while three appear in three centuries and five appear in all four centuries. The latter group includes Banavasi and Kolhapur which have yielded important archaeological evidence of urbanization and long-distance commerce in the early-first millennium; the significant Jain center of Sravana Belgola; the regional political seat of Talakadu; and the coastal site of Goa. These data suggest that a pronounced continuity in the occupation of central places and a major expansion of towns and trade after the year 1000 rested on a continuous history of urban development going back in some cases to the beginning of the first millennium.

The site of Aihole (Ayyavole) in northern Karnataka, which appears in Prasad's study only in the seventh century, demonstrates the continuing importance of 'guilds' in cities throughout the second half of the first millennium. Today the site is less than half a kilometer on each side, lying next to the unimpressive flow of the Malaprabha River, a tributary of the Krishna. Scholars have been interested in Aihole primarily because of the variety of exquisite stone temples that have survived here from the period of the early Chalukya dynasty (sixth–eighth centuries) which had its seats in nearby Badami and Pattadakal, created a peninsular-spanning empire, and survived through a cadet branch in Andhra Pradesh until the eleventh century (Gupte 1967; Rajasekhara 1985). The temples at Aihole are described typically as examples of 'Chalukya' art but their construction may result in part from resources donated by local commercial interests whose identity has been emerging from studies of inscriptions.

In imagining the setting of Aihole's temples in the seventh century, one must visualize the Malaprabha River (unaffected by modern dam construction) providing a wide waterway connecting all of peninsular India to a town that surrounded the shrines within primarily wooden residential and office blocks without fortification walls. This town was the home of a mercantile consortium calling themselves the Five Hundred or in some cases the Five Hundred of a Thousand Directions. They were active originally in Karnataka, expanded into Tamil Nadu, then moved into Sri Lanka, Kerala, Andhra Pradesh, and Southeast Asia. Their many donations to religious institutions eventually included references to dozens of articles that they transported, including many Southeast Asian luxury items. They interacted with other consortiums known as the Manigramam (Village of Jewels) or the Nanadesi (Those of Many Lands) that were also active in peninsular India and the Bay of Bengal littoral. It seems likely that the continued use of the title 'Ayyavole Five Hundred' in these varied settings took on the nature of a brand name, with various branches of the consortium functioning as independent companies and specializing in particular goods. The many find spots of their records and the dozens of references to places they frequented point to a ramified network of central places that was coming into existence by the ninth century, at the latest, and that was still expanding in size and complexity when the

Five Hundred were most active in the twelfth and thirteenth centuries (Abraham 1988; Champakalakshmi 2001).

In a short study of literary portrayals of early South Asian urbanization, B. D. Chattopadhyaya points out (2003: 122) that 'representations of the city are a requirement' in Sanskrit fiction of the late-first millennium. These fictional works aimed at an audience consisting primarily of city-dwelling princely families, government administrators, and wealthy merchants and the main characters come from similar backgrounds. If part of the action in a story takes place in a non-urban environment (on the battlefield, at a sylvan hermitage, or in the Vindhya Forest, for example), the heroes and heroines have traveled there from a city and eventually return to a city. A prime example is Banabhatta's *Harshacharita*, composed by a contemporary of Harshavardhana; most of the activities in the text take place outside of Kannauj, but the capital (possession of which defines the king) exerts throughout the text a powerful centripetal force. In Banabhatta's *Kadambari* the base of operations is contemporary Ujjayini which appears early in the tale with standard characteristics: It is surrounded by a moat, has suburbs, possesses turrets reaching the sky, is crisscrossed by avenues lined with bazaars, is adorned with many temples, includes groves, parks, and ponds, and displays a wide range of architecture (assembly halls, houses, well, watering sheds, way stations, bridges, and machinery). Its (male) citizens are urbane and sophisticated, and good-looking too:

> The city is inhabited by a pleasure-loving people whose fame is celebrated in all the world. They, like the moon in the locks of the Destroyer, have wealth in the tens of millions... Though they are bold, they bow to others. Though their speech is sweetly spoken, they are truthful. Though they are handsome, they are content with their own wives. Though they rise to greet guests, they do not petition others... They are exceedingly learned, liberal, and intelligent. Their speech is accompanied by a smile; their humor is charming; their dress bright; and they have mastered the languages of all countries. They are clever at witty speech, wise with the study of narratives and tales, and know all scripts... They enjoy skill in all the arts, such as gambling.
>
> (Banabhatta 1991: 52).

Clearly, the social world addressed by literature of this type (which has exerted a huge impact on subsequent writing) remained vibrant during the late-first millennium. The decidedly elitist perspectives appearing in Sanskrit fiction and the subordination of servants, workers and 'tribal' characters that occurs repeatedly therein reflect the class divisions developing within South Asia, increasingly characterized as aspects of *jati* or caste.

By the end of the first millennium the process of state formation, which had been occurring for centuries through the mobilization of resources at the regional level, had produced a sub-continental array of regional polities controlled in some cases by old princely families (e.g. the Chalukyas) but also including an influx of upstart lineages. The largest polities engaged in a constant struggle to construct a sub-continental empire but in practice this policy required a constant accommodation of sub-regional and local interests. The result was a peculiarly South Asian configuration of compartmentalized sovereignties that historians have defined with terms such as 'feudalism' (Sharma 1965) or the 'segmentary' state (Stein 1980). Within a 'core' or 'nuclear' region, that typically included a productive agrarian tract, it was possible for rulers to eliminate alternative sources of power and to appoint officials within bureaucratic or proto-bureaucratic systems. On the periphery of the kingdom there was a greater tendency to coerce or to attract the loyalty of 'feudatories,' described in many inscriptions and contemporary texts as *samantas*, who often controlled their own resource bases and who were always ready to make their own bids for supreme power. Imperial ambitions typically involved the consolidation of an array of *samantas*, or the 'samantisation' of the state (Kulke and Rothermund 1986: 129–30; Kulke 1995). Conquest, involving coalitions of feudatory forces and elements of a paid, standing army, aimed at the control of additional core regions or, more often, at the acknowledgement of subordination by defeated rulers who were allowed to retain their thrones. Thus the term for emperor was 'the primary king among great kings' (*maharaja-adhiraja*) and textual sources describe the ruler's feet as glowing with the light reflected from the crowns of defeated rulers bowing before him. The home base(s) of the hegemonic ruler, as well as the bases of the *samanta* circle, all served as courtly magnets for officials, commercial groups, artisans, and service workers of all kinds. This process of state formation and the concomitant creation of central places remained underway in some regions of South Asia even in the early-nineteenth century (Tanabe 1999; Schnepel 2002).

2 The sacred city and the fort

The opening action of the blockbuster film *Mughal-e-Azam* (1960, dir. K. Asif) shows a bearded, barefoot man who we know is the emperor Akbar, walking toward the camera through a desert wasteland, followed in the distance by a large caravan including his state elephant and a number of bullock carts with tents that shelter the ladies of his court. We learn from the narrator (who is the land of India personified) that the emperor is without son and heir, and is traveling to the shrine of a great spiritual leader to seek his intervention. After the emperor arrives at the shrine (in Ajmer), he kneels with his wife before the tomb of the saint in the presence of its bearded custodians, who sit kneading their prayer beads. Acting on their advice he addresses the saint as the lord of both material and spiritual worlds (*donon jahan ke malik*), saying 'You are the emperor of emperors' (*shehanshahon ke tum shehenhsah hai*). The narrator then describes the kneeling petitioner: 'And our emperor, before whom the whole world had bowed, bowed his own head in the presence of a fakir's authority' (*aur us shehenshah ne jis ke age sari duniya jhukti thi ek phakir ki sarkar main apna sar jhuka diya*). At the end of his prayer, we see the hands of a custodian placing flowers in the hands of Akbar's kneeling wife. The next scene, nine months later, portrays the celebration at the palace at the news of the birth of a son and heir, Salim, who will become the emperor Jahangir.

This chapter will examine the recurring theme of the interactions between sacred power and administrative authority (so often portrayed and enacted in South Asia) and sketch its impact on urbanization since the late-first millennium. It will concentrate first on manifestations of what we may call the sacred city, which connotes not only the urban as a realization within the mundane world of a cosmic plan or a potent spiritual force, but also suggests that specific locales exude a spiritual power that attracts human settlement and coordinate recurrent, dense human activity around them. The chapter then considers major changes that occurred in the military and political landscape of South Asia around the year 1000 that enabled a more intensive extraction of resources by the state and resulted in a new array of fortified administrative centers, culminating in the Mughal Empire, and that has become, in part, the precursor of contemporary urbanization. During the following presentation it may be possible for analytical purposes to consider either the sacred city or the administrative center as separate entities, but in reality, as in the film, they operated simultaneously. The interpenetration of the sacred and the state, accompanied by the dynamism of commercial groups, amplified the processes of city formation.

Temples and pilgrimage sites

The temple had begun as hut or small quadrilateral building with the image of a deity in its center viewable or accessible through a single doorway typically on the east side. Constructed in brick or stone, with the addition of a pillared porch or hallway in the front and a vertical extension of the roof, the temple began its transformation to the most impressive architectural form in South Asia at the beginning of the second millennium. As political and commercial patrons funneled more funds into larger temples and their growing ritual staffs, centrally placed temples became the hubs for the redistribution of ever larger amounts and types of resources, including precious metals and currency, agrarian produce, animals, art, and even people. At the political seats of regional rulers, temples became gigantic monuments testifying to the power of their political overlords (Michell 1977). The Rashtrakutas had led the way with the massive rock-cut temple at Ellora (late-eighth century). The response came from the Chola kings in the Rajarajesvara Temple at Tanjavur, and from the Ganga kings in the Lingaraja Temple in Bhubaneswar (both constructed in the early-eleventh century). In a similar fashion, political leaders at a variety of levels within the regional state funneled resources into the construction of smaller temples. This process that combined piety with public legitimacy led to a spate of temple construction that transformed the built environments of urban sites (see Map 5).

The quest for movement through space toward a location of spiritual power, simultaneously a sacrifice of self and a satisfaction of desire for travel, has established over time a practically infinite series of South Asian pilgrimages, providing cash flow and employment for specialists at single sites or at multiple destinations conceptualized as components within a sacred array. This drive toward pilgrimage, manifested in all religious groups, came to support sizeable percentages of the workforce in places like Varanasi, and has provided a primary stimulus for urban growth in hundreds of locations. The very existence of many small towns in hilly or mountainous regions depends on the pilgrimage traffic attracted to famous sacred centers (e.g. Badrinath and Kedarnath in Uttaranchal). Destinations in the Himalaya, in other hilly tracts, or along the scenic banks of water bodies demonstrate the advantage for potential pilgrim towns of strategic or physically attractive locales. The greatest example is Allahabad (Prayag), where the confluence of the holy Yamuna and Ganga Rivers attracts a regular stream of bathers, but every 12 years at the Kumbha Mela attracts major gatherings of devotees (estimated conservatively at more than 20 million in 2001) to the world's biggest festival.

Religious specialists with a systematic bent have long attempted to group and quantify such phenomena. In this manner Prayag becomes one of four sites for the Kumbha Mela (along with Hardwar, Nasik, and Ujjayini). The 'Seven Cities'

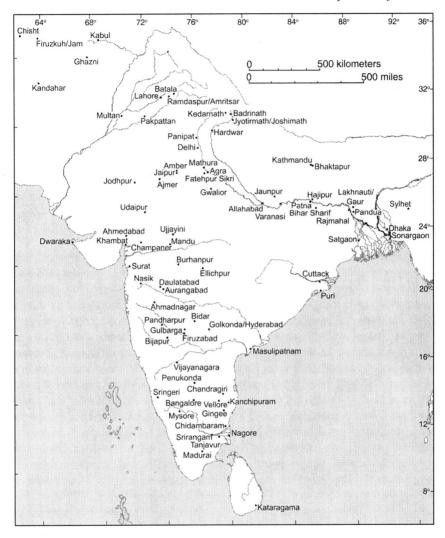

Map 5 Sacred sites and administrative centers, ca. 800–1800

leading to liberation include Dwaraka, Kanchipuram, Hardwar, Mathura, Ujjayini and Varanasi; the 12 important sites of the 'lingas of splendour' (*jyotirlinga*) attracting pilgrimage for Shiva include Kedarnath; there are 108 seats of female energy (*shakti pithas*), etc. Similarly, each region and sub-region boasts a wide range of polycentric networks attracting devotees from different religious paths and, in many cases, devotees from all religious paths. In only the best-known Maharashtrian example, the Vaishnava shrine of Vithoba (Vitthala) in the otherwise unassuming city of Pandharpur (population ca. 60,000) attracts an influx of half a million during four points during the year, many devotees walking in caravans from other towns associated with the ministries of famous saints active between the thirteenth and seventeenth centuries (Mokashi 1987; Feldhaus 2003). In Sri Lanka, Hindus, Buddhists and Muslims travel annually by the tens of thousands (since the 1950s mostly by car or bus, although some thousands still may walk hundreds of kilometers) to shrines at Kataragama, a small township in the southeastern part of the island, where Murugan, the son of Shiva, has his seat near a Buddhist institution and a mosque (Harrigan 1998).

The combination of site-based sacrality and local or long-distance movement toward it have created the conditions for a concentration of resources, commercial interests, and state intervention within specific settlements or neighborhoods that have become magnets for long-term human settlement. We will now examine examples of such phenomena first in southern India, and then in the north.

The south Indian temple city

In southern India, and particularly in Tamil Nadu, the survival of hundreds of temples and associated settlements dating back to the late-first and early-second millennium, along with the accessibility of thousands of inscriptions, allow an in-depth understanding of the evolution of urban form, the model of the sacred city, and the social groups responsible for the growth of unique, polycentric city regions. The classic settlement plan involved a quadrilateral space at the heart of a village, dedicated to a shrine for the god and/or goddess, with different high-caste groups living along the surrounding street. As a settlement grew in size, funding from political authorities or from mercantile groups supported the re-construction of the shrine in brick or stone and the erection of a surrounding wall with cardinally oriented entranceways. With expansions and artistic embellishments to the central shrine, establishments for other deities, pillared halls and administrative offices, and additional surrounding walls featuring a radical vertical extension of entrance towers, the temple could grow to become effectively a separate city – a phenomenon that occurred at important sites such as Srirangam (78 hectares) or Chidambaram (16 hectares). The prototypical example of the embedding of this model within the larger urban fabric is Madurai, where the sacred precincts of the city's main temple dedicated to Shiva as Sundaresvarar and his consort Minakshi cover 6 hectares while a series of quadrilateral streets surround the temple in a nested pattern (Lewandowski 1977: 190–6; Michell and Ramamrutham 1993).

Kanchipuram in Tamil Nadu demonstrates the phenomenon of neighborhood growth around multiple temple sites that resulted in an important sacred city. Kanchipuram today is a growing sub-district headquarters famous for silk textiles, exhibiting a distinctive L-shaped plan that probably has changed little during the last millennium. It existed as a small town associated with monastic institutions during the early historical period, served as the capital of the Pallava kings (seventh–tenth centuries), and became a secondary seat for the Chola kings (ninth–thirteenth centuries). The city plan features neighborhoods surrounding several dozen major temples constructed under the Pallava and Chola kings and enhanced by later donations. The original city center, perhaps fortified in the early historical pattern, lay around the shrines for Kamakshi, who became the city's goddess, and the Ulagalanda Perumal Temple for Vishnu, 'the lord who resides within the interior of the holy settlement' (*tiruvurakattu alvar*). Additional nuclei lay around the Ekamranatha Temple for Shiva on the north side of the settlement; a Jain neighborhood in the southwest (even today called Jina Kanchi); and the Varadaraja Perumal Temple for Vishnu in the southeast. Pallava-period constructions of the Vaikunta Perumal Temple on the east side and the Kailasanatha Temple on the west completed the basic outlines of the city. Until the recent past, open spaces probably separated the various neighborhoods surrounding these and smaller shrines. Garden lands and agricultural fields began at the very edge of the town, with water obtained through irrigation systems originating in a group of artificial tanks and a small rivulet branching from the Palar River – a pattern reminiscent of Anuradhapura in Sri Lanka (see Chapter 1). The high walls of the individual temple compounds provided security for the images and ornaments of precious metals and for other treasures accumulated through endowments (Champakalakshmi 1996; Shanmugam 2000).

The 'place histories' (*sthala purana*) or 'praise texts' (*mahatmya*) associated with specific temples or with sacred cities often describe their origins in forest hermitages of holy brahmanas, but by the Pallava period kings were creating endowments for groups of brahmanas that defrayed taxes or transferred ownership of blocks of land in order to support ritual activities and scholarship. By the Chola period, assemblies of brahmanas who received support from such grants were active in donations and administration of temple endowments, and the state was creating special administrative endowments dedicated for the support of temple rituals, carried out by bodies of temple officials. Separate assemblies of merchants calling themselves Nagarattar, or 'people of the city' – some handling local retail and wholesale trade, others working with long-distance traders like the Five Hundred – were interacting with bodies of skilled artisans to manage the commercial economy and also provide donations to temples (Hall 1980; Ramaswamy 1993). The settlement assembly (*Urar*), consisting mostly of leading members of local agricultural groups, provided probably the largest channel of resources to support religious institutions. By the twelfth century, these corporate bodies were giving way to private donors who often bore high honorific titles associated with the state and who controlled their own resource bases. Female members of the royal households and other high-ranking families, along with multi-generational groups of women controlling resources dedicated to temple service, played leading roles in the creation of temple endowments and the maintenance of ritual activities (Orr 2000).

The Chola state intervened locally to disburse funds for major expenditures such as temple construction, renovation, or architectural expansion, and periodically adjudicated disputes over resources, but allowed considerable local autonomy in the regulation of religious affairs and urban governance. The edifice of state power rested in part on ritualized gift giving to religious institutions, which allowed local notables to establish their leadership credentials and their loyalty to the state through ostentatious display at sacred centers. The resulting spatial pattern of small, unfortified settlements clustered around temple sites exhibited the economic and social dynamism one might expect from the concentrated population clusters characteristic of early historical urbanization – a distinctively distributed quality that would remain typical of many South Indian cities. Communication and transportation among distributed settlements occurred through a dense network of roads. The terminology appearing in inscriptions differentiates between small 'paths' (*vati*) that traversed fields, 'roads' (*vali*) that ranged from the often quadrilateral patterns of urban sites to routes connecting contiguous settlements, and 'big roads' (*peruvali*) that served as highways between major sites. The latter categories were unpaved but often ran along causeways raised above surrounding agricultural tracts, and in many cases still serve as the roadbeds for contemporary paved roads (Deloche 1993: 79–81; Heitzman 2001b; Heitzman and Rajagopal 2004).

In the early-fourteenth century, a coalition of Telugu-speaking warriors began a process of conquest that would bring the former Chola territories and all of southern India under a single kingdom for the first time, with its capital in northern Karnataka at Vijayanagar, the City of Victory – the largest city ever seen in the south. Located next to the Tungabhadra River amid spectacular, rugged hills and bottomlands, the urbanized landscape still covers 25 square kilometers oriented around discrete sacred precincts (see Map 6). Following the analysis of John M. Fritz *et al.* (1984), we may distinguish a zone stretching along the south bank of the river as a 'sacred center' with a series of four major temple complexes forming the nuclei of urban quarters (*pura*) with dedicated commercial malls. To the south, flanked on both sides by rocky ridges, lies an agrarian zone still irrigated by canals originating in the river several kilometers to the west; this zone seems to pre-date the metropolis, but became an integral part of the urban fabric. Farther to the south lies the residential and administrative heart of the city, the 'urban core' protected by massive defensive walls and fortified gateways. Within this core, the 'royal center' is a rough ellipse about one kilometer north-south and 1.5 kilometers east-west, consisting of 31 enclosures surrounding the Ramachandra Temple complex. Here we find some of the earliest palace structures surviving in South Asia, including the 'great platform' and the base of a hundred-pillared hall 40 meters square (which at one time supported multistoried wooden superstructures), and subsidiary structures including massive elephant stables capped by some of the earliest true domes extant in southern India. Residential neighborhoods surround the royal center on its north (e,g, the 'noblemen's quarters') and east (e.g. a 'Muslim quarter' marked by a series of stone tombs), and occupy the space on the southeast that was bounded by an outer defensive wall tied into the bund of the Kamalapura Tank, which also features several bastions. By the sixteenth century, this large, man-made lake fed agricultural fields to its north and periodically provided water for the royal center through aqueducts and pipes that fed a number of pools, including the 'great tank' measuring 67 by 22 meters. The remainder of the city drew its water from canals, wells, and a number of tanks storing runoff water – the latter essential in one of the driest areas of southern India (Davison-Jenkins 1997). Archaeological evidence of lime processing, stone working and ironworking aligns

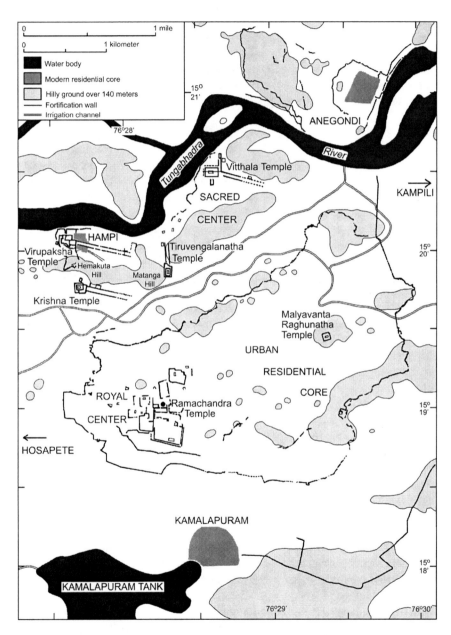

Map 6 City and region of Vijayanagara. Adapted from Survey of India sheet; Fritz *et al.*
1984; Morrison 1995.

with travelers' accounts of peninsular India's largest commercial market to indicate a multifaceted economy surrounding a large military encampment (Morrison 1995: 64–6, 86–8). The road network (including a bridge across the Tungabhadra) linked the city to a number of suburban sites including Hosapete (the 'new market') to the west, a group of fortified villages to the south, the older fortified site of Anegondi to the northeast, and the old Chalukya center of Kampili 11 kilometers to the east.

Archaic memory associated the site with the worship of the goddess Pampa, who later was said to marry Shiva in his form as Virupaksha at a temple that became a magnet for pilgrims. A Chalukya-period record referred to the town around the Virupaksha temple (today Hampi/Hampe) as Virupaksha *pattana* – the latter term typically signifying a commercial center. The earliest dynasty of rulers at Vijayanagara, the Sangamas (1336–1485), were primarily Shaivite in orientation, and followed the practice long established for local lords in using donations for the Virupaksha temple and for shrines on nearby Hemakuta Hill as a means of legitimizing their authority (Wagoner 1996, 2001). They promoted a second level of sanctity by using their association with a mendicant preceptor, Vidyaranya, to create narratives of the city's foundation that confirmed its identity as an imperial capital. According to these narratives, Vidyaranya had traveled to the most sacred of all cities, Varanasi (see below), where he achieved knowledge allowing him plan the urban core with its base on Matanga Hill. His actions, surrounded with miraculous events and governed by the ritual prescriptions of architectural treatises, led to the alternate naming of Vidyanagara, the 'City of Knowledge.' A third level of sacrality became salient under the Vijayanagara rulers after 1485, who were more Vaishnava in their orientation, and who tapped into older associations of the area with events occurring in the *Ramayana*. This led to the construction of the Ramachandra temple at the heart of the royal enclosure, which became the pivot of the city's architectural and transportation network. The annual Ramanavami Festival, described in detail around 1520–2 by the Portuguese visitor Domingo Paes (Sewell 1962: 253–69), became the most important public event in the capital, an occasion when the leading personages of the empire assembled to link the king as representative of Vishnu with architectural gigantism, conspicuous consumption, artistic performance, and military review.

The result of these approaches was the embellishment of Vijayangara with religious architecture ranging from the large temples with royal connections to the many smaller shrines in the urban core apparently established by various occupational groups. A recent survey of surviving monuments has identified 350 temples, including 91 Shaiva and 93 Vaishnava sites (Verghese 2004: 426–7). The spatial alignment of various temple groupings toward each other and toward the movements of celestial bodies created relationships between the cosmos, the city, the bodies of the ritual specialists and the royal family (Malville 2001). The concatenation of sacred associations with the city was so powerful that catastrophic military defeat in 1565 and the sack of the city led the surviving members of the royal family to describe (unsuccessfully) their later seats at

Penukonda and Chandragiri – decidedly smaller and unimpressive centers – as the new Vijayanagaras (Wagoner 1993: 33–50).

The varying combinations of state intervention, commercial interest, and the fulfillment of devotion through movement and the sensory experience of the divine have created at least one public religious performance or civic ritual in every major city that in some sense defines its urban quality. One of the more famous examples is the annual festival occurring in Madurai during the first month of the solar year, falling during the hot season before the summer rains. This is a classic portrayal of unity through the wedding of its god, Sundaresvarar, with its goddess, Minakshi, the latter constituting the main focus for devotion. A steady amplification of ritual activities over a number of days culminates in the circumambulation of the city's main streets by the gigantic cars (*ratha*, *ter*) carrying the images of god and goddess, bringing out hundreds of thousands of observers. Through an innovation attributed to Tirumalai Nayaka (1623–60), the most impressive ruler of one of the successor kingdoms to the Vijayanagara Empire, the car festival ends just as the traveling image of the Beautiful Lord, Vishnu, is arriving at the Vaikai River after a 20-kilometer trip from his hill shrine north of the city. In this elaboration of the wedding narrative, Vishnu is Minakshi's brother, and he has to give her away in marriage. A concourse of perhaps 500,000 persons, including many from the agrarian region surrounding the city, welcomes Vishnu upon his arrival at the river, annually connecting the city-defining celebrations with a ritualized regional identity (Binford *et al.* 1976).

A different version of city definition occurs annually in Bangalore, which eventually succeeded Vijayanagara as the leading metropolis of the southern Deccan. Unlike the wedding of Minakshi in Madurai, which remains the responsibility of temple brahmanas, Bangalore's leading celebration lies in the hands of a backward caste group called the Tigalas associated with horticulture, who train regularly for their demanding physical roles in wrestling clubs throughout the city (similar clubs play a major role in many of the festivals mounted in Varanasi as well). The goddess Draupadi, who as the heroine of the *Mahabharata* was married to the five Pandava heroes, manifests herself in aniconic form, represented by a pot carried by the main Karaga priest surrounded by sword-wielding hero-sons, preserving for posterity the martial image of the Tigala performers who served in the armies of the kings of Mysore as early as the seventeenth century. During successive days of the festival, culminating in a final processions attracting over 100,000 persons, the Karaga icon visits many locations in the old city of Bangalore that have long served as centers of spiritual power, including the tomb of a Sufi saint, and also visits a number of (now defunct) water bodies formerly important in the horticultural economy of a small city. In an informative reversal of regional demographic trends, the Karaga format that originally seems to have migrated to Bangalore in the seventeenth century with Tigalas from northern Tamil Nadu has been spreading recently from the old city of Bangalore to smaller enactments in its exploding suburbs, through ritual entrepreneurs from local Tigala communities (Srinivas 2001).

The northern sacred center

The quintessential sacred city in South Asia is, of course, Varanasi (Banaras) or Kashi, which lies on a ridge overlooking the northern-flowing Ganga River between the small Varana River on the north and the smaller Asi River 6.4 kilometers to the south. West of this ridge, a series of lowland basins until the nineteenth century featured about 25 small, interlinked lakes draining north into the Varana or east into the Ganga. This topography left the ridge area almost an island, with dry land only to its southwest, during annual summer flooding. The earliest identifiable city lay on the highest section of the ridge called Rajghat (the 'steps of the King'), protected on its west and north by the final bend of the Varana River and on its east by the Ganga. Here was the major ford across the Ganga, part of the great 'northern path' that ran west toward Gandhara and east toward Bengal. The intersection of land and water routes was undoubtedly one of the attractions of this site, and until the nineteenth century the Rajghat area was still the berthing area for river traffic (Singh 1955: 43). The old city, sparsely inhabited in more recent times, was still the capital of the Gahadavala kingdom (which also briefly controlled Kannauj) during the eleventh and twelfth centuries. Expansion toward the south along the ridge fronting the river and into the zone to its west, a process occurring over hundreds of years, created the contours of the contemporary city (population 1.3 million in 2005).

Varanasi achieved a venerable reputation as a *tirtha*, or ford, leading from material to spiritual consciousness, and thus attracted pilgrimage (*yatra*) culminating in a personal encounter with powerful sacred forces and a purifying contact with water. The earliest locales for this encounter were sylvan hermitages located along the Ganga and around natural or artificial water bodies to its west. By the late-sixteenth century, donations from wealthy donors throughout India were transforming the riverfront through the construction of *ghats*, or steps, along with a number of palace structures. A Gahadavala inscription mentioned only five ghats; a mid-seventeenth century text mentioned 25; and an enumeration at the end of the twentieth century yielded 84. Simultaneously, the re-construction of earlier temples that had disintegrated or been destroyed, and an increasing pace of construction for new temples, was transforming the architectural landscape of the immediate riverfront area and the habitation areas behind it. A source from the mid-twelfth century had already listed 350 shrines in Varanasi; in the late-twentieth century there were at least 2,500 (Eck 1982: 82; Singh 1993: 67, 215). The density of habitation around these shrines steadily increased with the construction of contiguous houses of three to five stories on both sides of streets just wide enough to allow access by animal-drawn carriages, producing a concentrated built environment that offers a dramatic contrast to the more distributed habitation patterns of many older towns in southern India. In the center of the contemporary city, near the Chauk or main market neighborhood, lies the densely populated Vishveshvara or Vishvanatha sector oriented toward the city's most important Shiva temple. Two wards in the northern part of the city have long been home to a highly concentrated Muslim population, who constituted over 30 percent of the inhabitants of Varanasi in the mid-twentieth century, and still provide most of the labor for the famous silk and brocade industry (Singh 1993: 63–4, 82–3).

The visits of thousands to Varanasi daily, or the tens of thousands on auspicious occasions determined by heavenly bodies, rest on an understanding of the city as an array or circle (*mandala*) of spatial relationships that manifest divine attributes. The physical alignment of shrines in different neighborhoods displays a regulated geometry connected to celestial positions. Maps or diagrams sold to pilgrims portray the city as a circle or a quadrilateral, with the physically variegated patterns of rivers, streets, and shrines rendered as a geometrically symmetrical display. Energetic pilgrims may experience this phenomenon directly by tracing the subtle infrastructure of the city on the *panchakrosha yatra* of 88.5 kilometers that includes stops at suburban temples constituting an outer rim of sacred space. More typically, pilgrims visit a more limited array of shrines on the boundaries of the built-up city, within the city's sacred sectors, along a series of bathing ghats, or at specific locations where resident priests may guide them through ritual actions. These activities appear efficacious because the physical characteristics of the city, which may demonstrate irregular or downright unpalatable features, are expressions of ordered, universal forces leading the devotee toward liberation. It is in this sense that Varanasi encapsulates for devotees all sacred sites, or stands where the spiritual forms of all other *tirthas* come together. The consciousness of entering a circle of sacred power motivates the many people who come to Varanasi to die (Eck 1982: 283–303; Singh 1993: 37–64; Lannoy 1999: 437–60).

The encounter with Varanasi as sacred city for its permanent citizens may include elements of the cosmic circle that attract pilgrims from elsewhere, but ordinary practice privileges movement toward city- or neighborhood-based centers that, as in Bhaktapur (see below), provide localized senses of identity. The localized sacred city may develop, as we have seen in our earlier examples, from initiatives springing up through the devotion of citizen groups or through manipulation by the state. In the former category, we may include the many hundreds of small shrines in Varanasi dedicated to Bir Babas, or 'hero fathers,' which claim to commemorate the memory of deceased persons, and thus channel the energy of ghost spirits, but in practice demarcate the domains of protective deities that control domains corresponding to urban neighborhoods. These types of shrines demonstrate continuity with old-fashioned village practice, but more directly exemplify attempts by low-caste and often impoverished citizens to find social order within expanding cityscapes (Coccari 1989).

At a higher level within the hierarchy of sacred locales are the temple celebrations (*sringar*) proliferating, with the assistance of local merchant associations and working-class devotees, at neighborhood shrines throughout the city, providing opportunities for musical performances by professional musicians and local groups. The revolving annual series of such celebrations increase business and enhance neighborhood fame and solidarity by attracting visitors from different parts of the city. In addition, Varanasi stages over 40 annual festivals (*mela*) attracting city-wide audiences, and annual Moharram processions, including competitive parades featuring models of Karbala (*taziya*) and even fire-walking, that engage the city's substantial Muslim population. As Nita Kumar has pointed out (1988), the gradual withdrawal of first royal, and then upper-class patronage from many of these events has given them an increasingly working-class character, making them appear to spontaneously grow from an alliance of a petty urban bourgeoisie and popular, neighborhood-based devotion.

At an even higher level, we have the example of *Ramcharitmanas* recitations, based on the sixteenth-century Hindi reworking of the *Ramayana* story by Tulsidas, who lived in Varanasi. These mostly small-scale performances achieved a grander scale of visibility after 1740 under the quasi-independent kings of Varanasi, who established a fort and palace across the Ganga southeast of the city, and pumped resources into an annual Ramlila performance enacted on an extensive nearby campus called Ramnagar, the 'city of Rama.' After the eclipse of the kings in the twentieth century, mercantile patronage fueled the growth of the Ramnagar performance into a gigantic festival attracting hundreds of thousands of devotees; the multiplication of venues within Varanasi created an entire sub-culture of specialized performers and connoisseurs; and the popularity of recitations spread throughout the Hindi-speaking regions of northern India to become perhaps the most widespread genre of public religious narrative (Lutgendorf 1991).

A more detailed examination of the lived environment in a sacred city is possible in the Kathmandu Valley of Nepal, where a distinctive style of urbanization has developed over the last 2,000 years. The fertile Valley, about 22 kilometers east-west and 17 kilometers north-south, lies at an average altitude of 1,340 meters surrounded by peaks between 1,800 and 2,700 meters. Until the twentieth century, the Valley was isolated from India between March and November by malarial conditions in the marshy piedmont of the Tarai, and was isolated from Tibet by snows between October and May; but in practice an annual rhythm of extensive trade along mountain footpaths made the Valley one of the great commercial centers of the Himalaya. Probably the earliest major settlement lay south of the Bagmati River at a place that came to be called Lalitapura or Lalitapattana (today called Patan), where four peripheral 'Ashokan' stupas demarcated the outer limits of a trading center (today the Patan or Mangal Darbar) surrounded by villages that eventually coalesced as urban neighborhoods. North of the Bagmati River, on a bluff east of the Vishnumati River, a separate commercial center grew along the northeast-tending route linking Pataliputra to Tibet, around a rest stop known as the Kashtamandapa, leading eventually to the coalescence of Kathmandu from at least three separate settlements. About 11 kilometers to the east, a third commercial settlement known as Bhaktapur or Bhadgaon grew up around a separate road to Tibet, expanding from an original 'upper' town to a 'lower' town toward the west. The intermittent political union of the entire Valley occurred under Lichchhavi kings after the third century, and under Malla kings after the eleventh century, forging a unitary linguistic and cultural milieu. By the seventeenth century, divisions within the Malla dynasty resulted in the establishment of separate royal lines based in the three main cities of the valley, each the capital of a miniature empire and each the beneficiary of royal largesse that made them artistic and architectural jewels. In the eighteenth century, the hill state of Gorkha conquered the entire valley as part of its drive to create modern Nepal, leading to the establishment of Kathmandu as a national capital under the Shah dynasty. The usurpation of power by Prime Minister Jang Bahadur Rana in the 1840s preserved the unity of the nation against British imperialism, but the hereditary line of Rana prime ministers that ruled the country until the 1950s deliberately limited exposure to the outside world. When the Shah dynasty took power again, it inherited a well-preserved spatial and cultural environment in Kathmandu, Patan and Bhaktapur. These sites provide views of the urban environment assembled during seventeenth century, in turn preserving elements of an even older Malla order.

The very high density of habitation in the cities of the Kathmandu Valley (Levy 1990: 58–9) rests on a building style typical of the Himalaya that preserves precious agricultural land by minimizing architectural footprints (see Figure 3). The standard house in the old style uses a rectangular plan with a timber frame including a dividing wall along the center of the long axis, supporting up to five stories including an attic under a double-pitched roof covered in thatch, tile, or metal. The use of wood for doors and windows, including the elaborately carved specimens visible in well-to-do homes or public buildings especially on upper stories, presents a rich assemblage of public art for which these cities are famous. The basic house plans may be aligned in groups of four in order to create quadrilateral internal compounds; this design may bring together different private residences to create mini-neighborhoods, appears in older palace complexes, and also provides the space for 'monasteries' (*vihara*). The latter feature more complex wooden embellishment of entranceways and upper stories and preserve shrines or stupas in their central courtyards, in a pattern reminiscent of quadrilateral monastic institutions elsewhere in South Asia. The older sections of Patan still include many of these compounds, often interlinked and mutually accessible through narrow lanes; in Kathmandu, the patterns of streets and lanes in the old city are still oriented around the major cloisters. In practice, since the later Malla period the inhabitants of these complexes have no longer been celibate mendicants, but the families of hereditary castes that preserve ritual custodianship over their shrines (Slusser 1982: 128–30; 286–95). The ostensibly monastic architectural heritage lies intertwined with a large number of temples (a survey of Bhaktapur in the 1980s (Levy 1990: 205) revealed 120 'active' sites) ranging from the abodes of neighborhood deities to the formidable monuments dominating the public squares in each city assembled over hundreds of years through the donations of the Malla courts. The habitation patterns exemplified by Bhaktapur reveal a concentration of brahmanas (tracing their ancestry to Kannauj) and other high castes associated with former royal administrations around the main public squares; a tendency for other high-ranking castes connected to professional or commercial services to live in a surrounding ring and along major commercial arteries; the close association of outer neighborhoods with specific castes or sub-castes of mainly agriculturalists; and the relegation of lower or 'untouchable' castes to peripheral neighborhoods or locations outside the now-demolished city walls (Gutschow and Kölver 1975: 34–6, 56–8).

Figure 3 Aerial view of Bhaktapur. Reproduced by permission of Niels Gutschow.

Kathmandu, as national capital, has undergone radical expansion into a metropolitan region (population 250,000 in 1971, 1.23 million in 2005) encompassing Patan, nationalizing and modernizing elements of sacred geography and ritual cycle. Bhaktapur (population 40,000 in 1971), as a more peripheral city, has preserved the more archaic characteristics of its 24 neighborhoods along with an annual rhythm of approximately 80 festivals conforming to lunar and solar calendars. Within the household, a series of life-cycle rituals provide markers of identity for the individual, while 20 annual events confirm the individual's roles within the extended patrilineage and the caste. The organization of household space around domestic rites, centered on family shrines and periodic sacrifices involving priestly specialists, finds its spatial expression in the sometimes elaborate rituals performed during house construction, which associate different components of the built environment with divine beings, and includes the installation of a Hidden Shiva in the form of a linga hidden in the house's rubbish heap

(Slusser 1982: 133–4; 216–32; Levy 1990: 191–2). At these levels, practice in Bhaktapur is comparable to that of many villages in the Valley, and demonstrates the cultural continuity between urban and rural environments.

In public space, the inhabitants of Bhaktapur have developed an array of performance that embeds religious practice within the definition of the citizen. The centerpiece is the temple dedicated to Taleju, a form of the goddess Durga, who served as the primary deity for the Malla kings in all three kingdoms and still plays an active part, along with human representatives of the Malla/Shah king, in important annual events. In fact, all-city celebrations, headed by the solar New Year and autumn harvest festivals, may involve the pan-South Asian divinities representing aspects of the moral order, but highlight deities of power, particularly the terrifying form of Shiva as Bhairava and various manifestations of dangerous goddesses. These include the Nine Durgas, who appear as masked dancers on multiple occasions in order to trace processional routes through the city and enact dramas in the squares associated with each neighborhood. The goddesses also include the Eight Mothers, whose humble shrines on the edge of the city bound urban space and stand as pilgrimage sites connected with specific neighborhoods. The identity of neighborhoods is further strengthened through the presence of Ganesha shrines in each, the installation of stones at street crossings serving as disposal sites for polluting substances, and perennial connections with specific cremation grounds outside the city, accessed by funeral processions of family, friends and neighbors treading customary routes (Gutschow 1982). The density of ritual action at the neighborhood level and at the all-city level, expressed as movement and involving varying constituencies as participants and observers, defines the boundaries and the subdivisions of the city while establishing and renewing the entire urban collectivity. The association of these actions with mythic narrative, the 'transformation and civic "capturing" of the forces portrayed in the legend,' regularly reinforces the representation or mapping of social space and relationships through divinities, and 'reaffirms the special quality of an urban as opposed to a rural environment' (Gutschow and Basukala 1987: 155; Levy 1987: 114; Levy 1990: 612).

Sacred persons as the focus for urbanization

Until now our discussion has touched upon the disposition of urban space, or travel to the central place, in order to maximize contact with personal deities or with impersonal supernatural forces. In practice, the sacred power of important human beings has exerted an equally decisive role in South Asian urbanization. Through the ministry of the great philosopher Shankara (probably active in the eighth century), new lineages of renunciants adhering to a non-dualist interpretation of the 'End of the Veda' (*vedanta*) were attracting resources that allowed them to influence demography within specific locales. Shankara is credited with the establishment of four monasteries that served as the seats for his leading disciples: at Sringeri in Karnataka; Dwaraka in Gujarat; Puri in Orissa; and Jyotirmath (Joshimath) in Uttaranchal, while a separate seat associated with Shankara also came up in Kanchipuram – establishing yet another network of sacred cities spanning the subcontinent. Each of these institutions pulled in donations from important devotees (the Sringeri monastery, for example, was closely connected to the Vijayanagar rulers) that allowed them to become magnets for local service personnel and thus for population growth. The multiplication of monastic orders, which was in full swing by the thirteenth century throughout the subcontinent, created new constellations of regional and sub-regional institutions that served as the nuclei for neighborhoods within pre-existing towns, or became the focus for new town growth.

The process that allowed spiritual leaders to become catalysts for sacred city formation, either during their lives or after their deaths, is visible in the case of saints typically associated with Sufism. Perhaps the most important example is Shaikh Muinuddin Sijzi, who brought to the subcontinent the teachings and practice of the Sufi order originating in Chisht, a town in Afghanistan. In the late-twelfth century, he established his teaching retreat (*khanqah*) in the oasis center of Ajmer in Rajasthan, below the Taragadh Fort that served as a power base of Prithvi Raj III, the last ruler of the Chauhan dynasty. Living to a ripe old age, earning the epithet 'Benefactor of the Poor' (Garib Nawaz), he attracted a group of dedicated disciples and lay supporters through a message of universal love, service, discipline, and ecstatic devotion. After his death in 1235, his tomb (*daragh*) became a site of healing and intercessory power that attracted the devotion of political leaders and ordinary people from all faiths and walks of life. This was the shrine that attracted the attention of the Mughal emperor Akbar. More recently, in addition to a daily flow of pilgrims, the extensive architectural complex around his tomb has attracted perhaps 200,000 to the annual celebration of his death (Currie 1989). Muinuddin's leading disciple, Shaikh Qutbuddin Bakhtiyar Kaki (d. 1236), brought the devotional message of the Chishti order to Delhi, which was rapidly becoming the seat of a rising Turkish military power. His dargah became a major pilgrimage destination even earlier than that of his teacher by the late-thirteenth century. His disciple in turn, Shaikh Fariduddin Ganj-i-Shakr, eventually settled in the old town of Ajodhan, a ferry across the Sutlej River on the route between Delhi and Multan. Through his composition of devotional songs, Baba Farid became one of the progenitors of the Punjabi language; through his teaching and the distribution of amulets charged with spiritual power, he became the patron saint of southern Punjab. After his death in 1265 and the inheritance of his spiritual power by his descendants, his *dargah* attracted donations from the powerful and became one of the most important institutions in a place that became known as Pakpattan, the holy city (Eaton 2000: 203–4). Baba Farid's most important disciple was Shaikh Nizamuddin Auliya (1238–1325), who relocated to the small village of Ghiyaspur near Delhi and became a force in the spiritual life of the growing capital. After his death his *dargah* became the nucleus of a compact commercial center and attracted pilgrimage from people of all faiths. And finally, Nizamuddin's main disciple was Shaikh Nasiruddin Chiragh (d. 1356), the 'Lamp of Delhi,' whose death brought to a close the heroic era of the 'Five Guides' (*panj pir*). The annual celebration of the death anniversary (*urs*) of each saint became a major feature of the commercial environment that their ministries had helped to create (Siddiqui 1989).

The transmission of Sufi saints' power to dozens and then hundreds of disciples, combined with the ministries of separate Sufi orders and the independent activities of other charismatic spiritual leaders, created opportunities for a multiplication of shrines throughout the subcontinent along with their catalyzing role in settlement formation. Every major city, and many smaller towns, became the loci for tombs of Sufi saints; the very definition of a city came to include the presence of such tombs in its environs. In Varanasi alone, Nita Kumar (1988: 53) traced at least 28 shrines where graves dedicated to *pirs* and to martyrs (*shahid*) serve as sources of spiritual power, local identity, and annual festivals. In Bangladesh, the process of agrarian expansion and urbanization that accelerated after the twelfth century was intimately tied to the managerial roles of men connected (often loosely) with Sufi lineages (Eaton 1993). One of the most significant of these leaders, known today as Shah Jalal, settled during the early-fourteenth century in Sylhet (originally Silahatta or Srihatta, the 'auspicious market town'), where a trade route to Assam intersected with the navigable Surma River. Shah Jalal eventually became a patron saint of Islam in Bangladesh, and his shrine still attracts massive numbers of pilgrims. In southern India we have the example of the sixteenth-century saint, Sahul Hamid, who settled on the outskirts of Nagapattinam in Nagore (Nagur) which became a thriving coastal emporium during the eighteenth and early-nineteenth century. The shrine that grew up around his tomb, the Nagore Sharif, developed into an important suburb that attracts tens of thousands of pilgrims and has become a major social service institution. During the aftermath of the 2004 tsunami that ravaged this section of Tamil Nadu's coast, the shrine stood on the first line of social response, providing food and clothes to survivors and burial to victims (Saheb 1998; Balakrishnan 2004).

Since the fifteenth century independent religious movements have adopted and reconfigured elements of the spiritual lineage and the veneration of the enlightened master, with implications for spatial transformation. A primary example is the movement of those who followed the path of Nanak (*Nanakpanthis*), later called Sikhism, which venerated ten masters (*Guru*) beginning with Nanak (1469–1535) and ending with Gobind Singh (1675–1708) whose legacy included the holy book (*Granth Sahib*) established within the 'door to the guru' (*gurdwara*). Important *gurdwaras* eventually came up at many sites associated with the deeds of the Ten Gurus throughout the subcontinent (e.g. Patna), which became anchors for entire neighborhoods. The most significant locale was at an independent site in Punjab that became known as Ramdaspur, founded by the third Guru, Amardas, and endowed with a tank by his son-in-law and successor, Ramdas. The next Guru, Arjan, constructed in the tank a 'House of God' (*Harmandir*) and, after compiling the Granth Sahib, installed it there. The construction in the early-seventeenth century of the Immortal Throne (*Akal Takht*) nearby for the conduct of temporal affairs and the addition of the Iron Fortress (*Loh Garh*) about 1,100 meters to the west brought together the religious and administrative components that supported bazaars and dense residential quarters (*katra*) springing up between them. During the late-eighteenth century, as political centralization in Punjab disappeared, independent Sikh chiefs began constructing stately buildings called *bunga* around the tank of the Harmandir, while a series of neighborhoods associated with bazaars, tanks and gardens developed mainly to the north. Ranjit Singh (1780–1839), who consolidated control over Punjab and created an empire stretching from Kashmir to Sind, welded all these settlements into a single city protected by a 12-gated double wall with a circumference of about 8 kilometers, and renamed the city as the 'Pool of Nectar' or Amritsar, his second capital (Grewal 1981; Gauba 1988: 1–16). Sikhism spun off a number of independent movements, but one that is of interest for us here is the Radhasoami community, which grew from the ministry of Swami Shiv Dayal Singh (1818–78), and expanded primarily among an emerging middle class. After his death, the movement split into several wings, each founding intentional communities or colonies: Soamibagh and Dayalbagh at Agra and a settlement along the Beas River in Punjab that became large enough to achieve the status of an independent township (Juergensmeyer 1991: 145–80).

A recent example of urban growth around a master's shrine appears at Shirdi, which was a small Maharashtrian village in the early-twentieth century, when an itinerant holy man, who called himself only the 'fakir' but became known as Shirdi Sai Baba, settled there. The tales of his spiritual power circulating during his life and after his death in 1918 resulted in the coalescence of a major pilgrimage site attracting devotees from all over India and from a transnational diaspora, while the resident population of Shirdi grew to 26,169 in 2001. Closely related to this phenomenon is the career of Sathya Sai Baba (b. 1926), who announced during his teen years that he was the reincarnation of Shirdi Sai Baba, and later announced that he was an incarnation of God. His native place of Puttaparthi, originally a village in Andhra Pradesh with about 200 households, grew into a pilgrimage center with 3,461 persons in 1961, the focus of a transnational following of 10 million devotees and the site of a university, hospital, railway station and airport. In 1992, the government of Andhra Pradesh established the Sri Sathya Sai Urban Development Authority that brought Puttaparthi together with five nearby villages in a single planning unit that included 25,672 persons in 2001 (Srinivas 2008).

The builders of the sacred city

Since at least the first millennium, the persons responsible for the conceptual frameworks that have viewed space as a manifestation of divine principles have been lineages of professional architects or builders, organized as castes, known generally as *shilpin* or, more recently, as *mistri*. These groups seem to have played roles in almost all major construction projects, regardless of the religious affiliations of their patrons, well into the nineteenth century. The transmission of the theoretical, technical, and organizational knowledge required for their work occurred orally, but the survival of a number of texts dating back at least 1,500 years indicates that a shared classificatory and scholastic discipline informed their work (Thakur 1994). A brief look at one of the most important of these texts, the *Manasara*, demonstrates the position of this discipline in their production of space.

The *Manasara* is primarily an exposition of the structural characteristics and the exterior and interior design for individual buildings, mostly religious monuments, and of their artistic embellishment; these monuments are primarily temples, and production standards exist for a variety of statuary, including Jain and Buddhist images. The early chapters of the book are of greatest interest for us here, for they deal with city plans and with the underlying principles of site preparation. The explicit treatment of cities is disappointingly limited (Chapter 10), consisting only of a typology of urban settlements and fortified towns, ending with a statement that road systems should be cardinally oriented and that the layout of buildings should resemble that described for villages. The treatment of villages, in turn (Chapter 9), describes the settlement site as a quadrilateral divided into an even or odd array of squares, with sections allocated for public or private use, and with professional or caste groups segregated by sector. Earlier chapters, which describe in detail the preparation of the quadrilateral site, offer the greatest insights into knowledge (*vidya*) of architecture as essence (*vastu*). The builder is to conceptualize space as a cosmic person (*purusha*) expressed through the positioning of different divinities, or expressions of cosmic principles, at specific locations on the periphery and within the site, creating squares imbued with differentiated spiritual powers. The ritual establishment of the divinities, meditation upon them, and sacrifices directed toward them, activate spiritual correspondences between the cosmos, the site, and ultimately the human organism (*Architecture of Manasara* 1980). The precision required for the measurement of the site's quadrilaterals establishes a direct link from architecture to mensuration for the deity-invoking Vedic sacrifice, and another link to the so-called tantric paths becoming manifest during the first millennium that propounded techniques for activating and exploiting correspondences between physical arrays and spiritual powers. From the standpoint of the patrons funding the architect's consultancy, the correct alignment of the spatial and the spiritual would maximize auspicious potentiality and thus prosperity, a result similar to that expected from support for sacrifice, gifts for mendicants, or donations for temples.

It is uncertain whether the vast majority of the self-built housing within villages or among the urban poor made use of architectural consultants operating within the *vastu* paradigm, although the data from Nepal suggest that the principles preserved in the *Manasara*, expressed in regional manuals, were employed regularly. It is certain that the significant percentage of urban space devoted to religious institutions, public buildings including palaces, and the workplaces or residences of the more well-to-do citizens needed the services of professional builders and thus brought into play the understandings of space embedded within the shilpin's profession. This means that, in addition to the public performances that regularly re-enacted the drama of the city as a sacred *organum*, a large percentage of the individual buildings within the city were perceived as sacred spaces right from their origins.

In his exhaustive study of this issue in the Kathmandu Valley, Niels Gutschow provides evidence of the *mandala* concept as an interpretive tool regularly applied by intellectuals, and tacitly accepted by non-intellectuals, in order to map the diverse aspects of the built environment as a regulated, geometric diagram. According to his analysis (1982: 15–27, 179–85) this is not planning, but the application of a model after the fact to an urban pattern that grew slowly over the centuries as an expression of the variegated economic or social interests of the citizens, with state intervention occurring within limited contexts (e.g. construction of the palace or city walls, regulation of public spatial parameters). In a similar manner, the replicated settlement patterns in southern India that establish a quadrilateral array surrounding a central shrine (no matter how large that shrine could become) indicate the long-term application of culturally specific concepts, including to some extent the drive toward the *mandala*, rather than the direct implementation of a planning apparatus.

In practice, the opportunities for the foundation of a single settlement as a whole were so few, state power was usually so limited, and the vagaries of topography were so many, that one can find very few examples of *vastu vidya* application in a complete form. Departures from an ideal were inevitable and easily accepted even where the full panoply of state power could come to bear on the formation of cities. The city of Jaipur founded by the Kachchwaha kings of Amber after 1727 is the best-documented case where a unitary plan based on *vastu* principles underlay the construction of a major city. Even here, the presence of pre-existing roads, shrines and hills caused significant changes in the balanced geometry recommended in architectural texts (Sachdev and Tillotson 2002: 11–49). *Vastu vidya* thus has been regularly applied but rarely expressed as an essentialist paradigm in urban planning. The current situation in India, where *vastu* consultants with varying levels of competency in the classic texts have been enjoying an upsurge of demand from middle-class homeowners while remaining excluded from city planning exercises, mirrors a long-term trend.

Military and administrative centralization under the sultanates

The struggles of regional kingdoms in South Asia during the late-first millennium had stimulated the maintenance of shifting lines of fortified encampments on or near the borders of antagonistic states (the early Cholas called them 'houses of the army' (*padaividu*)), although these temporary or semi-permanent bases have left few traces on the ground. In addition, the maintenance of strongholds at strategic spots, primarily on hilltops, was a standard practice (Sharma 1965: 287–92; Joshi 1985: 51–92; Yadava 2001: 82). After the year 1000, more durable forts serving as the nuclei of permanent settlements became more important because South Asia was experiencing the consequences of a technological and organizational revolution that made cavalry the most effective striking arm of the military. This revolution had underlain the successes or early Arab armies and the rapid expansion of Turkish empires in Central Asia beginning in the seventh century, affected

Europe in the form of the mounted knight, and culminated in the unparalleled success of the Mongols (experts in the deployment of mounted archers) during the thirteenth and fourteenth centuries. The safety of permanent forts was a response to the mobility of mounted formations. The dissemination of gunpowder technology after the fourteenth century was a response to permanent forts, which in turn resulted in the strengthening of walls and the transfer of citadels to even more inaccessible locales. The consequence for military logistics in South Asia was the evolution of the siege train alongside massive cavalry and elephant formations. The consequence for central places was the increasing role of fortified enclosures – an amplified version of the role fortifications had played during early historical urbanization (Gommans and Kolff 2001: 26–39).

The cavalry revolution came to South Asia in full force through the agency of Turkish polities established originally in Afghan cities. Central Asian military strategies pushed a steadily expanding wave of conquest that led to the progressive installation of Turkic or Afghan warrior elites at the head of well-entrenched regional polities. Because these conquerors found themselves a highly visible minority in a hostile land, and often fell out over the disposition of power, it was incumbent on them to appropriate and upgrade pre-existing fortified sites to serve as their bases of operation, or in some cases to found new fortified centers that served as secure administrative hubs and also magnets for service providers. The role of military adventurers and dynastic politics in city formation thus assumed greater importance in South Asia during the early-second millennium. Installed at the head of their mostly inland regional states, the new warrior elites established relationships with indigenous administrative groups in order to appropriate sources of state revenue, including the major taxes on agrarian surplus. At this point the Central Asian administrative institution called *iqta*, which allocated control of public offices and their revenues to loyal subordinates, intersected well with extant bureaucratic or proto-bureaucratic institutions within the South Asian regional state, allowing military leaders styling themselves as sultans to reward their lieutenants with provincial or sub-provincial governorships. The locations of those lower-level political seats, which also served as military bases, allowed the growth of pre-existing or new market centers that processed state revenues either in kind or, increasingly, in monetized forms (Verma 1986: 39–42). Historical sources in South Asia after the year 1000 provide evidence of the importance not only of fortified capitals, but also an array of secondary and tertiary administrative nodes that later became the backbone of the modern urban system.

As Central Asia assumed greater political significance, it exerted a powerful influence on the configuration of cities within the corridor of urbanization stretching from Bengal to Afghanistan, and pulled the center of gravity toward the northwest. The new triad of Lahore, Delhi and Agra became the linchpins of an imperial network controlled by Turkish, Afghan, and later Mughal militarists.

Lahore was already a fortified town on the Ravi River with a mosque and an Arab quarter when Mahmud, Sultan of Ghazna/Ghazni in Afghanistan, began a series of military campaigns (998–1030) into Pakistan and northern India. Eventually Mahmud annexed Punjab and made Lahore his second capital, renaming it

Mahmudabad or Ghazna-i-khurd. The Sultan appointed a city prefect (*kotwal*), a market superintendent (*shahna*), and a governor who erected a masonry fort. Lahore remained an imperial capital until Muizz al-Din Muhammad bin Sam (1162–1206), the Sultan of the Ghur region in Afghanistan with a summer capital in Firuzkuh/Jam, took this last stronghold of Ghaznavid power in 1187. Soon thereafter the star of Delhi was ascendant, while Mongol armies appeared to the northwest. The Qarlegh tribe, affiliated with the Mongol camp, settled down and made local alliances allowing them to block vital passes between Lahore and Ghazna. Then the Mongols seized and pillaged Lahore, followed by an extension of Qarlegh power all over Punjab. The disruption of trade caused by these events enhanced the role of an alternative route from Delhi through Multan and toward Kandahar, leaving Lahore in decline during the middle of the thirteenth century (Naqvi 1986: 5–10, 130).

Delhi's moment was at hand. In the mid-eleventh century a local Rajput chieftain had established a refuge located about 10 kilometers south of the present center of New Delhi just north of the forested, rocky Ridge on the edge of the Aravalli range (see Map 14). This first version of the Red Fort (Lalkot) became the southwestern part of a more extensive defensive work later called Qila Rai Pithora constructed under the Chauhan polity based in Ajmer (Kaul 1985: 22–8, 298–303; Singh 1999: 97–107). That polity ended with the death in 1191 of its last king, Prithvi Raj III, in battle against Muhammad of Ghur, who was conquering of an empire stretching as far as Bihar. After Muhammad occupied Ajmer fort, the conqueror's sudden death made possible a power grab that re-established a more strictly South Asian polity. Qutb al-Din Aybeg, though officially a military slave and in fact only one of a number of claimants to the title of sultan, declared himself an independent ruler in 1206, initiating what we now call the Delhi Sultanate. He constructed a new Friday Mosque, measuring 66 by 46 meters with a rectangular plan surrounded by colonnaded arches that included components recycled from former temples, and also constructed nearby a massive minaret (*minar*) with a base 14.3 meters across. His successor, Shams al-Din Iltutmish (1210–36), oversaw suburban expansion on the southeast side of the old settlement, excavated a reservoir measuring about 200 by 125 meters south of the city, and introduced the practice of constructing monumental tombs for rulers and their families. He also expanded the Friday Mosque and added three stories to its minaret, bringing it to a height of 72.5 meters. The later association of this monument with the nearby tomb Qutbuddin Bakhtiyar Kaki, regarded by devotees as the axis (*qutb*) around whom the world revolved, led to its appellation as his 'staff' (*qutb sahib ki lath*), and in popular parlance as the Qutb Minar (Kumar 2002: 1–61).

The period of Delhi Sultans who were military slaves ended in 1290 with the accession of Jalal al-Din Firuz Khilji, who faced the first incursions by the Mongols. Then the usurpation in 1296 by his nephew, Ala al-Din Khilji, brought to power a personality who oversaw the defense of the northwestern frontiers against Mongol invasions, campaigned successfully in Rajasthan and Gujarat, and sent expeditions that penetrated as far south as Madurai. Now a truly imperial capital, Delhi witnessed the construction of a new palace and oval fort at Siri, about

3 kilometers to the northeast, along with a quadrilateral reservoir measuring about 600 meters on each side called Hauz Khas, about 5 kilometers to the north (Athar Ali 1986: 22, 26). A revolt in 1320 brought to power Ghiyas al-Din Tughluq, who faced considerable opposition within the empire and renewed Mongol threats on the frontier. He established a new capital called Tughluqabad about 8 kilometers east of Lal Kot, with a roughly trapezoidal plan bounded by walls 6 kilometers in length, including an attached fort and more heavily defended citadel, on a hill surrounded by a basin that collected water during the monsoon season. Despite the construction of a giant lake to the south, this was a site with limited access to water and never took off as a major population center (Shokoohy and Shokoohy 1994).

His successor, the charismatic but erratic Muhammad bin Tughlaq (1325–51), avoided his father's city and concentrated instead on the unification of the earlier cities of Delhi, constructing walls that joined the old city around the Qutb Minar with the more recent settlement of Siri, an extension called Jahanpanah (Refuge of the World). Then he attempted to solve the problem of ruling a pan-South Asian empire by shifting his capital in 1328 to the fortress of Devagiri (Deogir, renamed Daulatabad) in the northern Deccan, an experiment abandoned after only seven years. The decision to return to Delhi and expand it marked an acceptance of the infeasibility of ruling a vast empire stretching to Bengal (independent 1301–22 and again in 1342) and Madurai (independent in 1336), and the necessity to maintain Delhi as the linchpin of a defensive and communication/trade system still oriented as much toward Afghanistan as the east or south. The great Moroccan traveler, Abu Abdullah Muhammad Ibn Battuta, in addition to detailed descriptions of Delhi during this period, has also left us portrayals of the trade routes from Sind through Multan to Delhi, and then from Delhi to Khambat (Cambay), portraying the secure horse-relay couriers maintained by Sultan and also the insecurity encountered by caravans on the roads of central India (Gibb 1971: 593–767).

From an imperial perspective, the Delhi Sultanate continued to disintegrate with the loss of its Deccan possessions in 1347, when Zafar Khan, taking the title Alauddin Bahman Shah, declared himself an independent Sultan. Nevertheless, the rule in Delhi of Firuz Shah Tughlaq (1351–88) marks the high point of this city's early role as imperial capital. He constructed a suburban capital called Firuzabad on the bank of the Yamuna River northeast of today's New Delhi. The small fortress here occupied a roughly rectangular plan (800 × 400 meters) encompassing public and private audience halls and palaces (Alfieri and Borromeo 2000: 40–5). He also constructed a major canal that brought water from father north on the Yamuna River to the city and its surrounding gardens. The importance of Delhi during this period appears in contemporary sources, which refer to it simply as 'the city' (*shahr*) or *hazrat* (revered or respected, denoting the sanctifying presence of Sufi shrines); one estimate of its population counts 512,000 inhabitants in the various settlements founded during the preceding three centuries.

The economy of Delhi had become the largest in the subcontinent. Its main market for cloth lay next to the campus of the Friday Mosque. Separate bazaars existed for food grains and cloth. Smaller markets existed throughout the city, where brokers controlled much of the exchange. Goods reached the city from the outside through the activities of Banjara caravaneers, whose rest areas existed outside the city walls. City merchants were not allowed to intercept caravans before they entered the city gates and thus make purchases at lower rates. Food grains reached the city and were unloaded and stored at the grain market (*mandavi*) next to Mandavi Gate before distribution to smaller grain markets. Market superintendents fixed price ranges of each commodity, while *muhtasib*s worked in neighborhoods to regulate prices, weights and measures (Naqvi 1986: 135–8, 146).

Delhi's prosperity would be short-lived. Benefiting from the decay of the long-established defenses on the Afghan border, one of the great conquerors of all time, Timur Lenk (Tamerlane), brought an army from his base in Samarkand (present-day Uzbekistan) through Lahore and into Delhi in 1398. Rioting in the conquered city escalated into general pillaging and mayhem (Kaul 1985: 320–33), a blow from which the early city never fully recovered. The Lodi dynasty (1451–1526), originally hailing from Afghanistan, eventually succeeded in recreating an imperial Sultanate based in Delhi that stretched from Pakistan to Bihar. The monuments of the Lodi Gardens, now surrounded by New Delhi, remain a testimonial to their rule, but Sikandar Lodi (1489–1517) shifted his seat to a new city in Agra – the first sign of the latter's imminent rise.

The collapse of the Delhi Sultanate, the first concerted attempt for centuries to transform a regional power into a South Asian empire, allowed the re-emergence of a multi-regional political configuration in which fortified capital cities played crucial roles.

In Bengal, the imposition of rule from Delhi had resulted, in 1211, in a shift of the political center to Lakhnauti (Lakshmanavati), also known as Gaur (Gauda), an older administrative center located near the Bhagirathi/Ganga River's confluence with the Mahananda (Mahanadi) River. In 1301 Shams al-Din Firuz Shah declared himself an independent Sultan over Bengal and Bihar and conquered independent kingdoms based at Sonargaon and Satgaon, but he transferred his capital north to the old town of Pandua, which he modestly renamed Firuzabad. After temporary re-imposition of control from Delhi, a tripartite struggle broke out among former officials of the Delhi Sultanate based in the cities of Lakhnauti, Sonargaon, and Satgaon. The struggle culminated in the triumph of a military adventurer who took control of Lakhnauti/Gaur in 1345, with the title of Sultan Shams al-Din Iliyas Shah. He eliminated his opponents within Bengal, campaigned as far as Cuttack, Kathmandu and Varanasi, and shifted the capital again to Pandua. There, within archaeological remains scattered over an area seven by 3 kilometers, we find the Adina Masjid (plan 155 × 87 meters), completed in the 1370s, the largest mosque hitherto built on the subcontinent. A unique style of monumental architecture, utilizing primarily brick as its medium, began to blend Central Asian elements with the curved cornice reminiscent of Bengali buildings constructed with bamboo and hay (Alfieri and Borromeo 2000: 80–93).

Gaur remained an important administrative center, even while the capital of the independent Sultanate of Bengal was at Pandua, and during the mid-1400s the capital shifted back to Gaur, which functioned as the capital of Bengal until 1575. Most of the extant archaeological remains at Gaur date from this period, marked by fortified embankments stretching about 11 kilometers north-south along the east bank of the Bhagirati River and about 3 kilometers east-west. The royal center with an L-shaped plan, located next to the river about 4 kilometers south of the old governors' fort, was protected by an earthen rampart about 9 meters in height and 58 meters thick at the base, with round bastions and a moat 61 meters in width, encompassing an area 1.6 kilometers north-south and 800 meters east-west on its southern extension. In the southwest corner of this citadel stood a palace compound measuring 640 meters by up to 274 meters, surrounded by its own brick wall 4.57 meters wide at the base. To the east and south of the royal center, extensive mounds, numerous tanks, and some outstanding examples of mosques and Islamic schools indicate the presence of what archaeologists have called a nobles' quarter and the urban core. Under Sultan Ala al-Din Husain Shah (1494–1519) another zone to the north, between the old seat of the governors and the royal center, became the seat of power. The far northern part of the city enclosed by fortifications shows little sign of habitation, and may have been used mostly as agricultural land protected during times of siege. Southern suburbs also exist outside the city walls within what would have been one of the largest cities of its time in South Asia (Husain 1997; Sinha 2002).

In northern Maharashtra, the Yadava dynasty in the late-twelfth century had established their capital at one of the great forts of South Asia, the 'Mountain of the Gods' or Devagiri (Deogir). The final capture of this fort (renamed Daulatabad) by the Delhi Sultanate in 1318 and improvements in its defenses elevated it to a position of great strategic importance for peninsular India. Bahman Shah's declaration of independence in 1347 took place at Daulatabad, but he quickly shifted his political seat to Gulbarga, a site poorly endowed with natural defenses, where he constructed a citadel enclosing a massive rectangular keep. In Gulbarga a Deccani style of architecture started to blend the *shilpin* tradition with influences from the Delhi Sultanate and contemporary Persia. At Gulbarga and also at the nearby palace-capital of Firuzabad (constructed between 1399 and 1406), the Bahmani rulers brought to peninsular India the standard sacred geography of the sultanate city, revolving around a central Friday Mosque and the peripheral shrines of Sufi saints, who according to popular notions bestowed temporary sovereignty and legitimacy on the sultans (Michell and Eaton 1992: 14–16). The capital of the Bahmani dynasty shifted in 1429 to the more centrally located Bidar, located 96 kilometers to the northeast, positioned on a slope with the detached citadel at the upper end and the walled town below. The collapse of the dynasty resulted in the emergence of independent successor states identified with fortified capital cities – Bijapur (1489–1686), Berar (1490–1572), Ahmadnagar (1494–1636), and Golkonda (1507–1687) – built on centuries-old provincial administrative seats (Michell and Zebrowski 1999: 23–52; Alfieri and Borromeo 2000: 144–73).

Bijapur (earlier Vijayapura) exemplifies the organization of the Deccan fort-capitals (see Map 7). It was the site of a Bahmani provincial governorship until

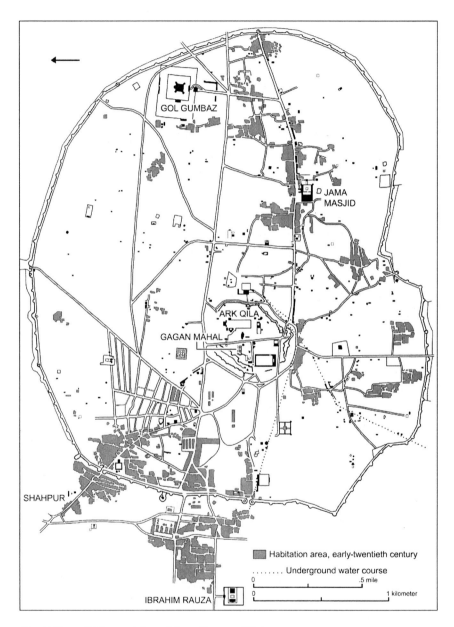

Map 7 Plan of Bijapur. Adapted from Cousens 1916.

Yusuf Adil Khan revolted and declared himself Adil Shah, an independent Sultan (r. 1489–1510). His son and successor, attempting to consolidate the defensive posture of his capital, completed an almost circular citadel (Ark Qila) protected by a stone wall and moat, where a mud fort had stood earlier. His grandson, Ali Adil Shah (1557–80), pulled together the coalition of Bahmani successor states that destroyed Vijayanagara in 1564. Buoyed by resources obtained through that victory, he embellished his new palace within the citadel (the Gagan Mahal) and constructed a new Friday Mosque, a nine-meter high fortification wall with 96 bastions and moat enclosing the entire city (encompassing in the process six independent villages), and the large suburb of Shahpur to the northwest of the city. In 1599 work began at Nauraspur, about 6 kilometers west of Bijapur, to construct a new capital with better access to water and a more defensible position – a project abandoned after military defeats in 1624 resulted in the wrecking of the construction site. Nonetheless, the Sultans continued to embellish Bijapur with monuments that brought to a peak the Deccani style of Indo-Islamic art: the tomb of Ibrahim II (d. 1627) or Ibrahim Rauza, which translated wooden architectural forms into stone; and gigantic tomb of Muhammad (d. 1656) or Gol Gumbaz, which at a height of 84 meters displayed the largest domed space in the world. The Sultans of Bijapur and their nobles funded extensive hydraulic works designed to provide water to a constantly expanding population in an environment that remained arid during much of the year. Water facilities included a number of wells and step wells embellished with rest houses located near public thoroughfares and mosques; artificial lakes to the west that watered the city and its suburb, Shahpur; aqueducts supported on towers that served the citadel, Shahpur, and the neighborhoods around the Friday Mosque and the Gol Gumbaz; and a Persian-style underground tunnel (*qanat*) conducting water from the environs of Nauraspur to Bijapur. On the urban periphery lay the irrigated and cultivated properties of well-to-do citizens, where they raised tombs for their families and also funded tombs with attached endowments in memory of the lines of Sufi masters that made Bijapur their home.

The military disadvantages of this prosperous capital city, commanded by higher ground to the east and north, were minor when measured against the capabilities of fifteenth-century artillery, but they became fatal flaws by the late-seventeenth century, when ordnance was considerably more advanced (Cousens 1916; Rotzer 1984). The elimination of the independent Bijapur state and its reduction to a provincial capital left behind a heritage of Sufi institutions associated with the Chishti, Qadiri and Shattari orders in the form of tombs scattered within the city walls and in its suburbs, a rich literature in the composite Dakhni language originally developed at the court but popularized through Sufi folk literature, and a number of shrines (*dargah*) that remain important scenes of devotion today (Eaton 1978). A steady decline in population resulted by the early-twentieth century in pockets of habitation corresponding to the locations of older bazaars, preserving the pattern of main avenues and smaller side streets winding through residential quarters, amid a pattern of major monuments, smaller mosques and tombs that serve as a skeletal reminder of the formerly thriving capital.

Of all the capitals of Bahmani successor states, Golkonda was to enjoy the most glorious history. Its origins lay in the strategic importance of a formidable rock standing several kilometers north of the Musi River within an oasis surrounded by defensible, rocky uplands, along a major trade route leading from the east coast toward the western Deccan. By at least the thirteenth century a mud fort existed on this rock, which came to be known as Golkonda. It had fallen under the control of the Bahmani dynasty in the late-fourteenth century, but in the early-sixteenth century the Bahmani general Qutb ul Mulk announced his independence by assuming the title of Sultan Quli Qutb Shah and making Golkonda his capital. He and his successors spent the next 60 years extending the boundaries of their kingdom to the north, east and south, enhancing the scale of fortifications at Golkonda and adding outer defensive works that made it an almost impregnable castle. Residential areas began spreading along the Musi River 5 kilometers toward the east, where a bridge was constructed in 1573. Muhammad Quli Qutb Shah (1581–1611) then ordered the construction of a new city further to the east on the south bank of the Musi River, along the trade route to Masulipatnam, which was emerging as the kingdom's main port. The comprehensive plan of this new city, originally called Bhaganagar/Bhagyanagar, was a quadrilateral with main thoroughfares crossing approximately in the center, where the Sultan constructed the famous Charminar ('Four Minarets') monument. The general market, or Chauk, lay to its west. During the seventeenth century the entire urban complex stretching about 10 kilometers from Golkonda to Bhaganagar (renamed Hyderabad/Haidarabad) enjoyed a period of unparalleled prosperity as a political and commercial center, fabled for its diamonds (Rao 1989: 1–6)

In Gujarat, the governor under the Delhi Sultanate, Zafar Khan Muzaffar, assumed the title of Muzaffar Shah and established an independent Sultanate in 1407 that lasted until 1583. His son, Ahmed Shah I, set up a new capital in 1411 on the Sabarmati River at the old Chalukya trading center of Ashaval/ Asapalli/Karnavati. The story of four pious men named Ahmed who laid out this new city of Ahmedabad suggests that they must have stood at the four corners of a planning area within visual range of each other and delineated a fortified palace and administrative area that became the Bhadra Fort. The Friday Mosque outside the royal enclosure was the initial magnet around which a series of markets and residences for commercial groups coagulated. Suburban quarters called *pura*, founded by notables of the court or rich merchants and growing around religious institutions, developed during the fifteenth and early-sixteenth centuries in a ring around the administrative and commercial core. In these *pura*, the mansions and gardens of the well-to-do were magnets for the humbler dwellings of numerous service personnel and for markets. By 1487 the city was enclosed within a wall 10 kilometers in circumference, including 189 bastions and 12 gates (Mehta 1987). Funding by the sultans and other wealthy donors was enabling the construction of architectural complexes including *khanqahs*, mosques and assembly halls at the shrines of eminent Sufi saints on the outskirts of denser neighborhoods within the walled city and its environs, forming nuclei for small *qasbas* (Desai 1989). The spatial pattern of several dozen well-constructed step-wells that have survived indicates the direction of at least nine major highways emanating from the city (Deloche 1993: 188–9).

Within Ahmedabad, most people resided within localities that became known as *pol* after the gates at their entrances. The built environment therein consisted of high wooden houses with overhanging eaves lining small crooked lanes and dead ends. The inhabitants of the *pol* might belong to a single occupational/caste group, but in any case they allowed residence only by families with related backgrounds. Common funds maintained law and order and funded common festivals or social expenses such as weddings or funerals. The strength of the city's economy never depended solely on its role as a capital (the seat of the sultan's government lay at Champaner fortress between 1484 and 1536), but rested instead on its commercial position. It became a trading center on the route between Rajasthan and the major port at Khambat, and a manufacturing center for textiles, with specialties in silk and cotton. Merchant and financial guilds (*mahajan*) and artisan guilds (*panch*) exercised considerable influence in public life. By the seventeenth century, the population of the Ahmedabad peaked at 250,000 to 500,000 persons (Gillion 1968: 25–9; Habib 1982a: Map 7B; Mehta 1987; Singh 1985: 21–2).

Urban expansion under the Mughals

The early-sixteenth century witnessed events that re-established the significance of the Lahore-Delhi-Agra triad in the affairs of South Asia. The 1526 intrusion from Afghanistan of the Mughal war leader, Zahiruddin Muhammad Babur, which led to his surprising victory at Panipat, denoted the continuing strategic importance of the Delhi region, but afterwards he moved on to Agra and retained it as his new capital. Babar's son and successor, Humayun, was crowned in Agra as Mughal emperor in 1530, but he proceeded to construct a new capital in Delhi called Din Panah (Refuge of the World), a site known today as the 'Old Fort' (Purana Qila) just west of the Yamuna River and midway between the north-lying Firuzabad and the shrine of Nizamuddin Auliya (see Map 14). When the sometimes-alcoholic Humayun suffered defeat at the hands of Islam Shah Sur, the former subordinate of the Lodi kings whose military ability made him a formidable contender for supreme power, the latter chose Agra as his capital and relocated there from his base in Jaunpur. As Sher Shah, he also supported urban growth in Delhi around Purana Qila and had constructed the fortress of Salimgarh on an island in the Yamuna River (Chenoy 1998: 24). The miraculous return and triumph of Humayun, and his sudden accidental death in a fall down his library steps at Purana Qila, brought to the throne his young son Akbar (1556–1605), the greatest of the Mughal emperors. Akbar returned to Agra in 1558, renamed it Akbarabad, ordered the demolition of the old Lodi fort, and supervised the construction of a new, invulnerable fort made of red sandstone in 1565. Although Akbar personally was often on the move with the army, and resided in Lahore much of the time between 1584 and 1598, Agra became the unquestioned hub of an expansive Mughal military and administrative machine that transformed center-periphery relations from Afghanistan to Bengal, and inexorably spread into peninsular India.

The layout of imperial Agra typifies the major Mughal city. The massive walls and moats of the roughly semicircular Fort, which used the Yamuna River as a defensive barrier on the east, encompassed military compounds and the workshops of imperial artisans as well as administrative and palace buildings, the latter ornately embellished with marble. Adjacent to the Fort on was an open exercise and parade ground, the Maidan-i-Shah. To the northwest was the Friday Mosque constructed in 1648. The main shopping arcade of the city, the Chauk Bazaar, lay between the Fort and this mosque. An outer wall, originally with five, and later with 16 gates, surrounded the residential space of the city in a semi-circular plan. Residential space was interspersed with temples, mosques, gardens, public baths, and specialized markets for grain, animals, and slaves (Naqvi 1974: 87). As the empire expanded, so did Agra as its capital city: Population is estimated at 200,000 by end of sixteenth century, when the city circumference was about 32 kilometers, and perhaps 700,000 inhabitants in the mid-seventeenth century, when it was about 58 kilometers. On the outskirts of the city stood mausoleums (including, after 1648, the Taj Mahal) and, stretching north and east of the fort along the Yamuna River, the residences of the leading nobles of the Mughal court. A major road led northwest past Akbar's mausoleum at Sikandra (on the Mathura-Delhi Road). Ribbon development extended 8 kilometers southwest toward Fatehpur Sikri, Akbar's audacious experiment in the planning of a palace city, occupied only between 1569 and 1584 (Brand and Lowry 1985, 1987). Another ribbon stretched almost 5 kilometers south along the road to Gwalior, that major stronghold protecting the right flank of Mughal power. Expansion to the opposite bank of the Yamuna became possible through access on a pontoon bridge. Shaded rest stops stood along the roads radiating from the city. As an industrial center, Agra became well known for textiles, carpets, metallurgy, stone cutting and inlay work. It lay at the heart of a major region for the production of indigo (Habib 1982a: Map 8B; Gupta, I.P 1986: 10–37).

Emperor Shah Jahan (r. 1628–58) was born in Lahore, which always remained his favorite among the three main Mughal cities. The plan of the city, where the fort with quadrilateral plan improved by Akbar lay on the northwestern side of the narrow, winding lanes of the old city (Rehman and Wescoat 1993: 187–9), would inform his later experiments in urban planning. He ruled from there for four years before relocating to Agra in 1632. The decision to found a new capital was among the most influential moves of his reign, for it shifted urban primacy to Delhi and eventually led to the eclipse of Agra. The site chosen for the new site of Shahjahanabad (referred to as Delhi's 'Old City' today) lay north of the capital established by Sher Shah in 1540, and incorporated in its design pre-existing tanks, earlier road patterns (i.e. the main route to Lahore), and some earlier structures such as the Kalan Masjid built during Firuz Shah's time and the Salimgarh Fort built under Sher Shah (Chenoy 1998: 33–8). The imperial household laid out the Red Fort (*Lal Qila*) and moat next to the Yamuna River along with the wall and gates surrounding the entire city, two main boulevards heading directly south and west from the Red Fort, a system of channels distributing water from an improved Paradise Canal arising 120 kilometers north on the Yamuna, and the Friday Mosque with endowed commercial properties in its surrounding bazaar (see Map 8). The north-south boulevard was the site of the Faiz Bazaar. The east-west boulevard was flanked by arched openings divided by brick partitions fronting warehouses; it included the Camp Market or Urdu Bazaar, the headquarters of the city magistrate (*kotwal*) and its open square (*chaburtala*), the Jewelers' Market or Jauhri Bazaar, the Silver Square or Chandni Chauk (which eventually gave its name to the entire street), and the Fathpuri Bazaar in the west named after the major mosque built near the Lahori Gate. Members of the royal family and members of the nobility laid out extensive gardens with Persian-style geometric plans north of Chandni Chauk and outside the city walls, endowed rest areas (*sarai*) and public baths, and established major mosques (e.g. the Fathpuri Masjid). The emperor first occupied the Red Fort in 1648 at an auspicious hour and amid festivities that expressed an understanding of the city as the center of the universe, the manifestation of macrocosmic and microcosmic principles embedded in its design and function, an archetype of a perfected and symmetrical reality (Blake 1991: 29–36, 64, 71–82; Chenoy 1998: 53–5).

The imperial household within the Red Fort may have supported about 57,000 persons (about 40 percent military personnel). The state also made land available to leading administrators for their construction of mansion compounds (*haveli*) that resembled smaller versions of the royal household, employed thousands of retainers and artisans, and created subsidiary hubs throughout the fabric of the city. The average mansion compound could have supported about 16,000 persons, including similar proportions of security personnel; this means that the economic and spatial organization of most of Shahjahanabad revolved around the state and its grandees (Blake 1991: 44–51, 86–7; Chenoy 1998: 46–51, 72–91).

The state left remaining sections of Shahjahanabad in private hands, which allowed the growth of neighborhoods (*mohalla, mahallah*) that often featured dead-end alleys or winding, narrow lanes providing a secluded, personalized interface between public and private space, similar to the *pol* in early Ahmedabad. Gates separated each neighborhood from the rest of the city, and individual homes also included gates that provided privacy to the family. Each neighborhood took on the name of a prominent aristocratic or mercantile family maintaining a mansion (*haveli*) therein, or the name of an occupational group well represented there (Tillotson 1994), although it was most typical that a variety of professions were practiced in the various neighborhood lanes. There was minimal spatial division between home and work, so that different neighborhoods or lanes therein became associated with industrial/artisan production or with stages in the division of labor; Shahjahanabad became famous for its cotton fabrics, indigo, brass, leather goods, and weapons (Naqvi 1974: 76). The center of the neighborhood was often a shopping center also offering lodging, although religious institutions served as important sites for the reinforcement of local identity. For example, in addition to eight elite mosques founded by notables, Shahjahanabad had approximately 200 neighborhood mosques in addition to numerous Sufi shrines for a population somewhere between 150,000 and 500,000 (depending on the presence of the imperial household) that was perhaps half Muslim (Blake 1991: 66–8;

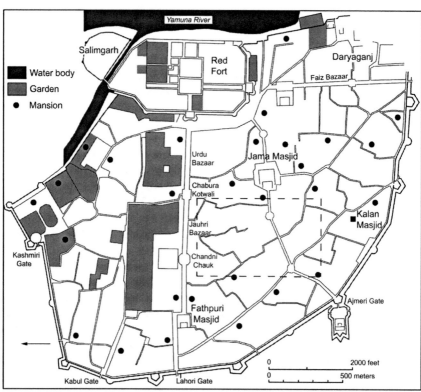

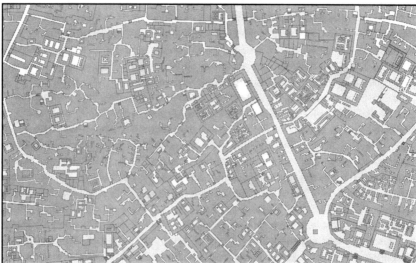

Map 8 Above: plan of Shahjahanabad ca. 1850. Adapted from Blake 1970: 72–73. The hatched lines indicate the boundary of (*below*) neighborhood details. Adapted from Ehlers and Krafft 2003.

Ehlers and Krafft 2003: 16–19). Security within the neighborhood was the responsibility of watchmen (*chaukidar*) paid by the residents. These watchmen were unofficially connected to neighborhood supervisors (*mahalladar*) who answered to the supervisors of the 12 wards (*thana*) of the city, under the direction of the city magistrate. The city judge (*qazi*) took care of legal problems, but in practice the vast majority of disputes achieved resolution at the level of the neighborhoods or within occupational/caste councils that were often coterminous with one or more neighborhoods (Quraeshi 1988: 183–5; Ehlers and Krafft 2003: 20–1, 32–3, 74–80). A remarkably preserved map dating to 1850 shows the plans of *mohallas* (see Map 8) that owed their origin in part to Mughal-period residential forms and in part to encroachment on eighteenth-century mansion compounds.

The rapid growth of the Mughal Empire under Akbar had created a single administrative zone stretching from Kandahar and Kabul in Afghanistan (viewed by the court as components of their original patrimony) to Bengal in the east (Gaur conquered in 1564) and Berar in the south (Ellichpur/Illichpur conquered in 1594). The slow evaporation of Mughal control in Afghanistan accompanied steady expansion into peninsular India during the seventeenth century, culminating in the conquests of Aurangzeb (r. 1658–1707) that extended the empire past the fort at Ginjee (Jinji) in 1698. The relatively pacific conditions within the parts of the empire where expansion was not actively occurring, along with the application of a single currency, created economic stability and demographic growth and contributed to quickened urbanization. The Mughals made administrative decisions within territories directly administered by them and political compacts with allied rulers that effected important changes in the upper echelon of urban sites organized around forts.

Lahore, which had enjoyed periods of prosperity under the Delhi Sultanate, alternating with catastrophic conquest, experienced approximately 150 years of generally peaceful patronage under the Mughals, who used the city as the staging ground for their activities in Afghanistan and Kashmir. Akbar built the massive Lahore Fort on the foundations of the Sultanate-period fort and enclosed the city within a red brick wall including 12 gates. Civic improvements culminated under Shah Jahan in the renovation of the Fort, the construction of a major canal that brought water to the city environs from farther up the Ravi River, and the laying out of the Shalimar (Shalamar) Garden. Aurangzeb constructed the Alamgiri gateway for the fort and one of the jewels of Mughal architecture, the Badshahi Mosque, in 1673. The principal industries of Lahore were carpets, shawls, woolens, silk, weapons, sugar, boats (Naqvi 1986: 17, 20, 34, 81).

Some fortress capitals founded earlier by independent sultanates in central India became even more important under the Mughals. For example, in the Sultanate of Malwa, conquered by the Delhi Sultanate in 1305 but independent under its own sultans in 1401, the plateau fortress of Mandu (elevation 632 meters: area 12,000 acres) had served as the capital and the site of monumental constructions including a wall that nearly surrounded the entire plateau, a huge Friday Mosque, palaces, and additional structures such as the Madrasa of the Heavenly Vault with its seven-story tower. After Akbar annexed Malwa in 1564, the capital became a pleasurable way station on the route to Mughal possessions in the Deccan. Emperor Jahangir (r. 1605–27) spent seven and a half months there and allocated large sums for the renovation of its buildings (Brand 1991).

In the Sultanate of Khandesh (Kandesh), which had seceded from the Delhi Sultanate in 1382, its second ruler, Nasir Khan Faruqi, had founded a new capital near the Tapti River called Burhanpur after the Sufi teacher, Burhanuddin Garib. The main defense of the city was the Asir Fort about 20 kilometers to the north, which controlled passes leading between the Narmada and Tapti valleys. After its final submission to Akbar in 1600, Burhanpur was the staging zone for imperial campaigns in the Deccan and remained under the close supervision of the imperial household. While Khambat remained the dominant port on the Gujarati coast, access from the interior through Ahmedabad was superior; the rise of Surat during the seventeenth century (see Chapter 3) brought with it the resurrection of Burhanpur, which was an important way station on the route to Agra (Naqvi 1972: 125–6; Gordon 1988a).

In the Sultanate of Ahmadnagar, its founder Ahmad Bahri Nizam Shah (1496–1510) had not only acquired Daulatabad Fort but also built a new capital named after himself near an older garrison town that lay on an important east-west commercial route about 100 kilometers south of Daulatabad. During the following century the city of Ahmadnagar was the scene of extensive architectural elaboration and hydraulic improvement, and although originally unfortified, it eventually enjoyed the protection of a massive fort constructed to its east in the 1560s. The kingdom came under intense pressure from the Mughals, who took Ahmadnagar and its fort in 1600, but initially the conquerors could not control the entire province, and a new capital came up at a village called Khirki (later Fatehpur) about 15 kilometers south of Daulatabad. After the Mughals completed their conquest of the sultanate in the 1630s, Aurangzeb occupied the newly founded capital, renamed it Aurangabad, and made it the linchpin of his military operations in peninsular India and the *de facto* capital of the empire between 1693 and his death in 1707. He commissioned extensive public works including a great market in the center of the city, fortifications, gates, and a royal palace. His wife's tomb, the Bibi ka Maqbara, stands in Aurangabad as a southern response to Agra's Taj Mahal (Gadre 1986; Michell and Zebrowski 1999: 10, 39–40, 54, 80–5).

Some fortress capitals that had enjoyed regional primacy under independent sultanates declined under the Mughals. We have already seen the example of Bijapur. In northern India, Jaunpur had been a Tughlaq provincial capital that became the seat of an independent sultanate in 1394, emerging during the fifteenth century as one of the most important Gangetic cities under a series of independent rulers who embarked on an impressive building program. After the sack of Delhi in 1398, it attracted artists and scholars to one of the most brilliant courts in South Asia. Sikandar Lodi, resenting Jaunpur's competition, sacked the city and damaged many of its buildings. Under Akbar, substantial renovation and improvements included one of the greatest achievements of Mughal engineering, a ten-span bridge over the Gomti River, but the city never regained the brilliance it had enjoyed during the fifteenth century. Jaunpur was demoted from a provincial (*suba*) leadership role to the position of a district (*sarkar*) seat, while Allahabad took its place and in 1583 became the site where Akbar built a palace and massive fort that projected the Mughal defensive system toward the east (Alfieri and Borromeo 2000: 94–103).

Despite their personal disinterest in affairs of the northeast, the Mughals understood that a steady shift in the economic balance of South Asia was elevating the importance of the cities along the lower Ganga River and increasing the income from their provinces there. Recognizing the increasingly unhealthy character of the Bengali capital at Gaur, where shifting of river courses had allowed the expansion of swamps, the Mughals constructed a new capital in 1592 at Rajmahal or Akbarnagar, with a fort, Friday Mosque, and extensive suburban gardens. This site originally seemed appropriate for mediating affairs in Bengal and Bihar, but in 1610 the Mughals accepted the greater importance of security operations and a burgeoning agrarian frontier toward the east. They shifted the capital of Bengal province to Dhaka/Dacca (renamed Shahjahanabad), a site on the north bank of the Buriganga River, a 40-kilometer offshoot of the Dhalesvari River, with water-borne access to the entire delta. In addition to sheltering the provincial administration and headquarters of the army, Dhaka became the center for customs payments in the eastern province, and thus a wholesale mart and trans-shipment spot. It also became a node for coordinating village-based weaving networks, with the finest muslins reserved for imperial and provincial households. Even after the return of the provincial capital to Rajmahal between 1639 and 1659, Dhaka's advantages supported a second period as provincial capital until 1704, while Rajmahal went into permanent decline during the eighteenth century after the Ganga River shifted its course. Dhaka's population, estimated at about 200,000 in 1640, remained relatively stable through the eighteenth century (Karim 1964: 83–90).

In the province of Bihar, which oscillated politically between the orbits of Bengal and provinces to the west, by the sixteenth century few could remember that old Pataliputra once had been the most important city in South Asia (see Chapter 1). Its name had evolved into Patna (*pattana*, the market town), pointing to a continuing commercial role, but it was an unremarkable place with a Friday Mosque built only in 1511. The provincial capital during the late Sultanate period lay at Bihar Sharif, which featured the standard configuration of brick and stone citadel, market, mosques and temples, shrines (*dargah*) and tombs of officials and saints. The most important regional commercial center remained Hajipur, near the confluence of the Ganga and Gandak Rivers, which had been the commercial hub and political capital during the early Sultanate period. In 1541, however, Sher Shah noticed the potential strategic value of Patna and allocated funds for the construction of a fort there, making it a provincial capital. This was the beginning of an extended period of prosperity for Patna, where Akbar built a fort and palace, and where a regional version of the Mughal courtly culture developed during the seventeenth century. Along with Varanasi, Patna developed a reputation for cotton textile manufacture. Its population peaked by the end of the century at about 200,000 persons, most of them living (as in all contemporary South Asian cities) in humble homes with thatch or tile roofs (Naqvi 1974: 104, 161; Askari and Ahmad 1983: 444–6; 1987: 50–1, 405–6, 448–9).

The Mughal state at its height maintained in good condition the 'northern path,' which the British later called the Grand Trunk Road, through the planting of a continuous double row of shade trees from Lahore to Agra and points east, and also through the erecting of pillars marking distances (*kos minar*) along main highways. The Mughal nobility also provided periodic rest stations (*sarai*) equipped with wells. The actual construction technique of even the most important thoroughfares, however, involved only the leveling of earth with a slightly convex profile to allow water to run off to the sides, wide enough to permit, at most, the passage of two carts. Communication along these routes for state dispatches sometimes still depended on horse relays, but most often on relays of runners whose progress varied, but could exceed 200 kilometers daily. Groups of human carriers were typically employed for overland transport of small loads and persons. Transportation by ox-cart was more common in the north than in the south, and camel caravans were common in the northwest, but for long-distance overland transport of bulk commodities the most effective agents until the nineteenth century were specialized castes of cattle drivers (Banjara, Lambadi), sometimes traveling with tens of thousands of animals. In addition to carrying goods for merchants, cattle caravans accompanied armies with provisions as they moved on campaigns very slowly, at the rate of perhaps 10 kilometers daily. The generally unimproved character of roads everywhere severely limited movement by land during the rains. The transportation of larger loads was possible within the reticulated water channels of Bengal, on the Ganga River as far as Allahabad, and during much of the Mughal period far up the Ganga and Yamuna Rivers. Waterborne freight also moved considerable distances along the Indus River and for limited distances on its tributaries and on the great rivers running west-to-east in peninsular India. Water transport was negatively affected by monsoon runoff, and thus experienced seasonal peaks and lows. Even in the best of times, traffic moved slowly; a one-way trip along the Ganga River could take several months. South Asia thus appeared to contemporaries, as it had for several thousand years, to be a gigantic expanse that required considerable effort to traverse, and its major cities remained separated by many days' travel. In this sense South Asia was no different from other macro-regions until the nineteenth century. Some European commentators found travel within the Mughal Empire to be superior to movement in their homelands (Deloche 1993, 1994: 5–39).

The urban hierarchy of the late Mughal period

We have been considering mostly the bigger cities that developed as fortress-administration centers under the aegis of various sultanates, independent kings, or the Mughal Empire. Between 1550 and 1750 there were perhaps 250 primary and secondary sites in this category (Chaudhury 1978: 88), ranging from the imperial capitals such as Agra or Delhi with several hundred thousand inhabitants to regional capitals or seats of provincial (*subah*) and sub-provincial (*sarkar*) officials with perhaps 10,000 to 20,000 inhabitants. All these centers became the arenas of a cosmopolitan imperialist cadre that communicated in Persian and patronized an Indo-Islamic culture generating the highest forms of artistic expression. They did not, and could not, exist without a hierarchy of smaller urban locations, described in Arabic, Persian, and Urdu literature as towns or *qasba* (*qasbat, kasba*) in distinction to city (*shahr* or *mada'in*), lying in turn within a vast and expanding agrarian economy based officially on villages. In Akbar's time there were between 2,700 and 3,200 places within the expanding empire described by this terminology as towns (Naqvi 1986: 77; Hambly 1982: 442; Rehman and Wescoat 1993: 51). An example is the Punjab settlement of Batala, founded probably in the early-sixteenth century, which evolved into a walled city about 3 kilometers in diameter with several dozen neighborhoods grouped around two bazaar thoroughfares with an old fort and congregational mosque at its heart – a smaller version of the pattern found in more metropolitan locales. The population of Batala by the early-eighteenth century probably ranged between 15,000 and 20,000, making this one of the larger places classified as a town. It was, perhaps, half that size 100 years earlier (Grewal 1975: 18).

If we conservatively estimate that there were 3,000 small towns with an average population of 3,000 persons in each, we would find approximately 9 million people living at the lowest level of the Mughal-controlled urban hierarchy at the beginning of the seventeenth century. Because the Mughals controlled, at the most, two-thirds of the subcontinent's population at that time, we could extrapolate to about 13.5 million persons living in all the smaller towns of South Asia (Subrahmanyam 1990a: 71–7). If we then very conservatively estimate an average population of 20,000 persons in all 250 primary and secondary cities, we find an additional 5 million urbanites, and arrive at *a total urban population of at least 18.5 million around 1600.* Comparing these numbers to scholarly guesses of the entire human population of South Asia in 1600 between 100 and 125 million, one could propose that somewhere *between 15 percent and 18.5 percent lived in central places.* Irfan Habib (1982b: 167–72), estimating a total population of between 140 and 150 million, similarly estimates that approximately 15 percent (i.e. up to 22.5 million persons) lived in urban centers. Through computations based on detailed tax statistics, Shireen Moosvi (1987: 299–307) also estimates an urban population of 15 percent and the value added by urban manufactures excluding trade and transport was 9.6 percent of total agricultural production.

Based on previous sultanate procedures, and consonant with practices through-out South Asia, the Mughals divided their realm into sub-districts (*pargana*) that contained many villages organized around, and named after, settlements where they based a small staff of administrators and accountants who regulated the flow of land revenues. Batala, for example, had been a *pargana* headquarters under the Lodis and remained one under the Mughals. The number of such units controlled by the Mughals expanded as a result of conquest and also because of agrarian growth; in Bihar, for example, there were 200 under Akbar in 1582 and 246 under Aurangzeb in 1685 (Singh 1985: 116–18; Askari and Ahmed 1987: 309–10). Each new pargana meant the addition to the state's administrative system of at least one town, connecting a mostly agricultural world to an urban economy based increasingly on monetary transactions, denoting the ability to extract resources for military campaigns and for conspicuous consumption. The tabulation of 4,716 parganas within the Empire in 1720, when it encompassed most of the subcontinent, would thus provide a rough baseline indicating the number of small towns in South Asia, although in practice a number of sub-districts seem to have included multiple sites functioning as *qasba* (Sato 1997: 60–1). Again estimating very conservatively an average population in each *pargana* seat of 3,000 persons, we would find approximately 14 million people living in the lowest level of the Mughal urban hierarchy as the Empire entered its senescence. We could once again add a conservative figure of 6 million persons living in at least 250 primary or secondary centers to arrive at *a South Asian urban population of, at the very least, 20 million in the mid-eighteenth century*. Measured against estimates of total South Asian population in 1750 between 100 and 200 million, we could expect the urban population to fall *between 10 and 20 percent of total population* (Visaria and Visaria 1983: 466).

The pressure exerted by the Mughals at the sub-district level to monetize local revenue collections and the enhanced security provided by their local police posts or fort garrisons allowed the empire to support the activities of merchants, brokers, and moneylenders in order to stimulate local-level urbanization. In addition, the grandees of the empire funded infrastructure or founded new settlements and markets (Hambly 1982: 441–6; Richards 1993: 62). The Empire, the most formidable representative of the fortress-administration model, thus stood as a city-based agency that actively encouraged the formation of towns. It was not the only political agency doing this. Competing states – the independent or allied polities in Rajasthan (based, for example, in Jodhpur or Udaipur), the successor states to the Vijayanagara Empire in southern India (at Gingee, Vellore, Tanjavur and Madurai), the emerging state of Mysore (which bought Bangalore from the Mughals), and the emerging Maratha state in Maharashtra – implemented similar initiatives (Tillotson 1987; Deloche 2000). Hundreds of 'little kings' within and outside the empire pursued such goals. Various 'stratified lineages' that we may generically label Rajput threw up lineage leaders (*raja, chaudhari, babu, zamindar*) whose bases of operations were 'lineage urban-like centers' that featured mud forts, served as intermediate revenue-collection nodes, and attracted merchants or artisans (Fox 1970: 178). The combined activities of these states or proto-states, interacting with commercial firms and households within an institutional environment that since the thirteenth century had become increasingly paper-based, created what Frank Perlin (1993: 40, 55–6) terms an 'invisible city,' characterized by practices that were spreading throughout Afro-Eurasia, pulling settlements at all levels within a monetized matrix. Hundreds of the towns drawn into this sphere of interaction or created by it would eventually become the district and sub-district centers of modern South Asian states.

3 Emporiums, empire, and the early colonial presence

Anthropology and history meet in Amitav Ghosh's book *In an Antique Land* (1992), where he describes his fieldwork in an Egyptian village and his parallel fascination with the Geniza Documents, a priceless collection discovered in the storeroom of an Old Cairo synagogue. His tale of a person of Indian origin living in late-twentieth-century Egypt becomes a counterpoint to the story of a slave from twelfth-century Karnataka who became the agent in Mangalore for a Jewish merchant based in Aden, Yemen, and Egypt. The author's involvement in the distant past conjures a vision of the Indian Ocean as it once was: the greatest trading zone in the world, where ships and peoples from all shores traveled freely to market raw materials and precious items at open ports. And as the book progresses we begin to feel the sadness of this scholar who finds himself a stranger in the strange land of contemporary Egypt, where citizens have no experience of travelers from India, where the state locks people and consciousness within national ideologies and specific flows of capital and labor. We come to realize that a world has been lost here, and that the loss began with the voyages of European traders and imperialists who reached out to the Indian Ocean in the late-fifteenth century and made new rules that re-channeled regions and macro-regions within a global capitalist mode. The ports of the ocean littoral became nodes of colonialism and then achieved freedom only as components of the nation-state. Within this new dispensation, Egyptians and Indians (or persons of Indian origin via the United States) would rarely find opportunities for direct contact across the sea.

This chapter will concentrate on a 300-year period until about 1800 when the imperial project emanating from Europe was devised, very slowly polished, and then imperfectly implemented within South Asia. It will describe in particular the entrepots for Indian Ocean trade as first encountered by the Portuguese, and then trace the processes that allowed the Portuguese, followed by the Dutch, English and French, to establish trading outposts within a commercial world that was still controlled by Asian merchants and the agents of powerful kingdoms marshaled by the Mughal Empire. Finally, it will examine the most sophisticated city-states created by the European trading interests, and the policies that allowed them to become the most dynamic examples of urbanization within South Asia as the system coordinated under the Mughals underwent a painful transition. Our journey begins, however, with a heterarchic configuration of open ports and regional kingdoms – a type of openness that has become alien to Ghosh and to all of us.

The coastal emporiums in the late-first millennium

Commerce was always a major factor in the formation of South Asian cities located far from the ocean, even if political and military interests appeared to dominate. A consideration of coastal sites demonstrates more clearly a preponderance of commercial interests. Unlike the tributary system of East Asia, trade in the Indian Ocean developed without any attempt by land-based administrations to regulate the system as a whole. Although piracy was a constant threat and ships required security personnel, the sea was demilitarized. Ports were open to any ships ready to trade, assuming their captains and crews were willing to abide by local regulations and, most importantly, pay customs duties. The income from those duties was a crucial component in the budgets of the many independent kingdoms that grew up along the coasts of South Asia, and it was therefore in the interests of their little kings to attract traders with reasonable customs rates and access to regional trading communities along with adequate hospitality. Even when coastal towns became parts of larger empires, port administration enjoyed considerable autonomy. The traders of the Indian Ocean created this pattern at least 2,500 years ago, and perfected it during the late-first millennium. We will look briefly at four regional examples (see Map 9).

In Sri Lanka, the continuing importance of Anuradhapura was matched by the prosperity of its main port, Mantai, which operated until the eleventh century, eventually evolving a horseshoe-shaped plan protected by fortifications and a double moat. From occupational debris up to 10 meters deep, archaeologists have obtained evidence of imported glass and ceramics from the Red Sea, Persian Gulf, East Africa, South Arabia, India, and China. Mantai was a major bead production site, with artisans working on materials from Sri Lanka and abroad, the latter including glass and lapis ornaments (Carswell 1991). Comparisons of assemblages from Mantai, Banbhore/Daybul in Sind, and the port of Siraf (modern Taheri), which became one of the leading emporiums of the Persian Gulf, indicate a production and commercial nexus linking the three locations with a peak between 800 and 1000 (Tampoe 1989: 106–9). Literary descriptions and the patterns of Chinese ceramics at the three ports indicate that Persian merchants may have gone to Southeast Asia and China until the eighth century, and direct sailing may have become more common by the ninth century, but the most common strategy for long-distance trade was a segmented, regional division of labor, with Sri Lankan ports playing the role of linchpins until the end of the millennium (Hourani 1995: 40, 61–8). By that point, as attested by changes in the pottery from Mantai, direct imports of Chinese ceramics were catering to the tastes of the well-to-do within Sri Lanka and were becoming part of an ongoing trade toward the west that involved mariners from southern India, China, Southeast Asia and the Arabic-speaking world (Charvat 1993). Thus the emporiums of Sri Lanka became important trans-shipment points in Indian Ocean commerce.

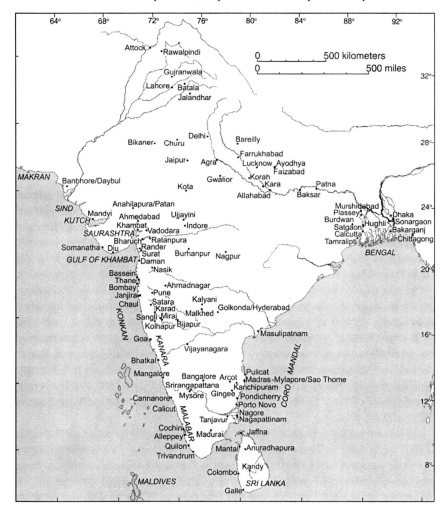

Map 9 Commercial centers, ca. 800–1800.

Arabic writers described a number of cities on the coast and within the interiors of Maharashtra and Gujarat. The most important inland center for these writers was Manyakheta (modern Malkhed), a seat of the Rashtrakuta dynasty (eighth–tenth centuries), viewed as the greatest rulers in South Asia. The collapse of the Rashtrakutas brought a line of later Chalukya princes to power in their home territories with a new base in Kalyani (Kalyanapura), and a separate line (sometimes known as the Solankis) to power in Gujarat in 941 with a base in Anahilapura alias Anahilavada (modern Patan). A study of economy under the Chalukyas of Gujarat by V. K. Jain (1990: 116, 120, 129–32) suggests that towns and trading networks were already well developed before the dynastic revolution. For example, Anahilapura apparently supplanted the earlier site of Srimala or

Bhinamala as the chief center of inland commercial activity. The eleventh-century foundation of Karnavati as a major trading center rested on a pre-existing town called Asapalli, earlier controlled by Bhilla rulers. On the coast, the site of Somanathapattana with its important temple was already an 'old town' before it reached its height during the tenth century. Bharukachchha or Bharuch/Broach, formerly one of the premier ports on the west coast, seems to have suffered an eclipse but never disappeared, re-emerging as one of the chief commercial centers. The port of Thane/Thana, located on the navigable creek bounding Salsette Island on the north, rose in the seventh century as a premier port of the Chalukyas and later the Silahara dynasty that controlled much of the western coast of Maharashtra between ca. 800 and 1265 (Hebalkar 2001: 115-17).

Inscriptions have revealed a concentration of commercial groups and administrative personnel interacting from at least the beginning of the tenth century along the west coast of India (Chakravarti 2001). We have begun to understand the long-term history of one market segment well known to Arabic writers – the western Indian stone bead industry – which had emerged by at least the early-first millennium. The industry rested on the mining of agate nodules around Ratanpura (the Jewel City) on the south bank of the Narmada River. Processing of its raw materials was an Ujjayini specialty until the late-first millennium, when the industry shifted to Limudra, about 5 kilometers from Ratanpura, and later shifted to Khambat (Khambayat or Cambay), a harbor town on the north shore of the Mahi River estuary founded by the sixth century and well-known to Arabic writers by the early-tenth century. The distribution of beads from this industry reached as far as Scandinavia, along with thousands of Arab *dirhams* discovered in coin hoards (Wink 1990: 307–8; Arasaratnam and Ray 1994: 119–21; Francis 2002: 103–11).

As for coastal emporiums in Bengal, although archaeology suggests that older deltaic ports such as Tamralipti reached their peak in the third century, literary references describe it as a functioning port as late as the seventh century. A large cluster of commercial sites were thriving along the original channel of the Bhagirathi (Ganga) River and near the intersection of the Padma and Meghna Rivers between the tenth and twelfth centuries (Sengupta 1996: 124–5). Thereafter Bengal's main ports lay at Satgaon (the seven villages), accessing the Ganga River system, Sonargaon (the village of gold), accessing the Padma/Meghna River system, and Chittagong (Chattagama) on the estuary of the Karnaphuli River (Prakash 1998: 14–22).

Shifts in the configuration of coastal emporiums, ca. 1000–1500

South Asia entered a new phase of economic expansion around the year 1000, manifested in an amplification of its ocean-borne commercial activities. Western trade through the Red Sea, with Aden and Cairo as the coordinating centers, flourished under the Fatimids and Ayyubids (969–1250), eventually tied to the rise of Italian intermediaries and a resurgent economy in Western Europe. Contacts with

Southeast Asia continued to intensify, initially through the intermediaries of the Srivijaya state (seventh–twelfth centuries) based in Sumatra, and then through the maturing systems associated with the Khmer empire (ninth–fifteenth centuries) based at Angkor and the first empire of Myanmar/Burma (eleventh–thirteenth centuries) based in Bagan/Pagan. Further afield lay the booming economy of China under the Song (960–1279) and Ming (1368–1644) dynasties, which led to direct Chinese trading with ports in Sri Lanka and on the west coast of southern India. Internally, South Asia was experiencing accelerated agrarian growth, e.g. in what is now Bangladesh or in the Kongu region of northwestern Tamil Nadu. The interactions between long-distance trading corporations and hundreds of central places serving as local market centers accompanied, and sometimes intersected with, the growth of political seats for kings and subordinate political leaderships.

Discussions of coastal emporiums during the second millennium use a regional nomenclature to describe different segments of the Indian Ocean littoral. In this sense we differentiate in Pakistan between the Makran coast of Baluchistan and the coast of Sind at the delta of the Indus River, the latter linked ultimately to the Punjabi river port of Lahore, which gained a reputation for shipbuilding. In Gujarat, there were major differences between Kutch in the west, the main block of Saurashtra or Kathiawar, and the Gulf of Khambat on the east dominated by Khambat/Cambay, the primary port serving northern India. The Konkan coast of western India corresponded roughly to what are now western Maharashtra and Goa, linked commercially to the inland kingdoms of the Chalukyas and Yadavas and their eventual successor, the sultanate of Ahmadnagar. The Kanara coast of Karnataka was linked commercially to the kingdom of Vijayanagara and the sultanate of Bijapur, with its major emporium located at Bhatkal, 3 kilometers up the Skandaholeya River (Subrahmanyam 1990a: 121–35). The Malabar coast of Kerala was a major producer of black pepper, the most desired of spices, and also served as the main region for the trans-shipment of goods at the intersection of routes from the Arabian Sea and the Bay of Bengal, linked ultimately to the supply of other spices in demand: cinnamon from Sri Lanka, cardamom, mace and nutmeg (and more pepper) from Indonesia. Toward the east was the Coromandal (or Coromandel) coast, a term derived from Cholamandalam, the 'circle of the Cholas' who had ruled until the thirteenth century, including Tamil Nadu and part of what is today Andhra Pradesh. The ports there came to serve the empire of Vijayanagara and, after its demise, its successor states and the sultanate of Golkonda.

We may visualize the principle commercial pattern on the Indian Ocean during the early-second millennium as evolving toward a 'triple segmentation,' or three trading circles covering an area from eastern Africa to southern China, with intersections along the western coast of India and the Malay Peninsula/Sumatra (see Map 10). Within this larger pattern, long-distance routes moved high-value, low-volume items alongside bulk goods used as ballast. Shorter-distance coastal traffic, later called the 'country trade,' moved the largest amount of consumer goods and bulk items such as grain. The roles of particular ports within this configuration

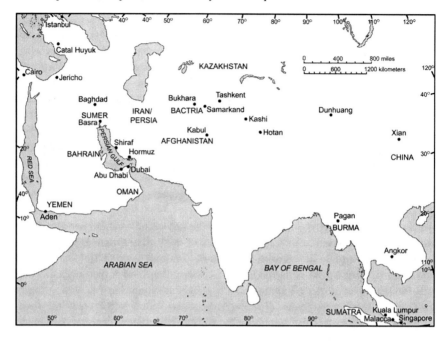

Map 10 Eurasian connections with South Asia.

shifted in the short and long terms, depending on variations in political economy, demand from participants in the larger system, or accidents of geography. After the thirteenth century, Malacca (Melaka) in Southeast Asia and Khambat in Gujarat became linchpins of long-distance transportation. Calicut (Kozhikode) became the largest trading emporium in Malabar by the fifteenth century, although it experienced competition from alternative ports led by Cannanore (Kannur), on a small bay protected by a promontory, and Cochin (Kochi), a shipbuilding center that lay near the estuary of the Periyar River at the entranceway to an array of inland lagoons and waterways. In Sri Lanka, the focus of Indian Ocean trade was relocating from the north to the southwest coast. Siltation would cause the decline of Khambat, Satgaon and Sonargaon after the sixteenth century (Chaudhuri 1985: 41, 108–9, 208; Arasaratnam 1994: 35–40; Prakash 1998: 8–12).

The voyages of exploration funded by the Ming Empire of China and led by Zheng He between 1405 and 1433, which investigated conditions at least as far as the eastern coast of Africa, involved the largest fleets ever witnessed on the Indian Ocean (Ray 1987; Levathes 1994). The decision to cancel those expeditions – certainly one of the most fateful strategic choices in history – preserved the Indian Ocean as a neutral zone during a period of increasing state absolutism, rapid technological change in oceanic transportation, and the military revolution involving gunpowder weaponry. In an amazing quirk of fate, the exploiters of this situation were the Portuguese, who were steadily creeping down the west coast of Africa.

The Portuguese impact

When the expedition led by Vasco da Gama rounded Africa and obtained a guide, who directed them across the Arabian Sea, they headed for Calicut. Anchoring in 1498 at the more protected inlet of Pantalayini-Kollam north of the city (where today one may randomly pick up fragments of fifteenth-century Chinese pottery), the Portuguese visited the coastal emporium of the Zamorin (i.e. the Samudri, or Lord of the Ocean). Although Calicut lay on an unprotected expanse of beachfront, it enjoyed the advantage of a semi-permanent offshore 'mudbank,' a colloidal suspension of sediment, which dampened wave action and provided a screen to ships anchored on its leeward side, protecting landings to the north of the port (Deloche 1994, 2: 85–9). The city – still unfortified at that time – stretched for several kilometers along the coast, consisting mostly of walled compounds enclosing one-story houses, gardens and groves. Behind the beach were shops and warehouses, and beyond them the habitation-and-storage compounds of traders segregated by place of origin. Although he maintained a coastal domicile, the ruler's main palace was several kilometers distant from the coast, in close proximity to the main fonts of political power – Nambudiri brahmana and Nayar landowning elites and the sources of agrarian production. Access to spices or other trade goods would require the standard payment of customs duties to agents of the king's government, and interactions with local brokers and merchant princes who maintained networks of commercial intermediaries in the port's hinterland. Muslim trading communities were prominent competitors, including 'foreigners' who controlled long-distance maritime commerce and native-born Mapillas who controlled coastal traffic. The entire complex presented all the functionalities of an urban site without dense habitation patterns, architectural concentration or monumentality, in contrast with inland cities (Arasaratnam 1994: 16–17, 23–4; Bouchon 2000: 42–3).

The Portuguese demonstrated a disinclination to participate in the conventional trading pattern evidenced at Calicut, aiming instead to establish themselves as a colonial power with monopolies over seaborne trade. As early as 1499 the King of Portugal was calling himself the 'Lord of Guinea and of the Conquests, Navigation and Commerce of Ethiopia, Arabia, Persia and India' (Hart 1950: 202). Their second expedition led by Pedro Álvares Cabral left Lisbon in 1500 with 13 ships and 1,200 men, and upon arrival at Calicut reinforced local perceptions of their arrogance and hostile intent. Fighting erupted and the Portuguese proceeded to the bombardment of Calicut, a state that thereafter opposed their policies. In 1503 two Milanese cannon makers deserted the Portuguese and found immediate employment with the ruler of Calicut; within three years they cast 300 cannon and the Zamorin had a fleet of 200 ships with cannon (Pearson 1987a: 60). Meanwhile, the Portuguese had established alliances with competing Malabar city-states, setting up their first fort in South Asia at Cochin in 1503, followed by another at Cannanore in 1505, although they remained incapable of controlling the movement of spices to the coast. The tenure of Francisco de Almeida (1505–9) as commander of the fleet coincided with the Portuguese defeat of the combined fleets of Mamluk Egypt and the governor of Diu (Diva), an appointee of the sultanate of Gujarat, thus eliminating the only major threat to their presence on the Indian Ocean. Thereafter, the Portuguese under Afonso de Albuquerque (1509–15) and successive Viceroys implemented a militaristic policy designed to control strategic ports across the Indian Ocean, from which they could regulate the entire trading system. They took, lost, and regained Goa in 1510. They took Malacca, the gateway to Southeast Asia, in 1511, Hormuz (Bandar-e Abbas), the gateway to the Persian Gulf, in 1515, and Colombo in 1518. Their only major failure was an inability to take Aden at the entrance to the Red Sea in 1513; they subsequently attempted to control access there through regular sea patrols (Aden fell to the Ottoman Empire in 1538). The Viceroy of this emerging Estado da India resided originally at Cochin, but later more often at Goa, which became the capital of Portuguese ventures in the East in 1530.

Aside from Sri Lanka, where they found themselves involved in a debilitating war with interior lordships led by the mountain kingdom of Kandy, the Portuguese used fortified ports in order to mount a seaborne protection racket. Their passport or *cartaz* system forced ships sailing in the Indian Ocean to purchase safe passage from Portuguese authorities; any ship intercepted at sea without a passport was subject to attack and confiscation. They also tried to force ships to sail in convoys (*khafila, cafila*) under the direction of their fleet, requiring stops in ports administered by Portuguese customs collectors. They attempted a complete monopoly over the trade in spices to Europe, a scheme that was foiled at the outset by their failure to close the Red Sea. In practice, the trading economy was so large and multifaceted that they were only partially successful, and Portuguese personnel regularly engaged in private trade and corrupt practices that undercut official policies. In any case, after the 1540s the Portuguese crown began withdrawing from direct management of trading voyages, instead granting concessions to private individuals (Pearson 1987b: 36–81; Prakash 1998: 28–9; 1999: 178–81).

Portuguese traders began to tap into the textile trade on the Coromandel coast in 1517, near the small temple-town of Mylapore/Meliapur, where they founded an enclave known as São Tomé, and set up a second base at Nagapattinam, which had long served as the staging area for trade with Southeast Asia (Subrahmanyam 1990a: 194–206; 1990b: 47–95). On the Konkan coast, they became major players in the transport of horses, with a presence at Chaul and Bhatkal; later, Goa became their major conduit for horses going to the Deccani sultanates. In 1528 Portuguese forces gained control over the island groups of Bombay and Salsette (where they began to develop the important port of Thana/Thane), and the following year they took Bassein (Baçaim/Vasai) on the mainland just to the north. Their main strategy was to isolate or gain control over the great emporium of Khambat, and thus regulate the foreign trade of Gujarat. The Sultans of Gujarat resisted until they came under irresistible pressure from the recently created Mughal Empire. The island-fortress of Diu, 11 kilometers long and separated from the mainland by a narrow channel, controlled the western side of the Gulf of Khambat; it finally fell completely into Portuguese hands in 1555. Daman, on the other side of the Gulf, fell in 1559. Thereafter the commerce of Khambat followed the trading fortunes of the Portuguese. The Mughal Emperor Akbar, lord of Gujarat after 1572, obtained from the Portuguese one free pass annually and generally ignored their presence, although the double brick walls at Khambat were strengthened to forestall their raids (Naqvi 1972: 124; Arasaratnam and Ray 1994: 121–33). In Bengal the Portuguese maintained an important presence in Chittagong and targeted Satgaon originally, but the gradual silting of the river there prompted them to move to Hughli (a presence legitimized by Akbar in 1579, three years after the Mughal conquest of Bengal), where about 5,000 persons were residing in the early-seventeenth century (Subrahmanyam 1990b: 96–127; Arasaratnam 1994: 149–52).

At Goa, the Portuguese had obtained outstanding port facilities where the estuaries of two rivers – the Mandovi on the north and the Zuari on the south – entered the Arabian Sea at the same location. The estuaries and their tributary streams bounded the island of Tisvadi, creating a combination of safe harbors and defensibility that had attracted traders for centuries. The Portuguese established their main settlement on the northeastern corner in bottomlands at beginning of the Mandovi estuary – in the long run a poor choice, since the low topography contributed to health and sanitation problems that were never resolved. This site had been one of the main ports of the sultanate of Bijapur, and represented a relatively recent transfer of commercial centrality from a much older location on the southern side of the island that had accessed the northern shore of the Zuari estuary. In 1524 there were 450 householders labeled Portuguese at the conquest site that today is known as Old Goa. The Portuguese by 1543 had consolidated their hold over buffer zones – Bardesh/Bardez sub-district on the north (264 square kilometers) and Salcette/Salcete on the south (335 square kilometers) – which together with the island constitute what they eventually termed the Old Conquests. Their concern for naval security prompted construction of forts that protected the mouths of both estuaries and backup forts halfway up the Mandovi estuary.

Coming by sea to Old Goa at its height in the late-sixteenth century, one sailed past the large royal shipyard and arsenal, the quay of Saint Catherine (the landing site for the fishing fleet), and the galley yard on the south shore of the Mandovi estuary. Disembarking at the quay of the Viceroys, one entered the old fort area and saw to the left the main customs house and the factory/warehouse for imports. Directly behind lay the palace of the Viceroys (reconstructed in 1554 on the site of the older Bijapuri harbor fort) with the grand bazaar to its east. Passing through the Waterfront Gate, after 1597 called the 'Arch of the Viceroys,' on the west side of the palace, one walked south down the Straight Street (Rua Direita), flanked by one of the livelier markets in South Asia. A short distance down this avenue two smaller roads headed west to a small square surrounded by public offices, a former palace of the Bijapur sultans (acquired by the Inquisition in 1560), and the archbishop's seat. Back on the Straight Street, at the heart of the city one entered the square of the Church of the Holy House of Mercy, behind which lay another large market. Following the main street toward its end, one came to the plaza of the 'Old Pillory,' where six streets came together at another market, and finally to a steep climb leading to the church of Our Lady of Light, beyond which lay the suburbs. As in other Portuguese cities on the west coast of India, Goa's city plan came to be influenced by Renaissance concepts of city planning with orthogonal streets and blocks, but in practice the neighborhoods, without a public water supply, were a maze of small, filthy streets and alleys flanked closely by two-story homes with red tile roofs. A number of roughly semicircular streets in concentric arcs around the Arch of the Viceroys were generally inhabited by groups specializing in specific lines or merchandize or trades (with artisans organized in confraternities modeled directly on Portuguese craft guilds). The main city, roughly triangular in plan, had a circumference of about 7.2 kilometers. A wall enclosed city and suburbs, with six strong passes on the east along the river separating the island from the mainland, and two additional passes at the wealthy suburb of Raibandar and Panjim/Panaji (which would become Goa's capital in 1843) on the west. Habitations spilling out toward the west and south covered the island with a series of villas and country estates (De Souza 1979: 109–14; Hutt 1988: 66–8, 107–15; *Cidade de Goa* 1994; Rossa 1997: 41–53).

Among the relatively small, but rigorously hierarchical, community of Portuguese living in Goa, churchmen came to dominate social life. Approximately 50 churches, convents and other Christian religious foundations came up in the city. The largest building, the Cathedral of Santa Caterina (76 meters in length), the fifth of six cathedrals fixing the skyline, replaced an original parish church to become the episcopal see. The Jesuits made Goa the base of their Asian operations, setting up the first printing press in South Asia in 1556. All temples in the city were destroyed, followed by temple destruction in Bardesh and Salcette. Efforts to Christianize the population were partially successful; by the early-seventeenth century about two-thirds of the city population and about 20 percent of the 250,000 persons in the Old Conquests were officially Christian. In practice, the administration was never able to dispense with the services of non-Christian personnel. Furthermore, the Portuguese applied European racist categories to social organization. Stratification generally occurred on the basis of the blood's 'purity' as marked by skin color and facial features. Most Portuguese men in Goa, however, took lovers from the local populations, leading to the growth of a large *mestiço* community. The population of Old Goa in the early-seventeenth century was about 75,000, including 1,500 Portuguese or *mestiços*, 20,000 Hindus and the remainder local Christians. By the end of the century, when the city was in steep decline and the entire population was about 20,000, there was also a substantial community of slaves and freed persons of full or partial African origin constituting perhaps a quarter of the city's inhabitants (de Souza 1979: 115, 124–6; Pearson 1987a: 92–3, 107, 116–21; 2003: 155).

The early imperialism of the Dutch and English companies

The decline of Old Goa occurred because the Portuguese were encountering stiffer resistance to their version of imperialism from South Asian powers, and also because of mounting interference from European competitors, especially the Dutch and the English. Whereas the Portuguese effort in Asia always retained the character of a crown undertaking and involved close connections with the Church, the activities of the northern Europeans more closely resembled those of modern capitalist organizations. Their funding came from private joint-stock investors who wanted dividends from successful mercantile voyages, and territorial gains were considered an unnecessary drain on profits. Their merchants, living in a post-Reformation society, were disinterested in expenditure on religious monuments or conversions. Their companies did, however, share with the Portuguese a desire for monopolies that would guarantee stable returns, and they adopted the tactics of seaborne protection rackets and closed access to raw materials or artisan production within territorial spheres of influence backed up by military power. They also moved as quickly as possible to construct port-enclaves guarded by their own security forces, which grew into substantial coastal trading towns. Thus these early transnational corporations exerted a profound impact on the configuration of urbanization in South Asia.

Expeditions mounted by nine joint stock companies from the United Provinces of the Netherlands began arriving in Southeast Asia in 1596, initially pursuing the spice trade in cloves, nutmeg and mace. In 1602 these companies amalgamated as the United East India Company (Vereenigde Oost-Indische Compagnie, or VOC). Their main goal was to supplant the Portuguese at the sources of spices in eastern Indonesia, but they discovered that exchanging silver for cloth on the eastern coast of India gave them something marketable in Southeast Asia. Thus they obtained from agents of the Golkonda Sultanate permission to establish their first warehouse/factory in 1606 at Masulipatnam (Machchhilipattanam), located at the eastern end of the Krishna River Delta and commanding one of the better anchorages on the Coromandel coast. It became Golkonda's main port and the east coast's leading emporium until the middle of the seventeenth century (Subrahmanyam 1993; Arasaratnam and Ray 1994). The Dutch established a second factory in 1610 at Pulicat (Palaverkadu), an old port on an inland lake with access to the sea, where they constructed Fort Geldria (Arasaratnam 1989: 80–2). Hostilities then broke out with the Portuguese based in Nagapattinam and São Tomé, but the Dutch held their own militarily and benefited from Portuguese inability to control the indigenous political forces along the east coast (Subrahmanyam 1990b: 188–215). The Dutch learned to interact with indigenous merchants who in turn worked with secondary brokers who contacted direct producers. In southern Coromandel their partners were Komati, Beri Chetti and Balija merchants, and in the northern part, Muslim Chulias. In this manner the Dutch endeavor rapidly evolved in the same direction as that of the Portuguese; from the simple transport of spices to Europe into a major commitment to intra-Asian trade (Winius and Wink 1991: 18–19; Prakash 1998: 186–7).

In England, the Crown issued a charter for 'the Governor and Company of Merchants of London Trading into the East Indies' in 1600, before one of their ships had even lifted sail. The preliminary expeditions mounted by the company focused on Southeast Asia, where their ships arrived to find the Dutch busily engaged in the elimination of Portuguese bases. The English captains quickly learned the well-established practice of trading goods from eastern India in Sumatra, which led, despite some initial resistance from the Dutch, to the founding in 1611 of the

Company's first South Asian factory/warehouse at Masulipatnam. Meanwhile, clashes between English and Portuguese ships occurred off the coast of Gujarat, with the former uniformly successful. In 1613 the Mughal governor at Surat (Prince Khurram, later Emperor Shah Jahan), impressed with their mettle, granted the English company permission for trade. This led to the establishment of English factories at Ahmedabad, Broach, Burhanpur, Khambat, Vadodara (Baroda), and Surat, with branches in northern India at Agra, Lahore, Patna, and (for six years) Lucknow. The success of the English gave the Dutch an opening, and in 1618 they also obtained permission from the Mughals for trading in Gujarat and other north Indian centers (Forster 1998: 144–72, 208–16, 314–15).

The failure of the Estado da India to check the inroads of the Dutch and the English was followed by disasters that shook the Portuguese enterprise in the East. The Persians (in alliance with the English) took Hormuz in 1622. In Bengal, the Portuguese established at Hughli had been engaging in a variety of troublesome behaviors, leading to a decision by the newly crowned Emperor Shah Jahan to wage war against them. Mughal forces captured Hughli in 1632 and imprisoned its inhabitants for several years before allowing them to return. The Dutch benefited from the Portuguese discomfiture by obtaining permission to set up a presence in Bengal, eventually fixing on the site of Chinsura near Hughli as their main base of operations. The success of the VOC and the perception of declining Portuguese fortunes prompted the Dutch to launch direct assaults on the Estado da India in its strongholds. Malacca was besieged and fell in 1641. In Sri Lanka, a Dutch alliance with the kingdom of Kandy led to several decades of bitter and expensive conflict ending in the siege and capture of Colombo in 1656, followed by the capture of Jaffna two years later.

The Portuguese had decided on Colombo as their seat not because of the superiority of its harbor, which was a shallow lagoon exposed to the southwest monsoon and possessed of a dangerous bar, but because of its defensibility and its proximity to cinnamon production in the wet, southwestern zone of Sri Lanka known as the Low Country. Their fort in Colombo lay on a hooked spit west of the lagoon, almost entirely cut off from the interior by marshes. The Portuguese raised the water level in these marshes to expand Lake Beira, across which a single road provided access to the fort, the latter protected by a single line of ramparts built of timber and mud with a dozen bastions, a ditch and a moat on the landward side. The Dutch remodeled the fort with projecting, sloped glacises overlooking fields of fire kept clear of buildings or large trees. They reorganized the internal layout of the fort around a rectilinear road grid; outside the fort on the east grew a settlement for traders and service personnel that became known as the Old City (*Oude Stad*) or the Pettah (Tamil *pettai*). The Dutch renewed contractual arrangements with intermediary lords for the delivery of cinnamon, cardamom, and elephants to the seat of the Governor at Colombo, or the seats of Commanders at Galle and Jaffna. The Dutch also used Sri Lanka as the base for the centralization of the trade in cowry shells coming from the Maldives and disseminated as currency as far as western Africa. The alliance with Kandy weakened with every Dutch success, and led eventually to a protracted guerrilla war ending only with a peace treaty preserving the independence of the central kingdom (Brohier 1984; Perera 1999: 29–30, 48–9; Pearson 2003: 151).

Turning to mainland South Asia, the Dutch took the Portuguese fort at Nagapattinam in 1658 and instituted typical restraints on local shipping that pushed much of the country trade to nearby Nagore, which began its rise as a mid-sized town. In Malabar, the Dutch had established favorable relations with the ruler of Calicut, the inveterate enemy of the Portuguese, during the first decade of their operations in the east. After their success in Sri Lanka, the VOC decided to eliminate Portuguese monopolies in the Malabari city-states of Cochin, Cannanore, and Quilon (Kollam). These maneuvers were also successful in 1663, as the Dutch cooperated with the king of Cochin to throw out the Portuguese. The ruler of Calicut, a desultory ally in the operations, immediately invited the English to establish a factory at his capital, thus dashing Dutch expectations for a monopoly over the Malabar pepper trade. In any case, the Dutch were never able to eliminate smuggling, even in Cochin where they had negotiated near-monopoly rights, and the Kanara coast was already becoming an alternate pepper source (Winius and Wink 1991: 36–9; Arasaratnam 1994: 97–110; Prakash 1998: 43–4).

The English profited in other regions from the decline of Portuguese fortunes in South Asia and the exertions of their Dutch competitors. English traders in Masulipatnam had discovered that desirable chintzes were procurable farther south; so in 1639 they obtained from a local ruler a grant of beachfront at Chennaipattanam which they called Madraspatnam or Madras. The Company's first exclusive possession in South Asia, it stretched only 5 kilometers north from the mouth of the River Cooum, and about 1.5 kilometers inland, and lay about 6 kilometers north of the older Portuguese settlement at São Tomé. To command the completely unprotected beachfront-port, they immediately commenced construction of a castle called Fort St. George, originally a quadrilateral measuring roughly 100 by 80 meters, with bastions at the corners and a factory house at its center, partially protected on the landward side by a portion of the river. They attracted 300 to 400 weaver families, and transferred the headquarters of all their east coast operations there, making Madras a Presidency (headed by a President-in-Council) in 1652; its population grew to about 50,000 in 1674 (Brush 1970). Meanwhile, by 1651 English agents had consolidated a factory in Bengal at Hughli, a base allowing them to move up the Ganga River to Patna. On the west coast in 1661 the Portuguese crown ceded Bombay to the king of England, Charles II, as part of the dowry of his Portuguese wife; in 1668 the Crown rented these islands to the company. These English maneuvers, of course, would have a huge impact in the future.

The 'Blessed Port' and the acme of the Mughal urban system

The big urban story on the west coast during the seventeenth century was the rise of Surat, originally a small port about 22 kilometers from the ocean built on the curving south shore of the Tapi (Tapti) River where it flowed south, and then west. As access to Khambat became more difficult, and the sultanate of Gujarat collapsed, Surat enjoyed the support of the Mughals and the visits of European companies that funneled capital into the hands of indigenous trading communities. The 'Blessed Port' became the wholesale market for textiles produced in the Gujarati hinterland and, later, imported from northern India, Coromandal or Bengal. Surat also became the embarkation point for persons going on the Hajj. During the height of their prosperity around 1700, Surat's merchants extended investments eastward into Bengal and as far as the Philippines. The port was home to a fleet of over 100 vessels, mostly of 200 or 300 tons (Arasaratnam 1987: 107–6; Pearson 2003: 164).

Surat differed from most coastal emporiums because of its concentrated, fortified physical organization more reminiscent of an interior administrative center. Many large vessels coming to Surat anchored near the river mouth, protected by a sandbar, at a spot about 6 kilometers southwest of the port or at Suvali (Swally) about 8 kilometers to the north, where lighters loaded or offloaded goods and passengers. The imperial wharf and other piers, for a limited number of large commercial concerns, lined the south bank of the Tapi River up to the city limits. In the city's center, the Sultans of Gujarat had erected a castle near the riverside to protect against the Portuguese. A main entrance on the castle's landward side led to an open parade and caravanserais where merchants pitched their tents. The customs house, the mint, and the palace of the harbormaster stood upstream from the castle. A circular mud wall with a surrounding ditch, upgraded to a brick wall with bastions for guns after 1670, enclosed the inner city, and an elliptical wall enclosing the outer city was constructed about 40 years later. In 1689 the breadth of Surat stretched 5 kilometers and included three suburbs with extensive gardens maintained by wealthy administrators and merchant families. Already in the early 1600s Surat's inhabitants numbered between 150,000 and 200,000, with numbers swelling when shipping was most active – a population that remained more or less stable into the early-eighteenth century. At that time Surat administrative district (*sarkar*) included 425 villages and 15 towns in addition to the city, the latter providing between one-third and one-quarter of the revenue from the entire district. The most important second-level town was Rander, which had been a major competitor but became only a weighing and warehousing site for goods moving between Surat and Ahmedabad (Naqvi 1972: 112, 24; Gokhale 1979: 10–12, 20–1, 51; Das Gupta 1979: 20–9).

Surat during the seventeenth and early-eighteenth centuries exemplified the social and spatial hierarchy in the coastal emporium under the administration of an interior power. Urban government rested in the hands of managers imposed from outside: the fort commander who in turn cooperated with the district army chief, the port officer (*mutasaddi*), and the urban magistrate (*kotwal*). They moved within a Persian-speaking milieu, enjoyed family connections with imperial grandees, interacted with the court in Agra or Delhi, and at times engaged directly in commercial investments (Gokhale 1979: 51–5). A cosmopolitan elite comprised of ship-owning Muslim families, either local entrepreneurs or of Arab, Persian, or Turkish background, controlled much of the long-distance trade that drove the city's economy. Their large homes often featured elaborate wooden superstructures, fronting the streets with a large wooden door leading to an open interior quadrangle ringed by living quarters. A separate grouping of merchant families collectively called Baniya/Bania (*vanija*) and Jains specialized in brokerage, credit instruments, banking, assaying, money changing, supplies, and retail transactions. The homes of the small shopkeepers among this class consisted of brick, lime, and timber with clay roof tiles, but even families that controlled immense wealth might live in such relatively humble abodes. Collectively, the administrative and mercantile elites were responsible for the construction of the mosques, temples, educational institutions, and caravanserais that gave character to the urban landscape. Below these managerial/capitalist groups were communities specializing in textile production, shipbuilding and repair, and a variety of services ranging from water carrying to tailoring. Their homes (i.e. the vast majority of dwellings) typically consisted of mud cottages with thatched roofs. At the bottom of the social pyramid lived despised caste groups relegated to household or sanitation work, living on the outskirts of the city. All of the groups mentioned here manifested divisions based on sectarian religiosity or occupational specialization, and were capable of interacting with each other or with the state through councils of leading citizens, 'hinge' personalities, whose positions rested on hereditary qualities combined with personal influence (Pearson 1976: 118–54; Gokhale 1979: 27–55; Das Gupta 1979: 75–93). Violence directed by factions of the wealthy and involving contingents of client workers was a common mode of resolving disputes. Within this variegated urban fabric stood the factories of foreign merchants including the European and Armenian firms (Aghassian and Kévonian 2000).

There is a tendency to focus on the places where the European trading companies were active because so much of the historical source material on coastal emporiums comes from their records and because we know that colonialism later triumphed in South Asia. Certainly the early European impact was important at select sites such as Goa. We must note, however, that well into the eighteenth century indigenous mercantile houses remained the most influential commercial actors in South Asia. In sites such as Porto Novo, perhaps the best natural harbor on the Coromandel coast, or Mandvi (Mandavi), the leading port of Kutch, indigenous mercantile interests remained outside European interference, maintaining their own fleets and position in the long-distance or country trade into the nineteenth century (Arasaratnam 1986: 25–6, 162, 174–5; Raval 1988; Subrahmanyam 1990b: 224–37; Deloche 1994, 2: 41). Even in the places most frequented by the European companies, they remained competitors, rather than dominators; their share of Surat's trade around 1700 was perhaps one-eighth, with the Dutch controlling most of that (Das Gupta 1979: 18). European narratives repeatedly describe the careers of South Asian merchant princes, whose wealth surpassed that of their entire companies, who invested in shipping, brokerage, funds transfer, credit and banking, in addition to 'portfolio capitalists' who engaged in agricultural trade, revenue farming, and military mobilization (Subrahmanyam 1990a: 298–342). Aside from the limited Portuguese territorial incursions (inherited in Sri Lanka by the Dutch), the European companies were incapable of translating their naval superiority into empire; a disastrous attempt by the English East India Company in 1686–90 to wage war against the Mughal Empire highlighted their institutional and informational limitations (Arasaratnam 1994: 86–7).

The formidable production apparatus of the subcontinent, accessible to the Europeans primarily through translators and brokers, intersected with urbanization in several ways. The Mughal emperors and other kings maintained industrial workshops (*karkhana*), located mostly within or near major cities, employing hundreds or thousands of workers specializing in the provision of military equipment or luxury goods only for the state and its retainers. The much larger 'private' sector of production for the market, while ultimately involving the agency of urban merchants, remained a distributed phenomenon that increasingly involved coastal emporiums. In this context textiles, with the main centers of production in Coromandal, Bengal, and Gujarat, were the most important industrial sector in South Asia, which probably led the world during the late-seventeenth and the eighteenth century, fueled in part by a growing European demand. In Coromandal weavers lived dispersed in industrial villages, specializing in different products or quality levels, located within several hundred miles of the coastal emporiums and linked through long-established road systems to interior markets. A Dutch survey in the 1680s indicated that the numbers of weavers in each settlement varied between 40 and 900. The comparatively cheap river transport of Bengal allowed a similar decentralization of production for cotton goods and also for silk fabrics, unparalleled elsewhere in South Asia, in a zone around Dhaka and in a corridor stretching about 200 kilometers north from the area around Hughli. In western and northern India export-oriented weavers were clustered in urban centers, such as Ahmedabad and Surat, or in suburbs and nearby towns. Individual weavers and dyers, or associations that were often caste-based, received advances from merchants and enjoyed through the eighteenth century the ability to negotiate prices and the conditions of employment (Chaudhury 1985 202; Arasaratnam 1986: 39–63, 265–71; Prakash 1998: 163–74). A large amount of industrial production thus took place within a domestic sphere that appeared village-based, but in practice formed part of extended urban-based exchange matrices in which a hierarchy of towns served as distribution nodes.

The great transition of the eighteenth century

In any discussion of the South Asian city during the eighteenth century, one cannot get around the eclipse of the Mughal Empire, which resulted in a radical reshuffling of security arrangements that affected trade routes and production regimes. The last years of the long reign of Aurangzeb (1658–1707) were expended in the fruitless attempt to complete the conquest of peninsular India and to counter the rise of Maratha power in western Maharashtra, which resulted in intermittent dislocations or devastation of territories in an arc stretching from eastern Gujarat to Tamil Nadu. When Aurangzeb finally died, his sons were already men of advanced years who engaged in a destructive war of succession that resulted in the triumph of Bahadur Shah, who in turn died in 1712. A series of weak rulers and distasteful court intrigues followed, de-legitimizing imperial authority and resurrecting a pattern of regional polities throughout South Asia. The result was a radical alteration in the constellation of central places. Some cities closely aligned with the Mughals in their heyday experienced steady decline; new capitals and trade centers aligned with successor states enjoyed rapid growth.

In Maharashtra, the military strategy perfected by the Marathas under Shivaji (1630–80) rested on the occupation of hill forts (*gad*) along the ridges of the Western Ghats, abandonment of fortified cities (*kot*) to the Mughals, and mobile guerilla warfare designed to disrupt Mughal logistical support. Shivaji controlled about 240 hill forts, some of which were formidable construction feats and included appended bazaars; but with an average garrison of about 500 men, they qualified only as rudimentary examples of urbanization in comparison with the well-established fort-capitals of the former sultanates under Mughal control. Maratha light cavalry formations ranged extensively over peninsular India and by the mid-eighteenth century were able to gain control of Delhi. The success of the Marathas coincided with a palace revolution that placed the royal descendants of Shivaji under the control of a hereditary line of chief ministers called the Peshwas, who in turn found it increasingly difficult to control the behavior of military commanders campaigning away from Maharashtra. Instead of creating an empire, the Marathas became a confederation.

The headquarters of the Maratha confederation was Pune (Poona), which until the early-eighteenth century was a nondescript *qasba* on the right side of the northeast-flowing Mutha River, just before its junction with the Mula River and its eastward course, as the Mulamutha, to join eventually the Bhima River. When Peshwa Bajirao Ballal shifted his seat there in 1730 he found a population of 20,000 to 30,000 inhabitants living in six market-neighborhoods (*peth*) with an old fort guarding a river ford lying off the main trade routes through Maharashtra. He demolished the fort and established a new Shanwar Palace, attracting numerous brahmana administrators to the growing Maratha power. Population totaled 40,000 in 1764–5. By the end of the century the unfortified city housed nearly 200,000 persons living in 18 neighborhoods, extensive parklands, and a variegated, service-centered economy (Divekar 1981: 98–105; Gokhale 1988).

Observers from outside Maharashtra often stressed the disruptive effects of Maratha campaigns, but Maratha success exerted a threefold positive impact on urbanization. First: the more stable conditions they eventually guaranteed within Maharashtra allowed the re-emergence of an older pattern of central places along the leeward side of the Western Ghats at sites allowing access to the agrarian production of the Deccan and also trade and communication routes to the coast. Pune is the prime example, but Nasik, an ancient sacred city and commercial node on the upper reaches of the Godavari River, also enjoyed a renaissance as the secondary capital under the Peshwas. At the ancestral seat of the royal family in Satara, Maratha victories prompted the migration of a more secure population from the fort into the town at the foot of the hill. Meanwhile, Kolhapur became a secondary administrative seat of a dispossessed royal line, and Karad, Sangli and Miraj became seats of smaller Maratha principalities. Second: the leading Maratha generals established their own seats of power. The line of Pilaji Gaekwad (d. 1732) set up their base at Vadodara (Baroda), the line of Ranojirao Scindia (d. 1745) at Gwalior, the line of Raghoji Bhonsle (d. 1755) at Nagpur, and the line of Malharrao Holkar (d. 1766) at Indore. These towns, formerly of secondary significance, benefited from the presence of princely administrations to grow steadily into major cities. Third: an array of small Maharashtrian towns with market-neighborhoods, in many cases the older commercial centers of sub-district (*pargana*) seats, recovered to become centers of occupational specialization and the exchange of agrarian produce (Kosambi 1988: 11–17; Guha 1996).

The most important urban phenomenon in the north during the eighteenth century was the decline of Lahore, Delhi and Agra due to the eclipse of Mughal administration and a realignment of commercial relationships. Profiting from signs of military incapacity, Nadir Shah of Persia led an expedition in 1739 that disrupted Lahore and resulted in the capture and pillage of Delhi. The decade 1751–61 witnessed a civil war in Delhi, occupation by a second invading force led by Ahmad Shah Durrani of Afghanistan, and a further occupation by Maratha armies. Widespread insecurity caused the collapse of the canal system that had sustained agriculture and much of Delhi's water supply. A major famine around Delhi in 1783 completed the decline. With the Emperor reduced to the status of King of Delhi and the dispersal of the upper levels of the Mughal nobility came the abandonment or reapportioning of the spaces formerly allotted to city mansions, although the basic street plans remained relatively unchanged. Habitation disappeared from the suburbs to the relative security within the city walls. While Muslim artisan communities remained viable, the role formerly played by major merchants who provisioned the households of the emperor and his grandees became transformed through the immigration of non-Muslim trading communities (Bayly 1986: 128–35).

Shifts in military power or trade routes caused the decline of some older centers and the rise of others, but the overall urban profile of the north demonstrated realignment and modest growth, rather than general depression. In Punjab, where two lines of transit nodes had run roughly parallel to the hills, with the towns of Batala and Jalandhar between them and the fortified town of Attock providing access to the northwest, a large number of new centers such as Gujranwala developed around the headquarters of Sikh-dominated military confederations. Rawalpindi, for example, which until then was a small settlement of mendicants, became an important center within the polity of Milkha Singh Thepuria (d. 1804). The average population in each of these new towns was probably less than in locations prominent during the previous century, but 75 of them have survived until today as the substratum of Punjab's impressive urban transformation (Grewal 1984: 210; Grewal and Sachdeva 2005; Chopra *et al.* 2005).

In Rajasthan, the increasingly autonomous states of Jaipur and Bikaner raised duties on merchandize crossing their territory, but the semi-independent lords of the Shekhavati region declined to raise their own duties, resulting in a marked increase in caravan traffic through their kingdoms. Churu, for example, had been an overgrown village until 1715, when Thakur Kushal Singh constructed a fort and a city wall and inviting traders to relocate there, giving the settlement the character of a *qasba* oriented toward local agrarian produce. As trade routes shifted through its region, Churu became a market town with a population of at least 12,000. Three times during the eighteenth century its city wall was extended and rebuilt (Arora 1988). Within the kingdom of Kota in southeastern Rajasthan, a steady increase in the number of market towns occurred through the interventions of the state, its notables, and local merchants, but relied ultimately on increases in agrarian productivity and the local exchange of agricultural goods. In many cases this resulted in a shift in the pattern of settlement formation from sub-district headquarters that had been generating nearby villages to new *qasbas* that clustered in the peripheries of the older towns (Sato 1997). The merchants encouraged by the Rajput states to frequent these market centers accumulated capital at the lowest levels through petty retail trade, and at the highest levels through government banking and revenue farming. The commercial houses of Shekhavati, in particular, became noted during the late-eighteenth century for their ability to migrate in order to tap commercial opportunities within and outside Rajasthan, constituting the first wave of trans-regional business houses known as Marwaris (Timberg 1978; Sharma 1984).

In the Yamuna-Ganga valley, the general decentralization of political and military authority entailed the entrenchment of administrative and military retainers, artisans and merchants within hundreds of market towns with populations somewhere above 3,000, and within a sturdy group of 60 cities with more than 10,000 inhabitants in 1770 – altogether supporting perhaps 25 percent of the population who made their living in non-agrarian pursuits (Bayly 1983: 113). In some cases the commercial character of redistribution points for an agrarian hinterland or transit points for long-distance traffic was marked by the presence of a fixed market center or *ganj*. This was typically a quadrilateral enclosure made of earth, wooden planks or masonry, built originally around a crossroads or at a stopping-point for travelers, with gates, bastions, available water, and quartering for people and beasts. Stalls selling travelers' necessities, backed by habitations for their owners, fronted the main roads and distinguished these spots from simple *sarais* (Llwewllyn-Jones 2001). Depredations of raiding armies caused only temporary disruption or relocation of these commercial sites within a resilient mercantile/agrarian economy that was capable of operating with minimal intervention from an imperial state. The only northern towns known to have practically disappeared were Korah/Jahanabad and Kara/Shahzadpur, former provincial capitals that suffered from local agricultural disruption but mostly lost functionality as way-stations for caravan and river traffic, respectively (Bayly 1980; 1986: 126–8).

The relocation of military leaders to pre-existing sites adjoining *qasba* or *ganj*, and the founding of a market center near a military camp, were the time-honored signs of the transition to secondary urbanization. These signs were more prominent in the western section of the Yamuna-Ganga basin during the eighteenth century. The town of Bareilly (Bareli), for example, already established as a center for commerce and Mughal administration, became the seat of Afghan warrior groups known as Rohillas, whose power peaked in mid-century; their primarily urban way of life stimulated the development of towns throughout a region that became known as Rohilkhand (Bayly 1983: 117–22). The town of Farrukhabad rose as the seat of the Afghan warrior-chief Muhammad Khan Bangash (1713–93), who obtained the title of Nawab or 'Deputy' and organized a quintessential 'court and camp' city with a mud fort and dry moat, central mosque, and designated quarters for military dependents. An outer wall approximately 10 kilometers in length, made of mud with lime cement, featured 12 gates and enclosed 143 neighborhoods associated with specific occupational groups, a main bazaar 50 meters in width, and pleasure gardens. Seven gates were provided with sarais for merchants. Understanding the relationship between a capital city and subsidiary settlements, Muhammad Khan Bangash founded smaller commercial towns along the Ganga River and installed his sons and military slaves there as governors (Umar 2001: 23–7). The extinction of the nascent states based at Bareilly and Farrukhabad resulted in the medium-term decline of these cities, but their position as sub-regional marketing and administrative centers eventually spurred their resurrection: Bareilly's population in 2007 was about 875,000, and Farrukhabad's population was about 267,000.

The new cities versus the perception of decline

A tale of two cities, contextualized by the rise of the independent state of Avadh (Oudh), exemplifies the altered context of urbanization in eighteenth-century north India. When Akbar apportioned his realm into 12 provinces in 1590, he chose the town of Lucknow (Lakhnau, old Lachmanpur) on the south bank of the Gomti River as the seat of the province of Avadh, and during the next century the city became a regionally important commercial and administrative center. In 1722 the Persian-born Mir Muhammad Amin, later called Saadat Jang Burhan ul Mulk, one of the most powerful nobles within the unraveling Mughal administration, obtained appointment as the governor of the province. Faced with the opposition of local lords who had entrenched themselves in Lucknow, he fought his way into the city and gained control over the castle-like 'Fish Mansion' (Machchhi Bhavan), the administrative seat at the city center. Having established his authority there, however, he retired to a site about 130 kilometers to the east, where he set up his military camp about 8 kilometers west of the ancient city of Ayodhya. Burhan ul Mulk then demonstrated his intention to entrench himself as the Nawab of an independent principality by refusing reappointment to Agra. His nephew, Safdar Jang, inherited this position in 1739 and continued to reside mostly at the site near Ayodhya that had evolved into an administrative city named Faizabad. Safdar Jang's son, Shuja ud Daula, acceded to the position of Nawab in 1754, but initially fixed his residence at Lucknow. He allied with Emperor Shah Alam II (r. 1761–1806) to oppose the rising power of the British East India Company in Calcutta (see below), but the defeat of their combined forces at Buxar (Baksar) in 1764 reduced Avadh to the status of a 'princely state,' officially independent but in fact subordinate to British policies. The Nawab retired to Faizabad, where he greatly extended the fortifications, razed all buildings outside for 3 kilometers in all directions to create a firing range, laid out extensive gardens, and presided (while not traveling through his realm) over a major cultural revival. With his passing in 1774, however, the seat of the Nawabs of Avadh shifted irreversibly to Lucknow and Faizabad's importance decreased in the medium term (Sharar 2001: 29–36). It rebounded as a sub-regional marketing and administrative center, with a population of about 245,000 in 2007.

Lucknow was already becoming one of the largest cities in northern India, with an estimated population of around 250,000 at mid-century, and around 300,000 in 1800. Its heart was a business district or Chauk, a main street running roughly north-south with narrow winding roads branching off on both sides, crowded by the residential mansions or humble mud-and-thatch dwellings of traders and artisans who processed agricultural raw materials or produced textiles and copper utensils for which the city was famous. On the periphery of the residential quarters the Nawabs and other prominent administrators founded a series of market centers (*ganj*) that eventually became completely inhabited and blended into the fabric of the old city. The south end of the Chauk headed toward the port of Kanpur on the Ganga River. At the north end of the Chauk, fronting the Gomti River and a stone bridge, the castle-palace complex called the Panch Mahal evolved from the old Machchhi Bhavan. Flanking the original palace along the river grew up a number of additional palaces and administrative offices of the Nawab's government which combined elements of Mughal camp/palace architecture with European elements in a unique regional style; these included to the west the Daulat Khana and to the east the Farhad Baksh (Chattar Manzil) and Kaisarbagh. Between the latter two palaces, on land earlier owned by the French military consultant and trader Claude Martin, the British East India Company procured a complex of houses that became the seat of its Resident when the Nawab's government relocated to Lucknow in 1775. Simultaneously, on the north side of the river opposite the Panch Mahal, the British established a Cantonment for troops that it controlled but that were funded by the Nawab, ostensibly in payment for their assistance in Avadh's conquest of Rohilkhand. The combination of Residency and Cantonment expressed a political arrangement that, as we shall see, would influence future city planning throughout South Asia. Until the end of the eighteenth century, they still seemed like the appurtenances of a magnificent regional court that created a magnificent array of public architecture and became a magnet for Arabic, Persian, and Urdu scholars and Hindustani musicians in an outburst of late Mughal cultural creativity (Naim and Petievich 1997; Kippen 1997; Sharar 2001; Llewelyn-Jones 2001, 2006).

In the eastern Deccan the fate of the city of Hyderabad (Haidarabad) during the eighteenth century offers some remarkable parallels to the story of Lucknow. The 1687 Mughal conquest of the Golkonda kingdom devastated the city, and recovery was slow, as Hyderabad became merely a provincial capital. Under Emperor Farrukhsiyar (r. 1713–19), governor Mubariz Khan began construction of a fortification wall 9.6 kilometers in circumference to protect Hyderabad; this expressed the abandonment of the Golkonda fort as the defensible heart of the urban complex and formed part of a strategy to establish himself, potentially, as an effectively independent ruler. But Farrukhsiyar had also bestowed upon one of the leading members of the Mughal nobility, Qamar ad-Din alias Chin Qilij Khan (1671–1748), the exalted position of Nizam ul Mulk ('Governor of the Kingdom'), giving him control of the six Deccan provinces of the Empire. In 1724, disgusted by court atrocities in Delhi, the Nizam committed himself to carving out an autonomous role in those provinces, and killed Mubariz Khan in battle (Richards 1975: 264–305). Emperor Muhammad Shah (r. 1719–48) responded to this civil war among his nominal subordinates by bestowing the additional honorific title of Asaf Jah on the *de facto* ruler of the south, although everyone maintained the illusion of continuing imperial unity. Asaf Jah completed the wall at Hyderabad, but he followed well-established imperial practice by maintaining his capital at Aurangabad. His death in 1748 unleashed a period of struggle for the position of Nizam in which the French and British became enmeshed; but the final accession of Nizam Ali Khan (r. 1762–1803) and the transfer of his capital to Hyderabad in 1763 signaled the abandonment of a peninsular vision and a concentration on the buildup of a regional kingdom. It also meant the rejuvenation of Hyderabad, which experienced market expansion and suburban population growth, and served as the center of a continuing program of military activity. The closure of military options came in 1798 when the Nizam signed a treaty of subsidiary alliance with the British East India Company. Five thousand Company troops and their auxiliaries occupied a Cantonment about 10 kilometers north of the Charminar on a site northeast of the Husain Sagar, a large artificial lake dating from the sixteenth century. The courtly culture of Hyderabad would survive for 150 years as a Deccani expression of language, literature, art and music associated with the late Mughal Empire.

Southernmost India's formal conquest by the Mughal Empire (the fort of Gingee was taken in 1698) led to the installation of a Nawab, ostensibly a Mughal official, in a new fort at Arcot. In reality the most important power emerging in the south was the realm of Mysore, where the kings fell under the control of the dynamic general Haidar Ali (1722–82) and his son, Tipu Sultan (1750–99). The heart of this kingdom lay in the fertile regions of the southern Deccan plateau around the upper Kaveri River, which supported the rise of Bangalore as a commercial and textile production center, and also the rise of Srirangapattanam as military/administrative center on an island surrounded by the Kaveri. By the end of the eighteenth century this latter city had a population of approximately 150,000 persons. The Bangalore and Mysore regions became studded with an array of small commercial towns adjacent to strong points providing defense in depth for the kingdom. This resulted in numerous town names ending in suffixes denoting forts (*durga* or *kote*) or hills (*giri* or *kal*) on which forts were situated.

On the west coast, Mangalore (long an entrepot of the spice trade, but repressed during the sixteenth century by the Portuguese) experienced a resurrection as Haidar Ali's naval base. Like Goa, it lay at the intersection of estuaries for two navigable rivers, the Gurupura and the Netravati; here the rivers created two long bars separated by a single entrance to a protected anchorage, although access originally required clearing of a bar covered by only 2 meters of water at low tide. Improvement of the channel, installation of a military dockyard and shipbuilding facilities, and modernization of fortifications began during the 1760s and lasted until 1780s, when the British occupied the city and dismantled its naval capabilities (Lafont 2001: 4–3). A similar rise of a new port on the west coast occurred through the consolidation of the kingdom of Travancore based at Trivandrum (Tiruvanantapuram), which developed Alleppey (Alapuzha) as its main harbor during the late-eighteenth century. Two main canals running through the heart of Alleppey linked the ocean to inland waterways running just behind the coastline and thence to agricultural regions producing spices, copra and coconut oil (Deloche 1994, 2: 81, 91; Schenk 1997).

In Tamil Nadu, which had long maintained one of the densest concentrations of small urban sites in the subcontinent, the lively eighteenth-century market in textile production had contributed to the consolidation of commercial towns in the interior that lay within cotton-producing belts, such as Salem and Erode. The disruption of the security environment that involved the collapse of post-Vijayanagara polities controlled by Nayaka kings, the incursions of the Mughals, and interventions from Mysore, Hyderabad, and the Marathas generated numerous small polities controlled by 'protectors' (*palaiyakarar*) who, as in contemporary Punjab, established seats that also served as small commercial centers. This led to the growth of dozens of places with names indicating their role in provision of security (*palayam*); in the Coimbatore region, which had been developing as a major agricultural zone since the fourteenth century, there were 94 places with this designation. The most successful of the emerging warlords were able to install themselves as permanent landlords (*zamindar*) or as 'little kings' in the interstices of older urban network; they oversaw the development of capitals in relatively dry zones, as at Pudukkottai (the 'new fort') lying roughly midway between the older centers of Madurai and Tanjavur (Gupta 1991).

While imperial Europe underwent a relentless accentuation of urbanization beginning in the late-eighteenth century, South Asia may have experienced a period of urban stasis between 1750 and 1800 when the British were consolidating their position. Scholars suggest that about 11 percent of South Asia's population lived in urban sites at the beginning of the nineteenth century among a total population estimated at about 160 million, implying *a total urban population of 17.6 million persons in 1800* (Visaria and Visaria 1983: 466, 490). If we recall from the discussion at the end of Chapter 2 the estimate of South Asia's urban population in 1750 at about 20 million, we can posit an absolute decline in the urban population during the subsequent 50 years. This viewpoint is consistent with oft-repeated British perspectives of collapse caused by the worsening security situation. To some extent, however, the perception of urban decline results from a change in categories, which increasingly defined the city only in terms of population statistics and nucleation around the administrative and economic institutions of the colonial state. This reclassification process had a major impact on the understanding of the lowest levels of the urban hierarchy, so that, for example, many places that we have categorized as the smallest towns under the Mughals with average populations of 3,000 became rural sites. In a similar manner, networks of small sites that we have described as urban, defined in some cases by economies based on religious institutions or by extended textile production systems, appeared simply as groups of villages where older connectivity survived only in the form of religious architecture or chains of pilgrimage destinations.

The process of category change occurring during the late-eighteenth century is expressed in a genre of Urdu poetry called *Shahr Ashob,* or the 'city's misfortune.' This genre once provided an erotic, exuberant portrayal of urbanity, but now bewailed the transitory nature of existence through meditation on the collapse of city life, with the fate of the three imperial cities of Lahore, Delhi and Agra/Akbarabad as its primary subject (Petievich 1990; Umar 2001: 77–83, 105–10; Sharma 2004). Here are sections of a poem by Shaikh Muhammad Wali, known as Nazir Akbarabadi (1740–1830), who lived in Delhi during the Afghan invasion and later relocated to Agra:

On show in every land: display!
Look close: a one-man-band display!
Don't disdain such a grand display!
Look around, on every hand – display!
There isn't much, in short, to say –
The world is such a fine display!

I watch the show with stupefied eyes
I can't know truth, I can't know lies
It's the Magic Reality I can't understand
A marvelous sight – hooray, it's grand!
There isn't much, in short, to say –
The world is such a fine display!

He who panned for gold has a gold-shop of his own
The money-lender now sifts dust for rag and bone
He who used to steal now mounts guard at the doorsill
The earth revolves, and the sky stands still!
There isn't much, in short, to say –
The world is such a fine display!

The bearded are thought to babble without sense
The beardless are trusted for sound evidence
Darkness is light, and light is dark instead
A ruined city, ruled by the dead.
There isn't much, in short, to say –
The world is such a fine display!

Those without wisdom are sharpshooters still
Those who have wisdom are mentally ill
Women are eager for men's clothes and ways
Men are effeminate and eunuchs these days.

There isn't much, in short, to say –
The world is such a fine display!

Great ones are cut down to a small size
Small ones are great in everyone's eyes
Strange breezes blow, and strange effects appear
How surprising people are – beyond words, Nazir!
There isn't much, in short, to say –
The world is such a fine display!

> (Nazir Akbarabadi 1984: verses 1–2, 5, 12–13, 26). Reproduced by
> permission of Shamsur Rahman Faruqi and Frances W. Pritchett.

In a series of oppositions drawn from examples of everyday life, the author describes the 'strange' or 'magical' transformations visible in the social and cultural order, with the inversion of positions defined by class, age, gender, and status. The translators call this poem 'The Vile World Carnival,' but whereas a typical carnival produces such inversions or reversals of ruling hierarchies within a temporally bounded environment in order to produce laughter or irony, the poet sees no end in sight for the transformations he is witnessing. There is, thus, no humor but only a melancholy sense of loss. The poet witnesses the end of city life and culture as defined by the Mughal synthesis, while he remains incapable of recognizing the outlines of the urban world that was replacing it.

The new European city-states

The most drastic change in South Asian urbanization during the late-eighteenth century involved the capture of regional power, for the first time in history, by coastal emporiums, coordinated by a single entity – the English/British East India Company. The strange rise to supreme power of an early transnational corporation brought with it the unprecedented growth of its three power bases – Madras, Calcutta and Bombay.

Pondicherry: The French option

Until the middle of the eighteenth century, it seemed possible that the major European contribution to South Asian urbanization would come from the French, relative newcomers in the Indian Ocean. It was only in 1664 that the French East India Company received state support and began operations. They opened an office in Surat in 1668, at Pondicherry (Puduchcheri) on the Coromandal coast in 1674, and at Chandernagor near Hugli in Bengal in 1690. Governor François Martin at Pondicherry supervised construction of a roughly quadrilateral brick fort about 300 meters in length, with towers at the four corners, which enclosed their factory headquarters and which was flanked on the north and south by stone buildings constructed for about 200 French employees. The remainder of the settlement, in a rough L-shape about 1 kilometer in length on each side following the course of the Uppar River, was the town of the 'blacks,' with separate neighborhoods in the north and west for weavers, artisans, and a brahmana community, and in the south for trading castes, a Muslim community, and (on the outskirts) despised service castes. An enclosure, part parapet and part hedge, encompassed the entire settlement. Gardens and fields lay interspersed with habitation structures throughout the settlement, which may have had 50,000 people by 1690.

Military confrontation with the Netherlands led to the conquest of Pondicherry by the VOC in 1693. The Dutch immediately negotiated a purchase from the Maratha ruler of Gingee of villages in a roughly semi-circular arc with a radius of about 3 kilometers surrounding the original settlement. They also developed, as they had in their earlier settlements in South Asia, a plan for an orthogonal street grid surrounding the fort, and demonstrated an obsession with relegating different occupational/caste groups to exclusive neighborhoods. When, as part of a peace accord, Pondicherry and its surrounding villages reverted to French authority in 1699, the Company utilized the Dutch designs to plan a symmetrical fortress-town featuring the grid pattern that still forms the heart of the city (see Map 11). At the center near the coast was Fort Louis, re-designed with five bastions and one *demilune* encompassing the old fort. When François Martin died in 1706, Pondicherry had become a commercial center of 60,000 people with garrison, a tax system, and a governing judicial and religious establishment (Prakash 1998: 147; Deloche 2004).

Reorganization of the French commercial operations under the new Compagnie Perpetuelle des Indes in 1723 rapidly led to its growth as a major competitor to the British and Dutch interests in South Asia, and Pondicherry emerged as the capital of an incipient French imperial presence in southern India. Between 1724 and 1733 the entire settlement was surrounded by a masonry wall with projecting bastions. Buildings adjacent to the fort were eliminated to provide a free-fire zone around it. By 1740 the outer defenses of the town were supplemented with a moat, and a garrison of 700–800 men with 300 cannon protected the settlement. Governor Joseph François Dupleix (1742–1754), who took charge of a city with around 130,000 inhabitants, oversaw the construction of a magnificent palace within Fort Louis. He involved the French administration deeply in the affairs of Arcot and Hyderabad, while simultaneously fighting with the British East India Company based in Madras, a distant theatre of what the Europeans called the War of Austrian Succession (1744–8). The French were able to acquire control of more villages during the 1740s, creating a patchwork of holdings that survived for several centuries.

The map of Pondicherry at its peak in 1755 displays the quintessential Company emporium with central fort-castle, *bourg* and surrounding bastioned fortifications. This plan demonstrates the European penchant for assigning discrete spaces to occupational/caste groups as they perceived them. Europeans lived in the eastern third of the city, closer to the ocean. To their west lived the natives, some of whom were important commercial and political intermediaries meriting streets with their names, e.g. Chinnappayya or Timmu Chetti (numbers 20, 22). The military governor who officially represented the 'Mughal' administration was

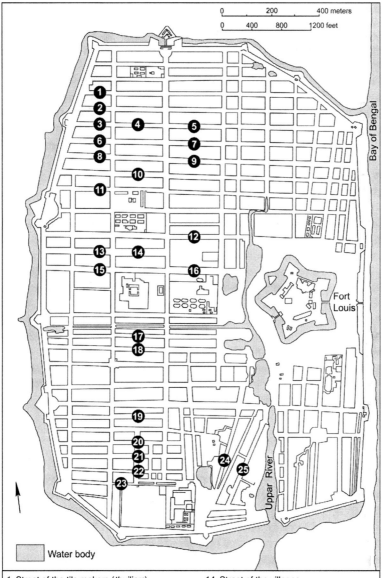

0   200   400 meters

0   400   800   1200 feet

Bay of Bengal

Fort Louis

Uppar River

Water body

1. Street of the tile makers (*thuiliers*)
2. Street of the mendicants (*mendians*)
3. Street of the metal-workers (*chaudronniers*)
4. Street of the Malabars
5. Street of the Komatis
6. Street of the goldsmiths (*orfèvres*)
7. Street of the weavers (*tisserands*)
8. Street of the blacksmiths (*forgerons*)
9. Street of the Komatis
10. Street of the Chettis
11. Street of the Company merchants
12. Street of Nayanappa (*Naynapa*)
13. Street of the coral-workers (*corailleurs*)

14. Street of the villages
15. Street of the brahmana Mudali (Modély)
16. Street of the brahmanas (*brammes*)
17. New street of the brahmanas
18. Street of Nayanapalli (Naynapouley)
19. Street of the *subedar* (*choubedar*)
20. Street of the Chinnappayya (Chinapaya)
21. Street of Ayyatti (Ayoti)
22. Street of Timmu Chetti (Timouchetty)
23. Street of Mallappa (Malapa)
24. Street of the Moors (*maures*)
25. Street of the Chuliyas (*choulias*)

Map 11 Plan of Pondicherry, 1755. Adapted from Deloche 2005.

the *subedar* (number 19). The brahmanas had separate quarters in the heart of the native town (numbers 15–17). To their north, commercial groups with separate streets included the Company merchants working directly for the French, the Malabars (i.e. Malayalam-speaking traders hailing originally from Kerala), the Telugu-speaking Komatis who were active in Madras and points north, and the Tamil-speaking Chettis (numbers 4–5, 9–11). Around them live the various artisan groups, including weavers (number 7), who provided the goods and services required for an export-oriented commercial settlement. In the southeastern part of the city resided Tamil-speaking Muslim merchants called Chuliya and the 'Moors,' or Muslim merchants whose ancestry lay elsewhere in the Indian Ocean littoral (numbers 24–25).

Hostilities during the Seven Years War (1756–63) led to the failure of French policy in India, the capture of Pondicherry, and its systematic demolition by the British in 1761. The city was restored to the French two years later, and reconstruction of the built environment and the commercial connections supporting the city brought the population back to about 60,000 by the end of the decade. Its role as a token in continuing French-British struggles led, however, to periodic occupation by the British and a decline of population (26,000 in 1777, 36,000 in 1791) until the final defeat of France after the Napoleonic Wars returned it to a stabilized French administration in 1816 (Vincent 1992; Deloche 2005). In a demilitarized form, retaining its French cultural orientation, the city center preserved the formal characteristics of urban planning informed by the rational principles of the European Enlightenment. The very decline of Pondicherry has allowed preservation of the street pattern laid down 300 years ago.

Madras: The first English colony

If Pondicherry represented what might have been the urban future of southern India, the British settlement in Madras represented its unexpected reality.

During the 1660s Coromandal had replaced Gujarat as the most important venue for the textile trade with Europe, a position that peaked in the 1680s just as the English East India Company was consolidating its colony at Madras. With Fort St. George as its nucleus, the original English settlement (which came to include Portuguese attracted from nearby São Tomé and also an Armenian community) grew up in a 'white' town characterized by a grid plan and brick houses that were sometimes several stories high. The 'black' town for native inhabitants, led by the Komati, Balija and Beri Chetti trading communities who served as intermediaries for the Company, grew up farther to the north. The relatively exposed security environment of the city became apparent when Madras fell in 1746 to the French; it reverted to British control only through a clause in the 1749 peace treaty ending the War of Austrian Succession. The reinstalled British administration proceeded to strengthen the fort's defenses, and after the resumption of hostilities they withstood a French siege in 1758–9, although nearby residential neighborhoods were plundered. During the 1760s the French menace was replaced by a new threat from the armies of the Mysore kingdom which ranged freely up to the walls of Madras. These events prompted a complete reconstruction of the fort according to a polygonal plan with a free-fire zone or esplanade surrounding it on the landward side. During the process of fort remodeling much of the old town was dismantled and the native population re-located north in the former suburbs called Muthialpet closer to the ocean and Peddanaickenpet to its west. The two neighborhoods were separated by a strip of marshy or 'garden' ground. A defensive wall with bastions dominating a surrounding free-fire zone, completed in 1772, protected the expanded native town.

The two wings of the native settlement, and specific streets within the wings, became associated with Left Hand and Right Hand caste groups that established temples as the foci for their ritual life and engaged in sometimes-violent inter-caste conflicts. With the reclamation of the central marshy strip and the northward shift of the port (in 1799) from its location on the beach behind the fort, Muthialpet became surrounded by Europeanized neighborhoods along with a settlement of Muslim traders hailing from Kerala and southern Tamil Nadu in its northeast. The southern portion of Peddanaickenpet attracted Gujarati commercial castes, while its central sections attracted substantial minorities of brahmanas and agriculturalist castes originally displaced by the conflict with Mysore. The settlement as a whole became known as George Town by the end of the century (Lewandowski 1977; Neild 1979; Mines 1994).

The defining character of Madras was not its concentration in a central business district but a distinctively distributed urbanization that long preserved features of the rural environment and a variety of neighborhoods that retained special socio-spatial markers. The creation of this pattern occurred partially through the official establishment of suburbs such as Washermanpet (ca. 1720), designated for cloth washers north of the city, Chintadripet (1735), designated for weavers on an ox-bow of the Cooum River southwest of the Fort, and Royapuram (1799), designated for boatmen north of the city. In addition, the Company pursued an aggressive policy of expanding its holdings in surrounding settlements. By 1672 it had appropriated the old temple town of Triplicane south of the Cooum River, along with three villages, originally on leases. By 1708 a Mughal edict gave the Company control over an additional five villages and several others were obtained in 1742. The old urban center of Mylapore/São Tomé fell under their control after the French withdrawal in 1749. Recognizing his inability to control the political destiny of the south, the Nawab shifted his seat from Arcot to Chepauk, northeast of Triplicane, in 1768, leading to the growth of a predominantly Muslim settlement there under the protection of the Company. As the security situation improved around Madras in the 1770s officials of the Company and well-to-do citizens ,who had made their fortunes by cooperating with the Company, began re-locating their residences to suburban estates purchased in surrounding villages. By the end of the century the Company controlled a colony of 55 square kilometers including 15 villages, with a population of about 300,000 (Brush 1970) located in an array of communities, each retaining its historical identity. The Madras Board of Revenue in 1798 established an area of 70 square kilometers, including ten of the villages, subordinated to the authority of the British legal system. Officials referred to the new legal entity as the 'Collectorate,' subsequently as the 'District,' and eventually (in the mid-nineteenth century) as the 'Municipality' (Neild 1979; Basu 1993).

Calcutta: The reach for empire

At the beginning of the eighteenth century Madras remained the most important South Asian possession of the Company, but the main source of textile trade with Europe was shifting toward Bengal (Arasaratnam 1986: 139–41, 191). The emerging metropolis in Bengal was Murshidabad, a significant site for silk production and exchange on the east bank of the Bhagirathi/Hughli (or Ganga) River. A sub-district headquarters since the 1660s, Murshidabad became the seat of the Nawab of Bengal in 1704, and thus the capital of the most prosperous province in the late Mughal Empire. European firms that maintained factories farther downstream also established subsidiary factories 10–15 kilometers to the south of Murshidabad, including the English presence at Kasimbazaar, the Dutch at Kalkapur, and the French at Saidabad. The population of this extensive, polycentric urban complex was about 200,000 in the mid-eighteenth century (Mohsin 1980).

The English East India Company's confrontation with the Mughal Empire in the late 1680s had prompted its agents in Bengal to look for a main factory site farther south on the Bhagirathi, distant from the provincial seat of political power, but also possessing an adequate anchorage for oceangoing ships. The site chosen in 1690 was Kalikata on the east bank of the river, protected from floods by high levees and screened on the east by extensive salt lakes. The sparsely inhabited tract, officially controlled by the Mughal emperor, lay bracketed between the village of Sutanati on its north (site of a lively annual yarn market) and the village of Gobindapur on the south (where lived merchants who controlled the local textile trade). The Company commenced construction of a fortified factory in 1696, although legally it was squatting on an imperial estate, and named it Fort William after their reigning monarch. In 1698 the Company obtained a more secure legal hold to these premises by purchasing *zamindari* rights over Kalikata, Sutanati and Gobindpur (a tract amounting to approximately 770 hectares stretching about 5 kilometers along the river), and paid rent on these lands for the next six decades. Commerce grew so quickly that in 1699 Kalikata, until then directed from Madras, became the seat of an independent Presidency. In 1717 the Company, without going through the Nawab of Bengal, purchased a charter from the Mughal Emperor Farrukhsiyar that allowed it to trade duty-free in the province; the Company interpreted this charter as allowing its servants also to trade freely while claiming Company status, and they extended the privilege to their native associates as well. These arrangements gave the British a marked commercial advantage over their competitors, and deprived the provincial government of revenues at precisely the moment when the Nawabs were establishing an independent administration in Bengal while attempting to fend of Maratha military incursions. The boost to the Company's business attracted a growing population to a native town north of their fort, oriented around the

'Gran Bazaar' or Bada Bazaar (first mentioned in records from 1703), which began its evolution into a conglomeration of smaller, specialized markets associated with specific lanes or locales. The Maratha threat stimulated the Company, in cooperation with local citizens, to construct in 1742 defensive works including a 'Mahratta Ditch' that stretched from the Chitpur Creek north of Sutanuti along the east side of the three villages (The southern side was never completed). This ditch came to form the eastern edge of a growing city with a population of 117,000 in 1752, although most of the land inside the ditch remained semi-rural through the eighteenth century (Brush 1970; Losty 1990: 10–33).

The famous confrontation with the Nawab of Bengal, Siraj ud Daula, came in 1756 when attempts to improve Fort Willam resulted in an ultimatum, military intervention, and the sacking of the Company's city. The Nawab changed the name of the settlement to Alinagar, and temporarily seemed to re-establish the sovereignty of a Mughal-style successor state (Ray 1992). At this point the Company was able to call upon its extensive military establishment assembled in Madras during confrontations with the French and their allies, political connections forged with members of the Nawab's administration, and links with leading merchants in Bengal. The defeat of the Nawab's army at the small village of Plassey (Palashi) on 23 June 1757 and the speedy murder of the Nawab resulted in a revolution in the administration of the province that produced, in 1765, an agreement with the Mughal Emperor bestowing the title of Diwan on the Company, pulling it officially within the Mughal system as the financial manager of Bengal. The Company used its position as Diwan to centralize all government functions in its renamed capital of Calcutta, relegate to insignificance its foreign competitors, shift its financial base from commerce to the manipulation of land revenue, and utilize these vastly expanded resources to support a military establishment that proceeded to conquer northern India. The seat of the provincial government shifted from Murshidabad, which slowly declined to the level of a district seat; in 1829 the city magistrate there recorded a population of 146,176, in 1837 there were 124,804, and in 1872 there were 46,172 (Mohsin 1980). The family of the Nawabs retained their title until the twentieth century, but controlled only a palace compound in Murshidabad.

In 1773 an Act of Parliament recognized Calcutta as the seat of government for all British holdings in South Asia, and the Company's President there became the Governor General of India. The bestowal of provincial power and imperial status on Calcutta contributed to profound changes for the city. The Company shifted the site of Fort William to an open field or *maidan* south of the city's principle anchorage, constructing modern defensive works planned as an octagon with five landward glacises and three oriented toward the river; this most powerful European fort in South Asia could mount hundreds of guns and accommodate 15,000 troops (Lafont 2001: 108–11). The areas of the 'white' town along the river north, east and south of the old fort became the locations for private mansions, large public buildings and churches influenced by Georgian and neo-classical architectural styles. South of the old fort, the commercial and administrative center stretched from the Great Tank (Lal Dighi) or Tank Square (laid out in 1709), with

Company offices ranged along its peripheries, to the northern edge of the Maidan or Esplanade Row, which became the site for an impressive row of official buildings including Government House (completed 1803), Council House, and the Supreme Court. Along the eastern edge of the Maidan and north into the European city ran Chowringhee Road, which became the fashionable avenue for well-heeled residents (Sreemani 1994: 25–8; Banerjea 2005; Chattopadhyaya 2005: 82–7, 11–19).

North of the European sector in Calcutta was an intermediate zone that included large percentages of Muslims and Eurasians, as well as communities of Persians, Arabs, Parsis, Armenians, Jews, Greeks, and Gujaratis, who established their own religious and philanthropic institutions. A Chinese community began in the 1780s (Sinha 1978: 39–3). In the 'black' town farther to the north, there was already a tendency for groups identified with caste, occupation or region of origin to settle within the spatially bounded quarters (*para* or *tola*) that were typical of many Bengali towns (Islam 1980: 232–5). Now individuals or families, who made their fortune through commercial connections with the British, joined those who became rich as landlord-tax collectors (*zamindar*) in the countryside to construct large city homes characterized by impressive frontages blending Indian and European elements and internal courtyards that included large pillared halls for family deities and annual religious festivals. The vast majority of the native population lived in small, thatched homes in neighborhoods that shaded into rural environments or on blocks of rented land that sprouted densely packed assemblages of huts called *basti* (bustee), which were oriented around the great houses controlled by the colonial elite. Thomas Daniell's painting of *View on the Chitpore Road* (1792), for example, displays a series of bucolic hutments surrounding a palatial dwelling, with a temple roof in the background, on what would become a major north-south artery for the metropolis (Losty 1990: Plate 9).

A proclamation by the Governor General in 1794 fixed the boundaries of the city for 73 years south of Chitpur Creek and inside the Maratha Ditch on the east – boundaries marked by the partial filling of the Ditch and construction of a Circular Road in 1799. The entire complex, which counted perhaps 160,000 persons in 1801 (Brush 1970; Sreemani 1994: 177–8), displayed a tendency to grow in a north-south orientation along the river. The British regime stimulated suburban development around Barrackpur to the north, where native troops of the Bengal Army bivouacked and where the Governor Generals constructed a mansion for summer retreats; around Dum Dum to the northeast, which was the site of the artillery park for the Bengal Army; and unofficially to the south in the form of suburban mansions for the British elite. As a commercial hub Calcutta pulled toward it all import-export trade of the province and transformed the towns of Burdwan and Bakarganj into regional poles that funneled trade and supplies toward it (Marshall 1985; Evenson 1989: 15–27). The rise of Calcutta meant the eclipse of Dhaka as a commercial and administrative center, resulting in a decline in population from about 450,000 in 1765 to about 200,000 in 1801 and 68,610 inhabitants in 1838, when the city began its slow resurrection (Ahmed 1986: 14).

Bombay: The unlikely metropolis

On the west coast, the colony of Bombay originally consisted of seven islands, bordered by mud flats, running in two lines north-to-south. The eastern line included Parel, Mazagaon, eastern Bombay, Old Woman's Island, and Colaba; the western line included Mahim, Worli, and western Bombay (the latter featuring the ridges of Cumbala and Malabar Hill). The population consisted of 10-20,000 fishing people and farmers. This collection of high spots (see Map 15) was a relatively unimportant appendage of Salsette to its north, which was a separate and larger archipelago with one big and six small islands separated by creeks that were undergoing a slow process of siltation, separated from the mainland by Thane Creek. The harbor of Thana/Thane on the northeast coast of Salsette Island had functioned as an emporium since the mid-first millennium, but since 1533 had been a Portuguese town with its own cathedral (Kamerkar 1988). Across Thana Creek near the coast was the fortified Portuguese settlement of Bassein, which stood as the capital of their north Konkan operations. The remainder of the nearby mainland was ostensibly under the control of the Mughal Empire, but in reality was coming under the rule of the Marathas, who normally put up with the foreigners but periodically manifested an interest in driving them out. When the Marathas conquered Bassein and eliminated the Portuguese from Salsette in 1737–39, they became the immediate neighbors of the Company.

The uncertain security environment prompted the Company to locate its base on the southeastern corner of the main island of Bombay, as far away as possible from Salsette, on the site of a Portuguese manor house and garden overlooking the extensive bay and deep-water anchorage to its east. The Company transformed the manor house into a diamond-shaped castle with four projecting bastions, while a neighborhood of English habitations straggled to its south and a larger native neighborhood rapidly developed to its north. The castle was the only part of the island to hold out during the confrontation with the Mughal Empire during the late 1680s, when the Sidis of Janjira, commissioned as the Mughal admiral on the west coast, occupied the island of Bombay and cut off supplies for a year (Kosambi 1985: 35). Between 1716 and 1725 the English and native neighborhoods became enclosed within a fort extending in a crescent, about 1.5 kilometers north-south and about a half kilometer east-west, that came to include 13 bastions and an additional envelope of demilunes on its northern side. The occupation of Salsette by the Marathas prompted local citizens to contribute funds for the digging of a moat around the fort walls, commonly called the 'Maratha Ditch,' between 1739 and 1743.

Within the fort, the Bombay Green located west of the castle was the main open space. Churchgate Street, named after St. Thomas Church on its southern side, headed west of the Green toward Church Gate, the main entrance to the fort on its western side. The southern section of the fort stretching toward the wharves of Apollo Bunder evolved into the central business district including the headquarters of European firms, banks, shipping and insurance companies, and warehouses. The northern fort evolved into a residential neighborhood of native merchants and financiers. Outside the northern wall of the fort, accessed through Bazaar Gate, a separate native settlement developed into the neighborhoods of Mandvi and Chakla, fronted by docks, warehouses and wholesale shops – an area that would become known as the Old Town. The temporary closing of the Great Breach, between Worli and Mahalakshmi in 1715, was a major step toward the reclamation of the muddy Flats, or the low-lying areas in the center of the Bombay archipelago, and made possible the gradual settlement of areas to the north and northwest of the fort that became known as the New Town (Dossal 1991; Masselos 1992: 275–86).

The English East India Company had transferred its west coast headquarters from Surat to Bombay in the late-seventeenth century, when the population of the colony was about 60,000, but Surat's position as the premier port on the west coast continued throughout the eighteenth century (The latter's population in 1800 was still between 400,000 and 500,000) (Subramanian 1996: 207–8). Surat's relative prosperity was declining, however, as Mughal collapse and Maratha inroads eroded the overland trade connections with northern India, markets accessed through the Red Sea and the Persian Gulf shrank, and English private traders muscled in on the shipping business. Meanwhile, as the Company achieved west-coast naval supremacy through its military arm known as the Bombay Marine, traders who had occupied subsidiary niches in Surat's commercial circles began to relocate in Bombay. By the 1730s this migration included many Parsis, who worked primarily in small and mid-level businesses including the supply of provisions to the Company. A clear sign of the growing power emanating from Bombay was the Company's 1759 military intervention in the disintegrating administration of Surat itself, resulting in the procurement of a Mughal imperial order approving the Company's title as fort commander (*qiladar*) responsible for the city's security – a revolution supported by many from Surat merchant communities collectively known as Banias. Bombay's power was not accompanied by fiscal stability, however, which led to the consolidation of what Lakshmi Subramanian (1996) terms an 'Anglo-Bania order' in the late-eighteenth century; as the Company utilized Surat-based networks of credit and bills of exchange transferred through Varanasi to obtain funds from Calcutta in order to finance increasingly ambitious political projects. The cooperation of indigenous financiers and the British stimulated an ever greater presence of the former in the island city. These arrangements became even more significant after 1784, when Bombay became the primary coordination center for the export of Gujarati cotton to China, a business that involved Bania intermediaries in lower-level centers in Gujarat and in Surat, generating fortunes for British and native entrepreneurs in Bombay.

During the early 1770s the threat of hostilities with the Marathas and the French prompted the creation of an open Esplanade extending about 400 yards around the fort, resulting in the razing of plantations and buildings that were clustering close to the town center. The security situation then improved with the acquisition of Salsette, Elephanta Island and several smaller islands in the harbor during the First Anglo-Maratha War (1775–82). The less necessary Esplanade came to be used as an open space for summer tents pitched by European military officers escaping from the heat of enclosed buildings. Improved security also prompted a general expansion of population outside the fort, assisted by the permanent closing of the Great Breach with a vellard (from the Portuguese *vallado*, 'a mound or embankment') during the administration of William Hornby (1771–84), who was the first Governor to move his official residence outside the fort to Parel, which was an early site for suburban retreats of the rich. The Hornby Vellard allowed additional reclamation of the Flats and the creation of garden plots or 'oarts' which subsequently underwent urbanization almost entirely through private initiative, with wealthier inhabitants occupying street frontage while poorer renters occupied interior areas. The native population thus became concentrated in an expanding 'black' town to the north, while new garden suburbs grew up farther north and west for the European and native elites. Premier sites included Malabar Hill, which would become one of the most exclusive residential areas on the island. A causeway at Sion linked Bombay to Salsette in 1805, when the population of the colony was approximately 200,000 (Dossal 1991: 23; Evenson 1989: 30–8; Dwivedi and Mehrotra 2001: 18–56).

Urbanization as system

World systems theory, identified most closely with the work of Immanuel Wallerstein (1974, 2004), describes the origin and intensification of capitalist relationships in Europe and, through imperialism, their expansion until the nineteenth century, when the earth became a single operational field for corporate interests and the nation state. One may witness the earliest phases of this radical shift in the world's political economy by the fourteenth century, with the solidification of agrarian production regimes and business practices in a European corridor stretching from the city-states of the Netherlands to those of northern Italy, and their linkage to an Atlantic economy by the early-sixteenth century under the auspices of the Iberian kingdoms.

The Atlantic economy in a sense accidentally resulted from the one of the primary thrusts of Iberian exploration as it attempted to access the already dynamic commercial world of the Indian Ocean. Building on the Mediterranean work of Fernand Braudel (1972) and the later work on the Indian Ocean by K. N. Chaudhuri (1985), Janet Abu-Lughod (1989) has shown how the interacting circles of trade within the Indian Ocean were already linked by the late-thirteenth century to a Mediterranean/northern European circle and to an East Asian circle – a fact that was well understood by the early European explorers. Within this Afro-Eurasian configuration, which still did not exhibit the characteristics of unitary control, South Asian commercial entrepots with their roots in the first millennium functioned as linchpins, and thus it was that the Europeans were seeking the entrepots of the Indies.

With command over naval technology, designed to navigate the Atlantic Ocean, the Iberians were able to adapt to the seasonal rhythms of the Indian Ocean monsoon and thus found themselves in a position to bring under a single management the various circles making up the Afro-Eurasian commercial network. Because they were simultaneously gaining control over the Atlantic, they were the first wave of Europeans assembling a world system. The consolidation of this system under true capitalists, instead of royal functionaries, occurred after the formation of the militaristic Dutch and English companies, which (with the assistance of their new national governments) suppressed the Iberians and exerted an ever-increasing influence over external trade in the many regions where they operated. During the seventeenth or Dutch century, we may thus trace the appearance of the world system's 'core' in northwestern Europe, its 'periphery' in those regions where European commercial interests dominated access to resources and capital, and its 'semi-periphery' in those regions where European economic interests were interacting with those of indigenous agents who controlled independent fields of action. Following this line of argument, we may describe global history since the eighteenth century as the expansion of systemic relations and the agonistic shift of core, peripheral, and semi-peripheral conditions among different world regions. Within South Asia, the changes set in motion through the destabilization of the Mughal Empire cleared the way for the macro-region's semi-peripheral encompassment within the European-dominated world system.

Wallerstein's perspective on the world system, while acknowledging the role of 'centers' such as Amsterdam, ultimately shows greater concern with regional and macro-regional interactions that eventually co-evolve with the modern nation-state. My approach here has been to start instead with the centers, i.e. cities, and demonstrate how the slow process of building extended configurations of urban hierarchies – perceived as arenas of physical expression and human interaction – is a different and fruitful manner of understanding how systems can exist and change. Traders, early capitalists and the state confronted patterns of urbanization that already existed on the ground. They then attempted to alter them through their own spatial decisions or city-building exercises. The results of their actions were a new configuration of urbanization that supported and in an important sense constituted the arena for system-building on a global scale. In this manner the productive apparatus within village-like textile production webs, the administrative functionality of secondary and primary cities, and the growing importance of the three Presidency city-states were the basis for regional or macro-regional inclusion within the world system. We might even say that urbanization with all its complexity *became* the system.

4 Space, economy and public culture in the colonial city

In Shyam Selvadurai's postcolonial novel of manners, *Cinnamon Gardens* (1999), we enter Colombo's southern suburbs inhabited by the colonial elite in 1927, the high water mark of colonialism in Ceylon/Sri Lanka. We meet several related families whose first language is Tamil but who communicate easily in English, and whose livelihood depends ultimately on the income from remote tea plantations in the hills or rubber estates in Malaya. The most influential character for these families is the septuagenarian Navaratnam, bearer of the honorific title of Mudaliyar (the 'first' or the 'chief') bestowed by the Government of Ceylon, who controls most family assets and the old family temple in the Pettah or Native Town, and autocratically expects obedience from the many petitioners requiring his administrative intervention, from his many servants exploited for physical labor and sexual favors, and from his extended family members. His arrogance has already driven his eldest son into exile in Bombay; his interference has brutally ended the relationship between his younger son, Balendran, and the love of his life, Richard, during their school years together in London. Now Balendran is in his forties, married and with a son studying in England. He expends much of his energy earning his father's trust in business matters and dedicating himself to his supportive wife – while paying men for casual sex near the railway tracks. His cousins living in the nearby estate include Annalukshmi, graduate and now teacher in an exclusive English-medium missionary school, whose great love is the reading of English literature. Balendran finds his brittle reality challenged by Richard's visit to Ceylon during the governance inquiries of the Donoughmore Commission and then the impending death of his exiled brother; Annalukshmi's world is perturbed by pressures to marry and by encounters with individuals representing the hitherto distant world of labor unions and the hitherto unimagined world of modern art.

This is a story about everyday struggles for personal liberation from the looming presence of Cinnamon Gardens, this enclave of privilege and self-proclaimed progressiveness, where physical labor is a hobby rather than a necessity, and where the cost of comfort is a multi-layered cushion of proprieties, exclusions, and constrictions. Against a backdrop of palatial homes set back from the road amid luxuriant gardens, the tattlers and the elders and, indeed, the younger generation, are ready to note and censure the smallest behavior that may challenge the segregation of sexes and classes: the exchange of glances, the uncomfortable sitting posture, one's presence in the wrong room or the wrong part of the city. Gender roles and power relationships are interconnected and over-determined through the slightest linguistic clues which send victims into paroxysms of doubt and alienation, masked by unrelenting civility and politeness. This environment is in one sense a British creation; although the direct reminders of colonial limitations are irregular (the sudden appearance of the brutal police chief, the sudden reminder that career advancement is impossible for a non-European), during everyday interactions the Ceylonese middle classes create their own cultural subservience through the constant imitation of European manners. Despite the constant pressure to live according to the seemingly eternal rules of this middle-class enclave, we know that it is, in fact, a purely colonial creation less than a century old. We also witness the social and political pressures that will lead toward radical change – Independence, democracy, civil war – within the near future. The characters in this book find agency against this backdrop of change, and utilize the fractures that inevitably appear over time to pursue personal rebellions and transgressions. But in the end Cinnamon Gardens remains unscathed, and the author, who has pronounced the impossibility of living in a Colombo where homosexuality remains a crime, sees the work as a parable for contemporary South Asia.

This chapter will investigate the historical processes that created the colonial city and neighborhoods like Cinnamon Gardens during the nineteenth and early-twentieth centuries. It will first consider the large-scale changes that attended the final conquests of the British and the enmeshing of the political economy of South Asia within an imperial system which led to the imposition of specific spatial models and architectural forms. It will then present four case studies on the evolution of the colonial edifice: in Calcutta where colonialism hit hardest; in the 'tribal' belt where it was most attenuated; in the Punjab where it reached late but displayed its ambitions most intensely; and finally in Bombay which became the quintessential expression of a new urbanization. These examples, which could be multiplied almost indefinitely, demonstrate imperialism's range and its varying tool kit, as well as the different ways urbanization served as the venue for an imperial, and increasingly national, production of space and society. Finally, we will examine some of the innovations in social organization and culture that changed the performative space of the city and attended the transition to South Asia's postcolonial modernity.

The path of urbanization under the Raj

The conquest of South Asia by a European colonial power, in the form of the British East India Company, was a process with precedents dating as far back as 1498 and rested on the slow growth of the British presence beginning in 1602. In effect, the Company evolved from an early transnational corporation into an imperial power within a period of almost exactly 100 years, between the 1757 battle of Plassey and the 1857 outbreak of the 'Sepoy Mutiny' or 'War of Independence' – the latter allowing the Company during its last year of operations to eradicate all vestigial organizations that might oppose its total domination. Within this century the decades of its midpoint, between 1798 and 1818, witnessed the crucial victories over formidable military opponents that were alternative imperial contenders within South Asia, including the 1799 destruction of the military capabilities of the Mysore state; the 1803 occupation of Delhi; the 1816 restriction of the Kathmandu-based Gorkha empire, which had been expanding through the Himalayan region, to the boundaries of modern Nepal; and the final defeat of the Marathas in 1818. The coincidence of these two decades with the French Revolution and Napoleonic Wars which resulted in British ascendancy over France, their most dangerous European opponent, allowed the British to exploit their South Asian advantages with little outside interference. The unlikely success of the British East India Company was the accomplishment of Presidency city-states that made the transition from coastal emporiums to military bases, and that increasingly coordinated their strategies allowing them to operate (unlike any of their opponents) at a sub-continental scale. Once the British had achieved a position of dominance, the period up to Independence (1947) witnessed a steady expansion of the Presidency capitals and the imposition of a colonial model of urban development on secondary cities throughout the British Raj (see Map 12).

The colonial impact on South Asian urbanization during the height of the British Raj is inseparable from profound technological innovations linked to organizational change. First, the transportation revolution, appearing initially as refinements of sailing and road construction, rapidly evolved into the application of steam power to shipping and railroads. Energy generation from steam, followed by conversion to fossil fuels, contributed to the radical extension of urban primacy in the Presidency capitals and also privileged specific interior transportation nodes. Second, the industrial revolution, long in gestation but emerging in full view by the end of the Napoleonic Wars, transformed Britain into the workshop of the world and established the conditions for the centralization of South Asian production facilities in the vicinity of large population centers, characterized by new configurations of social class and professionalism. Third, developments in communication media (initially the post office, later the application of electricity), shifted the 'information order' toward colonial forms of knowledge (Bayly 1996), and the spread of printing along with new educational institutions altered paths of social mobility, making inevitable the transition to city life as one of the primary vectors of social change. These phenomena signaled the assembly of a global hierarchy of cities under the aegis of imperialism. Calcutta, which became the second largest city in the British Empire, was the most important center that funneled resources from South Asia to London and through which British administrators introduced European administrative, technological and social experiments to their greatest colony.

The nineteenth century witnessed stasis in the *rate* of urbanization in South Asia. In this context we may recall the discussion from Chapter 3 that suggested a decline in urban population between 1750 and 1800 and a rate of urbanization at the latter date of 11 percent, implying an urban population 17.6 million persons among an estimated total population of 160 million. By 1872 the percentage of urbanites had

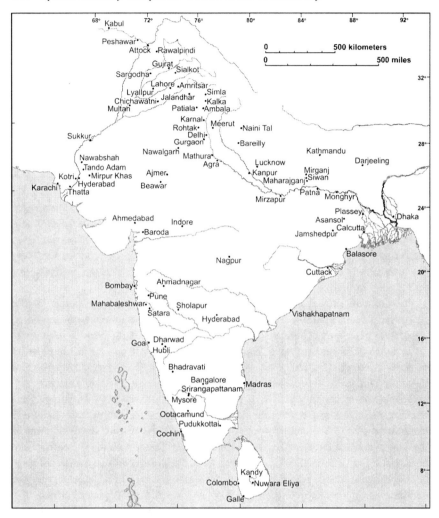

Map 12 Urban sites, 1800–1947.

declined to 8.7 percent, and did not rise to 11 percent again until 1911. But because overall population increased to 298 million in 1911, the number of urbanites had risen to 32.8 million, *an absolute increase during the nineteenth century of around 15 million persons, or almost a doubling of urban population* (Visaria and Visaria 1983: 466, 490). Significant expansion of the rate of urbanization began in the 1920s and picked up just before Independence, propelled by increases in migration from a countryside experiencing rapid demographic growth and slow economic development. During the decade of the 1930s, the population of British India increased 15 percent, while its urban population rose 40 percent. By 1941 there were 55 cities with populations over 100,000 and 863 additional settlements with populations greater than 10,000 (Koenigsberger 1952: 96; Sahai 1980: 25; Ramachandran 1989: 60–2).

City expansion under the British Raj occurred in the regions most intensely affected by imperial policy, particularly along improved transportation routes. The pull of three primate coastal cities – Calcutta, Madras and Bombay – suppressed second-level city formation and prevented the emergence of a new metropolis. The Bengal Presidency was the most extreme example of hyper-primacy: at the end of the nineteenth century, for example, the proportion of urban to rural population there was only 4.8 percent, compared to 9.9 percent in Madras and 19.5 percent in Bombay. The domination of Calcutta was partly responsible for the stagnation of secondary cities like Patna, which the early-nineteenth century was still one of South Asia's largest cities with a population of about 300,000 and a built environment extending more than 14 kilometers along the Ganga River. By 1921, commercial stagnation had contributed to a population decline to about 120,000 persons (Chaudhuri 1990: 35; Kidwai 1991: 163, 170–1; Yang 1998: 92–3).

Important changes were taking place, however, due to the dispersal of market functions and administrative offices (e.g. police stations) to towns with populations less than 50,000, which became hotbeds of nationalist politics in the early-twentieth century. Northwest of Patna, for example, interior market centers like Siwan, Maharajganj and Mirganj (the latter originating, as their names' suffixes indicate, in small trading centers) served as collection points and trans-shipment sites while maintaining groups of specialty artisans. Siwan in the late-eighteenth century was already the site for manufacture of metal commodities, calico cloth, birdcages, soap and silver links; its population was about 11,000 in 1872 and almost 18,000 in 1891, and although it subsequently experienced a half-century decline, it was growing again by the time of Independence. Maharajganj by the late-nineteenth century was a distribution center for agricultural produce, cloth, and metals, supporting multiple bureaucratic offices and religious institutions; by 1921 it was influencing an 'intermediate marketing area' with a 20-kilometer radius that included more than 86,000 persons (Yang 1998: 180–4, 194–7). This pattern of expansion in 'intermediate' sites, occurring throughout the subcontinent, set the stage for a tremendous increase in the number of towns and small cities after Independence.

Acts of Parliament in 1813 and 1833 divested the East India Company of its trade monopoly and then its commercial functions, opening fields for private enterprises. A business form known as the managing agency house came to dominate British investment in South Asia during the next century. Such a firm was typically a partnership with a headquarters in Britain and administrative offices in one or more Presidency capitals, providing complete management solutions for other companies (which might be joint-stock organizations) operating in specific business fields; in return, the managing agency passed on all expenses to the companies and charged commissions on sales and profits. The earliest fields entered by the managing agencies reflected the East India Company's older maritime orientation, with connections along transportation corridors to the interior in order to guarantee raw materials for export or markets for import. Thus they specialized in seaborne and river shipping; services for railroads; insurance; timber; and plantation-style agriculture aimed at export and requiring the coordination of large work forces (e.g. tea, indigo, jute, sugar, and coffee). They later moved into the processing of agricultural commodities, mining, paper, engineering, and the generation of electricity for urban sites. In many cases the managing agencies acquired equity in the companies they represented, at times they also provided purely agency services and charged only a fee, and they were always ready to start their own ventures. This flexibility, often aimed at achieving vertical or horizontal integration (e.g. tea estates in Assam, steamboats on the Brahmaputra River, coal mines, and export offices in Calcutta), made them aggressive and creative forces in economic expansion until the late 1930s. British-controlled banks worked closely with managing agencies to furnish capital. Independent British firms of solicitors, accountants and brokers cooperated with them, seconding personnel for interlocking boards of directors. With their many headquarters, in and around Calcutta's Clive Street or within the old forts of Madras, Colombo and Bombay, the concentration of British enterprises proved formidable competition for native firms attempting to penetrate the most profitable fields of modern capitalism. Only on the west coast, primarily in Bombay and in Ahmedabad, did indigenous capitalists compete effectively with the British to carve out independent empires of wealth.

The upper level of administrators within British firms enjoyed connections with the firms' founders. Mid-level administrators obtained their positions as covenanted servants through personal contacts and relationships cemented in British public schools or the Oxbridge circuit. Lower-level office personnel, numbering in the hundreds within the larger firms, were almost entirely natives, forming a new class of bureaucratic, English-speaking functionaries. Until the 1930s most British firms offered few opportunities for the advancement of non-Europeans to upper levels of management and did not allow natives membership in the exclusive clubs where trust-building could occur through shared leisure activities (Jones 1992). In this sense British capitalists under the Raj created an organizational culture similar to that of the military and civil wings of the colonial state.

Indigenous firms organized as family, sub-caste and caste coalitions dominated the 'bazaar' economy of the Presidency capitals and, within regional strongholds, coordinated the linkages between the agrarian economy and small or mid-level towns. They controlled interior money market, and distributed artisan or factory-produced manufactures. They thus constituted an intermediate level of business enterprise between the European-dominated firms based in major cities and the peddlers or pawnbrokers providing commodities and finance to the peasantry. They were also the chief employers and creditors of the urban poor (Morris 1983: 558–9; Ray 1995; Gooptu 2001: 34–41, 63–4). Opportunities provided by the colonial economy allowed some of these regional groups to migrate toward the Presidency capitals and to secondary cities, initially building trans-regional finance, and later transforming themselves into a new, indigenous capitalist class. We may describe three major migrations that also had consequences for global urban economy (Ray 1984):

1   The traders of the 'Bania heartland' of Gujarat and upper and central India used Bombay as the coordination center for particularly strong involvement in Maharasthra with extensions in the western Indian Ocean and Africa. The global 'Sindworki' network of handicraft distribution, a 'sphere of circulation' based in Hyderabad in Sind, was a minor but not insignificant stream flowing through Bombay (Markovits 2000).
2   Khatri traders from the Punjab led the way down the Ganga Valley toward Bengal, giving way to a more massive movement of trading groups originally hailing from Rajasthan who collectively became known as Marwaris. They concentrated on Calcutta and from there moved into Assam and Burma. They also extended their influence throughout central India, Bombay and its Maharashtra hinterland, and Hyderabad in southern India. Between 1860 and 1930 families of successful Marwari merchants returned profits to the small towns of their putative homeland in Shekhavati such as Nawalgarh and built elaborate neighborhoods of ornamental mansions (*haveli*), serving as the sites for periodic ritual gatherings (Timberg 1978; Cooper and Dawson 1998: 89–96).
3   Chetti and Chettiyar traders used Madras to expand their well-developed banking, money-lending, and investment capacities to Sri Lanka and South-east Asia. The Chettiyars, describing themselves with the archaic title of Nagarattar, built hundreds of mansions within towns and villages around their ancestral homelands near Pudukkottai, utilized almost entirely for extended kinship rituals (Hardgrove 2004: 91–126).

By the late-nineteenth century native entrepreneurs, including a disproportionate number of business leaders representing these three migrations, were shifting capital from financial and trading operations to a modern industrial sector. Some formed alliances with the nationalist movement, benefited from enhanced speculative and industrial investments made during First World War, and utilized opportunities afforded by protective tariffs during the 1930s to specialize in fields as varied as heavy industry, engineering, motor vehicle parts and repairs, agricultural processing, and soap. The leaders of this 'bazaar industrialization' found themselves well positioned for the great expansion of industries, including large numbers of small-scale units, during Second World War. By then British and native firms alike faced competition from multinational corporations attracted by markets among South Asia's urban populations whose purchasing power doubled between 1900 and 1940 (Goswami 1992: 249–57; Kling 1992).

Nodes within the imperial economy

Cities were the nodes and transportation systems were the channels enabling the control functions and movement of people and goods that made colonialism economically viable. Interior cities became coordinating and bulking centers for raw materials forwarded to a limited number of major ports where oceanic transports moved them to the colonial metropolis, returning with manufactured goods that were then distributed along the same lines throughout the urban network – the entire process managed by British administrators who drew their income from South Asian sources.

Initially the initiatives of the British administration in South Asia to extend the transportation systems – in order to penetrate the interior – concentrated on road improvement with paving in crushed gravel that significantly increased the movement of cart traffic and eliminated the cost-effectiveness of the great pack-bullock caravans that had dominated long-distance trade for centuries. During the 1830s, for example, the government began a 40-year project to grade and pave an improved Grand Trunk Road running from Calcutta to Peshawar; during the decade 1840–1850 alone, it constructed about 50,000 kilometers of roads through Company territories (Varady 2001: 257–8). Then the railroads came. By the late 1840s, responding to pressure (among others) from the Manchester Commercial Association, which wanted to assure a steady supply of Indian cotton for its mills, the East India Company had come to agreements with British capitalists on subsidies for railroad development that guaranteed specific rates of return to investors regardless of the lines' profitability. British citizens would occupy all major managerial posts in the railroad system, and components requiring machine production ranging from rails to locomotives would be imported from Britain. These ground rules, of great benefit to British financial and manufacturing interests and to the British engineering and administrative professions, supported a heroic period of railroad expansion in South Asia that by 1947 produced a total of 91,000 kilometers of track, the world's fourth largest and Asia's largest railway system, employing about 1,050,000 persons (Gumperz 2001: 105; Thorner 2001: 92).

We may examine the improved transportation systems in South Asia under the Raj in terms of their general or more specific impacts on urbanization. In general, by accelerating the incorporation of agrarian production within global trade, they altered agricultural regimes in wide reaches of the subcontinent and amplified the transactional centrality of district or sub-district marketing centers while offering opportunities for British or indigenous traders to establish new patterns of capital formation. The presence of railroads stimulated road construction and enhanced contacts for small commercial centers and rich landowners (Yang 1998: 50–2). The ability to move or, through telegraph, to communicate over wide distances facilitated the operation of new educational systems and enabled a class of highly educated urbanites to dominate an emerging public sphere that, by the end of the nineteenth century, was oriented around a nationalist discourse. Periodical literature, especially in South Asian languages, grew in tandem with these changes. In specific cases, cities that found themselves on improved transportation lines or became hubs enjoyed an advantage over potential competitors for central place functions and witnessed greater commercialization and/or industrialization. Thus the railways invigorated smaller, older settlements, which came to play important roles as servicing and switching spots, such as Waltair (Vishakhapatnam), Bareilly,

Meerut, and Nagpur (Ramachandran 1989: 67). A new industrial working class came together at railway workshops that also became colonies for employees, often including planned residential layouts and support facilities. The Lahore railway workshops, for example, had over 2,000 employees in 1880 and 4,500 in 1906. The workshops next to Monghyr (Munger) in eastern Bihar had 11,000 employees in 1921 (Das Gupta 1994: 27). The railway workshops opened in Ajmer in 1879 and employed 8,000 people by 1911, stimulating an increase in urban population from 35,111 in 1872 to 68,489 in 1891, mostly in suburban areas. The railroad also brought large numbers of pilgrims year round to Ajmer's shrine of Shaikh Muimuddin Sijzi (see Chapter 2) – just one example of the massive increase in pilgrim traffic throughout the subcontinent. The management of the railroads kept detailed statistics on pilgrims and organized lines to provide access to pilgrimage sites (Yang 1998: 135–6; Kerr 2001: 40, 53–6).

The example of Maharashtra demonstrates how a dramatic expansion of transportation systems during the nineteenth century affected regional patterns of urbanization. Increasing involvement of the Bombay Presidency in the affairs of the Maratha Peshwa, based in Pune, prompted initial efforts to improve ground transportation between the two cities. During the Second Anglo-Maratha War (1778–9), for example, the British expedition from Bombay had required six weeks, involving a boat trip across the bay to Panvel (see Map 19) and then construction of a road for guns leading to the Bhor Pass, followed by additional road construction through marshes to the east. The improvement of the military road in 1804 reduced the trip to four or five days. The creation of a macadamized road through the Bhor Pass in 1830 still required special sets of coaches for the steep ascent but allowed the first mail cart to run between the two cities (Kosambi 1985: 36–7). During the next decade, similar improvements in east-west running roads transformed the transportation of cotton from Dharwad to the coast, augmenting its importance as the headquarters of the Presidency's southern division. The improvement of the Bombay-Agra military trunk road running through Nasik contributed through the 1840s to a massive increase in pack-bullock and, later, cart traffic, moving cotton from Malwa and Khandesh and English cloth and other finished goods from Bombay. Meanwhile, at Bombay, road construction originating as elevated causeways created by the 1830s a single island-spanning web (see Map 15). The Colaba Causeway, using Old Woman's Island as a steppingstone south to Colaba Island, was completed in 1838 – thus linking together all seven of Bombay's islands for the first time. Another causeway constructed through Parsi benevolence connected Mahim to Bandra on the southwestern corner of Salsette in 1845 (Chandavarker 1994: 35).

The first railway track in South Asia was laid between Bombay and Thana in 1853, and ten years later the Great India Peninsula Railway was extended through the Bhor Pass towards Pune; Nagpur was connected in 1867 and the link to Calcutta by 1870. Meanwhile, the Bombay Baroda and Central India Railway connected Bombay to Ahmedabad and Baroda (Vadodara) by 1864. The Southern Mahratta Railway linked Pune with southern Maharashtra districts and to Bangalore by 1884–5. With its legacy as an educational and administrative center, and its role as both transportation hub and summer capital of the Bombay Presidency, Pune overcame a population decline in the early-nineteenth century to experience growth from about 90,000 inhabitants in 1872 to 153,000 in 1901. Bombay's export economy, which had hitherto depended mostly on Gujarati and Konkan connections, now had direct, fast access to agricultural districts on the Deccan Plateau and commercial agents of Gujarati or Marwari background used telegraphic communications and extended kinship networks to penetrate regional markets past the Western Ghats. As the railroad successively reached Sholapur, Ahmadnagar, and Hubli, these market towns began to outstrip others as the major commercial centers in the interior. In Sholapur, where the railroad reached in 1859, a former bulking center for the export trade witnessed the foundation of the Sholapur Spinning and Weaving Company in 1877 and a continued concentration of textile firms; population rose from 61,000 in 1881 to 277,000 in 1951, with 31,605 persons working in the textile industry (Pethe 1988). Satara, on the other hand, which was as well situated as the others to control neighboring commerce, remained off a rail line and experienced an absolute decline in population by the early-twentieth century (Kidwai 1991: 163; Gumperz 2001: 97–125).

The intersection of rail and steamship terminals at coastal entrepots, primarily the Presidency capitals, was a major reason for their continuing growth during the British Raj. For Bombay, the opening of the Suez Canal in 1869 dramatically increased its role as a berthing spot for ocean-going steamers. Between 1875 and 1914 over 40 hectares of new water area were created and over 9,100 meters of quays with 50 berths. Workers and managers for the Bombay Port Trust (founded 1873), along with employees of the railroads and a variety of organizations utilizing port facilities, settled on the eastern side of the island (see Map 15). This trust also planned and executed the highly successful commercial development called the Ballard Estate by 1923, built on the fill excavated from the construction of the Alexandra Docks during the previous decade. It reclaimed on the eastern side of Bombay a total of 1,880 acres of land which in the 1930s comprised one-eighth of the land area of the city (Dwivedi and Mehrotra 2001: 184–91, 205). Dramatic changes also occurred at Calcutta, where South Asia's first port trust was established in 1870, and continued improvements provided 49 hectares of wet dock space by 1929, while the establishment of the main rail station at Haora (Howrah) on the west bank of the river formed the core of a massive population increase (Banerjee 1987: 38–60, 193; Chaudhuri 1990: 238–40). At Madras, where cargo had always been transferred to and from ships in surf boats, the construction of an entirely artificial harbor after 1877, complete with railway sidings and office space, ensured the city's continued dominance of South India's import-export economy. Outside the Presidency capitals British expansion of major port facilities included the improvement of the harbor at Cochin between 1920 and 1941 through removal of its sandbar and the shifting of harbor facilities to Willington Island (an artificial land mass created from the sand dredged during the deepening of the channel). The commissioning of a new harbor at Vishakhapatnam in 1933 aimed at the export of manganese ore transported by the Bengal-Nagpur Railway (Broeze *et al.* 1987; Broeze 1991; Corporation of Cochin 2007). At Goa, where the main settlement shifted during the nineteenth century westward to Panaji (Panjim), the Portuguese developed a deep-water port on the other side of the peninsula at Mormugao during the 1930s.

The classic example of a colonial economy and its impact on port urbanization comes from Sri Lanka and the growth of Colombo. The 150 years of Dutch rule had introduced plantations for cinnamon and some coconut production along with a preliminary road system that linked Colombo to plantation areas in the Low Country, the southwestern part of the island. After the British government took direct control of Sri Lanka at the end of the Napoleonic Wars and then completed the conquest of the kingdom of Kandy (1815–18), they took steps to encourage coffee cultivation on plantations that spread into the mountain foothills at the center of the island. This plan required the more effective linking of Colombo to the interior through the postal system (the first service opened between Colombo and Kandy in 1822); paved roads (3,000 miles in length by 1860); a rail system that reached Kandy in 1867; and a telegraph system that allowed direct communication from Colombo to London markets in 1870. The population of Colombo which, with about 31,000 persons in 1824, was still about the size of Galle, grew to 111,000 in 1881 and 154,000 in 1901, far outstripping any other city on the island. Although the coffee leaf fungus caused the collapse of the coffee economy during the 1870s tea rapidly took its place, followed closely by commercialized coconut production and then, after the automotive revolution began in the twentieth century, by rubber production. By 1900 these three crops accounted for 90 percent of export values, almost entirely funneled through the ramified transportation network to the port at Colombo. Major improvements to Colombo's facilities through the extension of breakwaters – to create a sheltered harbor in 1912 – and the construction of coaling stations allowed it to surpass Galle as the island's major port. It became the seventh port in the world in terms of entering tonnage, the third largest imperial port, and the largest port in South Asia (Broeze *et al.* 1987; Dharmasena 1989; Pearson 2003: 216). By the 1940s, when its population was 362,000, Colombo was the only urban place in Sri Lanka with more than 65,000 persons; the second, third, and fourth largest towns were its suburbs (Murphy 1997).

When the British took control of Sri Lanka, they appropriated the Colombo Fort for their administration and originally pushed the descendants of Portuguese and Dutch colonial elites (collectively known as the Burghers) into the east-lying Pettah. Native inhabitants, including a large representation from Muslim trading communities, tended to relocate farther east in the Outer Pettah beyond which country houses came up for colonial administrators. When the city expanded its role as colonial capital and transnational port, the fort and Pettah areas witnessed the replacement of the old-style Dutch buildings by more massive public offices, hotels, banks, and exchanges. The fort walls came down between 1869 and 1871 and the esplanade along the west coast called Galle Face became a promenade stretching 1.5 kilometers south along the seafront, the site of colonial parades, races and games (Roberts 1989: 179–83). To its southeast the new suburban settlement known as Cinnamon Gardens became the site for museums, cricket grounds and a racecourse amid low-density residential blocks that attracted the colonial administrative elite. The massive influx of immigration, consisting mostly of Sinhala-speakers from the Low Country, resulted in an expansion of denser neighborhoods, mostly characterized by class and caste segregation, to the east and south. An additional level of segregation appeared after the 1880s in the formation of the enclave called Wellawatta on the outskirts of the city, housing mostly Tamil-speaking migrants, along with smaller Tamil-speaking business enclaves in the central areas of the city – a trend that would have momentous consequences during the late-twentieth century. The tendency of migrants to preserve small garden plots, even in shanty towns, combined with the suburban configuration of elite neighborhoods and the influence of British garden-city planning concepts, gave the city a distinctively low-rise and distributed character that it shared with Madras and other South Indian cities (Perera 1999: 49–52, 75–89, 112–15).

At the other end of South Asia, Sind became incorporated at a relatively late date into the British colonial order but the rapid growth of Karachi as its leading city was the most astonishing urban phenomenon in South Asia under the Raj. At the beginning of the nineteenth century no one would have predicted Karachi's illustrious future. The main city in southern Sind for hundreds of years had been the inland site of Thatta and which remained a regional seat under the Mughals (Shah Jahan oversaw construction of several world-class monuments there). The decline of Mughal power in Sind brought with it the eclipse of Thatta and the devolution of political power to a constellation of lords owing loose allegiance first to Persia and then to Afghanistan. The political center shifted to the new town of Hyderabad, constructed after 1768 east of the Indus River. Karachi, meanwhile, was beginning as a fishing village on the south bank of the Layari River, which formed the westernmost extension of the Indus River Delta, but in fact provided no certain waterborne link to the Indus. As a minor commercial center, Karachi's traffic from the interior consisted of camel caravans that arrived at a *sarai* lying adjacent to a walled town housing between 8,000 and 10,000 persons. In the sea about 3.5 kilometers south-southwest of Karachi lay Keamari Point, the western end of a narrow island that protected a large lagoon comprised of shallows with mangrove forests crossed by Chinna Creek. About 3.5 kilometers further south lay Manora Point, the eastern end of an even longer, narrower island running toward the northwest that protected a similar but larger lagoon. The gap between the two points provided ingress to the lagoons and a narrow but deep channel leading toward the Layari River, although a bar made access difficult for larger craft (Lari and Lari 1996: 15, 23, 34, 91; Hasan 2002: 15–16).

The British East India Company occupied this unprepossessing site in 1839 as a staging area for its military intervention in Kabul. Following complete disaster in Afghanistan the Company contravened all treaties signed with the lords of Sind and, in a fit of pique, annexed the entire region in 1843 – a move so unscrupulous that even many Company officials decried it – and in 1847 placed control of the newly acquired region under Bombay. A cantonment came up east of the old city and the British launched a program of harbor improvement and regional road construction. The population of the city, around 14,000 at the moment of annexation, increased to about 57,000 by 1856. The first big opportunity for Karachi came with the American Civil War (1861–4) when Sind became a site for cotton production and export. Karachi attracted capital and capitalists from Gujarat and Maharashtra, including Parsi, Goanese, and British entrepreneurs, who helped create a dynamic business district adjacent to the old city. The full panoply of Gothic and Indo-Saracenic architecture (see below) came to dominate the major public and commercial buildings and schools in the city (Lari and Lari 1996). The opening of the Suez Canal made Karachi the first major port of call for ships arriving from the west, enhancing its role as a transit node and facilitating large increases in wheat exports. Radical improvement of the port facilities, coordinated after 1887 by the Port Trust, included construction of a mole stretching south from Manora Point to protect the channel entrance; dredging of the main channel; and the filling of a land bridge from Karachi to Keamari Point for a large berthing area, warehouses, and rail yards. Meanwhile, the completion of railway bridges at Sukkur and Kotri improved rail connectivity within Sind and with other regions. Further port improvements in the early-twentieth century created an entirely new berthing and transportation extension on the west side of the channel. In 1901 Karachi's population was 117,000 and its municipal area included a further 109,000 persons (Banga 1992; *Karachi under the Raj* 2004, 1–2).

Giant irrigation projects undertaken between the 1890s and 1930s, including the Jamrao Canal and the Sukkur Barrage (opened 1932) transformed the agricultural profile of Sind and dramatically increased the cultivation of wheat and cotton; area devoted to the latter rose from 121,400 hectares in 1930 to 303,520 hectares by the end of the decade. A component of these projects was the planned construction of a series of new towns or 'barrage towns' such as Nawabshah, Tando Adam, and Mirpur Khas which throve initially as agricultural processing centers and became components of a more ramified urban hierarchy within the province. Immigration from other provinces, especially from Punjab, transformed the demography of these project areas. Simultaneously, Karachi's importance as a transportation hub was augmented by the inauguration of air transport; in 1924 its airport became the South Asia's first node for service provided by Imperial Airways. The steady increase in the trans-regional connectivity of the province, and Karachi in particular, was accompanied by what many Sindhis viewed as the unacceptable influence of non-Sindhis. The 1936 separation of Sind from the Bombay Presidency with Karachi as its provincial capital only exacerbated debates within the new Legislative Assembly and the press on the definition of the true 'Sindhi.' Karachi's population, in the meanwhile, rose to total about 387,000 in 1941 when the city was assuming further responsibilities as a hub for British and U.S. logistical efforts (Ansari 2005: 25–39).

The colonial disposition of urban space

Ashis Nandy's famous essay, *The Intimate Enemy* (1983), explores the psycho-social processes that occurred within colonial South Asia as the eighteenth-century heyday of the British 'bandit-kings' gave way to the promotion of what he calls the 'secular hierarchies' by those who were imbued during the nineteenth and early-twentieth century with the modernizing spirit of the West. The promoters, who were mostly male and who included significant segments of public opinion among 'native' leadership, came to believe in the progressive supplanting of the traditional by the modern, the obscurantist by the enlightened, and the indigenous by the universal. British imperialism was the agency that would allow the modernizing transition to occur, if painfully; even the opponents of imperialism could achieve limited success only through the adoption of the categories of the modern, through becoming Western. Categorization under colonialism, a variant of nineteenth-century power/knowledge that claimed to rationalize its program through mathematical precision, fixed upon South Asia grids of time and space, self and other that profoundly affected the spatial and social organization of human groups. What seemed earlier to be transitory excrescences of the Western project – the security psychosis, racism, sexism, environmental degradation, ethno-nationalism – in retrospect appear to be fundamental components of its categorical imperatives. We will briefly explore three features of the colonial South Asian city – the cantonment, the hill station, and public architecture – that demonstrate this mixture of progress and racist chauvinism, the impact of this 'second colonization.'

As the British enterprise evolved from a mercantilist community toward a militarized bureaucracy governing vast territories, their strategies for organizing urban society and space applied concepts that had hitherto informed the policies of all European trading companies, with an increasingly overt fixation on military affairs and racist perspectives. Eschewing its earlier deferential attitude toward continental powers, the Company militant applied the lessons of eighteenth-century planning in Presidency towns – characterized by strong, isolated fortifications and segregation of 'whites' and 'blacks' – to urban sites throughout the interior of the subcontinent. The first major manifestations of the British military presence in places like Lucknow and Hyderabad (see Chapter 3) provided the template for the Cantonment: a self-contained encampment of Indian and European troops that included 'lines' of tents or barracks along with parade grounds and shooting or practice ranges. In areas that the British controlled directly, they established the lines on public land, at times in places of strategic military value but without substantial pre-existing native populations. Within the territories of princely states, officially allied to the British Raj, they established the lines in consultation with the princes' governments on tracts that became, in effect, extraterritorial enclaves located typically on the outskirts of earlier settlements. By 1863 the British maintained 114 cantonments in South Asia (mostly in the north) serving as the bases of 227,000 military personnel that included 85,000 Europeans scattered in detachments ranging from 50 to over 4,000. Thirty cantonments housed over 1,000 European troops, and two housed over 4,000 (King 1976: 98).

Distinguished from, but closely aligned with, the 'military lines' or 'military station' were the offices and residences of the 'civil lines' or the 'civil station.' In princely states the latter included, at first, the establishments connected with the British Resident and his staff, which originally had tended to lie within capital cities, but which tended to migrate (especially after the rebellions of 1857–8) out toward the cantonment. As the British administrative presence expanded during the nineteenth century its civilian presence encompassed a wider range of colonial personnel: collector, magistrate, judge, police superintendent, surgeon, missionary, teacher, and businessman. Near the civil and military lines grew a discrete bazaar catering to the needs of colonial personnel but usually created and staffed by natives who were immigrants from Presidency centers or represented business communities specializing in the colonial economy-in effect, immigrants to the regions where they did business. Thus the colonial pattern of urbanization could involve three components: the 'old city' inhabited mostly by indigenes; the native bazaar in a discrete location near the European quarters; and the civil and military station(s) with a predominantly European cultural ethos.

During the nineteenth century the British – always aware of their higher mortality rate in South Asia – embraced ethno-medical theories that identified environmental factors, and particularly airborne miasmas coming from crowding and poor sanitation, as the cause of many diseases. The old cities and native bazaars were the sites most often associated in the British conceptual system with these negative qualities. Traumatized by the subcontinent-wide cholera epidemic of 1817–21, and its regular recurrence along with typhoid and malaria, the British perceived the relationship of contagious disease and crowded conditions although they had not yet traced their linkages to specific microorganisms or insect carriers. They quested, therefore, for open spaces and healthy, arterial corridors that allowed circulation of air within major cities. For example, a Lottery Committee established in Calcutta in 1817 to fund civic improvements through regular public lotteries concentrated until 1836 on sanitation and drainage issues and, as part of its concerns about public health, constructed north-south arteries through the native city. Strand Road along the bank of the river became the site for prestigious public buildings. A boulevard east of Chowringhee Road also ran from south to north, extending Wellesley Street as College Street in the neighborhood of the Hindu College (founded 1817) and Sanskrit College (founded in 1824) and then becoming Cornwallis Street. The Conservancy Act of 1842, which allowed the formation of sanitary committees for garbage disposal, became the first formal measure of municipal organization applied in the Bengal Presidency (Chaudhuri 1990: 171; Gupta 1993).

The belief that South Asian cities were heavily populated and dirty intersected at Lucknow with a quest for security after the military disasters of 1857–8, leading to the driving of broad boulevards through the old city and the consolidation of a series of esplanades, along with expansive civil and military lines, on the eastern side of the city. The municipal committee that administered Lucknow accepted the necessity for 'lung spaces' that facilitated air circulation (and riot control) but severely disrupted the fabric of older neighborhoods. In its quest for sanitary rationality, agents of the British administration interfered with social space that hitherto had remained within the private sphere, in networks as diverse as Muslim burial practices, household toilet facilities, and models of home construction (Oldenburg 1984: 96–116).

The most intense ethno-medical intervention by the British administration occurred in response to a major epidemic of bubonic plague in 1896 which, after a particularly virulent initial period, raged intermittently for several decades affecting mostly urban environments. By this point a microbial explanation of the disease was accepted by British officials, but because the disease vectors were imperfectly understood, explanatory frameworks that stressed locality-specific aspects of the plague affected the government's response. Officials forcibly washed or quarantined urban buildings; conducted intrusive house-to-house searches for plague cases; enforced segregation of those who came in contact with victims; and authorized compulsory medical examinations of the native population. Because conditions of squalor and lack of fresh air were seen as predisposing causes that supported the genesis of plague organisms, the government targeted neighborhoods of the poor for demolition of structures deemed insufficiently sanitary. Only after 1900, when a report of the Indian Plague Commission declared such measures counter-productive, did officials begin to curtail such intrusive policies (Arnold 1993; Chandavarkar 1998: 234–65; Kidambi 2004).

The British tried to preserve for themselves plenty of space and fresh air, along with protection from the sun and the heat of the tropics which they described as particularly dangerous for Europeans. They were also concerned with combating problems of intemperance and sexually transmitted disease that might occur through contact between natives and their own personnel, and attempted to relieve boredom or to inculcate positive attitudes by providing opportunities for recreational activities and games requiring specialized playing areas. Thus the civil and military lines came to be serviced by up-to-date utilities for the supply of fresh water and power, with churches, clubs, libraries, theaters, parks, racecourses, and museums. Broad, tree-lined avenues with paved streets and spacious intersections gave access to residential developments designed for officers and professionals. The characteristic architectural form was the bungalow, a style derived originally from rural habitations encountered by the British in Bengal: a single-story building internally divided into living, dining, and bedroom areas with separate bath, and often including an extension of the low thatched or tiled roof over a verandah that could surround the building on all sides. The bungalow stood at the center of a compound, often walled with an entranceway for a drive leading to the main house, with separate areas for servants' quarters, carriages, and gardens. After the establishment of the Public Works Department in the 1840s–1850s, the design of the bungalow adopted various features of cottage architecture coming from European models, and became enshrined in a Military Board style that affected all official buildings of the Government of India. This protean bungalow went on to enjoy success among the middle classes worldwide; in South Asia, the bungalow-and-compound combination characterized a low-density planning model that stood in sharp contract to 'native' urbanization, leading to formidable problems of integration after Independence (King 1976: 109–25; 1995: 14–64).

Kanpur (Cawnpore) exemplifies the trajectory of the Cantonment model as the nucleus of a completely new urban site. The Treaty of Allahabad in 1765 had made arrangements for the mutual action of the East India Company and the state of Avadh against the Marathas. As a result, the Company set up a temporary military base near a small village on the south bank of the Ganga River, a screen for Lucknow only 72 kilometers to the northeast. The base never moved thereafter and developed as a permanent military presence complete with officers' bungalows and bazaars. In 1801, when the Company pressed campaigns against the house of Scindia, Kanpur lay within Ceded Provinces taken from Avadh and amalgamated with the Bengal Presidency. It became a district headquarters as well as the biggest British army base in India. Success against the Marathas and the general pacification of northern India led to a growing British commercial presence. The Grand Trunk Road reached Kanpur in the late 1830s and the telegraph in 1854. By that point a complex of civil and military stations spreading about 6 kilometers along the river surrounded on three sides a bazaar area that had become Kanpur city (an area of 280 hectares), the entire complex housing about 109,000 persons, with 55 percent crammed into the city alone (Yalland 1987; Singh 1990: 9). Although Kanpur was already serving as a bulking center for cotton and indigo, its export position in the heart of the Gangetic plain still remained secondary to Mirzapur, which during the first three decades of the nineteenth century had become known as the 'Manchester of India' and which supported a population of 75,000 in 1853 dependent primarily on trade (Bayly 1983: 338–41).

The struggles of 1857–8 resulted in the annihilation of the European population of Kanpur, and general devastation when the British re-occupied it. Thereafter the city enjoyed a remarkable rebirth as a major manufacturing center, aided by its established base of tanning and leather firms supplying products for the military and by the arrival of the railroad in 1859, which allowed Kanpur to usurp the position of Mirzapur as the leading regional hub for cotton bulking. The American Civil War, which cut off cotton supplies to industries in Great Britain, gave Kanpur and other South Asian cities an enhanced role in the global textile industry, stimulating the cultivation and export of the raw material but also providing opportunities for factory production within the subcontinent. With the rail head booming, the Kanpur Cotton Committee was formed in 1861 and led to the creation of the Elgin Cotton Spinning and Weaving Company which began production in 1864. This company failed in 1871 during the post-Civil War depression and restarted under new management in competition with the Muir Mills established in 1874 and the Cawnpore Woolen Mills Company established two years later to manufacture army blankets. These plants led a takeoff into factory-based textile and leather goods production, closely followed by a major expansion of agro-industrial plants (e.g. in sugar processing, flour mills), managed almost entirely by British capitalists with capital assistance from Marwari firms that also served as sales agents (Timberg 1978: 150). The number of workers employed in manufacturing rose to 13,324 in 1911 (accounting for 20 percent of the workforce), doubled again by 1931, and quadrupled during the 1940s due to enhanced demand during Second World War. The 1941 Census recorded Kanpur as the eighth largest city in South Asia, with a population of almost 490,000 (Bayly 1983: 436–41; Singh 1990).

Another example, on a smaller scale, of the city-founding qualities of the Cantonment model comes from Beawar or Naya Shahar, the 'New City,' in Rajasthan. In 1818, when the British acquired Ajmer, they became concerned with the Mairs or Mers, people of the dry, hilly tract to the southeast called Mairwara/Merwara, who made their living (in the British view) as plunderers. The tract was subdued in a campaign 1819–21, leading to its complete acquisition by the British through elimination of princely claims in 1825. They then established the Mair battalion and set up a cantonment for it about four miles from the village of Beawar. To support this site the British attracted merchants (*mahajan*) and in 1836 constructed a bazaar that became the core of Naya Shahar. Within 12 years 1,599 families had settled there as the spread of cotton production made the growing town a center for its trade. In 1871 the battalion was transferred to Ajmer but the commercial centrality of the town stimulated its continued growth. The railroad reached there in 1880 and the Krishna Cotton Mill followed a year later. By 1901, when the population reached 21,928, manufacturing accounted for 48.6 percent of the work force, with cotton textiles employing 38 percent. Metalwork and calico printing became regionally famous and the grain trade was important. Beawar/Naya Shahar thus evolved into one of the important industrial towns in Rajasthan, with a population of ca. 134,000 in 2007 (Joshi 1988).

Bangalore exemplifies the impact of the Cantonment model on a pre-existing settlement. After the British defeated the Kingdom of Mysore the former thriving city of Srirangapattanam never recovered from its sack in 1799. It became a village lying amid ruins near the main road running from Mysore, which remained the seat of the restored Odeyar kings, to Bangalore, which continued to evolve as the kingdom's leading commercial city. The British occupied Bangalore's old fort, which stood just south of the old city (*pete*), and also created in 1807 a separate cantonment that occupied lands northeast and east of the old city. The Cantonment Bazaar (later called Shivajinagar) grew adjacent to the main cantonment offices and attracted a substantial contingent of Muslim traders along with mostly Tamil-speaking service personnel and Anglo-Indians (many of them Christians) from the Madras Presidency. The several kilometers lying between the city and the cantonment became a reserved parkland named after Mark Cubbon, administrator of the state between 1834 and 1862, and witnessed the construction of a number of public offices including the high court building and the jail along with the race course. Although the walls of the old city came down during the 1860s, it remained a separate social world where Kannada was the most common language. The city's main market catered to a population that was still concentrated within dense habitations while the cantonment (aside from the Bazaar and its Commercial Street) displayed the wide avenues and low-density housing of a bungalow culture, eventually generating a new market around Brigade Road farther to the south. The Karaga festival (see Chapter 2) was the main religious celebration in the old city while the annual festival at the Roman Catholic St. Mary's Church became the main public celebration in the cantonment. When the first textile factories appeared in Bangalore during the 1870s they located west of the old city, reinforcing its profile as an indigenous manufacturing center, while the cantonment retained its character as a professional and service-based economy. The two parts of the city maintained separate administrations until their 1949 union as a single municipality.

As late as 1971, only 37 percent of Bangalore's population spoke the official state language, Kannada, as their first language; 25 percent spoke Tamil and 3 percent spoke Malayalam (many of them still living on the east side), 17 percent spoke Urdu (associated with Muslims), and 18 percent spoke Telugu. Phenomena as varied as voting patterns, newspaper subscriptions and debates over architecture demonstrated the continuing impact of a bipolar history (Srinivas 2001; Heitzman 2004; Nair 2005: 23–76, 271–98).

British perceptions that the South Asian summer was excessively hot, humid, and unhealthy, combined with a Romantic attraction to picturesque highlands and new concepts of the health benefits gained from retirement to a sanatorium, spa or a bucolic resort, contributed to a vast expansion of urbanization in the hill station. During the nineteenth century the British founded up to 80 such centers at higher altitudes and made arrangements for the relocation of public offices and British military contingents there for extended periods. Beginning in the 1820s, officers of the Madras government retired to Ootacamund (Udugamandalam), or 'Ooty,' for up to six months annually. The Bengal government came to stay in Darjeeling, a planned development which between 1835 and 1850 increased in population from 100 to 10,000, and later became a coordinating point for tea production. The Bombay government shifted to Mahabaleshwar, the government of the Northwest Frontier Provinces and Oudh (later the United Provinces) to Naini Tal. In Sri Lanka, the resort of Nuwara Eliya became the preferred escape from Colombo after 1819. By the end of the nineteenth century the hill stations had become important components within the social life of the British in South Asia – places where they pursued matrimonial alliances; engaged in recreational activities with their families; educated their children; and participated in civic organizations, parties, and private interactions that reinforced their sense of separateness from the governed and participation in a cosmopolitan European culture. Wherever hill stations developed they led to the expansion of road and railroad systems in their vicinity, originally for the convenience of British elites and support of their leisure activities, but ultimately resulting in the stimulation of regional commercial capacities and strings of small commercial and transport centers. Thus the hill stations, originally conceptualized as British retreats and later developing into alternative sites of official functionality, encouraged the rapid increase in the indigenous service population and, during the early-twentieth century, witnessed an ever-greater influx of the native middle class as land investors and as participants in the vacation life-style (Kennedy 1996).

The greatest of the hill stations was Simla (Shimla), which began with the construction of a thatched cottage in 1819 by the East India Company's political agent dealing with the surrounding group of hill states. It grew up in the midst of six satellite stations, including several military cantonments, and gained a reputation as a sanatorium 2,100 meters above sea level. By 1864 the Viceroy was abandoning Barrackpur just north of Calcutta for Simla as his summer residence. After 1876 the Government of Punjab was retiring there and during the 1880s the headquarters of the Indian Army relocated there. The narrow-gauge rail line arrived in 1903. At its acme Simla displayed the typical features of many hill stations where spatial organization reflected social hierarchy. The upper part of the settlement, the Ridge, included a dispersed grouping of mansions and boarding houses, designed as imitation English cottages or Swiss chalets, allocated according to a strict protocol for various ranks within the Government of India. Below, emanating from the Anglican church, lay the Mall, a flat promenade featuring shops that catered to an English-speaking clientele and that remained off-limits for native service personnel during the early evening. The Bazaar stood further below: a dense collection of low-income housing and shops for the commercial groups, transport workers, sweepers, and household servants who took care of the practical necessities for their British masters and mistresses. Racial segregation and a constant round of social events (featuring a high percentage of women) contributed to a homey feeling for British vacationers and reinforced their social exclusivity.

The segregated ambience, of course, could not last. During the first two decades of the twentieth century the permanent population of Simla grew from about 36,000 to 45,000, including a doubling of the non-British population. Native ownership of properties within the town steadily increased. After 1939 the Government of India was keeping more of its people permanently in New Delhi and army headquarters similarly shifted there, reducing the importance of Simla (Kanwar 1990). But after Independence the Government of Punjab in India used Simla as its seat and in 1966, with the creation of Himachal Pradesh as a separate state, it was a ready-made capital (Population was about 192,000 in 2007). In a similar manner many hill stations throughout South Asia after Independence served as political seats or evolved into the preserves of the upper and middle classes, becoming honeymoon getaways and sites for public or private educational and training institutes.

The expansion of government bureaucracies in British India and in princely states entailed the construction of public buildings that exerted a major impact on the spatial fabric of cities where most of these buildings were located. Architectural designers in the early European settlements were originally military engineers and, later, staff members of the engineering offices of the British East India Company overseen by Military Boards. The utilitarian and cost-saving viewpoint that dominated the thinking of these organizations, inherited after 1845 by the Public Works Department, resulted in the application of standardized forms in hundreds of public structures throughout South Asia. The typical buildings were long, single-story (and more rarely multi-storied) structures that often included a sheltered walkway giving access to office cubicles – a ubiquitous plan for public office buildings throughout South Asia even today. The planning of more important public buildings sent engineer-architects to pattern books that reflected shifts in the popularity of styles in Europe while allowing some freedom for elaboration by individual designers. For example, the Viceroy's Lodge atop the Ridge in Shimla (occupied 1888), designed by Henry Irwin, Superintendent Engineer and Architect of the Public Works Department, bore a resemblance to an Elizabethan mansion or a Scottish castle (Kanwar 1990: 49–53). The architectural profession that was beginning in South Asia during the 1860s exerted minimal input on the decisions of the Public Works Department during the nineteenth century. Similarly, despite the reliance of British designers on native workmanship, the long-established role of the master builder (*mistri*) remained ignored or substantially downplayed in works commissioned by the British administration (Lang *et al.* 1997: 58–64).

A sequence of sometimes competing European architectural fashions came to characterize the major buildings constructed under the Raj, many of which remain functioning components of the South Asian city. During the late-eighteenth century a Georgian or baroque neoclassicism dominated British monuments, giving way to a simplified Greek classicism in the early-nineteenth century. The Romantic Movement then contributed to a Gothic revival that came to dominate church construction and heavily influenced the public architecture of Bombay. Attempts to formulate a more indigenous architectural mode that also included European inputs led by the 1860s–70s to the 'Indo-Saracenic' style, which self-consciously borrowed what its adherents viewed as 'Mughal,' or 'Rajasthani' contributions but which ultimately was a style of facades. Its features included the wide-projecting cornice (*chhajja*); the projecting balcony (*jharoka*); the pierced stone lattice-screen (*jali*); and the canopied roof turret (*chhattri*). This fashion exerted a strong influence on the palaces and offices constructed in princely states, but even there it was in decline by the early-twentieth century, giving way to Palladian or Italian Renaissance influences and then the Art Deco Movement. The steady increase in private clients after the 1850s and changing perspectives on architecture among public administrators resulted in more commissions for professional architects' firms from Britain and encouraged the growth of an independent architectural profession within South Asia that advocated a diversification and modernization of styles. By 1910 there were about a dozen practicing British firms. In 1929 the Indian Institute of Architects was formed with 158 members; it grew to 240 members by 1940 (Evenson 1989: 57–80; Metcalf 1989; Lang *et al.* 1997: 86–110, 140–5, 164–71).

Calcutta: New class formations

Personal accounts by men and women coming out from Britain to Calcutta during the early-nineteenth century tend to record a limited range of experiences: the strangeness of arrival; the round of social activities; the omnipresence of servants; and the restricted activity spaces of Europeans within the city (Thankappan Nair 1989; Chaudhuri 1990: 50–1, 123–7). Calcutta's central business district and adjacent neighborhoods to the east and south remained the arena for British-dominated administrative and commercial work and habitation where one could encounter the most pronounced cases of racial segregation. The promenades of the northern Maidan, for example, were long off-limits for natives in the early morning and evenings, allowing Europeans the illusion of freedom from association with their inferiors. The landscape painters that chose Calcutta as their subject in the early-nineteenth century often concentrated on public buildings that projected images of Company power, peopling the foreground with indigenous types in order to project authenticity, but effectively isolating British architecture and citizens from their socio-spatial matrix. This fascination with a spatial manifestation of dominance produced the Calcutta of the late-nineteenth century that functioned as the capital of the Raj: a massive array of state offices and monumental architecture projecting an imperial aloofness or racial pride funded from South Asian sources. The ultimate spatial expression of this project took shape when Lord Curzon, Viceroy of India at the height of the Raj, proposed a monument commemorating Queen Victoria after her death in 1901 to be sited in what was still the imperial capital. This led to the completion in 1921 of the Victoria Memorial, a gigantic domed museum in Romanesque style with Indo-Saracenic influences, on the Maidan south of the European-style public buildings (Chaudhuri 1990: 256–8; Farid 2001: 105–7).

In practice, from the beginning of British dominance there were varied opportunities for interaction with their subjects. Many of the homes inhabited by the British in Calcutta were rented from Indian landlords and they lay adjacent to the humble quarters of the numerous personal servants they employed and to retail establishments controlled by natives. One notes in Charles D'Oyly's 1835 painting of *A View in Clive Street* (see Figure 4) the centrality of the mounted and top-hatted European with his mounted and turbaned secretary (while a bearer follows on foot) but everyone else in the scene is a native. An accretion of thatched huts and collapsing two-storied wood-frame structures on the right, apparently serving as residential and retail sites, are juxtaposed with Greco-Roman structures in the left foreground. The painter has chosen his buildings as representatives of a passing order: the erection of thatched huts was prohibited after 1837 when almost 31,000 still existed in Calcutta; by 1850 there were none. In the background, the apparent destination of the main characters is the heart of a rising fashionable district represented by a two-storey

Figure 4 Calcutta's Clive Street, 1835. Reproduced by permission of The British Library.

commercial block (Banerjee 1987: 4; Losty 1990: 114). In such transitional zones there were many opportunities for cultural change and exchange. Interaction also occurred regularly between the British and the native elite, headed by the great houses of wealth originating in the successful brokers (*banian*) and secretaries (*dewan*) of the late-eighteenth century, along with the families supported by holdings of rural *zamindari* or urban land (Sinha 1978: 36–7, 62–94; Chaudhuri 1990: 56–61). At the office a growing number of lower- and mid-level functionaries encountered the British within racially-charged bureaucracies, where all the highest posts were denied to Indians, or within commercial environments where British firms enjoyed competitive advantages. A professional class including physicians, lawyers, and journalists provided alternative public voices in a non-European public sphere where newspapers, voluntary associations, and political organizations manifested a concern for the affairs of the city and the nation – expressed in Bengali but also in English-language forums that brought British and Indian face-to-face.

The first several generations of the great families, newly rich and conspicuous consumers, remained tied to the smaller towns of their origin where they maintained residential seats, spent much of their time and spent lavishly on religious rituals. Their children and grandchildren, dependant on rental income, often identified more closely with Calcutta as their cultural home; they gravitated toward cultural patronage and artistic production as commercial affairs fell more completely into the hands of Europeans and non-Bengali capitalists. The Thakur or Tagore family stood at the forefront of this movement, producing generations of philanthropists, artists and writes, including Rabindranath (1861–1941), winner of the Nobel Prize for literature in 1913. His Bengali poetry became iconic within a city where just over 50 percent of the population spoke Bengali as their mother tongue (Sarkar 1997: 166). As English education became the avenue for upward mobility a more sizeable middle-income grouping of bilingual professionals and government functionaries became a significant social force within Calcutta, constituting with the members of the older aristocracy and the wealthy families from the Bazaar the 'big people' (*bhadralok*) in distinction to the 'small people' (*chotolok*) who constituted the vast majority of the population. Within the Bazaar, restricted to domestic investments by British managing agencies, savvy entrepreneurial groups were prepared to allocate capital to issues of public import and for artistic production (Morris 1983: 558–9). The results included a precocious development of a nationalist critique and the nationalist struggle alongside a strengthening of religious roles in a new public sphere.

Deeply committed to the power of language and the written word, generating dozens of periodicals, encountering on a daily basis the inequities and frustrations of British imperialism and the disciplinary regime of the bureaucratic office, the middle classes became a powerful source of social and political criticism and a growing audience for cultural production. Thus it was that Calcutta witnessed not only the most precocious development of English-language competence and adoption of European styles in dress, architecture, etc. but simultaneously the growth of coffee house and book house habitats, music, drama, and literature that used the medium of the Bengali language. The Bengali novel expressed the debate lying at the heart of urban modernity concerning the nature of the autonomous subject and the relationship between an individual interiority and social norms, with its corollaries of the problematic body and the question of the nation (Chakrabarty 2000: 117–48). The neighborhood of College Street around Presidency College and the Medical College, which became part of the University of Calcutta established in 1857, became a hotbed of public dining, bilingual cultural production and political discussion.

Paradoxically, the acceleration of urban cultural production accompanied a tendency to represent a bucolic past or to associate the city with the evils of modernity (Chaudhuri 1990: 96; Sarkar 1997: 177). The attempt to reconcile what many felt to be the dichotomies of life under colonialism, the encounter between India and the West or between the traditional and the modern, coalesced with great intensity around discussions of women, ranging from women's education to their marriageable age or their ability to inherit property. Depictions of the life of the office clerk, subjected to the rigors of clock-time, racist confrontation, and limited prospects for advancement, accompanied satirical portrayals of his demanding wife who desired the material trappings of bourgeois success (Sarkar 2002: 10–37). The debates over women, which appeared in the Calcutta press and in a vast literary corpus by the mid-nineteenth century, reflected a subaltern concern to preserve inviolate a gendered sphere of private life that bore the signs of masculine power and cultural autonomy. The removal of women's issues from the emerging nationalist critique, taking place while exceptional real progress was occurring in middle-class female education and within the household, allowed the consolidation of a new patriarchy in opposition to colonialism and engaged in nation-building (Chatterjee 1997). Accompanying such debates were more assertive political behaviors, ranging from terrorism to the *svadeshi* or 'one's own country' movement, which propelled the Calcutta middle class to the leadership of the Independence struggle at the end of the nineteenth century (Sarkar 1997: 177–85). As a regional phenomenon, this movement was a strategy by the Bhadralok, earlier fixated on a 'defensive urbanism' amid an overwhelmingly agrarian environment, to extend its intellectual and organizational leadership to smaller urban sites and into the countryside (Sinha 1978: 101; Chaudhuri 1990: 40–1).

The locality or *para* in Calcutta, as in smaller towns, evolved during the early-nineteenth century into an interlocking system of densely inhabited, multi-functional neighborhoods organized around the mansions of the commercial and landed elite and the bazaars they controlled, or the city's many tanks and gardens (Islam 1980: 232–5). The 18 *paras* remained the fundamental administrative units for most of the city until the mid-nineteenth century, when they officially gave way to 31 police *thanas* and then to urban wards, but most inhabitants continued to identify themselves with a specific *para* and negotiated the city as a grouping of these neighborhoods well into the twentieth century. Within the *para*, public life evolved around religious festivals and the formal or informal meetings of men who met, often on the door stoops or in the sitting rooms at the front of private homes, to discuss public affairs and cultural issues—a form of sociability that evolved into gatherings at a 'place' (*adda*) that incubated political consciousness and Bengali intellectuality (Chakrabarty 2000: 180–213; Chattopadhyay 2005: 88–90, 182–224).

North of the Bazaar, along Chitpur Road and the new streets constructed originally under the Lottery Committee, stood the mansions of the Bengali business aristocracy, many of whom had shifted their investments toward urban land. North of this area until the limits of the city one encountered many localities named after trades as well as markets owned by Bhadralok investors (Chaudhuri 1990: 206–7). The professional and bureaucratic members of the new middle class were more likely to settle in the southern suburbs of the city like Alipore or Bhawanipur, and they became an ever more prominent force in municipal politics as cleavages appeared between their interests and those of the landlord councilors (McGuire 1983; 100–01, 108–21).

The development of a middle-class identity and political agenda took place amid omnipresent urban poverty. The city remained mostly a congeries of hutments in the 1850s housing a heterogeneous array of castes, occupations, and languages (Sinha 1978: 28, 30–1). By the 1880s approximately 400,000 persons lived within city boundaries that had not changed for decades (McGuire 1983: 7–8), faced with increasing land prices that encouraged investment in commercial properties and limited the residential land market. The majority of the population, therefore, crowded into dense slums (*basti* or *busti*) of single-story and often single-room mud or brick huts, their number increasing from 132 in 1878 to 486 in 1881, located in the northern and central wards and in high-growth suburbs. Health and sanitary conditions were horrific as British domination of municipal administration consistently under-funded infrastructure investment outside the city's center. The death rate for the general population was more than twice that of the British and child mortality exceeded 46 percent (McGuire 1983: 8–10; Chaudhuri 1990: 218). These crowded conditions occurred within an urban fabric that in 1911, when Calcutta as imperial capital was the most significant urban site in South Asia, was still a relatively compact city.

Against this already complicated colonial class background, during the late-nineteenth century Calcutta witnessed the emergence of an industrial proletariat along with the birth of a new, factory-based jute industry. Although jute items supplied by artisan production had long been present in the Ganga River basin for a variety of purposes, Scottish merchants from Dundee created between 1840 and 1870 an international market for machine-woven jute products used mostly in the transport sector. Dundee stood at the apex of an extensive production, procurement, baling and shipping business based in Calcutta. The first attempt to establish production facilities in Calcutta – which would benefit from low shipping costs and cheap labor – occurred in 1855, which stimulated other factories, leading to a penetration of international markets by the 1870s. Calcutta inexorably became the production and trading center for almost the entire industry. Jute's role in the Raj export portfolio peaked in 1927–8 when raw and processed jute constituted 26.39 percent of exports, followed by cotton at 17.81 percent. The work force in Calcutta's jute factories peaked in 1929 at 339,665 (Morris 1983: 566–72; Chakrabarty 1989: 10, 107; Gordon 1998b: 12).

Calcutta's mills lay within a 100-mile corridor along the Bhagirathi/Ganga River, radically altering the demography of older settlements such as Serampore that became satellites of an emerging Calcutta conurbation. New jute mill towns became cores around which suburban Calcutta could expand (Ray 1974; Banerjee 1987: 72–80). In the early stages of the industry's growth, when the majority of the workers were Bengali-speakers, they sought housing in villages surrounding the mills. Companies eventually provided housing to about 30 percent of the workforce in 'labor lines' where thousands of employees lived in rows of houses constructed back-to-back with no windows, each consisting of a single small room, perhaps with a small verandah and small space for cooking. The larger percentage of jute workers lived in temporary lines or slums (*basti*) where homes were constructed of mud, clay, or sacks, separated from each other by narrow lanes, often inhabited by shifts of employees whose off-time social life occurred in male-only clubs, tea and liquor shops (Das Gupta 1994: 8, 342–4; Fernandes 1997: 61, 111–19).

A big shift in the demographics of mill labor occurred between 1890 and 1910 when non-Bengali migrants began to outnumber employees from the immediate region. At the industry's high point in the 1920s the labor force was only 17 percent Bengali-speaking with most workers coming from the impoverished peasantry of the Varanasi-Patna region and from Cuttack and Balasore districts in Orissa – a clear indication that proximate urban centers were unable to absorb excess labor amid a collapse of their old textile industries. The workers in the Calcutta mills thereafter displayed a high degree of mobility between village homes and factory sites, articulating the rural and urban economies within a multi-regional economic space (Das Gupta 1994: 15, 79–89, 123, 223–42).

Factory foremen (*sardar*) enforced discipline within the jute factory and perpetuated patterns of patrilineal re-recruitment for a largely semi-migrant workforce. The best-paid jobs, such as spinning and weaving, were excluded from women who in the 1890s constituted between 17 and 20 percent of employees. High production volumes during First World War led to massive increases in total employees and also women, but during the 1920s and 1930s laws excluding long hours and night shifts for women, automation innovations and management attempts to keep labor costs down (which resulted in the elimination of low-skilled jobs allocated to women) resulted in a steady decline in the female workforce. In 1944 there were 110 jute factories in Bengal employing 231,121 men and 36,005 women (13.5 percent). While middle-class reformers and government agencies rationalized this trend as a positive relegation of women to child-rearing and housework, female workers participated in militant action culminating in general strikes in 1929 and 1937 (Chakrabarty 1989: 7, 118–20, 187–9, 216–17; Das Gupta 1994: 424–82; Fernandes 1997: 66–71; Gordon 1998b: 46; Sen 1999).

Initial investment in Calcutta's jute factories was an exclusively European activity, and the management staff was exclusively European, mostly Scotsmen. Only in 1918–19 did G. D. Birla and Sarupchand Hukumchand (the latter a major force in the industrial expansion of Indore) found the first Indian-owned jute mills in Calcutta, spearheading an influx of Marwari capital that began to transform the jute industry. Indian owned and managed firms grew to constitute 15 percent of looms at the beginning of Second World War (Timberg 1978: 65, 170–1, 215–17; Morris 1983: 615). Elements of the Bengali Bhadralok, who may have benefited as stockholders in these enterprises, did not fill managerial positions and thus exerted minimal influence over the direction of Calcutta's largest private firms or the disposition of their profits. This exclusion reflected a more general eclipse of Calcutta's older commercial groups by Marwaris, who after the 1860s replaced Bengalis and then north Indian Khatris in Calcutta's Great Bazaar, occupied positions as guaranteed brokers to European firms, and captured the trade of Calcutta's hinterland by 1920s–30s (Timberg 1978: 148–51; Chaudhuri 1990: 42–3, 205, 221; Gordon 1998b: 26, 234). Thus it was that the Bengali-speaking middle class, increasingly isolated from the commercial economy, remained peripheral in the creation of the industrial sector while the Bengali-speaking working class became excluded from the largest sources of industrial employment. Confronting the full force of European political and economic domination, Calcutta's nationalist politicians were 'the prophets rather than the agents of native capitalism' (Ray 1979: 35).

Calcutta's Bengali-speaking middle classes were among the most urbane in South Asia, with relatively high rates of female literacy, and its English-medium university system produced men and women who occupied the front ranks of the scientific, artistic, and political communities. They existed, however, amid a growing sense of crisis. The transfer of the capital from Calcutta to New Delhi after 1911 (see below) resulted in a decline of bureaucratic employment and a reduction of the city to a provincial administrative center where manufacturing growth peaked about a decade later. Elements of the Bhadralok who relied on landholdings in East Bengal, cultivated in large part by an impoverished Muslim peasantry, were finding their position increasingly insecure as Independence approached and Dhaka emerged as an alternative administrative node. The wealthiest entrepreneurial groups in the city were now Marwaris, viewed by many Bengali-speakers as outsiders, who self-consciously cultivated a Rajasthani, Hindu cultural heritage and who were engaging in a self-critique of culture and gender roles only after the 1920s – decades after the Bengali Bhadralok (Hardgrove 2004: 181–246). Connections between the non-Bengali business groups and the Bhadralok on one hand and with the leadership of the city's Muslim community (who in 1932 constituted 18.5 percent of the population) on the other were becoming more tenuous as the Muslim League attracted ever greater support. Under these circumstances, while a majority of the Bengali-speaking middle classes and progressive elements of the Marwari community supported the nationalist aims of the Indian National Congress, important elements of unemployable middle-class youth came to support alternative political goals ranging from the militaristic anti-colonialism of Subhash Chandra Bose to the Communist Party of India (founded 1927). Distinct cleavages existed, therefore, among the indigenous leadership of the city and the province, while the vast majority of the city's population remained in dire poverty and engaged in lower-level service occupations. Then came the disasters of the 1940s: Second World War, the Bengal Famine, the post-war communal orgy of the Calcutta killings, and Partition. The Calcutta middle classes never recovered their pan-regional leadership position (Ray 1979: 167p1226; Chaudhuri 1990: 44, 75, 216).

The men of steel and the 'tribals'

The rapidly changing character of the industrial and entrepreneurial landscape during the early-twentieth century is exemplified in the development of a modern iron and steel industry in relatively close proximity to Calcutta.

British and Indian entrepreneurs by the late-eighteenth century were aware of extensive coal deposits in a belt stretching more than 400 kilometers from the western hills of Bengal through the Chota Nagpur plateau in southern Bihar. The eastern section of these deposits became more accessible through the Bengal Presidency's re-routing of the Grand Trunk Road through Asansol instead of its older path along the Ganga River (Deloche 1993: 40–4). The first organized exploitation of coal mines in the Asansol area took place by 1820, which prompted the laying of a rail link in 1855. By the late-nineteenth century a series of coal mines were operational in western Bengal, supplying a market originally controlled by European and Bengali capitalists but increasingly penetrated by Marwaris. Surveys discovered additional mineral resources awaiting exploitation in the Chota Nagpur plateau including iron ore in a belt lying about 150 kilometers south of the coal belt and limestone deposits slightly farther to the west. These resources remained generally untapped in this non-urbanized region (Johnson 1966: 8–11). Almost all iron and steel used for industrial purposes within the British Raj was still imported, mostly from sources in Great Britain. Although Calcutta was the main market for the trade and consumption of iron and steel, it fell to capitalists from Bombay, not Calcutta, to begin an industrial revolution utilizing this mineral wealth.

In 1902 Jamshetji Nusserwanji Tata (1839–1904) visited the United States and Europe in order to gain an international understanding of the iron and steel industry. After his death his sons continued his efforts and registered the Tata Iron and Steel Company (TISCO) in Bombay in 1907. After an exhaustive survey to determine the optimal location of a plant in relation to raw materials, transportation and markets they signed a lease in 1908 on land located in the village of Sakchi, southeast of the intersection of the Subarnarekha and Kharkai Rivers, about 225 kilometers west of Calcutta. The factory's foundation was laid the following year and in 1910 a dam with pump house was delivering 1 million gallons per day. The population in 1911 was 5,672 with 75 percent immigrants and the remainder low-skilled laborers from the 'tribal' populations already living in villages around the factory. Rapid expansion of production and employment occurred during First World War, pushing the number of employees in 1921 to 25,669. Acknowledging the success of the endeavor, the Viceroy personally named the growing town Jamshedpur; the rail station and rail workshops on the line serving the settlement, located south of the plant, became known as Tatanagar. The steel industry went through tough times during the 1920s and the Great Depression but nonetheless the Tatas moved forward on a Greater Extensions scheme for expanding and modernizing production and for achieving vertical integration in the procurement of raw materials. The 1930s brought greater prosperity and protective tariffs, allowing the Jamshedpur plant to supply 75 percent of the country's demand.

The agglomeration of subsidiary industries took place in and around the village of Golmuri on the east. The disruption of tinplate supplies from Wales during First World War stimulated a British firm to set up a plant, which was the precursor of The Tinplate Company of India Ltd. (TCIL) established in 1920 as a joint venture of the Tatas and Burma Oil Company; production began two years later using imported Malayan tin. At the same time initiatives began for the establishment of the Indian Cable Company (Incab); Indian Steel and Wire Products Ltd. (ISWP); and the Jamshedpur Engineering and Machine Manufacturing Company Pvt. Ltd. (Jemco), which benefited from tariff protection to achieve a solid footing in the mid-1930s. Tata Pigments Ltd., a wholly owned subsidiary of Tata Steel set up in 1927, eventually became one of the largest synthetic iron oxide producing plants in India. These plants contributed to the agglomeration effect by attracting a variety of smaller engineering and construction firms that helped spur Jamshedpur's population growth from 84,000 in 1931 to 149,000 in 1941. Second World War then stimulated further expansion. In 1946 the Tata Engineering and Locomotive Company (TELCO) absorbed the railway workshops farther to the southeast and shifted production into automobiles, steam rollers, paper-pulp machinery and excavators. The National Metallurgical Laboratory (NML) began at the same time with support from Jamshedpur firms as the third in the Council of Scientific & Industrial Research (CSIR) grouping of research institutes. The number of workers employed by TISCO alone peaked before 1947 at 32,000 (Morris 1983: 652).

Within this company town, TISCO took responsibility for providing infrastructural needs for the population. The administration of the city between 1921 and 1923 fell under a Board of Works consisting of six representatives of the company and three representatives from subsidiary industries. In 1924 the Jamshedpur Notified Area Committee was formed which administered the city in cooperation with TISCO. From the beginning housing was a problem that the companies were willing to address only partially. Segregation by employment category, which was usually a racial/caste category as well, was the norm. The original technical management team came from the United States and Europe and lived on the northern side of the town in bungalows with infrastructural amenities amid a grid pattern of streets, in dramatic contrast to the mass of semi-skilled or unskilled laborers who lived in *bastis* comprised of single-room mud huts that they often constructed themselves because the company provided no facilities for them. Low-caste and tribal populations were disproportionately concentrated in these slums. During the growth of subsidiary industries in Golmuri, their uncertain fate meant that these plants initially provided few housing facilities for their lower-level workers, and only by the late 1930s and 1940s were they establishing 'colonies' or dormitories of single-room or two-room homes for these employees. Lateral sprawl characterized the entire city (Dutta 1977).

The problems of providing a livable environment for a workforce that was becoming less transient prompted the commissioning of a development plan for this New Town under the direction of Otto H. Koenigsberger, who had already done work on the iron-and-steel town of Bhadravati established in 1923 by the Government of Mysore, which was leading the way in state economic planning. Koenigsberger by training represented the Modern Movement in architecture and urban planning, altered through the encounter with South Asian realities and responding to the earlier Indian work (1914–23) of Patrick Geddes, who advocated the 'diagnostic survey' leading to 'folk planning' (Tyrwhitt 1947; Boardman 1978). Koenigsberger viewed low-density, ground-level housing within compounds that allowed for expansion and outdoor activities as the housing solution best suited to create 'village-like' neighborhood units that would allow walking access to daily amenities. These neighborhood units would be strung, as a chain or 'band-town', along arteries of motorized transport enabling short trips to the workplace. His concepts, aiming at the application of universal aesthetic or scientific designs in order to build a multi-ethnic socialist urbanism, intersected with the vision of J. R. D. Tata (1904–93), who viewed Jamshedpur as an experiment in the creation of a Garden City. Thus it was that Jamshedpur, despite the unpalatable realities of slum proliferation and recurrent labor unrest, became an important site for the application of transnational theorization that would exert a major impact on post-Independence urban planning (Koenigsberger 1952: 105–14; Kalia 1994: 126–36; Liscombe 2006).

Punjab: Regional colonial planning and urban development

Punjab, the last region in South Asia to submit to British control, experienced the long rule of Ranjit Singh, who welded the variety of Sikh confederations and Kashmir into a single state. The urban systems within this state included 100 towns with major markets serving as nodal points for thousands of villages with small markets dominated by sub-regional configurations of Khatri, Arora, Khoja, Pracha, Jain and Agarwal Bania merchants. Colonial policies and commercial groups in Punjab, which after the British conquest in the 1840s included a vast expanse that encompassed Attock, Multan, Delhi and Simla, stimulated a number of ambitious strategies for urban growth that resulted in a dramatic rise in the centrality of older capitals as well as multiple lower-level sites. Rawalpindi, for example, grew from 16,000 persons in 1855 to 88,000 at the end of the century; Multan grew from 25,000 to 87,000; Sialkot from 19,000 to 58,000; Jalandhar from 28,500 to 68,000; and Ambala from 22,000 to 79,000 (Grewal 1984). In considering the several urban trajectories of this province, we may differentiate its eastern part, organized around the cities of Lahore and Amritsar, from its western part, stretching north from Multan.

Eastern Punjab, which under the British included a number of princely states based in seats such as Patiala, had enjoyed a long history of urban development resting on trans-regional trade and an agrarian economy primarily based on non-irrigated cultivation. The old Mughal capital of Lahore, which after 1799 had been the seat of Ranjit Singh's empire, remained the administrative center of the entire province and it experienced another period of preeminence as a bureaucratic and educational hub, witnessing the foundation of Punjab University in 1882. By the end of the century, the city had over fifty printing presses, while 40 newspapers and 20 periodicals were published there (Grewal 1997: 448–50). Its population rose from about 94,000 in 1855 to 672,000 in 1941, when it was South Asia's fifth largest city after Calcutta, Bombay, Madras and Hyderabad.

Less than 60 kilometers to the east Amritsar had served as Punjab's ritual center and second capital under Ranjit Singh. It was the last of the great Mughal-style cities fortified under him and also endowed with the Gobindgarh Fort on its west along with the Rambagh Garden on its north. Amritsar was also a major manufacturing base for artisan goods and for textiles including shawls, with a population of about 112,186 in 1855. Under the Raj expansion occurred mostly in the north outside the city walls, around the Grand Trunk Road and railroad, and around the European Civil Station and a Model Town inhabited by middle-class citizens who relocated there after the 1920s. While its role as a pilgrimage destination (See Chapter Two) continued to grow the city's industrial and commercial economy retained its vitality in sub-regional trade and artisan production (as Punjab's top silk manufacturing center). Its wheat futures market became the largest in South Asia. The number of factories registered in Amritsar rose from 9 in 1901 to 366 in 1945, when it was South Asia's ninth largest city with a population was almost 400,000 (Gauba 1988).

In the western parts of Punjab agricultural communities had long existed close to the rivers, where irrigation was possible, and towns such as Gujrat had thrived along the Grand Trunk Road and other trade routes (Rehman and Wescoate 1993). But extensive upland tracts between the rivers experienced insufficient rainfall for permanent cultivation and remained the sphere of semi-nomadic animal husbandry. In 1885 the government initiated a massive program of canal construction that brought river water to these tracts and enabled their conversion to nine 'canal colonies' that increased the irrigated acreage of Punjab from 3 million to 5.7 million hectares and stimulated a large demographic shift from the eastern districts of the province. Exports of wheat from Punjab rose from 250,000 tons in the early 1890s to 561,000 tons in 1922 (Darling 1947: 114), much of it coming from the new colonies and heading toward Karachi on an expanded provincial road network (1,073 miles in 1873, 4,500 miles in 1934) and a rail network that began in the 1860s, linked to Karachi in 1878, and totaled over 6,000 miles in 1939 (Grewal 1997: 446). The most important nodes in the transport network of western Punjab consisted of some older settlements such as Sargodha that underwent a radical transformation under state planning alongside a series of completely new or model towns. The government auctioned residential plots and sites for shops, warehouses and factories that were purchased by entrepreneurs for investment and rental purposes or acquired directly by mercantile castes that came to dominate trade in agricultural produce and money lending business. In the larger canal colony towns, sites of between 1.3 and 1.6 hectares were alienated to members of commercial groups who set up saw and four mills and factories for ginning, soap, ice and bricks (Beazley and Puckle 1926: 255–62; Ali 1988: 89–91). The towns grew quickly, in some cases registering rates as high as 3,000 percent by the 1940s. They contributed to an increase of the urban population in Punjab from 10 to 14 percent of total population between 1881 and 1941 (Grewal 1997: 441–2).

The plan of Chichawatni exemplifies the planning ideals implemented in the new city of the canal colonies, with a rigid quadrilateral pattern of residential blocks and commercial establishments flanked by rail and road links and an industrial zone (see Map 13). The conservative social agenda of the British is manifest in the peripheral locations of separate habitation areas for 'untouchable' groups such as sweepers and leather workers, a peripheral location for the washermen's work area (*dhobi ghat*), and a separate (boys') school and girls' school. Arrangements for what the British viewed as the three main religious groups included sites for

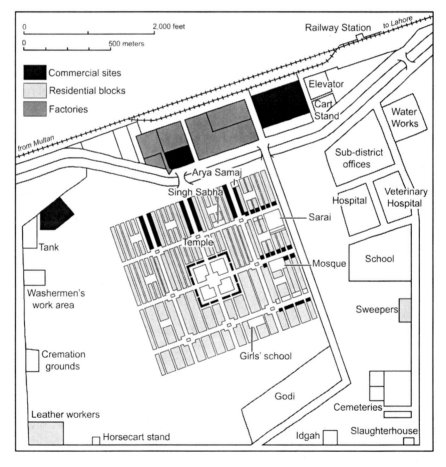

Map 13 Original plan of Chichawatni, a canal colony. Adapted from Beazley and Puckle 1926: 808, Appendix 9b, Appendix 10b.

a mosque, a Hindu temple, and centers for the 'reformist' Hindu organization of the Arya Samaj and also the (Sikh) Singh Sabha. Population of this successful planning initiative rose to ca. 91,000 by 2005.

The most successful of the canal colony towns was Lyallpur, founded in the 1890s and named after the incumbent Lieutenant Governor of Punjab, Charles James Lyall. It lay at the heart of the Chenab Colony, the largest project with an allotted area of over 800,000 hectares, between the Chenab and Ravi Rivers. Its business center encompassed 44.5 hectares organized around a central plaza in an unusual circular pattern. A clock tower, erected at the center of the main plaza through contributions by local notables, became the symbol of the township. Eight roads radiated from the tower through eight bazaars, housing wholesale and retail markets, that became surrounded by residential neighborhoods. The radiating roads intersected an outer road that encircled the perimeter of the settlement. The population exceeded 4,000 in 1902, and the following year the government established Punjab Agricultural College (later the University of Agriculture, Pakistan). In 1904 Lyallpur became a separate district and the city became its seat. The population in 1931 was 43,000, and by 1941 had grown to 70,000. Because the city lay within an emerging belt of cotton fields and supported cotton ginning plants and agricultural marketing institutions, Lyallpur Cotton Mills and 63 additional manufacturing units located there by the late 1940s (Waseem 1990: 208–10).

On the eastern edge of Punjab, Delhi, reduced to the level of a secondary center during the late eighteenth century, began its rise again during the nineteenth. In 1803, the British occupied the city and reduced the Mughal Emperor, Shah Alam II, to the position of a pensioner of the East India Company. Unlike the situation in the Presidency capitals, originally there was relatively little spatial segregation after the British took control; European troops occupied areas south of the Red Fort in the Daryaganj area and north of the Red Fort just inside the Kashmiri Gate, where a Resident was located in a palace modified according to neoclassical style with pillared portico (see Map 8). In order to supply water for the city and European functionaries alike, the canal system, last renovated under Shah Jahan, was refurbished during the 1820s. As the security situation outside the walls improved the British shifted the Cantonment in 1828 to a new site just beyond the Ridge lying about 3.5 kilometers west and north of the city walls (see Map 14). Here troops were billeted in huts or tents laid out in symmetrical lines near gardens, a racecourse, practice grounds for field battery and rifle, and a new Residency. The territory between the ridge and the north wall of the city began evolving into new Civil Lines. Meanwhile, within the city a new St. James Church (constructed 1829–36) rose inside the Kashmiri Gate for the use of the European community, and Delhi College (originating in the 1820s) developed a curriculum that combined 'Oriental' languages and literature with European mathematics and technical training – the heart of a 'Delhi Renaissance' that attracted support from colonial and Mughal elites. Following the conquest of Punjab, Delhi was transformed into a logistical center connecting territories in the northwest with older conquests along the Yamuna-Ganga Rivers. A detailed

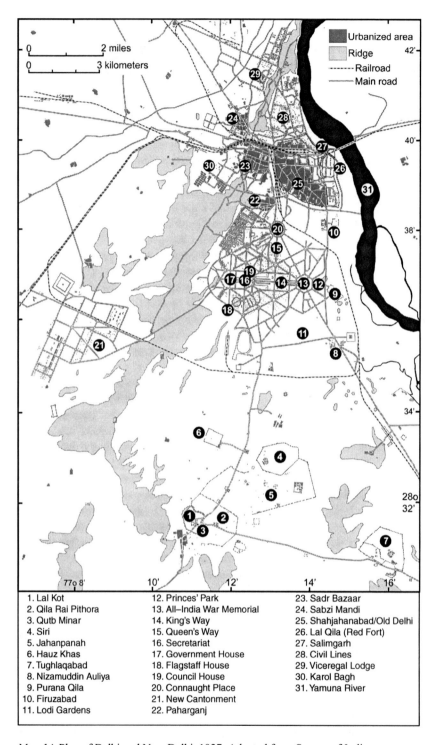

Urbanized area
Ridge
Railroad
Main road

1. Lal Kot
2. Qila Rai Pithora
3. Qutb Minar
4. Siri
5. Jahanpanah
6. Hauz Khas
7. Tughlaqabad
8. Nizamuddin Auliya
9. Purana Qila
10. Firuzabad
11. Lodi Gardens
12. Princes' Park
13. All–India War Memorial
14. King's Way
15. Queen's Way
16. Secretariat
17. Government House
18. Flagstaff House
19. Council House
20. Connaught Place
21. New Cantonment
22. Paharganj
23. Sadr Bazaar
24. Sabzi Mandi
25. Shahjahanabad/Old Delhi
26. Lal Qila (Red Fort)
27. Salimgarh
28. Civil Lines
29. Viceregal Lodge
30. Karol Bagh
31. Yamuna River

Map 14 Plan of Delhi and New Delhi, 1927. Adapted from Survey of India map.

census in 1833 indicated that there were 119,860 people in the city excluding the palace; a census in 1853 recorded a population of 151,000 (King 1976: 189–94; Gupta 1981: 4–16).

The Sepoy Mutiny or War of Independence of 1857 led to disaster for Delhi. Rebellious soldiers took control of the Red Fort in May, elevated the elderly Emperor Bahadur Shah II (1775–1862) to leadership of an anti-British coalition, and killed Europeans. Having lost control of the situation within Delhi the British fell back to positions along the Ridge and repelled assaults while slowly building up resources for a counterattack. When British forces recaptured the city in September, they launched an orgy of pillaging and recriminatory killing, followed by abolition of the Mughal dynasty the following year (Kaul 1985: 393–409). Major confiscations of property followed. Thousands fled the city, and the population was still only 141,709 in 1863. The British occupied the Red Fort, where they demolished many buildings, and appropriated the eastern third of the city for their Cantonment, now moved for security reasons within a walled environment; they demolished all buildings in an esplanade stretching about 425 meters around the Red Fort and 500 meters beyond the city walls. Many shopkeepers dislocated by these demolitions moved outside the western wall of the city, where they could obtain cheap alternative sites, initiating a new phase of suburbanization. The post-revolt decades witnessed the subdivision and sale of remaining mansions (*haveli*) in the old city and their transformation into multiple-unit apartments or single-courtyard units more appropriate for families drawing their support from small businesses and employment within the new British administration. The withdrawal of civil offices north of the city walls announced that overt spatial and social segregation had descended upon the ruined capital (Evenson 1989: 98–104; Hosagrahar 2005: 15–50).

The logistical advantages of Delhi within the emerging network of colonial urbanization led the city to rebound during the late-nineteenth century. In 1867, when water once again began running through the canal system, the first railway line came across the river and through the former Salimgarh Fort and then ran directly west through the wall north of the Kabul Gate. Corollary development of the castellated rail station, the parallel Queens Road south of the tracks, and Hamilton Road north of the tracks dislocated thousands of inhabitants, who crowded into the residential areas of the old city or relocated to the suburbs of Sadr Bazaar west of the city, Sabzi Mandi (the Vegetable Market) to the northwest, and Paharganj to the southwest (see Map 14). A new Delhi-to-Bombay rail link opened in 1872, the Delhi-Kalka-Ambala line began in 1890 and the link to Agra opened in 1906, making Delhi the largest railway junction in South Asia. These lines formed a major intersection within a gap in the ridge that divided the new western suburbs, and also ran down the esplanade along the west wall of the old city; this resulted in the increasing isolation of the remnants of Shahjahanabad pinned by the Cantonment in the east, the Civil Lines in the north, and the railroad in the west. The enhanced transportation system contributed, however, to the commercial importance of Delhi which became the leading market for Punjab and a major center for the distribution of English goods. Macadamized roads, adjuncts to the railroads, linked the city to a hinterland including Gurgaon in the south, Rohtak in the west, Karnal in the north, and Mathura in the east (Gupta 1986). The commerce of the city also began to attract an industrial presence through the foundation of a first textile factory in 1889; within two decades there were 2,500 textile workers employed in 20 factories. In 1884 the walled city's population was 127,711, and suburban population had risen to 61,937. By 1911, after the Cantonment moved again to an extensive site north of the Ridge, Delhi Municipality had a population of 232,837 (King 1976 213–30; Evenson 1989: 97–102; Gupta 1981: 45, 62–3, 161; Hosagrahar 2005: 115–42).

At a coronation audience (*durbar* or *darbar*) at Delhi that brought together 100,000 persons including all leading administrators and princes of the British Raj, King George V announced in 1911 that the Government of India intended to shift its capital from Calcutta to Delhi. The following year a Delhi Town Planning Committee consisting of British appointees began the work of choosing a site and general plan for a new administrative district. The committee originally considered an amplification of the civil lines to the north but eventually recommended an ambitious plan to develop a huge site to the south that would be surrounded by the monuments of Delhi's past. The committee was concerned less with indigenous models than with projections of geometric symmetry characteristic of sites in Europe and its colonies. The committee's final design visualized an axis pointing southwest from the Ajmeri Gate of the old city (with a line of sight to the Friday Mosque) to a shopping center consisting of concentric circles that would become Connaught Place with its colonnaded walkway facades and Palladian archways. Among the eight roads radiating from this circus the principle two – one called Queen's Way (later Janpath) heading due south and the other continuing southwest – would intersect the second main feature of the plan: an east-west axis called King's Way (later Rajpath) featuring the main government buildings. Throughout New Delhi, a series of traffic circles and radial roads would form a pattern of equilateral triangles and hexagrams (see Map 14).

British architect Edwin Lutyens, who was been a driving force in the Town Planning Committee, obtained the contract for design of the Viceroy's palace, or Government House (later Rashtrapati Bhavan), at the western end of King's Way on the eminence called Raisina Hill. As the main structure in New Delhi the Viceroy's four-winged palace, with massive pillared portico and central dome surmounting a Durbar Hall, reflected British faith in its own autocracy and culture. Concessions to the Indo-Saracenic included an abbreviated cornice and abstract roof turrets, plus a stylized railing around the central dome reminiscent of an ancient stupa complex; an extensive Persian/Mughal-style garden adorned the western side of Government House. Lutyens also designed the All-India War Memorial (later India Gate) that emulated ancient Roman arches and the Arc de Triomphe in Paris. Concentric mansions for the princely states were originally projected to surround this Memorial; eventually only five, headed by the houses of Hyderabad and Baroda, were constructed. Lutyens arranged an appointment for Herbert Baker as the architect for two Secretariat blocks that flanked King's Way, where the architect indulged his interest in Palladian influences that he had recently expressed in the Union Buildings of Pretoria, South Africa. After the passage of the Montague-Chelmsford Reforms in 1919 created provisions for the Council of State, Chamber of Princes, and Legislative Assembly, Baker also designed at the end of the main corridor coming from Connaught Place, just northeast of the Secretariat, a circular, pillared structure with three chambers called Council House (later Parliament House or Sansad Bhavan). Robert Tor Russell, Chief Architect for the Government of India, contributed in addition to Connaught Place 4,000 bungalows of varying size that connoted their occupants' ranks within the British administrative hierarchy headed by the residence of the Commander-in-Chief called Flagstaff House, later called Teen Murti Bhavan after the statues of three soldiers on the grounds, and more recently the Nehru Memorial Museum (Irving 1981; Volwahsen 2002).

Growth in the capital, which led to a population within the Delhi area of 696,000 urban and 222,000 rural inhabitants by 1941, increasingly took place outside the old city and in suburbs such as Karol Bagh (Buch 1987: 48–9). The area north of Shahjahanabad, which had served as the temporary location for government offices, became available for a variety of public institutions. In 1933, for example, legislation allowed the transfer of the old Viceregal Lodge grounds to the newly founded University of Delhi (Basu 1986). The Delhi Improvement Trust established in 1936 implemented a series of 'scientific' principles in maximizing tax returns and in the elimination of what it viewed as the overcrowding within the old city and its western extensions. It created new upper-class housing consisting of three-story townhouses on blocks with orthogonal streets in Daryaganj South and redeveloped the Faiz Bazaar commercial street; set up the Sabzi Mandi Vegetable and Fruit Market; and initiated an industrial estate to the west that would re-house many small and medium scale businesses. It also created a scheme for the elimination of what it termed slum housing and the razing of the old city wall around the Ajmeri Gate, and the construction of 'modern' residential blocks and open spaces fronting New Delhi (Hosagrahar 2005; 149–80). The often successful resistance of the residents of the old city to the implementation of municipal regulations and the schemes of the trust accentuated the relative isolation and crowded conditions there; the inability of the trust's schemes to provide housing and infrastructure needs of thousands of poor migrants squatting on the outskirts of the city presaged the post-Independence planning conundrums of the capital.

Bombay: *Urbs prima*

In Bombay we encounter a long tradition of planning motivated by the exigencies of an island location that experienced the most massive commercialization and industrialization within the subcontinent (see Map 15).

Bombay's planning issues came to a fore in 1803, when a great fire in the fort prompted the British to force more native inhabitants to reside outside its walls, stimulating the rapid growth of the entire settlement to the north of the fort. One year later, the British expanded the limits of the Esplanade to 800 and then

1,000 yards, thus accentuating the socio-spatial segregation of the administrative and business district from the native city and reinforcing settlement toward the north. A booming export economy, led initially by trade with China in cotton and opium, stimulated rapid population increase to 566,119 in 1846 and 773,196 by 1881 (Chandavarkar 1994: 30, 54–5). The economic opportunities presented by Bombay attracted immigrants from every region of South Asia and indeed all of Asia but at the top of the social hierarchy stood a small group of successful merchant families, mostly of Gujarati origin, who made their fortunes through cooperation with the trading activities of the Company and, after 1813, with European trading interests while investing in their own shipping, financial, and urban real estate enterprises. This class of entrepreneurs, collectively known as the *shetias*, maintained mansions mostly in the fort until the mid-nineteenth century although some constructed castle-like palaces elsewhere on the island (Dobbin 1972: 1–26). Most people lived within distinct neighborhoods of the native city that developed cohesive identities through shared caste, sect, religion, occupational specialization, place of origin outside the city, or language-although a complete monopoly of any neighborhood by a single group was never achieved. Close to the Esplanade native houses reached five to six stories with the ground floors allocated for shops and the upper floors used as residences characterized by distinctive overhanging balconies, often with screens, of finely wrought woodwork. In the more peripheral sections of the native town that stood on converted orchard land the more common building style was the two- to three-storied *wadi*, built around a central courtyard, and inhabited typically by an extended kinship group or sub-caste (Kosambi 1986: 45–6; Masselos 1991).

    After 1845 the infrastructural needs of this vast and varied population became the concern of a Board of Conservancy that attempted to deal with municipal administration and security while extracting limited revenues from native *rentier* and commercial groups who resisted all moves to increase taxation without representative government. The problems faced by the Board were acute. Water was still available only from tanks and private wells, which dried up during years of poor rain, while sewage mostly flowed into the main town drain which was simply a large ditch, formerly a tidal creek, which simply collected effluents without flowing anywhere. Some of the solutions implemented – over the protests of rate payers – augmented the government's role in the development of infrastructure. For example, in 1860 the state implemented a scheme for bringing piped water from an artificial lake created through a dam across the Vihar Valley on Salsette Island (see Map 19). This was a new level of public involvement in water provision that established the template for subsequent schemes in Bombay (Tulsi Lake in 1872, Powai Lake in 1890) and throughout the subcontinent. Other solutions, however, involved interactions with private firms, primarily in land reclamation. During the 1860s the Elphinstone Land and Press Company arranged with the government for the implementation of the Mody Bay Reclamation Scheme that created an estate of 276 acres on the eastern side of the island with provision of land for the neo-Gothic Victoria Terminus of the Great Indian Peninsula Railway (opened in 1882). Other public-private partnerships resulted in reclamations that extended the entire shoreline from Apollo Bunder to Mazagaon. An ambitious plan by the Back Bay Reclamation Company to reclaim the entire western foreshore collapsed during an economic crash after 1865, but added 24 acres and 2,400 square yards on the western side of the island with provision for a right-of-way for the Bombay Baroda and Central India Railway to the cotton depots on Colaba (opened 1899) (MCGB 1964: 94–6; Dossal 1991: 95–120, 50–63, 184–5).

The reclamation projects coincided with an industrial revolution resting on the growth of a textile sector and the development of an industrial proletariat. This story emerged from Bombay's position as the leading site for South Asian cotton exports (92 percent in 1860). Lancashire merchants, who hitherto had viewed the Indian market as a supplement to North American supplies, experienced a sudden cessation of supplies during the American Civil War and turned to Bombay for the coordination of a massive increase in cotton exports aided by the opening of the rail link through the Bhor Pass. The five-year cotton boom brought in 81 million pounds sterling to Bombay. But already the establishment of the Bombay Spinning and Weaving Company in 1854, followed by 12 additional mills by 1870, signaled the first major shift in the city's economy from a strictly import-export economy and toward a factory-based manufacturing sector. Bhatia and Parsi family firms, squeezed by European agency houses in the cotton export business and benefiting from technical experience accumulated earlier in the shipbuilding business, were redirecting mercantile capital toward industrial production. The crash at the end of the Civil War only temporarily dampened interest in industrial investment, and in 1874–5 alone 12 new mills opened (Guha 1984; Dwivedi and Mehrotra 2001: 88–90). Investment opportunities stimulated a massive influx of capital to Bombay (87 percent of Indian capital investment in 1914). The scale of Bombay's textile industry dwarfed developments in other South Asian cities where indigenous capital was mobilized for textile-based industrialization. In Ahmedabad, for example, where native entrepreneurs created a textile industry that underlay the city's growth to the sixth largest in South Asia, there were 49 mills working in 1914 compared to 85 in Bombay. Only after the boom during First World War did the expansion of Bombay's cotton textile industry end while the industry diversified spatially in South Asia, with Bombay's share of mill capacity declining from 31.4 percent in 1913–14 to 17.5 percent in 1938–9 (Gillion 1968: 96–104; Morris 1983: 575–6, 618, 661; Chandavarkar 1994: 23–6, 65–8, 78).

The Bombay mills came up on the city limits and their spatial pattern indicates the rough extent of the built-up area during the late-nineteenth century (see Map 15). The new industrial working class had to find accommodations within municipal wards including, and north of, Mazagaon, Byculla and Mahalakshmi. To house this burgeoning workforce (totaling about 140,000 in the early 1930s) property owners constructed the *chawl* or *chaul* (Marathi *chal*), a term literally connoting a corridor but in this context referring to a row of small, single-room apartments along a continuous passageway or verandah. Stacked in multiple stories as a narrow block which could contain 300 to 400 rooms (typically occupied by 5 to 10 persons each) such housing was multiplied to create high-density neighborhoods in proximity to mill districts or transportation hubs. Its typically male inhabitants

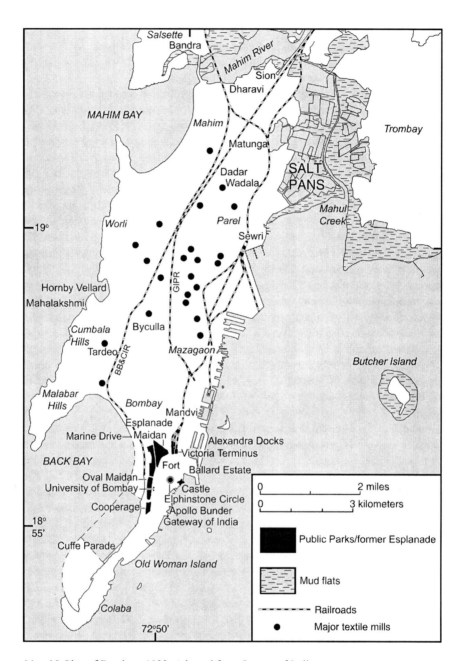

Map 15 Plan of Bombay, 1933. Adapted from Survey of India map.

shared water and sanitary facilities in environments that often degenerated into industrial slums within an island land market that made home purchase impossible for the workers and rewarded low construction quality. The Bombay Development Department established three- or four-story chawls in Worli, and the Bombay Improvement Trust built chawls closer to the docks for its workers and for municipal employees. In the outlying wards of Mahim, Worli and Sion large numbers of poor workers also set up makeshift neighborhoods of huts or sheds. The 1931 census counted approximately 250,000 tenements in the city, 80 percent of them consisting of one room, with an average of 4.4 persons living in them (Harris 1978: 11; Evenson 1989: 139–42; Lang *et al.* 1997: 111–13; Sharma 2000: 9).

Social organization at the factory became the sphere of intensive union organizing and the industry witnessed eight general strikes between 1919 and 1940. At the neighborhood level family connections stretching into the countryside remained primary for many workers who were semi-permanent migrants. The industrial working class included many from the Maharashtra hinterland, the Konkan, and later from northern India. Male-dominated patronage networks headed by jobbers who controlled access to employment, landlords, money lenders and crime bosses intersected with religious associations and membership within wrestling clubs. The courtyards at the center of multiple chawls became open plazas where varieties of cultural expression took place including musical performances and dramas that increasingly expressed nationalist and socialist agendas within a Marathi language format – about 46 percent of the city's inhabitants spoke Marathi as their mother tongue in 1941. This was a major shift from the earlier importance of Gujarati speakers whose mother tongue, the primary medium for business, declined as the first language of Bombay's citizens from almost 28 percent in 1881 to 19.5 percent in 1941. Hindi and Urdu, meanwhile, rose as the mother tongue from 11.5 percent in 1881 to almost 20 percent in 1941 (Morris 1983: 654–5; Kosambi 1986: 60; Chandavarkar 1994: 33, 168–238, 399; Dwivedi and Mehrotra 2001: 228–9). A parallel shift took place in the gender characteristics of the workplace in a trend similar to that affecting the jute industry in Calcutta – the secular displacement of female factory labor. In 1919 women constituted 20.3 percent of the textile workforce, and in 1930 their participation hit a peak at almost 23 percent, but thereafter their numbers declined steadily, constituting less than 15 percent in 1939 and 11.7 percent in 1946 (Morris 1983: 645; Kumar 1989: 142–3).

The cotton boom and an influx of additional municipal revenues coincided with a radical reordering of Bombay's central business district initiated under Sir Henry Bartle Edward Frere, Governor between 1862 and 1867. The public green, fronted by the town hall (completed in 1833) had become rather seedy; it was transformed into Elphinstone Circle surrounding a public garden and in turn surrounded by the four-storied, crescent-shaped Victoria Buildings which formed a single architectural ensemble (completed in 1873) reminiscent of the Circus designed by John Wood the Elder in eighteenth-century Bath. Frere also accomplished a project long contemplated by his predecessors when he oversaw the demolition of the fort walls in 1863–4 and the relocation of the bulk of the military establishment south to the tip of Colaba Island, where it remained the largest cantonment in the Presidency, with over 30,000 residents in 1881 (Kosambi1986: 53; Masselos 1992: 294–5). The sudden availability of open land and funds, obtained by sale of some former wall space, made possible a new scale of public monumentality architecturally influenced by Gothic and neoclassical revivals. Rampart Row and Esplanade Road traced the old line of the walls. West of the latter, in the central area of the former Esplanade, a row of imposing buildings completed in the 1870s included the High Court, the University of Bombay (founded 1857) Library and Convocation Hall, and the Secretariat. They overlooked the green space of the Oval Maidan to their west and afforded to persons in the new monumental line a splendid view of the ocean. The monumentality of the former Esplanade became anchored architecturally on the north by the Victoria Terminus of the Great Indian Peninsular Railway (GIPR) and the Municipal Corporation building (completed 1892) and on the south by the Gateway of India (constructed between 1911 and 1924), providing for the wealthy and influential a processional route of imperial spectacle. South of the Oval Maidan stood the open space known as the Cooperage. At the north end of the Oval Maidan stood the Indo-Saracenic offices of the Bombay Baroda and Central India Railroad (BB&CIR), separating it from the Cross Maidan to its north where the military staged parades. Farther to the northeast was the Esplanade (later Azad) Maidan, triangular in plan. A considerable extent of parkland thus remained in the expanded central business district (Evenson 1989: 30–45; Dossal 1991: 193–4, 200–1; Lang *et al*. 1997: 81–2; Dwivedi and Mehrotra 2001: 88–121).

The plague epidemic stimulated a new level of public awareness concerning urban planning and Bombay led the way in the establishment of a modern planning organization, the Bombay City Improvement Trust, in 1898 (Calcutta's Trust was initiated in 1911, Bangalore's in 1945). During its 35 years of existence, the trust in Bombay filled in low-lying land, built residential layouts, consolidated housing for police personnel and mill workers, and controlled land development. It remained fixated on increased sanitation and air circulation through the creation of open spaces in the built environment while continuing a process of channeling neighborhood growth along class lines. It constructed major arterial roads running south to north along future construction ribbons, including Sydenham Road (later Mohammedali Road) that opened a corridor from the fort to new northern suburban estates at Sion-Matunga, Dadar-Matunga, and Sewri-Wadala designed to house 205,000 persons. It cut Princess Street (1905) and Sandhurst Road (1909) on an east-west axis, ostensibly in order to bring the sea breeze to dense residential neighborhoods but in practice opening corridors enhancing access to the posh residential neighborhoods of Malabar and Cumballa Hills; the projects displaced in the process large numbers of persons who relocated to already-crowded adjacent neighborhoods (Dwivedi and Mehrotra 2001: 166–74, 177–9). Wielding freely its right to demolish pre-existing structures and to acquire land, the trust eliminated slums, evicting by 1909 over 50,000 people from demolished one-room apartments but simultaneously constructing more 'sanitary' chauls with only 2,844 rooms. It controlled all open land in the city (11 percent of the island) but left more than two-thirds undeveloped, and thus contributed to even greater pressure on land use and an increase in land values that benefited a small group of *rentier* capitalists who were motivated to add stories to already crowded buildings. During the first two decades of the twentieth century, while the city's population increased from 776,000 to 1.18 million, residential buildings increased only 11 percent while mills and factories increased 328 percent and commercial properties (i.e. warehouses, railways, tramways and docks) increased 400 percent, contributing to a perception of overcrowding. As in the case of Calcutta, Bombay remained a remarkably compact and congested city where, by the mid-1920s, trams, bicyclists, oxcarts and pedestrians shared the roads with 12,000 motor vehicles (Chandavarker 1994: 43–4; Hazareesingh 2001).

Responding to the crisis in working-class housing, in 1920 the Government of Bombay set up a Development Directorate, as an executive wing of a Development Department, with a mandate to plan residential schemes, improve suburban communications and lay out industrial estates outside Bombay. It quickly became embroiled in a scheme to reclaim the Back Bay in an arc stretching from a point west of the Oval Maidan to Colaba Island – a resuscitation of the original plans from the 1860s that received reinforcement through the financial success of a reclamation project called Cuffe Parade (completed in 1905 and named after T. W. Cuffe, a member of the City Improvement Trust) that provided upper-class residences on the west side of Colaba. Work began on an ambitious project that would fill eight blocks of land, but mismanagement and a depression in land prices resulted in the completion of only two blocks in the north and two in the south, with about 80 percent of the new land designated as residential and about 20 percent as commercial. The new Marine Drive, constructed between 1935 and 1940 on the beach of the northern blocks and curving northwest toward Malabar Hill, bounded an extensive zone of mid-rise residential complexes coming up during the 1930s. The wall of apartment buildings along Marine Drive became one of the most easily identifiable urban panoramas in South Asia (Evenson 1989: 132–47, 174–9; Dwivedi and Mehrotra 2001: 174–5, 193–201).

Bombay's island location and its rapid demographic shifts prompted an early consideration of the fate of its suburbs and sensitivity to a regional approach in urban planning which focused attention on the northern islands including Salsette and Trombay. Suburban residential layouts were beginning to come up in these northern suburbs by the 1920s; after the blow of the Great Depression, pressure on these suburbs was renewed as the population of Bombay grew to 1.49 million in 1941 with an estimated 50,000 persons without any home at all. At this point there were at least a quarter million people living in Bombay Suburban District in towns, administered as municipalities or 'notified areas,' strung out along rail lines (which made possible commuting to the city's business and administrative core) and along the coast at places like Juhu, a prominent locale for seaside bungalows for the well-to-do and the upper middle class. In 1932 J. R. D. Tata landed his private airplane at Juhu Aeordrome, carrying mail from Karachi via Ahmedabad; this act inaugurated regular commercial air service of Tata Airlines, leading to the construction of a larger airport at nearby Santa Cruz, site of a British airfield during Second World War, and the establishment of Air India. After submission of a 1945 report by the Bombay City and Suburbs Post-War Development Committee, the state government moved toward the creation of a new entity called Greater Bombay, which included the island city along with Trombay and the southern part of Salsette. Already planners were considering the possibility of urban expansion that would push the city past the islands and onto the mainland, as the greatest metropolis in South Asia (Dwivedi and Mehrotra 2001: 242, 288–9, 296–300).

Associational life and public culture

The urban experience created opportunities for the consolidation of new types of public institutions and performance, or of new norms of civility, affected by the peculiar conditions of colonialism. In the field of municipal governance the establishment of representative councils that progressively became more democratic provided a forum for persons for the upper and, eventually, upper-middle classes to participate in the planning of urban infrastructure, although property qualifications and the heavy hand of the British-dominated provincial bureaucracies cramped their fields of action – with important ramifications for urban governance in the late-twentieth century. A separate field of bio-moral philanthropic activity that followed parallel and sometimes intersecting paths of liberal and devotional discipline exercised the imagination and the pocketbooks of the wealthy; while the urban poor by the twentieth century were devising their own novel forms of self-help philanthropy that intersected with processes for mass identitarian assertion. Meanwhile, new types of mass audiences were coalescing around a technological innovation, film cinema, in a manner that challenged the physical and social segregations that still typified all population concentrations and that began to define a multi-class consuming public. And, finally, the transformation of specific types of athletic activities into modern sports with its heroes and giant venues redefined the public expression of masculinity.

A movement occurred throughout British India during the 1860s to set up urban municipalities with representative councils in order to address urban sanitation and infrastructure issues through local taxation, extracting revenue directly from rate payers and business interests with permission of provincial governments. The vision of operational democracy in municipalities prompted an 1882 Resolution issued by the British Viceroy, Lord Ripon, which became the basis for later discussions on governance throughout South Asia. The Resolution called for the creation of boards where elected members would sit with officials appointed by the government to exercise control over affairs within territorial constituencies. The ability to vote or to sit on municipal boards initially depended on property and degree qualifications that restricted the electorate to a tiny minority. Provisions for financing remained limited, therefore making positions on the boards only marginally attractive as sources of patronage and political mobilization. Members of the Indian Civil Service, which throughout the nineteenth century remained almost entirely a British enclave, retained wide-ranging executive powers and wielded them outside the authority of local boards. Rate payers observed a pronounced tendency to allocate resources to projects that benefited inhabitants of civil and military stations or the sections of cities where the British lived. Under these conditions, public response to local boards was mixed; seats that were available sometimes remained poorly contested and elected members often displayed little inclination to oppose nominated bureaucrats. But by the end of the century, municipal elections were serving as a public forum in which members of the up-and-coming professional classes could compete for limited public influence against representatives of the older landed and commercial classes (Tinker 1954: 43–63; Leonard 1973).

A report by a Government of India Decentralisation Commission in 1909 noted deficiencies in progress during the 25 years after Lord Ripon's Resolution on local governance, but made only tepid suggestions that elicited little official response as the Empire fell into First World War. Progress occurred after the Montagu-Chelmsford Report on constitutional reform in 1918 led to the enactment of the Government of India Act in 1919 that set forth the principle of 'dyarchy' – dividing political responsibilities between the central and provincial governments and making local self-government a 'transferred subject' determined by provincial legislation. Scheduled Tax Rules allocated revenues under 11 headings solely for local authorities and a generally buoyant economy during the mid-1920s allowed urban bodies to engage in more ambitious public-works schemes. Despite the importance of municipal elections for the provision of urban infrastructure, the qualifications for voting still restricted the electorate to a small fraction of the male population. In the United Provinces, for example, elections held under amended legislation led to a 300 percent increase in registered voters in 1922, although in Kanpur this meant that eligible voters had increased only to 16 percent of the urban population (Gooptu 2001: 74–5).

Participation in city government for several decades became a standard apprenticeship for national-level politicians like Sardar Vallabhbhai Patel in Ahmedabad, Jawaharlal Nehru in Allahabad and Subhas Chandra Bose in Calcutta. The policy of nationalist politicians after 1922 was to enter local and provincial councils in order to confront the imperial government from within, thus subordinating local political institutions to the larger national struggle. In Calcutta in 1924, for example, advocates of Self Rule swept moderates and European representatives from the Corporation, although in practice this led to an extended period of wrangling for power among factions within the nationalist ranks (Ray 1979: 104–7). After the onset of the Great Depression in 1929 and the Salt March civil disobedience in 1930, concentration on national issues and communal representation within councils intensified, resulting in the cancellation or adjournment of a large percentage of council meetings throughout the country. The Government of India Act of 1935, which extended the franchise and devolved more powers to provincial legislatures, reflected the concentration on national-provincial relationships, and led to the repeal of the Scheduled Tax Rules and thus to enhanced financial dependence of all local bodies on provincial governments. Issues of urban governance in general atrophied until Independence at precisely the moment that communal tensions and struggles within municipal councils became acute (Tinker 1954: 129–188; Bhattacharya 1974: 23–32, 74–81).

A separate arena of associational culture grew during the nineteenth century through the transformation of religious giving (*dana*) into philanthropy, and service (*seva*) into nation-building activities. Aristocrats, commercial elites based in the 'bazaar' economy, and the professional middle class continued to expend their organizational energies and money on the building and endowment of religious institutions which led to the proliferation of temples, shrines, gurdwaras, mosques, and religious schools in all cities of the Raj. In addition, they created new institutional forms outside the control of the colonial state that re-defined civic engagement from an individual act to a group process carried out by permanent, not-for-profit, voluntary entities that addressed what were now perceived as social problems. Publishing was one such activity and journals increased seven-fold between 1890 and 1912. Education, formation of youth collectivities such as the boy scouts and the girl guides, assisting at fairs and pilgrimage sites, founding hospitals, and helping sufferers during famines and epidemics were ways of building character and manifesting civic responsibility by helping the unfortunate, aiming at a new level of social efficiency. Charitable activities were often accompanied by the practice of bio-moral development or physical culture manifested as a restriction of physical desires, dietary regimens and group drill. The implementation of these 'upper-caste notions of civility, propriety, and hierarchy' aimed to uplift the depressed classes in order to construct a united and strong nation (Watt 2005: 16, 33, 68–9). The thousands of social welfare groups in existence by the early-twentieth century constituted a new public sphere characterized by institutional pluralism, associational depth and trans-regional scale that 'hollowed out' the monopoly over public expenditure arrogated to itself by the British Raj. The nationalist movement attempted to pull many of these activities within the orbit of the progressive or 'cosmopolitan' nation, but in practice by the 1920s many self-help, charitable and voluntary activities also had communal overtones.

The large pool of urban menial laborers, who comprised the overwhelming majority of city populations, included the Muslim poor well represented in the artisan trades; the 'untouchable' or Dalit poor who survived through low-status tasks such as leather working, domestic service and municipal sweeping; and the large population of the low-caste or 'shudra' poor migrating steadily from rural areas. The urban poor encountered upper-caste control of the urban economy linked to the latter's reformist or 'purification' initiatives, patronage of religious institutions and festivals, sectarian devotional programs and philanthropic uplift initiatives. They also experienced the impact of urban planning implemented by urban authorities that were dominated by the British and the South Asian middle classes, resulting in social and spatial exclusion plus insufficient housing. By the 1920s the urban poor were responding with religious assertion and a quest for status or political voice through self-help volunteer corps and militant public performance. The Muslim poor were attracted to a variety of Islamicist reform activities such as the Tanzim Movement that encouraged marches, prayer, and charitable activities, and the Tabligh Movement that linked Muslim devotion to physical fitness training for community defense. The Dalit poor joined primordial (*adi*) movements such as the Ad Dharmis of Punjab, the Adi Hindus of the United Provinces, or the Adi Dravidas of South India. The shudra poor claimed militant 'warrior' (*kshatriya*) identities, adopted sectarian devotional practices and projected a martial presence at religious festivals; in peninsular India many participated in 'non-brahmin' movements that re-defined their historical role as the true sons of the soil, visualizing the wresting of political and economic influence from colonial urban elites. Wrestling clubs (*akhara*), which for centuries had channeled masculine athleticism within restricted spaces and managed neighborhood- or city-wide competitions, increasingly became the recruiting grounds for caste-based and religion-specific groups whose members featured prominently during communal riots (Alter 1992; Gooptu 2001: 193–200, 262–89, 420–1).

The technology of film making was introduced by Europeans to urban South Asian audiences immediately after its invention at the end of the nineteenth century and it was rapidly adopted by European entrepreneurs who were closely followed by native businessmen. The first cinema house in southern India, for example, was the Electric Theatre opened in Madras in 1900 by a certain Major Warwick; and the first cinema house built there by an Indian was the Gaiety, opened in 1914. Within a decade houses in major cities could seat audiences of 500 or 600. Early cinema in rural areas consisted entirely of touring performances moving around on bullock carts, presented under thatched sheds or tents; when these performances took place also in major cities they reached an audience capacity of about 1,000. The introduction of sound led to the construction of veritable palaces of mass consumption that sported art deco ornamentation and became new landmarks within the urban fabric. In 1927–8 there were nine permanent cinema houses in Madras and 46 in the Madras Presidency, among 241 in British India; by 1941 there were 20 permanent houses in Madras and over 1,200 in British India (Gangar 1995: 221; Dwivedi and Mehrotra 2001: 246p153).

During the silent era 85 percent of showings were U.S. and European products, but Indian production companies entered the silent era in 1913 and engendered a new industry that was initially small and necessarily urban in location and marketing orientation. The first feature film was *Raja Harishchandra*, shot and released in Bombay in 1913. The first studio set up in southern India was the India Film Company in 1916, followed by the Star of the East Film Company in 1921. The production of Indian silent films until 1934 totaled 1,288, with 200 releases in 1931 making its biggest year. During the silent era until 1932 at least 73 films were made in Madras, but already Bombay was emerging as the major center for film production even for cinema aimed at regional audiences, with 19–20 studios in 1936. The introduction of sound resulted in a great expansion of the film audience and production facilities within South Asia and features produced between 1931 and 1947 totaled 2,716; the biggest year was 1947, with 280 releases. The main languages were Bengali, Hindi, Marathi, Tamil and Telugu, with a smaller number of releases in Punjabi and Gujarati. Bombay, and to a lesser extent Calcutta, supported film studios producing even for distribution in other regional markets (Rajadhyaksha and Willemen 1994: 32–3; Gangar 2003: 268–71; Bhaskaran 1996: 2–9; 2004).

Film acting had its roots in a new urban theatre that began in late-eighteenth-century playhouses built within the Presidency capitals for a mostly European audience and in nineteenth-century touring groups, including Parsi companies, which played mostly for a native audience and adapted elements of folk theatre including song and dance sequences (Hansen 2002). It was still possible to restrict the audiences for such performances to specific class or caste populations and members of 'untouchable' or 'scheduled caste' (i.e. Dalit) groups were typically not admitted to such events. Silent film was originally conceptualized as an extension or adjunct to live performances and showings that included footage of stunts often occurred on stage along with live entertainment. Although products from Europe and the United States were available in major cities, the South Asian products during the silent era mostly presented 'mythological' themes from epics such as the *Ramayana* and the *Mahabharata* or 'historical' themes with imagined reconstructions of the lives of famous personalities, a trend that continued during the five years after talkies appeared. In this context film cinema was an extension and amplification of trends within chromolithographic printing and photography, a dialogue of 'interocularity' that was framing discourse on the nature of the public and the nation (Pinney 2004: 34, 71–4).

By the late 1930s narrative-driven films portraying contemporary social issues were becoming more common. Simultaneously, songwriters and musicians who had been working in the field of stage drama brought to cinema the heritage of 'company drama music,' an alternative art form influenced by Hindustani and, especially in southern India, Carnatic music. The typical talking picture in the 1930s had 40 to 50 songs. Because cheap gramophone machines imported from Japan were also becoming available, an entirely new industry of film music was born which came to dominate a new pop music industry. The collective experience of film-going, which especially in the large urban theatres brought into the same space persons of varied class, caste, and religion and challenged gender segregation, popularized a democratization of space. The film advertising industry created a novel public sphere where film music and social commentary (or political propaganda) reached a mass culture. For decades the response of the upper classes was decidedly negative or, at best, apathetic, but as nationalist propaganda began appearing in talkies, writers began to take notice (Dwyer and Patel 2002; Bhaskaran 1996: 38–57; 2004).

Nothing exemplifies the strange contradictions of the colonial experience more than the spread of cricket to become a sub-continental masculine obsession. Unlike the history of cricket in England, which first developed as a form of recreation on village greens and then migrated to industrial towns where it remained territorially organized and supported county leagues, cricket in colonial South Asia began primarily in cities within clubs segregated by race and communal affiliation.

The first teams consisted entirely of Europeans, beginning with the Calcutta Cricket Club (reputedly founded 1792, now the Calcutta Cricket and Football Club), which obtained grounds in the northern Maidan that became known as Eden Gardens. The Colombo Cricket Club began in 1832. The Madras Cricket Club began in 1846 and shifted its matches in 1864 to grounds in Chepauk near the University of Madras. The Bombay Gymkhana amalgamated a number of European sports activities in 1875 and received an indefinite lease for its grounds on the southern part of the Esplanade Maidan. In these early stages women, natives and lower-class whites were not allowed membership and the teams played only against other Europeans-only squads. But on other sections of the urban maidans already there were numerous pick-up matches of native players.

The first natives known to play cricket on an organized basis were the Parsis in Bombay, who were imitating the Europeans as early as the 1830s and by the 1850s supported at least 30 teams. In 1877 the first match between the Bombay Gymkhana and a united Parsi team took place, in which the latter played so well that regular contests began. By 1886 Parsi cricketers were on tour in England and then formed their own Parsi Gymkhana which obtained a lease for grounds located on reclamation land on the western shore of the island, northwest of the Esplanade Maidan. Their team beat the Bombay Gymkhana for the first time in 1889 and the following year defeated a side of touring British amateurs before 12,000 fans. This signaled the coming-of-age of cricket as a South Asian sport with Bombay as its capital. In 1892 the newly formed Islam Gymkhana received a lease on land exactly the size of the Parsis' on the sea face a bit to the north, and the Hindu Cricket Club received their similar lease a bit farther north. The Presidency Match pitting the Europeans against the Parsis began in 1890 before 10,000 spectators. The format expanded to the Triangular (*tirangi*, or 'three colors') matches including the European, Parsi and Muslim sides in 1907; the Quadrangular (*chaurangi*) including the Hindu Cricket Club in 1912, which regularly attracted 20,000 fans; and then the Pentangular in 1937 with the inclusion of a side called The Rest, featuring Christian players. The venue for these matches was always the grounds of the Bombay Gymkhana which in fact was unable to accommodate the larger crowds; overflow spectators had to perch in trees, stand on neighboring rooftops, or wait outside to follow the action. Live English-language radio coverage was available by 1933 through equipment in hotels and other public places. Office work in the central business district often came to a halt during the finals (Guha 2002).

The growth of cricket as a mass spectator sport in Bombay was paralleled by its evolution in the other Presidency capitals, Colombo and secondary cities. The Sind Quadrangular at Karachi began in 1916, the Central Provinces Quadrangular at Nagpur began in 1919, and the All-India invitational tournament for the Viceroy's Cup began in Delhi in 1922 (Docker 1976: 7–11; Cashman 1980: 24–47). The first domestic competition in Ceylon was established in 1938 when 12 teams competed for the *Daily News* Trophy. The rulers of princely states, especially Patiala, played major roles in the cultivation of talented players as part of their 'aristocratic repertories' (Cashman 1980: 24–47). For example, the early superstar C. K. Nayadu, who led an all-India team on its first Test Match in England in 1932, was known as 'Colonel Saheb' to his fans because he eventually achieved promotion in the Holkar army; his duties in Indore, however, were limited almost entirely to cricket and he represented a new wave of professional cricketers. The formation of the Board of Control for Cricket in India in 1928, the first Test against England in South Asia (1933 in Bombay), and the inauguration of the all-India competition for the Ranji Trophy in 1934 presaged the national-territorial reorganization of cricket that would supplant the communal principle after Independence. The transformation of this English game into a facet of empire and then into an indigenized nationalist enterprise, while affected by political-communal politics off the playing fields, took place almost entirely outside the policy frameworks of the nationalist parties (Appadurai 1995).

Other games enjoyed great success under the Raj and had the potential to become the leading sports in South Asia. South Asian field hockey teams won every Olympic gold medal between 1928 and 1968. Football, organized along communal lines like cricket, in fact was far ahead of the latter as an organized force with the 1893 formation of the Indian Football Association (IFA) and the competition for the IFA Cup, still India's most prestigious football trophy. In Bengal football became particularly popular. Suburban towns became the recruiting grounds for a steady supply of football talent for teams in the city. In 1911 when Mohan Bagan defeated East Yorkshire in the IFA final a crowd of 80,000 to 100,000 were gathered around grounds that could accommodate only one quarter of them at best (Chaudhuri 1990, 2: 318). A rising public demand in Calcutta for a stadium never bore fruit before Independence, buried under the tide of communal strife and war, and Calcutta football was hard hit by the Partition that pulled away a large pool of talent assembled in Muslims-only teams (Bandyopadhyay 2005). In Bombay, on the other hand, the 41,000-seat Brabourne Stadium was inaugurated in 1937 on land of the Back Bay reclamation scheme, thus introducing to the South Asian city the primary congregational temple of modernity. The changed facilities and changing attitudes toward women's public roles meant that a crowd consisting of perhaps 5 percent women at the Bombay Gymkhana now included between 25 and 33 percent women. They were able to watch players recruited almost to a man not from villages, but from the towns, provincial seats and capitals of the Raj (Cashman 1980: 117–18; 173–91).

The cases of associational life examined here demonstrate that urban South Asia was generating spectacles of modernity that shared features with other world regions while retaining distinctive macro-regional characteristics. Arenas initially of male desire and the performance of citizenship occurred within narrow class and gender bases; the secular trend toward mass participation expanded the opportunities for the poor and for women to take part. We note here that earlier examinations of the public sphere (e.g. by Jürgen Habermas) concentrating on text and orality might find within the South Asian city cognate phenomena (e.g. publishing and coffee-house cultures) but the movements toward bio-moral mobilization, film, and sports suggest the theatrical nature of the public sphere and its inter-ocularity. These forms emerged from the carapace of colonialism to stake a claim on the nation, and thus one may juxtapose the cultures of urbanization with the national project. But they also took shape as expressions of an urbanization that was not strictly a manifestation or stage for nationalism or of imperial-systemic economic change. They were facets of a global city-culture with a unique dynamism that would dominate the life world of the late-twentieth century and the moral geography of relentless modernity and trans-modernity.

5 Languages of space in the contemporary city

Anyone visiting a South Asian city may be amazed at the huge number of pedestrians attempting to make their way on streets congested with vehicles of every type and description including (to name only a few) carts drawn by animals, carts drawn and pushed by men, bicycles, motorcycles (two-wheelers), cars, taxis, buses, lorries, and construction vehicles. Apparently paying scant heed to traffic laws, contributing to a giant rush that in mornings and evenings often leads to gridlock, the drivers of these vehicles are participating in a vast expansion of automotive transport that began in earnest during the 1990s and that has extended average trip times for everyone while seriously degrading air quality. Weaving in and out of the traffic are masses of auto rikshas, or three-wheeled taxicabs with space for the driver in the front seat and for three adults in the back seat. These are the automotive successors of cycle rikshas, bicycles with an attached rear seat protected from the elements by a collapsible hood, that move through the physical exertion of sweating young men (and some wiry older men). In fast-moving cities like Mumbai or Bangalore the auto riksha has eliminated its pedal-driven competitors, except for work along back roads, but in towns, smaller cities and even in some major centers like Dhaka, the slow-moving but cheap cycle riksha remains a major component of the transport industry. There are more than 600,000 auto and cycle rikshas on the streets of Dhaka.

Every year hundreds of thousands of men, facing poverty and joblessness in their villages, come to the cities looking for work. Many of them, without other skills, find jobs as cycle riksha drivers, renting from bosses who control fleets of vehicles, sleeping in dormitories run by the bosses or in the riksha's seat, perhaps hoping that eventually they may purchase their own vehicle or upgrade to an auto riksha. Possessing only their labor power, one step from the gutter and hustling for every coin, these drivers accumulate extensive knowledge of the city and often communicate in multiple languages; many have married young and support families who live in humble abodes within neighborhoods classified as slums. On the streets, the drivers are part of a massive crowd of working men and under-employed or unemployed male youth who people the everyday landscape of the South Asian city. The streets are the arena for public, i.e. male activity, and in many cities especially within Pakistan, Bangladesh and parts of northern India, women do not spend much time there, unless veiled or hurrying from one venue to the next, or forced to work publicly because of poverty. The harassment of women by groups of men hanging around on the streets, called 'Eve-teasing' by the English-language press, remains a problem everywhere.

The sights on the city streets – signboards, billboards, neon lights, tangles of telephone wires, dilapidated storefronts alongside post-modern office buildings, the wares – present an unending panoply of popular culture. The sights in the streets are no less variegated. A mass visual culture has grown around the painting of transport vehicles, especially the lorry's body and cab and the cycle riksha's hood, backboard and seat. During 25 years of studying Bangladeshi transport art, and that of the cycle riksha in particular, Joanna Kirkpatrick (2003) has identified a number of recurring styles and themes. The most widespread presentation is a symmetrical series of multicolored geometric forms that may cover every available surface of the vehicle and incorporate representations of animals and/or plants. Figurative art, more typical of the flat surface on backboards, includes scenes of wild or domesticated animals, human portraits juxtaposed with animals (e.g. woman with cobra), bucolic meditations on peaceful rural life, crossed swords, or media-inspired heroes/anti-heroes (e.g. Saddam Hussein, the 'bandit-queen' Fulan a.k.a. Phulan Devi) with military hardware. A separate genre deals with the contemporary city, or an idealized vision of what the city might be. A painted seat back, for example, shows a diesel engine and train roaring toward the viewer over a bridge, with flanking images of skyscrapers on the left and 'Indo-Saracenic' buildings on the right; an airplane fills the sky behind the train. The most provocative images, however, use film stars or star-like personalities to project the male world of heterosexual desire. In Figure 5 we see a backboard with the urban male and wifely lover on the left framed by a heart and the sultry (village) beauty on the right, with head covering and large earrings, staring provocatively at the viewer. On the hood above are the mirrored images of a scantily-clad vamp with arms raised, plenty of cleavage, and midriff exposed – the poor man's fantasy of the available female directed into the public sphere.

At the end of this chapter we will return to the relationship between the film industry and its representations of the city. We will begin, however, with a discussion of the period immediately following the withdrawal of the British colonialists in 1947–8 and the profound impact of the ensuing communal conflicts on public space, especially through the partitioning of the subcontinent. The discussion will then shift to a general consideration of the huge demographic changes that have occurred in South Asian urbanization during the subsequent 60 years and which sets the stage for a description of the built environment and class polarization. We will then look at the direct impact of the state in creating new cities and dramatically altering older sites, before examining urban planning initiatives since Independence, with a special focus on Bombay/Mumbai and its metropolitan region. We will change scale from larger sites to 'middletown studies,' i.e. the forces driving the growth of small and medium cities, before considering the recent impact of globalization through several case studies. There is plenty of empirical evidence here on the quantitative and qualitative changes brought about during an unprecedented experience of rapid urbanization, but the

Figure 5 Painted hood and rear of a cycle riksha in Dhaka. Reproduced by permission of Joanna Kirkpatrick.

subtext will always be the relationship between what the city could or should be and what it might become. As in the case of riksha drivers we will see people attempting to develop languages to describe the urban experience and to project these languages, for reasons of self-interest or in the name of civic responsibility, into the public sphere.

Partitioning the body politic

South Asia experienced rapid urban growth during the 1940s driven, in part, by an increased pace of industrialization in response to the exigencies of Second World War. With Independence for India and the two wings of Pakistan in 1947 the stage was set for an urban surge, but the form it took was unexpected. Partition caused a massive transfer of population along the borders with an estimated 10 to 17 million persons displaced – Muslims from what would be India moving to West Pakistan and East Pakistan, and Hindus and Sikhs moving from the latter areas to India. At least 200,000 and perhaps over 1 million persons lost their lives in the violence that attended this massive 'ethnic cleansing.' Programmatic violence aimed at women was an integral component of this catastrophe, which left traumatic memories that are still the subject of extensive research and collective therapy. Many of the survivors, mostly poverty-stricken refugees, drifted to camps in and around cities, creating a gigantic burden for new national governments that were attempting to reorganize with very limited resources.

The greatest impact of Partition occurred in the cities on both sides of the border between the West Pakistan and India. Karachi experienced perhaps the most profound changes. At the time of Independence its population was about 450,000, including 61.2 percent Sindhi speakers and 6.3 percent Urdu-Hindi speakers; 51 percent were Hindu and 42 percent were Muslim. The Government of Pakistan then established a Federal Capital Area in Karachi and appropriated most of the formerly provincial infrastructure for a national administration staffed mostly by Urdu-speakers who were immigrants from India and from Pakistani Punjab. By 1951, after the exodus of non-Muslims and the influx of approximately 616,000 refugees or *muhajirs*, Karachi's population had increased to 1.1 million with refugees comprising 58.5 percent. The Sindhi speaking population suddenly constituted 8.6 percent and the Urdu speaking population 50 percent; the Muslim population was 96 percent and the Hindu population was 2 percent (Hasan 2002: 24). Because Pakistani Punjab was already overrun with refugees, most of them from eastern Punjab, a large number of the refugees who arrived in Karachi were Punjabi-speakers or Urdu-speakers whose life-styles and even religious predilections diverged from those of long-term residents of the city. As the influx of refugees continued during the early 1950s, including thousands of 'Pathan' job-seekers from the Northwest Frontier Province, Karachi's infrastructure was incapable of supporting them all; in 1953 there were 250,000 persons described as homeless or living in all-refugee 'colonies' in makeshift habitations; in 1955 their estimated number had risen to 800,000. By 1960 more than 80 percent of Karachi's citizens were migrants of some kind. Efforts to create more substantial housing colonies often produced neighbourhoods consisting mostly of *muhajirs* hailing originally from specific cities or regions in India. Cricket and hockey, the main sports of the formerly north Indian migrants, replaced Sindhi-patronized football as dominant leisure activities and Urdu-Hindi films became the most popular forms of cinematic entertainment (Ansari 2005: 122–55, 210).

In Lyallpur, the most successful of the cities founded among the 'canal colonies' in western Punjab (see Chapter 4), 63 percent of the population migrated to India in 1947 with over 24,000 ending up in Delhi. In return, there was an influx of refugees including members of small-scale trading communities from Amritsar and Jalandhar, artisans from Ludhiana and Batala, and the Sehgal and Chinioti industrial families. By 1951 there were 148,564 refugees in Lyallpur, comprising 83 percent of the city's population. Refugee interests rapidly augmented the city's industrial base. With assistance from the Government of Pakistan, the Kohinoor and Crescent Textile Mills were founded in 1950 and four years later a coalition of textile industries created an Institute of Textile Technology that evolved into the National Textile University. Other industries that grew up in the 1950s and 1960s included beverages, fertilizers, clarified butter, jute, sugar, plywood, pharmaceuticals, agricultural machinery, and textile machinery. In 1941 industrial workers had formed 7.4 percent of the city's workforce, by 1961 they comprised 49.8 percent, a 4,000 percent increase in absolute numbers. By 1965 more than 3,000 industrial enterprises employed a work force of 65,000. The city attracted a reputation as the 'Manchester of Pakistan' and became the second largest industrial city in Pakistan. In 1977 the name of the city was changed to Faisalabad after the late king of Arabia, Shah Faisal bin Abdul Aziz, in honour of his bestowal of a grant for the development of the city. Its population was almost 2.7 million in 2007 (Waseem 1990: 208–11).

Before Partition, Lahore and Amritsar had evolved to a position of near parity in the administrative and economic configuration of eastern Punjab. The decision to lay down the new international border between Lahore and Amritsar led to massive riots in those cities that destroyed minority neighbourhoods. Then the refugees came. In 1948 there were 1 million in Lahore, mostly living in camps of tents or mud houses, and among the 836,000 persons living in the city by 1950 refugees comprised 43 percent. Although the Lahore Improvement Trust provided only a fraction of the housing needs for this massive influx, it nonetheless remodelled damaged sections of the old city and promoted schemes in the suburbs that laid the basis for renewed urban dynamism. Shahdara, a refugee camp in 1947, became one of the city's industrial zones. Refugees came to play major entrepreneurial roles in the growth of Lahore's pharmaceutical industry and the revitalization of the hosiery industry. Businesses founded by refugees also received considerable assistance from the Government of Pakistan, and Lahore retained its administrative importance as a provincial capital, even as the capital of West Pakistan in 1955.

Amritsar, on the other hand, experienced a 16 percent drop in population between the 1941 and 1951 censuses. Its Improvement Trust, established only in 1946 and reactivated in 1949, notified 20 schemes covering only about 29 hectares of commercial and residential developments during its first decade of activity. Amritsar's importance as an industrial and wholesale marketing center was disrupted through loss of raw materials, much of its customer base, and a large proportion of its skilled workers. Militarization of the border discouraged the location of new industries and administrative offices there and despite representations by its citizens it was never seriously considered as a candidate for capital of Indian Punjab. By the 1980s Ludhiana, farther from the border, became the state's industrial and commercial center as part of a generally south-eastern shift in urban growth (Talbot 2006). Thus Amritsar's population grew from about 332,000 in 1950 to 1.16 million in 2007 while Ludhiana's grew during the same period from 149,000 to over 1.62 million.

In Delhi about 329,000 Muslims fled toward Pakistan and more than 495,000 Hindus and Sikhs came as immigrants from Pakistan, almost 95 percent being former inhabitants of what were now Pakistani cities, led by 82,340 from Lahore. Originally these people camped all over the city in whatever space they could find, with major colonies in open public lands such as King's Way. Eventually 190,000 refugees occupied, in an extra-legal manner, properties abandoned by Muslims. Another 100,000 received homes in new constructions. The remainder established squatter communities that developed into new neighbourhoods on the edge of the city or within the interstices of pre-existing layouts. The majority of these persons, having made their living as shopkeepers, petty traders, moneylenders, small bankers and non-cultivating landowners, encountered initial difficulties in finding appropriate employment, but their business backgrounds eventually allowed them to become a force within the commercial and industrial growth of post-partition Delhi. For example, the government set up Okhla Industrial Estate south of Delhi primarily for refugee enterprises; by 1969 it had 1,800 units and employed 115,000 people, a major component in Delhi's emergence as an industrial center (Datta 1986).

The case of Faridabad about 25 kilometers south of Delhi, originally a small *qasba* founded in 1607 along the trunk road to Agra, links the refugee issue to the annals of New Towns. By 1949 about 16,000 persons, mostly refugees from the Northwest Frontier Province, had settled in tent camps there under the auspices of a special Development Board whose meetings until 1952 included participation by Jawaharlal Nehru. His interest arose from the encouragement allowed to refugee cooperatives of earth workers, brick manufacturers, road workers, brick layers, and carpenters who received subsidies from the Government of India for the construction of a new urban core with public and community buildings surrounded by residential neighbourhoods. Within two and half years, voluntary labor groups of 10-15 persons had built about 5,000 houses for a population of about 23,000 persons. The Development Board initially adopted a 'mixed economy' strategy of manufacturing cooperatives, private, and public sector companies but official support for the cooperative movement flagged and industrial units were auctioned mostly to private enterprises. Faridabad then became one of the major industrial towns surrounding Delhi, with about 150 large- and medium-scale units and 1,000 small-scale units by the early 1970s when its population had reached 86,000. A survey of Faridabad entrepreneurs in 1973 revealed that almost one-third were immigrants from Pakistan. The city population continued to grow about 1.4 million in 2007 (Koenigsberger 1952: 122–24; Panini 1978; Jain 1998).

In Gujarat the Government of India approved in 1948 a project for a new deep-sea port at Kandla on the Gulf of Kutch and here again the refugee problem became an opportunity for a New Town experiment. Gandhidham (see Map 16) began when a group of displaced persons from Sind (mostly from Karachi) decided to pool their resources to construct a 'New Karachi.' Land was acquired about 14 kilometers from the new port, a distance necessitated by the marshy ground surrounding the port facilities. A single corridor of transport linked the port, the initial source of employment, to residential areas strung as a band town along the transportation line. Construction in Gandhidham began with a plant for the manufacture of hollow concrete blocks. Housing schemes were laid 4.5 kilometers distant from each

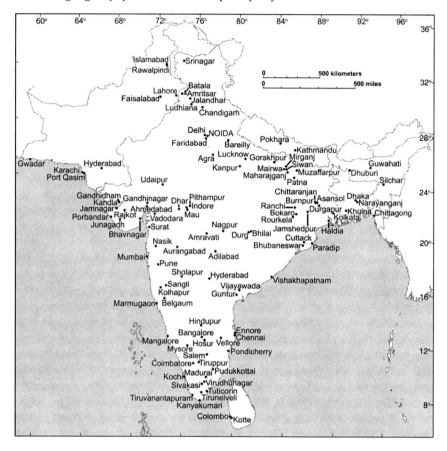

Map 16 Urban sites, 1947–2007.

other with the expectation that growth would eventually allow their fusion in a single city with a simple orthogonal street plan. The planners foresaw that business and industrial enterprises in Gandhidham would eventually outpace those of the port (Koenigsberger 1952: 126–31) and indeed Gandhidham's population reached approximately 141,000 in 2007 when Kandla's was about 27,000.

Partition did not result in a massive exodus of Muslims from Bombay but approximately 200,000 people, mostly from Sind, settled in 19 refugee camps and eventually found accommodation mostly around Bombay's suburban townships. About 5 kilometers from Kalyan the British government had set up a military transit camp during Second World War; it became a refugee camp housing about 100,000 refugees and in 1949 became the township of Ulhasnagar, which later developed into an important industrial and commercial hub. By 2001 it was home to about 350,000 persons claiming Sindhi background, the largest concentration of this group in India; the former 'Sindworki' community of Hyderabad, which had already developed a transnational commercial network, became a major player within the business environment of post-Partition Bombay (Kosambi 1986: 121; Dwivedi and Mehrotra 2001: 331).

Along the border between East Pakistan and Indian Bengal was still reeling from the 1943 famine and cities had already witnessed a surge of destitute famine refugees. Partition caused the migration of an estimated 1.5 million Muslims to East Pakistan and 4.2 million people, mostly Hindus, to West Bengal. The substantially lower number of Muslim refugees became distributed throughout a number of small cities including Narayanganj, Khulna, and Chittagong, and many found accommodation in properties abandoned by emigrants. In Dhaka, hitherto a sub-provincial city where Hindus constituted 59 percent of the pre-Partition population and Hindu administrative, professional, and business communities had played leading roles in community life. Partition eventually resulted in a population that was 95 percent Muslim (Hill *et. al* 2006). Calcutta bore the brunt of the incoming demographic wave in West Bengal. In the absence of adequate refugee resettlement camps most newcomers squatted on available public space, forming an army of pavement dwellers within the city and colonies of slums in the suburbs that transformed the social and spatial landscape and overtaxed infrastructure services. Many of the colonies were the fruits of self-help initiatives coordinated by committees of refugees. The Communist Party of India was able to tap into these units and organize successfully among refugee colonies as part of its effort to forge a political coalition that brought a United Front of left parties to power in the West Bengal legislature in 1967 (Tan and Kudaisya 2000: 165–75). Then a new influx of refugees fleeing the Bangladesh War of Liberation in 1971 swelled the number of people living in substandard housing and on the pavements of the city.

Post-Independence demography

By the 1950s the dust was beginning to settle on the aftermath of Partition – which in any case exerted a major effect only on a limited range of urban spaces in South Asia – and the anticipated urban explosion, a component of huge demographic changes throughout the macro-region, became manifest (see Table 1). In 1950, the total urban population of South Asia was about 71 million persons out of a total population of about 454 million, an urbanization rate of 15.6 percent and about 9.7 percent of global urban population. By 2005 urban dwellers in South Asia increased to 415 million, an urbanization rate of 30.3 percent and 13.2 percent of the global total, representing a 580 percent increase with an average addition of almost 7 million urbanites annually. In 1950, only two places in South Asia stood on the list of the world's 20 largest cities: Calcutta (ranked 9) and Bombay (ranked 18). In 2005, five South Asian cities stood on that list: Mumbai/Bombay (5), Delhi (6), Kolkata/Calcutta (8), Dhaka (11) and Karachi (13). South Asia's urban population lagged behind only East Asia (678 million) and Europe (526 million). It led Africa (347 million), South America (306 million), and North America (267 million) and exceeded the entire population of South America (375 million) or North America (331 million) (United Nations 2005: 1, 47–9, 53, 126–8).

Table 1 South Asian urban population, 1950–2007

	1950			1975			2007		
	Total population (thousands)	Urban population (thousands)	Percentage urban	Total population (thousands)	Urban population (thousands)	Percentage urban	Total population (thousands)	Urban population (thousands)	Percentage urban
India	357,561	60,936	17.0	620,701	132,406	21.3	1,049,874	350,658	33.4
Pakistan	36,944	6,473	17.5	68,294	17,985	26.3	164,541	68,186	41.4
Bangladesh	41,783	1,774	4.2	73,178	7,214	13.3	146,887	47,063	32.0
Nepal	8,643	231	2.7	13,548	654	4.8	28,196	7,184	25.5
Sri Lanka	7,782	1,193	15.3	14,042	2,736	19.5	21,064	3,501	16.6
Bhutan	734	15	2.1	1,161	53	4.6	2,259	479	21.2
Maldives	82	9	10.6	137	24	17.3	345	130	37.6
Totals	453,529	70,631	15.6	791,061	161,072	20.4	1,413,167	477,200	33.8

Source: United Nations 2005: 38–39, 48–49, 68–69, 79.

In 1950 the total number of urban sites in South Asia with populations of at least 100,000 persons was 91 including India with 79 and Pakistan with 10 places (see Map 17). In East Pakistan the only sizeable cities were Dhaka and Chittagong, the latter with about 290,000 persons. In Sri Lanka there was only one large city, Colombo, with just over 400,000 inhabitants. In Nepal also there was only one site, Kathmandu, with just over 100,000 inhabitants. The number of persons in all these places was about 31.5 million, which constituted about 45 percent of the entire urban population in South Asia. About 39.1 million people or 55 percent of the urban population lived in cities that had populations lower than 100,000. The urban system as a whole exhibited a distribution skewed toward a limited range of high-end central places. The population of the six cities with more than 1 million persons (see Table 2) totalled 12.4 million or 17.5 percent of the urban population. By comparison, the New York City-Newark agglomeration in the United States, the largest in the world in 1950, had as many inhabitants as these

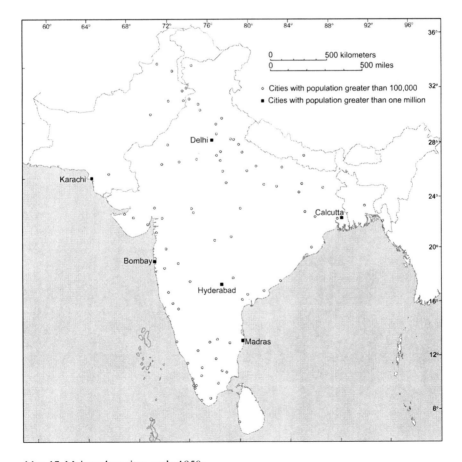

Map 17 Major urban sites, early 1950s.

six South Asian cities put together and the urban population of the United States alone was 101.2 million or 43 percent more than the entire population of South Asia's cities (United Nations 2005: 52, 126).

Looking at the situation in 2007 we see that an astonishing transformation occurred during the three subsequent generations (see Map 18). The urban population in South Asia reached approximately 477 million and accounted for one-third of the macro-region's total population. The number of cities with at least 100,000 inhabitants rose to 550, including 435 in India, 65 in Pakistan, 35 in Bangladesh, nine in Nepal, and six in Sri Lanka. The number of people living in these cities was approximately 308 million, which constituted 65 percent of the urban population and 21.8 percent of the total population. The geographic configuration of these places was relatively uniform except in environmentally challenging regions such as Baluchistan, western Rajasthan, southern Orissa and Chhattisgarh, and the Himalaya in the north. A concentration of cities stretched

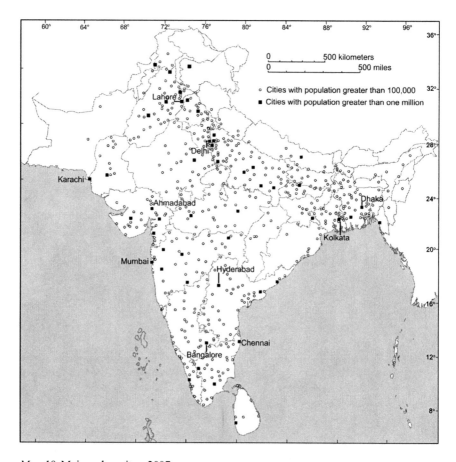

Map 18 Major urban sites, 2007.

from northern Pakistan all the way to Bangladesh with particular density in Indian and Pakistani Punjab, around Delhi, in West Bengal/Bangla, and Bangladesh. Density was greater also in the plains of Gujarat and in the South Indian states, especially Kerala and Tamil Nadu.

In 2007 there were 56 'million' cities or places with at least 1 million inhabitants. As a whole they included 191 million persons or 40 percent of the urban population and 13.5 percent of the total population. The category of 'million' cities included 46 places that we may describe as 'second-tier' (tier two) cities with populations of between 1 and 5 million, collectively including 84 million persons or 17.5 percent of the urban population and 5.9 percent of the total population. The category of million cities also included a special group of ten 'mega-cities,' which in the South Asian context refers to places with populations greater than 5 million, collectively including 107 million inhabitants or 22.5 percent of the urban population and 7.6 percent of the total population (see Table 2). Among the mega-cities the three former Presidency capitals had led the list in 1950, and although they all experienced massive expansion, the rate of growth for Calcutta/Kolkata and Madras/Chennai peaked in the 1970s and thereafter declined to the lowest in this group. The resulting growth rates of 'only' 327 percent and 480 percent, respectively, dropped them in the overall population rankings to third and sixth. The Bombay/Mumbai metropolitan region became the largest urban agglomeration in South Asia after growing by 662 percent to almost 19 million inhabitants. The most striking expansion took place in Dhaka, which increased in population from 417,000 in 1950 to almost 13.3 million in 2007, a 3,177 percent increase. Great size supported large absolute increases in population annually. Mega-cities had to accommodate at least 125,000 new citizens every year. Dhaka was experiencing the yearly augmentation of its population by about 439,000 persons, which meant that it was adding the equivalent of a million city every 2.5 years.

Moving down the urban hierarchy, we find a group of what we may call 'middle' cities with populations between 100,000 and 1 million, which included a total of 494 places with populations of approximately 118 million persons constituting 25 percent of the urban population and 8.3 percent of total population. Among the group of middle cities, more than half (294) had populations greater than 100,000 but less than 200,000, including 228 places in India, all cities in Sri Lanka aside from Colombo, and seven out of nine cities in Nepal. The majority of the places that appear on Map 18 fall into this category of towns or small cities that were experiencing fast population increases pushing them over the 100,000-person threshold. Extrapolations from census data suggest that 62 South Asian locales (47 in India alone) passed that mark between 2005 and 2007. In Bangladesh the average increase in their population during the decade of the 1990s was over 18,000 persons or a 24 percent rise. In India the average increase during that decade was over 23,000 persons or a 34 percent rise.

Approximately 169 million persons, about 35 percent of the urban population and 12 percent of the total population, were living in 'small cities' or 'towns' with less than 100,000 inhabitants. Populations were remaining stable in very few of these places, although the average annual increases seem tiny in comparison with

Table 2 Mega-cities in South Asia, 1950–2007

	Population 1950 (thousands)	Average annual growth rate 1950–55	Average annual population growth 1950–55 (thousands)	Population 1975 (thousands)	Average annual growth rate 1975–80	Average annual population growth 1975–80 (thousands)	Population 2007 (thousands)	Average annual growth rate 2005–10	Average annual population growth 2005–2010 (thousands)
Kolkata	4,513	2.27	108.40	7,888	2.71	228.40	14,769	1.71	254.20
Mumbai	2,857	3.67	115.00	7,082	4.02	315.20	18,905	1.93	368.00
Chennai	1,491	2.68	42.80	3,609	3.05	118.80	7,159	1.74	125.80
Delhi	1,369	5.26	82.60	4,426	4.56	226.40	15,785	2.42	387.00
Hyderabad	1,096	1.45	16.60	2,086	3.52	80.20	6,358	1.97	126.80
Karachi	1,047	6.09	74.40	3,989	4.71	211.80	12,231	2.65	328.80
Ahmedabad	855	3.27	30.40	2,050	3.74	86.80	5,348	2.20	119.20
Lahore	836	4.02	37.20	2,399	3.67	96.60	6,634	2.71	182.40
Bangalore	746	4.61	38.60	2,111	5.74	140.20	6,751	2.21	150.80
Dhaka	417	5.13	24.40	2,173	8.10	216.80	13,251	3.25	439.00

Source: United Nations 2005: 130, 135–6, 138, 147, 152–3, 155.

larger sites. In many cases, transformations of life style and the built environment were most pronounced at these lower levels of the urban hierarchy.

The high-rise and the slum

Most cities in South Asia with a history pre-dating the 1950s retained a section typically known as the old city, which preserved a dense concentration of residential cul-de-sacs within spatially self-contained neighbourhoods surrounding, and intermingling with, market areas. Although spatial identification with religious, class or caste groups was never complete, the pronounced tendency for close relatives and extended families to live in close proximity meant that communitarian identity remained closely associated with specific neighbourhoods in the old city. Some of its residents might work outside its boundaries but others found employment in the prominent bazaars where the street level was an array of retail and some wholesale establishments run by families of owner-operators. The tendency for multiple businesses to locate in clusters preserved the occupational specialization of streets and entire neighbourhoods, e.g. a jewellery district or a row of shops selling identical kitchenware. The old city supported an array of industrial activities in backroom family workshops (e.g. luggage manufacture and repair) or small factories (e.g. flour grinding mills) where workers were relatives or nearby residents and where working conditions were poor, job security limited, and child labor not uncommon. Within the old city or in contiguous neighbourhoods, storefronts with apartments upstairs in two-to-five story buildings alternated with mechanical workshops producing commodities ranging from textiles to diesel pumps or specializing in mechanical services such as auto parts.

Beginning by the 1930s, and accelerating after Independence, neighbourhoods described by Mohammad Qadeer (1983: 82–3, 181–4) as 'new indigenous communities' grew on the outskirts of the old cities and old cantonments for commercial and professional families often self-segregated by religion. These private housing initiatives transposed the residential styles of the old city within a more modernist paradigm. Municipal engineers or private surveyors laid out lots in rectangular grids with streets 4 to 5 meters in width to allow vehicular access. Three-story houses on both sides of the street covered entire lots and presented a continuous façade of screened windows and balconies with the ground floor designed to hold shops. Atriums or enclosed courts in the back, serving as middle-class versions of the central courtyards typical of defunct old-city mansions, provided a modicum of family privacy. Municipal services such as water and sewerage were nonexistent at the start but were extended when an area filled up; sometimes streets remained unpaved for decades. A second stage in the spread of new indigenous communities occurred when corporate groups or housing cooperatives began creating exclusive residential areas often termed *nagar*, which reserved spaces for parks, schools, mosques or temples, and clinics.

The deep involvement of the state in residential planning produced a range of characteristic forms. Public-sector firms and government departments created company housing. For officers and managers, development authorities allotted plots of land on the outskirts of the city within 'schemes' zoned for the construction of the post-Independence rectilinear bungalow in brick and concrete, either single-story or with an apartment upstairs, and featuring a small driveway along with garden space in the front and/or back. It was not unusual for entire streets within such schemes to house managers from different public-sector agencies. For lower-level staff from unitary public-sector departments lodging took the form of low-rise apartment-house clusters, often called 'colonies,' with single-bedroom or two-bedroom flats. A variety of state-funded authorities had the responsibility for providing housing for the poor described in India, for example, as the 'depressed classes' or 'weaker sections' and thus built on the outskirts of the city planned neighbourhoods with single-room apartments designed to take the pressure off the inner city. In Lahore, for example, the first of these projects was a satellite town called Lahore Township constructed in 1962 about 25 kilometers outside the city as a self-contained industrial workers' community on a 1,200-hectare site meant to provide 10,000 low-income houses locally called 'quarters' (Qadeer 1983: 87).

Suburban expansion even within planned schemes necessarily engulfed pre-existing villages whose inhabitants may have lost their agricultural livelihood but often retained their house sites. The compact collection of former peasant homes became low-income housing and supported a bazaar with inhabitants providing low-skilled services for the middle-class neighbourhoods on their doorsteps. Meanwhile, backfilling by private (and often illegal) arrangements in the form of new indigenous communities and squatter communities occurred after the first batch of households settled into a legally established scheme. Shacks or temporary stalls of bakers, tea sellers, and sweepers appeared on empty lots. As a scheme neared completion clusters of small shops appeared at intersections, along alleys, and in open spaces. Finally, the infiltration by offices along main boulevards occurred through unofficial commercialisation and later became rationalized through official re-zoning. The ability to find an array of goods and services close to home made this quasi-legal complex functional and even necessary where the time cost of transportation was becoming prohibitive.

By the 1990s the South Asian middle class, mostly living in cities, was variously estimated at somewhere between 200 and 400 million people commanding disposable income earned through commercial, administrative, political, military, and professional services (Nijman 2006). They represented a huge pent-up demand for housing, which until then had been inadequately met by lending institutions and urban development authorities. The middle class was poorly served by the housing market in South Asian cities until the intersection of economic 'liberalisation' and a slowdown in industrial growth in the mid-1990s pushed banks to seek alternative borrowers, and hundreds of private finance organizations entered the housing field to offer relatively low interest rates and fiscal incentives within a generally buoyant market. In India, where the transformation was the most striking and lending increased by 30 percent annually, the housing market remained small by international standards at only two percent of gross national product, compared for example to 13 percent in the Republic of Korea (UN-Habitat 2005: 72–3), but it made a large impact on the spatial organization of rapidly expanding suburbs.

For a mid-level middle class that included many first-generation urbanites, phalanxes of high-rise apartment buildings marching past ring roads and peripheral roads produced a heterogeneous social space that challenged entrenched patterns of clan, caste, religious, linguistic, or regional clustering. In Karachi, Laura A. Ring's study (2006) of an apartment building demonstrates the daily efforts of housewives to negotiate this alien terrain and to construct original forms of sociability amid an environment charged with ethnic enmity.

For the upper-level middle class, encompassing what Leela Fernandes (2006: 30) terms the 'new' middle class standing as a 'hegemonic sociocultural embodiment of liberalization,' residential enclaves and gated communities were components of a drive toward 'spatial purification' that protected/restricted the activity of women and shifted the poor out of sight. Visual surfaces allied to consumerist display, multiplexes and shopping malls, coffee shops and cyber cafes, automatic teller machines, and billboards accompanied the enhanced experience of consumption and family through interior design. Sites of consumption like Kathmandu's New Road or Bangalore's Brigade Road allowed the middle class to 'take place': to make itself and its forms of knowledge through consumerism, mass-media, and youth. Class practice within the city continually reconstituted key narratives of their differentiation such as 'suitability,' the body (i.e. its cleanliness, hygiene, nutrition and comfort), seclusion and exorcism of the 'evil spirits' of modernity, i.e. the poor, although these were absolutely essential for the preservation of middle-class distinctiveness through the services they provided. The expanding range of educational institutions or training institutes provided credentials for the middle class or aspirants to that class that allowed access to employment and a 'standard of living' that separated them from omnipresent urban poverty while mantling them in the glow of globalization (Leichty 2003: 35–8, 105–10, 213–52).

We may obtain a more nuanced appreciation of the human face of the contemporary city by looking in greater detail at a series of development indicators for all cities within major South Asian nations and also for five select cities (see Table 3). These statistics present a picture of poorer conditions than in 'developed' nations but we should note that in most cases they are higher than those for the rural areas of South Asia and in all cases represent tremendous progress since Independence. For Sri Lanka the statistical profile is complicated by the difficulties attending the civil war since 1983 but we may still glimpse a pronounced advantage over the other nations of South Asia in infant mortality, sanitation, and poverty eradication at the beginning of the twenty-first century. The situation was grimmer in Nepal, where the average life expectancy in cities as well as the countryside was in the low fifties (compared, for example, to the upper seventies in Seoul in the Republic of Korea) but where intense concentration of state welfare agencies in cooperation with non-governmental organizations resulted recently in rapid improvement in child mortality, child nourishment, education, and safe water. In Pokhara, Nepal's second largest city (population about 203,000 in 2007), under-five child mortality plummeted to 2.1 per thousand; we may compare this, for example, to the rate of 1.2 per thousand in Seoul. Urban infant mortality rates

Table 3 Urban human-development indicators, early-twenty-first century

	Bangladesh	India	Nepal	Pakistan	Sri Lanka
Infant mortality per 1,000 live births*	74.2	49.2	50.1	74.6	34.4
Under-five mortality per 1,000**	97.0	65.0	65.9	94.0	
Malnourished children under five years (%)**	39.8	39.2	33.1	32.3	
Population below poverty line (%)*	36.6	24.7	23.0	24.2	15.0
Population using improved drinking water (%)***	82.0	86.0	90.0	91.0	71.0
Population using adequate sanitation facilities (%)***	39.0	33.0	35.0	59.0	91.0

Notes:
*World Bank 2005: 278–79, 282–3.
**UN-Habitat 2006: 196–9; Government of Nepal 2002: 131.
***UNICEF 2006: 110–12.

Gross school enrolment ratio

City	Life expectancy		Under-5 mortality per 1,000	Primary		Secondary		Literacy rate	
	Female	*Male*		*Female*	*Male*	*Female*	*Male*	*Female*	*Male*
Chennai	68.5	65.0	37	49.5	50.5	50.7	49.3	69.0	72.0
Dhaka	60.9	61.7	96	77.9	80.4	62.3	65.9	60.3	60.3
Karachi	65.0	63.0	120	58.7	60.9	67.3	70.6	64.2	72.0
Lahore	65.0	63.0	63	66.2	68.5	73.3	71.9	65.1	72.7
Pokhara	50.0	55.0	21	88.0	83.3	35.4	26.6	42.0	66.2

Source: UN-Habitat 2005: 225.

of about 50 per thousand births in Nepal and India were just above those of Seoul at 47.8 and Chennai's rate of 37 was actually better than those of the Korean capital but Bangladesh and Pakistan lagged behind with about 74 per thousand births; the profile for infant mortality in the major cities of Bangladesh and Pakistan was similarly less encouraging. The problem of malnourishment, which affected over one-third of the children in South Asia's cities, was intimately linked to conditions of poverty. In India, Nepal, and Pakistan approximately one quarter of the urban population fell below national poverty lines, which were lower than the poverty lines in developed nations; in Bangladesh, one-third of the urban population was officially impoverished.

The state and private initiatives guaranteed improved drinking water to a substantial majority of city-dwellers – even if, on the ground, facilities in some low-income neighbourhoods might consist only of a public tap requiring a wait in a queue. Sanitation facilities were a different story, however, for in India alone only one out of three persons were serviced adequately and only in Sri Lanka did more than 59 percent of the urban population have adequate access. As for education, one should note that the rates displayed here represent mid-level accomplishments; statistics in certain cities such as Mumbai and Bangalore were noticeably higher. A consistent trend marked female literacy as lower than male although enrolment trends suggest that the literacy gap was narrowing. In no case did literacy reach the 97.9 percent of Seoul nor did the primary school enrolment rate compare to Seoul's 92 percent.

The national and all-city statistics here mask pronounced disparities in access to infrastructure linked to large and even widening differences in family incomes. The upper middle class lived at levels not dissimilar to those of middle-class citizens in Seoul or indeed anywhere else in the world. Members of these families might be literate in multiple languages; enjoy access to adequate water supplies and sanitation in the comfort of their homes; and expect longevity comparable to the middle class anywhere. The statistical profiles were lowered by the presence of large numbers of persons below and just above the poverty line whose living conditions remained more difficult.

According to the definition of slums devised by an Expert Group Meeting convened through the United Nations, slums housed 31.6 percent of the world's urban population or an estimated 924 million persons in 2001-a number that exceeded 1 billion persons in 2006 and would perhaps rise to 2 billion persons by 2020. South Asia presented an unenviable portrait within these estimates with 59 percent of its urban population living in slums, the highest rate in the world except for Sub-Saharan Africa (72 percent); in contrast, the slum population constituted only 6 percent of the urban population in Europe and 5.8 percent in the United States. The breakdown by country in South Asia: Bangladesh 84.7 percent, Bhutan 44.1 percent, India 55.5 percent, Nepal 92.4 percent, Pakistan 73.6 percent, and Sri Lanka 13.6 percent. Among these countries only Sri Lanka was described as 'on track' in coping with slum proliferation while India was a nation 'at risk' of losing control; Bangladesh, Nepal and Pakistan were 'off track,' facing rapid and sustained slum growth rates (UN-Habitat 2003, 2006: 38–41).

Although many slum families may have lived there for decades, their populations were augmented by a steady stream of migrants from the countryside, coming to the city with limited skills and low education (Mukherjee 2002). Among these migrants were many thousands recruited from rural areas as manual laborers for construction. Persons hereditarily categorized as bearing low status, described in India as scheduled or backward castes and scheduled tribes, were over-represented among slum dwellers. The 'informal' sector of the urban economy, including domestic service, regular employment in small-scale industries such as garment or spare parts manufacture or more irregular jobs ranging from begging to street vending, provided a livelihood for slum dwellers. In all major cities the informal sector comprised at least 50 percent of employment; in Mumbai estimates of its size ranged from at least 51 percent to as great as 66 percent depending on the database chosen for analysis (MMRDA 1999: 77).

Some disjunction existed between income levels and housing arrangements in neighborhoods described broadly as slums. For example, in Karachi at the beginning of the 1990s about 16 percent of households could be classified as high-income, 27 percent as high middle-income, 31 percent as lower middle-income, 15 percent as low-income, and 11 percent below the national poverty line. Simultaneously, 42 percent of the city's house stock was described as permanent (*pakka*), 49.6 percent as semi-permanent, and 8.4 percent as impermanent (*katcha*). One can easily imagine that all high-income families and perhaps half middle-income families inhabited permanent housing while most families living below the poverty line inhabited impermanent homes. But clearly a proportion of the very poor, around half of low-income families, and even some lower-middle families had to live within semi-permanent abodes. The crucial characteristic of such housing was its classification as non-legal occupation – an element within squatter properties, 'invasion settlements,' or 'informal subdivisions' – rendering problematic the delivery of basic infrastructure. In Pakistan such informal neighbourhoods, or *katchi abadis*, were classified as notified, i.e. scheduled for eventual regularization by the state, or non-notified, indicating that the state would eventually re-appropriate the land for other purposes. The state differentiated the *katchi abadis* from 'true' slums where infrastructure was collapsed or totally inadequate (Hasan 2002: 42, 62).

Among the 716 *katchi abadis* in Karachi the largest lay on the north side of the Layari River: Baldia, and Orangi (Aurangi) to its north, each with populations in the early-twenty-first century of over 1 million. Settlement in Orangi began about 1965 and coagulated around the Orangi Metroville project (Herbert 1982) designed to provide legal house sites with infrastructure to low-income groups including refugees. In practice most households could not afford the units and extensive squatter colonies grew near the delineated housing scheme, which was left vacant for years. Over 80 percent of the persons living in these *katchi abadis* obtained their income from the informal sector but this means that 20 percent, or more than 400,000 people, derived support from formal sector jobs but simply could neither amass the sums necessary for deposits on legal rental units nor offer sufficient collateral to obtain housing loans from registered lending institutions (Hasan and Mohib 2003).

The growth of large, contiguous informal settlements such as Orangi was the exception rather than the rule. Most grew within the interstices of the urban land market along railway lines and canals or near construction sites. In Mumbai, over 55 percent of the population lived in 2,500 slum settlements occupying 2,525 hectares or 6 percent of the city's total land area. Fifty percent of the settlements lay on private property, 25 percent on state government land, and another 25 percent on land of the municipal corporation. Households living along railway tracks totaled 28,000. Somewhere between 300,000 and 1 million people lived on the pavements (Das 2003; Sharma 2000: 17–18). In Kolkata, approximately one third of the population lived in 2,011 officially authorized (registered) *bustees* and in 3,500 squatter (unregistered) slums. Most rented from private owners. Typically each slum consisted of nine 'hutments' comprised of five huts, 90 percent of which contained one room of 45 square meters, shared, on average, by 13.4 persons. Refugee households from Bangladesh made up 17 percent of Kolkata's slum households (Kundu 2003).

The preservation of many stable homes within informal or slum settlements cannot obscure the generally unacceptable living conditions prevailing there. Health facilities were inferior to those available for higher income groups; sanitation facilities, in particular, were almost universally inadequate. The higher rates within slums of childhood diarrhoea and acute respiratory infection, for example, were important factors in the overall high rates of mortality for children under-five (UN-Habitat 2006: 198). Organizations officially described as criminal, headed by confederations of neighbourhood *dadas*, ran extortion and protection rackets more freely within informal settlements where police forces were unable or unwilling to penetrate. Alcoholism and drug abuse rates were typically higher than in other parts of the city. Domestic violence aimed against women was not uncommon, particularly among insecure migrant communities. Despite the necessity for many women living in slums to seek outside employment, poverty did not diminish the force of a patriarchal model that relegated them to the isolating tasks of the household and forced them to confront the major hurdles of household maintenance such as obtaining water (Haider 2000).

The dynamics of slum settlement, employment and processes of urban development are exemplified by Dharavi in Mumbai, once described as the largest slum in Asia, later surpassed by Karachi's Orangi Township. In the early-twentieth century Dharavi was a village on the northern end of Bombay island (see Map 15), inhabited mostly by Koli fishing people, which became the site of leather tanneries that obtained hides from slaughter houses located in Bandra. Much of the low-lying land in Dharavi's immediate vicinity was periodically flooded or supported marsh grass; rail lines bracketed it on the west and the east. Population increased through migration of low-caste workers including Tamil-speaking Muslims of the Labbai community long associated with the leather industry and Adi Dravidas who were relegated to this industry. Joined by low castes such as Marathi-speaking leather workers and potters who were pushed out of the southern part of the island by state authorities and private real estate developers, these depressed communities squatted in makeshift housing that they improved as best they could with mezzanines over the ground floor (Vora and Palshikar 2003: 172–6).

During the 1950s and 1960s Dharavi became an illegal dumping site for solid waste and hard fill, an unofficial land reclamation project that attracted the desperately poor to house sites that still flooded regularly. By the end of the century, the piecemeal accumulation of squatter settlements had spread over 175 hectares to include the entire area between the railway lines and the old village of Sion. Dense concentrations of hutments separated by narrow lanes filled every inhabitable space around older village sites and scattered *chawls*; guesses of the population here ranged from 250,000 to 1 million. Although residents came from all over India by the end of the century about one-third were native speakers of Tamil, another one-third were originally from Maharashtra, and about 10 percent hailed from Uttar Pradesh. A later wave of immigration was coming from Bihar. Because of the tendency of migrants to find homes near those of others who spoke the same language, and in many cases came from the same village or district, Dharavi was not a single slum but a collection of contiguous settlements each preserving some of the character of the original homes of its inhabitants. For decades the Hindu and Muslim populations, which were about evenly represented in Dharavi, lived interspersed and in relative harmony; the communal riots in 1992–3 led to a more pronounced communalisation of space and social interaction. This ghetto-construction exemplifies what Ranjit Hoskote (2007: 267–9) describes as the elimination of the city's 'interstitiality' and the strengthening of social marginalization.

Dharavi was notable for its heterogeneous mixture of industrial and residential space. After the state forced many stinking tanneries to move out in the 1980s, thousands of small-scale workshops grew within Dharavi specializing in finished leather goods; a factory run by Johnson and Johnson for the production of surgical sutures represented only the high end of this industry. Similarly, the collapse of the large textile factories created opportunities for hundreds of garment producers, a few serving the export market but most aiming at domestic consumption. Food-preparation businesses specialized in sweets, baked goods, and crisp, flat *papads* (the latter employing thousands of women working at home through affiliation with the women's organization, Shri Mahila Griha Udyog Lijjat Papad). Waste recycling through the hand sorting of metals and plastics, drum refurbishing, and motor oil reconstitution came to dominate a neighborhood in the northwestern part of the slum (Sharma 2000).

By the beginning of the twenty-first century this massive settlement was facing possible extinction – a phenomenon exemplifying the insecurity of tenure lying at the heart of the slum-dweller's condition. Because Dharavi was no longer a peripheral settlement of low-status persons but instead occupied a central location in Greater Mumbai with great potential for real estate redevelopment, the state and real estate agents evinced interest in providing enhanced infrastructure to parts of the settlement. This trend led to the construction of high-rise residences around the edges of Dharavi with arrangements to house earlier inhabitants (or more successful local business people) in some of the flats. The result was a skyline juxtaposing recent high-rise buildings with Dharavi's massive expanse of wood, tarpaulin, mud brick, and sheet metal. Then a Task Force of the Chief Minister's office advocated the development of at least one block within Dharavi as part of the drive toward a global city that would reduce the city's slum population from 50–60 percent in 2003 to 4 percent in 2013 (Bombay First 2003: 8; Government of Maharashtra 2004: 5). Inhabitants would come to occupy mid-rise or high-rise apartments, losing their involvement in localized manufacturing, or would find themselves relocated again to different low-income neighbourhoods within the metropolitan region. On June 1, 2007 the Slum Rehabilitation Authority of the Government of Maharashtra invited global tenders for a Dharavi Redevelopment Project that would affect 144 hectares in five sectors, providing 57,000 new homes, revamping business locations, relocating the leather factories, and reserving 15 percent open space – an approach focusing on 'health, income, knowledge, environment and socio-cultural integration' (HIKES). The long-anticipated announcement elicited widespread protests from slum-dwellers' associations including the Save Dharavi Committee (Dharavi Bachao Samiti) and the National Slum Dwellers Association, concerned primarily with the expected divorce between residence and workspace (Menon 2007).

Socialism and new towns

In all nations in post-Independence South Asia the influence of socialist concepts and programs peaked during the 1960s and 1970s and declined after the late 1980s. One of the most important features of socialism's 40-year run was a strengthening of the public sector at the national and/or state-provincial levels. Governments were not slow in allocating public funds for the provision of offices and housing for their own employees, which extended to the construction of new administrative zones with massive architectural impact on pre-existing cities and also to the foundation of entirely new planned cities. Governments also intervened directly within the economy to create public sector units, i.e. state-run corporations that provided services, produced commodities, and marketed goods. The rapid and sustained growth in bureaucracies at all levels of government thus exerted a direct impact on the character of political capitals and also on urban sites where major public sector units were located. In this section we will briefly examine state influence within new administrative centers, before turning our attention to the urban effects of public-sector industrialization in technology clusters, mining, and ports.

Constructing capitals

In independent India a regular program of state capital construction has occurred after the periodic establishment of new state governments, but the first three examples are most interesting because they led to completely new cities and introduced to the public sphere debates about the direction of architecture within a nationalist modernity. The first attempt took place in Orissa, which had attained the status of a province in 1936 after a lengthy agitation but which did not move toward the construction of a new administrative center because of Second World War and the final paroxysms of the nationalist struggle. The new state government finally decided in 1948 to avoid Cuttack, the state's largest commercial node with about 100,000 people, and to locate the new capital about 25 kilometers south at Bhubaneswar, the site of the eleventh-century Lingaraja Temple and a well-preserved example of a sacred pilgrimage center (see Chapter 2) with a permanent population of about 10,000 people. Otto Koenigsberger provided an initial city plan, which brought into play his 'neighbourhood units' roughly quadrangular in plan. Architect Julius Vaz and the Public Works Department executed the ensemble of the capitol, which became an exercise in public-sector monumental architecture. Between 3 and 10 kilometers north of the temple the regular grid of the new capital was an updated version of a cantonment with neighbourhoods graded according to rank within the bureaucracy (Seymour 1980; Kalia 1994). The inability to foresee what was ahead for the new city is exemplified by the initial projections of a population of about 20,000 persons; in fact, by 2007 Bhubaneswar had become by far the largest city in Orissa with about 827,000 within a metropolitan region of about 1.6 million inhabitants.

The second attempt at state capital construction, at Chandigarh in Punjab, elicited extensive and still-continuing public debate and commentary because it brought together Prime Minister Jawaharlal Nehru and Paris-based architect Charles-Edouard Jeanneret, alias Le Corbusier, who pushed an agenda of architectural modernism. The initial plan for the new city designed by the New York City-based Albert Mayer laid down the principle of the 'super block' or neighbourhood unit, similar to the ideas propounded by Koenisberger, for an initially projected population of 150,000 with allowances for expansion to 500,000 people. Le Corbusier's involvement after 1950 subordinated the Mayer plan to abstract architectural principles based upon European readings of modernity; for Le Corbusier, the signature form was the high-rise building resting on pillars and separated from other buildings by extensive plazas or parks: a design that he put into effect in the monuments of the capitol complex. The striking architectural embellishment in and around the capitol, the wide streets of the planned city, and the establishment of middle-class housing and infrastructure within the prearranged 'sectors' of the planned city were major accomplishments that made Chandigarh a unique achievement within Le Corbusier's corpus and a widely studied application of modern planning's successes and failures. His Indian associates later exerted a major influence over the architectural discipline within India and perpetuated the debate on modernity's impact. But in a city where the state owned all land and disbursed it according to pre-planned programs the unexpected and 'unplanned' settlements that subsequently cropped up inexorably shifted the city's economic profile toward commercial and industrial activities and pushed the population of the city past projections to about 972,000 in 2007 (Evenson 1966; Sarin 1982; Kalia 1999; Prakash 2002).

The movement in India toward the linguistic reorganization of states resulted in the separation of Maharashtra from Gujarat in 1960, which left Bombay with the former and a lack of administrative support for the latter. After careful consideration and rejection of Baroda/Vadodara and Ahmedabad, the new Government of Gujarat resolved to create a capital along the Sabarmati River about 25 kilometers north of Ahmedabad, naming it Gandhinagar after the late Mahatma, whose hermitage lay nearby on the river bank. H. K. Mewada, who had worked with Le Corbusier at Chandigarh and subsequently worked for the state governments of Uttar Pradesh, Assam, and Rajasthan, received the commission to design the city and its administrative core. The cantonment model continued its march in the rectilinear neighbourhood blocks or sectors divided by main roads accompanying infrastructure delivery to administrative personnel in separate status categories. The capitol complex, starting out as the architect's homage to Le Corbusier, became a functionalist example of late-twentieth-century public office buildings built by the Public Works Department. Construction began in 1964, the Secretariat shifted to Gandhinagar by 1970, and the assembly complex was inaugurated in 1982. Learning lessons from the earlier capital-building exercises, initial population estimates of 150,000 were raised to 300,000 with expectations of levelling off at about 500,000 in 2011. The population in 2007 was about 251,000 (Kalia 2004).

In Pakistan, attempts to conceptualize the architecture for a national capitol complex at Karachi ended with the 1958 military coup that brought Field Marshall Muhammad Ayub Khan to power. Within a year the new military government had decided to build a completely new capital along the old Grand Trunk Road southeast of ancient Taxila (see Chapter 1) and just 10 kilometers north of Rawalpindi (the latter's population about 330,000 at that time). Athens-based Doxiades Associates received the contract to design the new city called Islamabad, while bids for the various office buildings and neighbourhood housing went to international architectural consultants; coordination of the project rested with a Capital Development Authority founded in 1960. Konstantinos A. Doxiades, never bashful when it came to grand theorization, placed the Islamabad project firmly within his discipline called Ekistics or the study of connectivity between humanity, society, buildings, networks, and nature. He conceived the capital as a 'dynapolis' wherein growth would begin within the administrative enclave and four cellular 'segments' or 'polis' units – macro-neighbourhoods measuring 2 kilometers square, each housing 20–40,000 people oriented toward a communal axis featuring public services and commercial establishments. Expansion would occur through the addition of units in a south-western direction in order to avoid sprawl that would intersect with Rawalpindi. The dynapolis would operate within a bi-nodal 'dynametropolis' as Rawalpindi also would also grow toward the southwest (Doxiades 1968; Nilsson 1973: 139–81).

The success of the Islamabad plan depended on Rawalpindi as a staging area with the minimal infrastructure necessary to support a population of low-wage workers who would not find accommodation within the new capital. The municipal corporation of Rawalpindi remained the responsibility of the province of Punjab and the Rawalpindi Development Authority created a separate master plan, but the city accessed lower levels of resources. The Islamabad Capital Territory (ICT), redefined in 1992, retained much of its original character because expansion to the north was restricted by Margala Hills National Park and to the east by Islamabad Park with its artificial reservoir called Rawal Lake. Islamabad's growth toward the southwest preserved the original planning concept through the addition of segments or sectors while its commercial or Blue Area, named after its colour on planning maps, became the site of multi-story corporate offices. Islamabad found its iconic representation through the construction of the Shah Faisal Masjid, named after Shah Faisal bin Abdul Aziz, who arranged funding from Saudi Arabia. Designed by Ankara-based Vedat Dalokay and constructed 1976–86, this mosque with its tent-like center and delicate minarets framed against the Margala Hills could accommodate on its grounds 300,000 worshippers. Zoning regulations for the ICT created a new area southeast of old Rawalpindi dedicated to the private development of housing schemes; thus the ICT effectively surrounded more than half of Rawalpindi. The population of Islamabad (about 834,000 in 2007) enjoyed relatively adequate infrastructure and high levels of employment, while Rawalpindi (about 1.84 million) supported a low-income bracket comprising about 40 percent of its population (Maria and Imran 2006).

   Dhaka's orientation in a northwest-southeast direction along the Buriganga River had revolved around the twin poles of the commercialized Bangla Bazaar on the east and the administrative Chauk on the west with its fort, Friday Mosque, and large *sarai* called the Bara Katra. The British later installed their cantonment-and-railway zone called the Ramna farther inland to the north. The Pakistani constitution that came into force under Ayub Khan's regime in 1962 created a National Assembly that would convene alternately in Islamabad and Dhaka; the insufficiency of accommodations in Dhaka for this national body prompted the construction of a second national capital enclave (originally called Ayub Nagar) about 12 kilometers northwest of the Chauk and Ramna. Architect Mazharul Islam brought into the project Philadelphia-based Louis I. Kahn, who designed the assembly building on a diamond-shaped plan juxtaposed vertically with quadrilateral and cylindrical towers featuring his signature style of repeating circular, triangular, and rectangular apertures for light wells – the entire complex eventually surrounded by an artificial lake. The Bangladesh War of Liberation in 1971 followed by Kahn's death in 1974 delayed completion of the project, renamed Sher-e-Bangla Nagar, until 1983. The enclave as finally realized placed the assembly building and the parade ground/public park fronting it between diagonals of flanking hostel blocks, Secretariat, and office spaces. The assembly building, in concrete with horizontal marble strips inserted between poured sections, created an initially monolithic impression, set off against the brick of the surrounding buildings. Its interior provided a strikingly spacious and variegated pattern of light and the ensemble became one of the great achievements of late-twentieth-century modernism. By the early-twenty-first century Sher-e-Bangla Nagar had become encompassed within the Dhaka Metropolitan Area that was expanding rapidly as a 'peri-urban' sprawl toward the north and northwest (Nilsson 1973: 182–203; Gast 1998: 98–111; Brownlee and De Long 1991: 374–83).

In Sri Lanka the government decided in 1978 to relocate the national capital from Colombo fort to Kotte, about 10 kilometers southeast, where a fifteenth-century polity that briefly united the entire island had its base. An urban development authority was given the job of drawing up a master plan for the new city, which would be named Sri Jayawardanepura. Sinhala architect Geoffrey Bawa, who received the commission for the parliament building, designed a large main chamber in a central pavilion surrounded by five satellite pavilions, with each building surmounted by double-pitched roofs that provided a striking reference to indigenous architectural forms. The building complex, fronted by a ceremonial parade area, was accessible in the front and rear by causeways that traversed an artificial lake surrounding the entire site. Work was complete in 1982. Bawa and the government viewed the parliamentary ensemble as a component within a larger Garden City, but the intensification of ethnic warfare the following year stalled work on additional government buildings and forced the protection of the moat-bound parliament by a perimeter of defensive sandbags, barrels, and security posts. The war isolated the parliament architecturally and socially from the mostly unauthorized suburban sprawl that encompassed it and spread 10 kilometers to the east – the characteristic low-rise, low-density expansiveness of the Colombo Metropolitan Region (Robson 2002: 146–55).

Temples of production

In the 1980s, when the involvement of the central and state governments in direct production was still at its height, in India alone there were 226 undertakings that managed plants, most of them located in the vicinity of pre-existing cities (Bhatia 1991: 11). One of the most striking examples of clustering effects that occurred through the concentration of such plants was Bangalore (see Map 20). The first of the big undertakings there was Hindustan Aeronautics Limited (HAL), founded during Second World War to service aircraft and later becoming a major defense contractor, employing 21,000 persons during the 1960s on campuses in the eastern suburbs. In 1948 Indian Telephone Industries (ITI) was established with a national monopoly over production of phone equipment with a campus in the northeast suburbs, employing 3,700 persons during the 1960s. Bharat Electronics Limited (BEL) began in 1954 and became the nation's second largest electronics producer after ITI during the 1960s, when it employed 3,300 persons on a campus in the northwest suburbs. Hindustan Machine Tools (HMT) originated in 1955 to produce factory machinery, later expanding into watches; it employed 5,000 workers during the 1960s on its northwest campus. These plants maintained facilities on their extensive grounds for sports, social events, and health care, while providing housing for much of the managerial staff and a minority of their workers. They operated fleets of buses for line personnel who lived in nearby villages and in the outer edges of the city, thus stimulating suburban growth. The factories also stimulated the concentration of secondary industries, most notably on the Peenya Industrial Estate – once billed as Asia's largest – established by the state government during the 1960s. The presence of the Indian Institute of Science (IISc, founded under the leadership of Jamsetji Nusserwanji Tata in 1911) and the aerospace-electronics factories supported a group of research and analysis organizations including, to name just a few, the National Aeronautics (later Aerospace) Laboratory (NAL), which moved to Bangalore in 1960, and offices of the Indian Space Research Organisation (ISRO), established 1969. The presence of the state capital and numerous bureaucratic headquarters, in combination with the many public sector units, created formal-sector jobs in Bangalore for some 300,000 workers by the 1990s.

State intervention through public sector production facilities transformed the human landscape amid the coal fields around Asansol in West Bengal and in the 'tribal' regions that would become the Indian states of Jharkhand and Chhattisgarh. The experience of the private-sector steel industry at Jamshedpur (see Chapter 4) had already indicated the feasibility of building a large steel plant, adjacent planned city, related mining sites, and transportation infrastructure. Additional steel-town experience came from the private sector Indian Iron and Steel Company (IISCO) at Burnpur just west of Asansol, founded in 1918 and reorganized, finally achieving limited sustainability, during the 1950s. The foundation of a plant for locomotive production at Chittaranjan, a virgin site about 30 kilometers northwest of Asansol, indicated that the public sector was able to initiate industry- and city-building exercises on a fairly large scale. After its initiation in 1948, the plant turned out its first locomotive in 1950; population at Chittaranjan was about 16,000 in 1951 and peaked at around 45,000 (Mohsin 1964).

The Government of India, committed to heavy industry on a grand scale, began negotiations with a West German delegation in 1953 that led to the commissioning in 1962 of a big steel plant at Rourkela, lying within a 'tribal' village area in northern Orissa. Technicians from the Soviet Union began discussions in 1954 for a second plant at Bhilai in Madhya Pradesh that was commissioned in 1961 near Durg, a district town with a population of about 47,000. A British mission began discussions in 1955 that led to a third plant at Durgapur, lying 40 kilometers east of Asansol, which was commissioned in 1962. The socio-spatial decision making for these three complexes and appended model towns rested primarily on economic analysis of transportation and raw material accessibility. The Durgapur plant, for example, formed the eastern node of an industrial corridor stretching along the rail lines and Grand Trunk Road through Asansol and including Burnpur and Chittaranjan (Johnson 1966: 186–94; Sidhu 1983: 30–4). After negotiations with the United States reached an impasse, the Government of India signed an agreement with the Soviet Union in 1965 that led to the commissioning of the first phase of Bihar's Bokaro Steel City in 1978.

As in the township of Jamshedpur and on the campuses of public sector production units around Bangalore, the Government of India promoted itself as a model employer and visualized a self-contained living and working environment for its four steel cities. It thus provided status-ranked quarters (there were 18 types at Bhilai), sports facilities, club life, cultural events, educational, and health facilities. Wide, tree-lined streets with water and electricity in more reliable supply than in most other South Asian cities made the relatively secure employment in these plants and residence within their townships a mode of 'status enjoyment' providing social mobility for employees and their families. Additional factories located in and around the company towns, originally ancillary plants benefiting from input-output needs of the giant steel plants but slowly diversifying over time, generated jobs that also stimulated wholesale or retail cooperatives and commercial establishments, supporting the growth of tertiary-sector employment (Kumar 1986; Srinivasan 1988: 24–9, 78; Bhatia 1991: 235–40; Basak 2000; Dinesh 2003). But because the state could not provide residential and commercial space for all persons attracted to the magnet of the planned townships and because additional industries were expected to devise separate colonies for their workforces, an increasing percentage of the population found themselves on their own and 'unauthorized' constructions multiplied. Durgapur, for example, became 'a sprawling mixture' of factories and houses with unplanned infill along a 15-kilometer stretch of the Grand Trunk Road. Environmental degradation, marginalization of the original population (now landless) to the lowest paid jobs or unemployment, and a steady decline in the per capita provision of basic amenities characterized particularly those neighbourhoods outside the original model townships (Sivaramakrishnan 1982: 146–8; Meher 2003). As the percentage of the population who earned their income directly from the plants slowly declined, the townships as a whole took on the characteristics of the other large cities in South Asia. And large the steel towns became. By 2007 Durgapur was West Bengal's third city (after Kolkata and Asansol) with about 531,000 persons; Rourkela's population was about 533,000; Bokaro had a population of 539,000; Bhilai merged with Durg as a single planning authority for 1.1 million; and Jamshedpur was home to 1.2 million.

By the late 1950s the Government of India had relegated the job of managing the giant steel plants and their townships to a separate public sector company, Hindustan Steel Limited (HSL), which in 1959 relocated to a headquarters at Ranchi in Bihar – hitherto a slow-growing district headquarters and agrarian marketing node with a population of about 120,000 persons. Only one year earlier the public sector unit named Heavy Engineering Corporation Limited (HEC) had begun operations at Ranchi, with Czechoslovakian assistance, to supply capital equipment, machine tools, and spare parts to the surrounding steel cities. This was the basis of an engineering and manufacturing complex that employed 18,000 by 1971 (Crook 1993: 67). The foundation of the public sector giant called Steel Authority of India Limited (SAIL) in 1973, with authority over all public-sector steel plants and with its headquarters in Ranchi, accompanied the establishment of the Research and Development Center for Iron and Steel (RDCIS), which in turn joined a variety of educational and research institutes in Ranchi. A five-decade-long agitation for the creation of Jharkhand state, mobilized in and around Ranchi, led finally in 2000 to the carving out of Jharkhand from Bihar and a new concentration of state government offices in a city that had grown to almost 1 million by 2007 – an expansion occurring in large part because of public sector investments led by steel.

The new system of major ports

One of the stories followed throughout this book has been the changing pattern of ports in relation to shifts within Indian Ocean and global commerce. Independence brought ports within a paradigm of national economic development, creating a new macro-regional pattern that we will now examine.

In Bangladesh and Sri Lanka, over 90 percent of sea-borne traffic has gone through the major ports of Chittagong and Colombo, respectively, while in Pakistan about 60 percent has gone through Karachi and 40 percent through a second site within its metropolitan region, Port Qasim; all have been managed through central-government port trusts. In India, the Union List of the Constitution mandated central control over major ports. Eleven major ports in India were, therefore, trusts governed by the provisions of 1963 Major Port Trust Act; a twelfth was Ennore Port Limited, the first major port managed by a private corporation. India's 187 intermediate and minor ports were under the administrative control of the respective maritime departments of the state governments. The total volume of the traffic handled by all the Indian ports during 2004–05 was 521.58 million tons, of which major ports moved 383.75 million tons (around 74 percent) and minor ports moved the remaining 137.83 million tons. These ports were important components of national economy policy: about 95 percent by volume and 70 percent by value of India's international trade was carried on through maritime transport (Government of India 2005: 47, 55–56).

The left column of Table 4 portrays the 17 major ports of South Asia and their rank based on the amount of tonnage cleared within a twelve-month period. Among these sites are the port-capitals of colonial days – Kolkata (Calcutta), Chennai (Madras), Mumbai (Bombay) and Colombo – which were already multi-functional metropolises by 1947. Four additional ports grew under British rule as regional maritime hubs – Karachi, Kochi (Cochin), Vishakhapatnam and Chittagong – and advanced to million-city status after Independence. Mormugao was a Portuguese project of the 1930s that, after India's annexation of Goa in 1961, was declared a major port and experienced expansion after 1970. Kandla was a project of the Government of India immediately after Independence as a western replacement for Karachi.

The remaining seven major ports were post-1950 creations of their nation-states:

- Paradip, founded in 1962 and operational in 1966, was originally designed for traffic in iron ore but later diversified to handle coal, manganese ore, and a variety of stone or metallic raw materials. As a multifunctional port, it started handling containers and the trans-shipment of petroleum products in 1991.
- Haldia Dock Complex, the second of the dock agglomerations managed by the Kolkata Port Trust, is located about 50 kilometers southwest of Kolkata near the Haldi River and the mouth of the Hughli River. Conceived in the late 1940s, it became the site of a major petrochemical complex.
- Port Qasim (Bunder Qasim) originated in decisions by the Government of Pakistan during the late 1960s to relieve pressure on Karachi Port and also

Table 4 South Asia's major ports, 2004–07

Rank	Individual port	Tonnage	Rank	Port complex	Tonnage	Port complex population 2007***
1	Paradip	55,801	1	Mumbai–JNPT	67,995	18,905
2	Vishakhapatnam	50,147	2	Paradip	55,801	93
3	Chennai	43,806	3	Chennai–Ennore	53,285	7,159
4	Kandla	41,551	4	Vishakhapatnam	50,147	328
5	Haldia	36,262	5	Karachi–Port Qasim	49,894	12,231
6	Mumbai	35,187	6	Kolkata–Haldia	46,207	14,998
7	New Mangalore	33,891	7	Kandla	41,551	168
8	JNPT	32,808	8	New Mangalore	33,891	592
9	Mormugao	30,659	9	Mormugao	30,659	105
10	Karachi	28,613	10	Chittagong*	25,885	3,920
11	Chittagong*	25,885	11	Colombo**	18,737	2,559
12	Port Qasim	21,281	12	Tuticorin	15,811	328
13	Colombo**	18,737	13	Kochi	14,095	1,491
14	Tuticorin	15,811				
15	Kochi	14,095				
16	Kolkata	9,945				
17	Ennore	9,479				

Notes:
* Calendar year 2005
** Average based on figures for January 1–July 1, 2004 and January 1–July 1, 2005
*** In thousands (includes metropolitan region populations).

Sources: Basic port statistics of India. Government of India, Department of Shipping, Road Transport and Highways (http://shipping.nic.in).
Chittagong Port Authority (http://www.cpa.gov.bd).
Colombo Port handles highest ever container volume (2006) (Sri Lanka Ports Authority (http://www.slpa.lk)).
Government of Pakistan 2006 (http://www.statpak.gov.pk).

to support the public-sector Pakistan Steel Mills Corporation, established with assistance from the Soviet Union on a site about 40 kilometers east of Karachi. The Pakistan Steel plant, commissioned in 1985, spread over an area of 7,550 hectares northeast of the port and included 3,266 hectares for an industrial township. Bin Qasim Town developed during the 1970s and reached a population of 316,000 by 1998.

- The area around Tuticorin (Tuttukkudi) supported a harbour in ancient times and in 1920 Tuticorin still ranked sixth among South Asia's ports, although it slipped steadily to tenth by 1960 (Kidwai 1989: 213). Its port underwent a major renovation and in 1974 the Government of India declared it a major port, with two berths for container traffic.
- The main harbour of Mangalore (see Chapter 3) shifted 10 kilometers north of the old city to the New Mangalore project, started in 1962 and commissioned in 1974. The combination of port and refinery industries gave Mangalore the profile of Karnataka's main port and its most important coastal city.

- The Jawaharlal Nehru Port Trust (JNPT) located at Nhava Sheva was commissioned in 1989 as a component in plans to decongest Bombay (see Map 19). As a container port, JNPT became the first in India to handle more than 2 million twenty-foot equivalent units (TEU) in a calendar year and also ranked 32 among the top 50 container handling ports of the world during 2004 (Jacquemin 1999: 146–7; GOI 2005: 62).
- Ennore was originally conceived as a satellite port located 24 kilometers north of Chennai Port, primarily to handle thermal coal to meet the requirement of Tamil Nadu Electricity Board, but it was later expanded to serve additional industrial schemes. In the late 1990s, as part of its liberalization initiatives, the Government of India decided to gradually privatize port trusts in order to increase their responsiveness to market forces. The country's twelfth major port at Ennore accordingly began operations in 2001–2 as a private enterprise

The concentration of major ports on bulk raw materials goes a long way toward explaining their overall rank. In 2004–5, for example, 94 percent of Ennore's traffic consisted of coal, but it also constituted 47 percent of Paradip's tonnage. Meanwhile, 80 percent of the tonnage moved at Mormugao consisted of iron ore, which also comprised more than 30 percent of traffic at Paradip, Vishakhapatnam and New Mangalore. Petroleum, oils, and lubricants (POL), which made up 33 percent of all tonnage at India's major ports, totalled 73 percent of the tonnage at Kochi, 63 percent at New Mangalore, more than 50 percent at Kandla, Kolkata and Mumbai, and 45 percent at Haldia.

Eight of the major ports consisted of paired sites that lay within major metropolitan areas: Mumbai-JNPT, Chennai-Ennore, Karachi-Port Qasim, and Kolkata-Haldia. If we view these pairs as port complexes we find that that they occupy four out of the top six positions in tonnage moved during 2004–5, and that the Mumbai-JNPT complex was the largest in South Asia (see column 2 of Table 4). The lead of this latter complex increased further in 2005–6, when it registered traffic of 81.9 million tons followed only distantly by Chennai and Vishakhapatnam with about 56 million tons each. Placing this accomplishment in international context, one notes that the port of Singapore led the world with 1.15 billion tons and its container traffic amounting to 23.2 million TEU ('Singapore port' 2006).

Port growth connected with urban growth not only through the generation of direct employment but also through the state-sponsored clustering of industrial activities around the harbour in order to build a multifaceted source of formal employment. In Vishakhapatnam, for example, the population in 1950 was only 104,000. Subsequent public-sector establishments that accompanied port growth included the Dredging Corporation of India, Bharat Heavy Plate and Vessels Limited, Hindustan Shipyard Limited, Hindustan Zinc Limited, Coromandel Fertilizers Limited, and a refinery of Hindustan Petroleum Corporation Limited (HPCL). Plans were on the table in the late 1960s for a giant steel facility, but it was not until 1992 that the dedication took place for SAIL's 'Vizag Steel' plant reputed to be among the most energy-efficient in the world.

The plant included an attached 'Steel Town' or Ukkunagaram with a circular plan divided into sectors allotted to different ranks of employees, housing 11,000 in 2007.

The Government of Pakistan was anticipating a similar future for a brand-new major port in Baluchistan at the fishing village of Gwadar, where financial and construction assistance from the People's Republic of China included harbour facilities and the Makran Coast Highway link to Karachi (Ramachandran 2005). The foundation stone was laid in 2001 and the port became operational in early 2007, with management by the Port of Singapore.

Managing the mega-city

Following practices established during the colonial period, the management of South Asian cities after 1947 remained a state/provincial subject, which meant in effect that the organs of municipal governance enjoyed independent existence only through laws enacted at the state level and they could be changed or abrogated by state governments. Should a municipal corporation come into existence through state action its executive functions typically remained the prerogative of state-appointed bureaucrats, who interacted with elected city councils or mayors but in practice supervised administrative staffs that were not completely responsible to city officials. The state governments also reserved the right to abrogate the powers of municipal corporations or to disband councils at will, a power regularly exercised because of perceived incompetence or political deadlock or because of political machinations at the state and even the national level (The Municipal Corporation of Bombay was an exception until 1983, when the state of Maharashtra passed legislation that allowed it to supersede the elected city council). Municipalities demonstrated a chronic inability to gather sufficient income through the limited range of taxation available to them and most remained remarkably inefficient in allocating or collecting property taxes. Urban incapacity served as grounds for periodic state takeovers of city governments and also rationalized the creation of 'parastatal' authorities or directorates responsible to the state for the implementation and administration of water supply and sewerage, housing, or urban planning. Under these circumstances, citizen participation in decision-making or even the ability to affect the bureaucracy through democratic process remained limited (Buch 1987: 132–43).

Urban planning practice in South Asia responded to international trends in planning theory as well as indigenous perceptions of cities' roles within national and state/provincial development. The period immediately after Independence witnessed the hegemony of master planning exemplified by the London plans (1943–4) devised under Leslie Patrick Abercrombie. This approach focused on directed land use through zoning (e.g. residential, industrial, commercial) and attempted to mitigate the externalities of urban density through a redistribution of industries and populations to new towns or peripheral growth centers, separated from older urban cores by non-development expanses or green belts. Abercrombie brought this approach to South Asia when he produced a master plan for Colombo in 1948 that created a group of satellite suburbs on the edges of the city. The negative effects of concentrated settlement and industrialization were a special target of master plans, prompting attempts to push low-income housing and factories out of metropolitan regions into smaller cities serving as counter-magnets. An early example of this approach (1958–64) was the Greater Karachi Resettlement Plan prepared by the Greek architect Konstantinos Doxiades, which established two satellites (New Karachi to the north and Landhi-Korangi to the east) about 25 kilometers from the city center, designed as New Towns with industrial estates to provide employment for refugee populations.

By the late 1950s the states of South Asia were establishing public-sector 'authorities' to take over the job of 'developing' major cities – effectively divorcing planning from municipal responsibility. The Delhi Development Authority (DDA), for example, was set up in 1958 in order to produce a 20-year master plan that became operational in September 1962; the DDA remained the most powerful agency for urban growth in India's capital, with wide-ranging powers over transportation, land use, and construction. By the 1970s, the concept of urban development was becoming embedded within a perspective of the metropolis and its immediate hinterland as a single planning entity. This led to the creation of 'metropolitan' development authorities with a regional focus. By the 1990s, amid the drive toward economic liberalisation and a theoretical shift toward administrative decentralization, development authorities were accepting their limitations in micro-managing zonal development and providing required infrastructure investments, prompting a shift toward regional 'structure' plans that were 'indicative rather than mandatory' and describing current trends while sketching policy guidelines (Buch 1987: 2).

Here we will examine in more detail the post-Independence planning of Bombay (later Mumbai) as an example of the ambitions and limitations of state intervention within a city-region demonstrating unprecedented growth and complexity. This case study will involve us in a detailed look at the peculiar spatial characteristics of an island-turned-metropolis, where geographical limitations were encountered by limitless ambitions. One may note in this case study the interaction between a futurism that regularly encountered intractable demographic and economic realities exceeding its grasp on the one hand and the variety of voices claiming to project an overarching vision of the city on the other.

The story of Bombay's transformation into the largest city in South Asia rested primarily on expansion outside the original island city, which was already perceived as crowded at Independence (Jacquemin 1995: 83). The island was reaching a saturation point; the combined population of its western and eastern suburbs on Salsette Island surpassed the island city (see Table 5 and Map 19). Salsette's population was concentrated in two linear zones paralleling rail and road transport corridors that flanked Borivali (later Sanjay Gandhi) National Park, which covered 104 square kilometers stretching in a triangular plan north of Vihar Lake and included the ancient Kanheri cave monasteries (see Chapter 1). The sections of Salsette that lay outside the boundaries of the Metropolitan Corporation of Greater Bombay (MCGB) were experiencing rapid expansion, especially Thane

Table 5 Population of Bombay/Mumbai Metropolitan Region, 1971–2011

Planning Region	1971	1991	2011
Greater Bombay/Mumbai			
Island City	3,070,378	3,174,889	2,825,000
Western Suburb	1,705,494	3,947,979	5,910,000
Eastern Suburb	1,194,703	2,803,023	4,196,000
Region total	5,970,575	9,925,891	12,931,000
New Bombay/Navi Mumbai			
Municipal Corporation	40,063	307,724	1,533,000
Panvel	69,112	158,362	199,625
Uran	45,357	71,667	75,756
Three sub-region total	154,532	537,753	1,808,381
Region total	160,669	548,476	1,816,376
Northeast			
Ambernath	58,303	125,801	186,934
Badlapur	19,201	52,154	85,440
Bhiwandi	157,300	497,300	1,019,334
Kalyan	246,038	820,584	1,766,503
Thane	254,045	803,389	1,435,000
Ulhasnagar	172,947	385,095	613,400
Six sub-region total	907,834	2,684,323	5,106,611
Region total	1,054,207	2,921,172	5,283,177
West			
Mira-Bhayanar	31,860	175,605	617,000
Nallasopara	16,078	83,800	426,386
Vasai-Navghar	67,500	127,975	207,867
Virar	27,266	77,965	270,885
Four sub-region total	142,704	465,345	1,522,138
Region total	232,659	595,868	1,619,031
Alibag	81,602	107,811	188,061
Neral-Karjat	112,516	166,021	177,308
Panvel-Uran (outside Navi Mumbai)	108,679	180,828	287,327
Pen	56,624	88,297	138,693
Mumbai Metropolitan Region	7,777,531	14,534,364	22,440,973

Source: MMRDP 1999: 46.

and Mira-Bhayandar. Farther to the northeast, a cluster of small and middle cities was growing very quickly, led by Kalyan and Bhiwandi.

Part of the explanation for the attraction of Bombay along with its immediate hinterland lay in its relative economic dynamism. Working factories within Greater Bombay amounted to about 3,400 in the late 1950s, which constituted about one-third of the factories within the entire state; 76 percent of these were within the

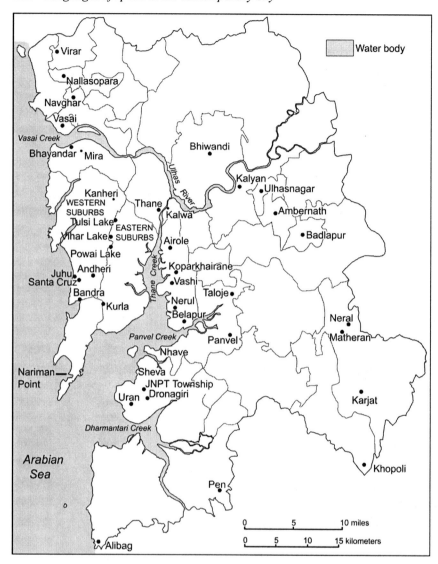

Map 19 Bombay/Mumbai Metropolitan Region. Adapted from MMRDA 1999.

island city (Study Group for Greater Bombay 1959: 74, 128). In 1980–1 the total domestic product of what officials came to call the metropolitan region amounted to Rs. 4,759.94 crores (US$5.23 billion) or about 35 percent of the entire product of Maharashtra, which in turn contributed 12.44 percent of India's production. On average, an individual could expect to earn more in and around Bombay, where per capita income was Rs. 3,638 (US$400) compared to Rs. 1,824 (US$200) in the rest of Maharashtra. The city had been the financial capital of India since the 1930s, when the headquarters of the Reserve Bank of India and the Bombay Stock Market were established; most of the country's banks and leading insurance companies were headquartered here (Harris 1978: 13–17). The continued concentration of workplaces on Bombay Island and of white-collar jobs in the central business district on the southern part of the island city put tremendous pressure on public transport and many thousands of daily commuters. In 1966–7 the Indian Railways reported that of the total of 2.2 billion passengers in Bombay who travelled on their national routes, 35 percent used only on the two main suburban lines in Greater Bombay. By the mid-1990s, there were 5 million rail passengers daily packed into, and hanging off, cars designed to accommodate half their numbers (Jacquemin 1995: 86, 91; Dwivedi and Mehrotra 2001: 188).

The amalgamation of new industrial zones on and beyond the northern administrative borders of Greater Bombay was underway during the 1950s and 1960s as the Maharashtra Industrial Development Corporation created industrial zones in the Taloja industrial estate covering 900 hectares and the Thane-Belapur Industrial Area (TBIA), a strip covering 2,105 hectares. The latter, one of India's main petrochemical belts, housed 44 industries in 1971 with a total work force of about 16,000, mostly commuters. By 1990 the areas of the metropolitan region outside Greater Bombay were supporting 37,173 factories employing 396,781 workers. Bhiwandi led the way with 129,000 manufacturing workers, followed by Thane with 73,000, Khopoli with 60,000, and Kalyan with 52,000 (MMRDA 1999: 56, 66–7, 76).

Consonant with approaches to urbanization that viewed density as the major problem, planning interventions in Bombay during the first few decades after Independence focused primarily on the problems of increased crowding within Greater Bombay and attempts to move industries away from the island city: originally to Salsette Island and later to the mainland. The unofficial 1947 publication of a Master Plan in Outline recommended expansion of the city limits into the northern suburbs and into satellite towns in order to relieve congestion, while banning light industries to Salsette and heavy industries to the mainland where satellite towns would be cultivated. The state in 1958–9 supported a study group that advised shifting industries off the island (opining that a new city on the mainland would be a 'master stroke'), recommended the creation of an office/commercial zone between Bandra and Kurla, and supported satellite towns and industrial estates on Salsette (Study Group for Greater Bombay 1959: 32–4, 108). In 1965 the Modern Architects' Research Group, including contributions by Charles Correa, Pravina Mehta and Shirish Patel, outlined a circular polycentric structure that would include the complete urbanization of land on the east side of Bombay harbour. Uneasy with the projected population of seven to 8 million people in Greater Bombay, influenced by the international trend toward regional planning, and affected by the bold MARG proposal, the state government in 1967 defined a new Bombay Metropolitan Region (BMR) and deputed a Planning Board (BMRPB) to draw up a document projecting a 20-year program. Government circles accepted the concept of a completely new mainland city named New (Navi) Bombay (after 1995, Navi Mumbai).

The Planning Board of the Bombay Metropolitan Region created in early 1970 a regional plan (sanctioned by the state government in 1973) that included the MCGB, the remaining land on Salsette Island, and adjacent areas on the mainland within a total of 4,375 square kilometers (see Map 19). It positioned a new city directly opposite Bombay linked to transportation infrastructure already underway, including the Thane Creek Bridge (opened 1973), a road-and-rail corridor to Pune, and the port facilities projected at Nhava and Sheva. In March 1970 the Government of Maharashtra also set up the City and Industrial Development Corporation (CIDCO) to develop Navi Bombay. When the state government formally constituted the Bombay (later Mumbai) Metropolitan Region Development Authority (BMRDA-MMRDA) in March 1975 it was committing to a model for future growth aiming at the mainland rather than the islands. The state was contemplating the largest South Asian city-planning exercise since Independence and one of the largest in the world.

Navi Bombay was conceived primarily as a site for tertiary employment, and the relocation of state government offices would provide a major impetus for its rapid growth. But in contravention of its own planning initiatives the state government, in collusion with real estate developers, also supported expansion of the commercial district in south Bombay. In 1958 it accepted a report from a one-man committee recommending the completion of the Back Bay Reclamation Scheme that had been halted in the 1930s with only four of its eight blocks complete (see Chapter 4). Subsequent study groups recommended abandonment of the scheme because of the pressure it would exert on transportation and other infrastructure, but the state government ignored the advice. The result was reclamation of a strip of land along the entire shore, plus the completion of block three in the north and about 40 percent of block five at Cuffe Parade. The northern block included Nariman Point, which featured a grouping of skyscrapers and facilities for the Government of Maharashtra (a new state assembly building and state administrative offices along with residences for assembly members). The block at Cuffe Parade included another grouping of skyscrapers that eclipsed the formerly genteel, low-rise environment of its upper-class residences and attracted commercial clients such as the World Trade Center (Banerjee-Guha 1995: 103–8; Dwivedi and Mehrotra 2001: 306–16). Decried in many public forums, the grouping of skyscrapers nonetheless gave the city another distinctive image, regularly reproduced and promoted as a vision of the contemporary city.

The main action was supposed to take place in Navi Bombay, which would cover an area of about 344 square kilometers including 294 square kilometers (56 percent in private hands) that became the responsibility of CIDCO. The project area stretched 25 kilometers south from Kalwa, flanked by Thane Creek to the west and hills to the east, as far as Panvel Creek and the industrial estate at Taloja. It then stretched southwest about 30 kilometers to include the already existing towns of Panvel and Uran. Within the new city a linear 'nodal settlement pattern' along transport corridors in the form of 20 new residential townships or 'nodes,' each projected to house 50,000 to 200,000 persons, would in theory support a total population of about 2 million by the end of the century.

The 365 hectares around Vashi village, an 'early development area' chosen because of its proximity to the first Thane Creek Bridge and to the Thane-Belapur industrial area, comprised CIDCO's first node taken for development (Verma 1985: 92–3, 100–4). CIDCO, however, could not assemble and develop a mix of affordable residential zones fast enough, which led to a steep rise in land prices and, in its effort to cover massive expenses, alienation of land to private real estate developers resulting in a bedroom community for middle-class citizens and a commercial zone in Vashi that became the real central business district of Navi Bombay. Displacement of lower-income groups through resale was also higher in Vashi than in other nodes where CIDCO-constructed residential blocks for low-income groups remained more stable. This early tendency for Navi Bombay to attract middle-class citizens who could afford housing (running against a model of providing housing for the 'common man') became more pronounced by the end of the 1990s as the Thane-Belapur industrial complex stagnated – part of the general shift from secondary to tertiary employment within the metropolitan region. The opening of the Millennium Business Park east of Vashi with 'intelligent' buildings signalled an attempt to shift employment toward information technology with its primarily middle-class work force (Shaw 2004: 107–20, 162–88).

As CIDCO completed nodes it would transfer them to the authority of the Navi Bombay Municipal Corporation (NBMC, later NMMC), activated in 1992. The first nodes completed – Vashi (population 108,000), Nerul (58,000), Airoli (41,000), Koparkhairane (30,000), and Belapur (29,000) – were transferred in 1995. The takeoff of land prices and the completion of a second Thane Creek Bridge at Airole stimulated a more rapid growth of Navi Bombay, but in fact the municipality's population at the turn of the century was still less than 1 million with a projected population in 2011 of about 1.53 million (see Table 5). Its expansion remained, at least in administrative circles, inevitable, stimulated through projects such as the New Mumbai Special Economic Zone (NMSEZ) within the Dronagiri, Kalamboli, Ulwe and JNPT areas.

While the initial planning work on Navi Bombay was underway the area on the mainland north of Salsette, including Vasai, Virar, and Nallasopara, had remained primarily agricultural. But pressure from major real estate developers was already resulting in the sanctioning of massive residential projects, in contravention to planning documents and without preparation of road systems or utilities. A tract of 8,500 hectares earlier labelled as green belt became available for urbanization. Population of the area shot up to almost 600,000 during the 1980s. When CIDCO became the special planning authority for the area in 1990 its interim plan showed 55 percent of the land categorized as urban already in use for residential purposes (Banerjee-Guha 1995: 114–18). Although the area had presented a low profile in earlier planning documents it was expected to house about 1 million people in 2011 (see Table 5). As in the case of Navi Bombay, the state backed off and allowed market forces to dictate the pace of change.

During 30 years of post-Independence discussions on the relocation of industries outside Bombay, the continuing presence of textile mills on the island city, mostly in its central part, remained off the table. Since the mid-nineteenth century these mills had defined the city as an industrial power (see Chapter 4) and a distinctive working-class culture within neighbourhoods surrounding the mill district had become an integral component of Bombay's persona. A work force of several hundred thousand, including a majority of permanent employees and a large minority of temporary workers, had deep roots in the city while retaining contact with native villages, mostly in the hinterland of Maharashtra (Adarkar and Menon 2004). Warning signs, however, pointed to the fragility of this ageing industrial cluster: technological obsolescence, payroll padding, challenges from East and Southeast Asia or from mills elsewhere in India, and the rising competition from thousands of power looms (including India's largest concentration in Bhiwandi). Cotton textiles absorbed 28 percent of the work force in 1977 but only 17 percent in 1981.

Militant labor actions had been a regular feature of Bombay's textile landscape, but a wildcat strike beginning in January 1982 shut down all the mills simultaneously. Although some production re-started after a few months the strike officially dragged on until October 1983. A number of mills never re-opened. A total of perhaps 75,000 workers lost their jobs (Van Wersch 1992). Commentators blamed the strike for delivering a death blow to Bombay's textile mills, but the nearly simultaneous decline of the mills in Ahmedabad suggests that industrial reorganization was underway producing a South Asian version of the 'rust belt' characterizing many industrial cities in the northeast part of the United States.

The moribund condition of the Bombay mills by the 1990s contributed to the formation of dense neighbourhoods with hundreds of small workshops and power looms as the 'informal' sector and substandard housing became the norm for perhaps 70 percent of the population, now increasingly divided into segregated religion-based or language-based enclaves (Hansen 2001: 162–6; Punwani 2003). Competing viewpoints came from the mill owners, the government, land developers, citizens' groups, and the mill workers about the disposition of 280 hectares of mill land that supported little economic activity but that had become extremely valuable (Bombay ranked consistently among the world's top ten cities in the price of office space). In practice, mill owners colluded with land developers to gentrify piecemeal sections of Mumbai's textile factories. Phoenix Mills in Parel produced the 28-floor Phoenix Towers, Phoenix Mall, and the Bowling Company, an entertainment arcade attracting the affluent scions of the upper middle class. Twin 60-story skyscrapers, the tallest in India, came up in the compound of M. P. Mill in Tardeo (D'Monte 2002: 120–52).

The gentrification of the mill district resonated with the dream of turning Mumbai into another Hong Kong or Singapore or, later, into another Shanghai (Mukhopadhyay 2001) imagined as 'global' cities oriented toward services, transportation-communication, and transnational corporations. The commitment to producing such a city rested in part with the Mumbai Metropolitan Region Development Authority (Verma 1985: 122–7), which helped create the Bandra-Kurla Complex covering 370 hectares. This attracted the International Finance and Business Center, the National Stock Exchange, the Diamond Bourse, a Convention and Exhibition Center, multiple banks, the U.S. Consulate, and the Mumbai

Cricket Association (allocated 5.2 hectares for an indoor cricket academy). Like Nariman Point, the Complex exemplified what its advocates believed was the service-oriented direction and global orientation of the city.

Among the agents promoting the global city concept was the Bombay Chamber of Commerce, which created a think tank called Bombay First (later Mumbai First, modelled on a London First initiative from the early 1990s) to cooperate with international consultants McKinsey & Company in order to devise a plan entitled *Vision Mumbai*. This approach utilized 'international benchmark levels' obtained from other urban success stories to rank Mumbai on its global profile. It visualized the city as 'one of Asia's leading service hubs' specializing in high-end services (finance, information technology, health care, media), low-end services (retail, recreation, construction), and middle-class consumption. It described six central business districts – Nariman Point, Kurla, Andheri, plus three Navi Mumbai nodes of Vashi, Belapur, and Dronagiri – and advocated massive expenditure on enhancement of rail and road connections among them. Mumbai was to upgrade and expand its housing stock, eliminate most slum housing, and create 'islands of excellence in world-class housing and commercial complexes' (Bombay First 2003). The Chief Minister of the state government responded by setting up a Task Force that expressed dismay over Mumbai's score of 'poor' in five categories of the global city, 'average' in four, and 'above average' only in health care. The Task Force reiterated much of the language coming from Mumbai First, accepted the estimate of Rs. 200,000 crores (US$40 billion) necessary to bring the city up to speed by the year 2013, and recommended the creation of a Mumbai Development Fund, a new post of Secretary (special projects), a cabinet sub-committee, an Empowered Committee, and a Citizen's Action Group to oversee progress. According to the Task Force, the focus should remain on 'the end customer, the citizen' (Government of Maharashtra 2004: 20).

The fixation on Shanghai as global service center, which offered many historical parallels to Mumbai but which – unlike Mumbai – rocketed within only one generation to international urban stardom and a potential role as the world's largest city, was in a sense merely a discursive gesture within the maturing boosterism of Mumbai's business community. The comparison does, however, offer an opportunity to evaluate the post-Independence performance of urban planning in Mumbai and, by extension, in South Asia as a whole. In this context the extremely rapid transformation of Pudong in eastern Shanghai from a predominantly agrarian zone into the poster child of Chinese urban modernism seems to offer a striking contrast to the less dramatic transformation of Navi Mumbai. One explanation for the disparity lies within the different trajectories of socialist development in China and India. In the former, urban affairs enjoyed low priority until the 1980s when shifts in public policy brought to bear on a single planning problem an almost unlimited amount of public resources from the state and central governments, allocated with little public debate. In India, by contrast, the decision-making process that allowed the Navi Mumbai option to achieve organizational form was marked by multi-faceted debate within the public and the bureaucracy, so that when the project finally got underway in the 1970s it was simultaneously precocious and institutionally weak. Thus the state government and its planning organ (in Navi Mumbai's case, CIDCO) may have entertained ambitions of acquiring, developing, and distributing all the land in the suburbs, but in effect they never commanded adequate funds and the 'capacity' to execute a totalised planning exercise. Meanwhile, an independent and increasingly powerful private real estate industry was busy with its own projects, and eventually came to supplant the state as the delivery mechanism for residential and commercial land use. The result was a slower and more variegated realization of the suburban dream.

The larger institutional context of the metropolis in South Asia also contributed to the unspectacular performance of urban planning. Unlike Singapore or Hong Kong, Mumbai was no centralized city-state but operated within the democratic political system of the State of Maharashtra where agrarian interests and those of the urban working and middle classes were competing for scant resources. Unlike the People's Republic of China, where a powerful central government coexisted with weak state governments and thus allowed the center to carry out super-prestigious urban projects and purposefully encourage state-level regional disparities, in India the constitutional framework distributed important preroga-tives to resource-deprived states while allowing them to compete democratically for central allocations, resulting in a more level distribution of funds for capital projects. The result in India was a slower, if inexorable, unfolding of the metropolitan region and a pronounced tendency for mega-projects like Navi Mumbai to occur simultaneously (and slowly) in multiple states rather than in a single city, state or grouping of states.

Middletown South Asia

This book has regularly departed from consideration only of larger cities to explore their relationship with a much larger number of small and medium cities that are home to substantial populations of urbanites and that are essential to the formation of multinucleated urban networks. Here we will examine several aspects of these 'middle cities,' ranging from their roles as marketing centers and sites for grassroots capitalism to their intersection with state-sponsored industrial policies. We will also glance at initiatives that are linking middle towns within urban corridors, with potentially great implications for future urban growth.

A large percentage of the small and middle cities in South Asia existed primarily as marketing nodes and, to a lesser extent, as administrative hubs for rural hinterlands. As such, they stood atop hierarchies of lower-level central places that provided a more limited array of services for villages, in patterns amenable to analysis through central place theory – an intellectual approach that stresses the economic basis of urbanization.

A case study that exemplifies this phenomenon (Thakur 1985) around Siwan in Bihar has portrayed the settlement pattern in a roughly trapezoidal study area approximately 100 kilometers across. By the early 1980s the economic activities within this study area with more than 3.5 million persons and 3,000 villages were still predominantly agricultural, with 91.2 percent of the employed workforce engaged in primary activities and the small percentage of industrial workers engaged mostly in agro-processing activities. The ubiquity of peddling activities at periodic markets, especially in the eastern section of the study area, indicated that linkages to higher-order central places were difficult for many villages in the absence of paved, maintained roads and regular bus services. Most of the study area was part of Siwan District, which even at the beginning of the twenty-first century featured only 5.5 percent of its population in settlements classified as urban and a literacy rate of 68 percent for males, 37 percent for females. We are looking here at the outer edges of South Asia's urbanization within a state with the second-highest population in India, but with one of the country's lowest urbanization rates (10.47 in 2001) and notoriously low developmental indices.

Eighty settlements fell within the three lowest levels of central places within the Siwan study area. At the bottom were 63 'service villages' that attracted purchases from their surrounding villages for food and other items of daily subsistence. Above these stood 13 'service centers' that provided convenience and shopping goods plus access to lower-level administrative functionality. Above them were three 'service towns,' each about 25 kilometers from the district headquarters of Siwan, including Mirganj with a population of about 17,000, Maharajganj with a population of about 15,000, and Mairwa with a population of about 12,000. The city of Siwan directly dominated eight service centers and 33 service villages, while Mirganj, Maharajganj and Mairwa dominated their own pyramids including four service centers and 30 service villages. Within a district population growing at a rate of two percent, the estimated 2007 population for Mirganj was about 26,000 (53 percent increase in about 25 years), for Maharajganj 23,000 (53 percent increase), and Mairwa 21,000 (75 percent increase). The population increases did not fundamentally alter the marketing relationships of these towns with their hinterlands.

Siwan during the early 1980s was a 'fourth-level' market town with a population of about 51,000 persons. It lay on the main route of the rail line between the cities of Gorakhpur (population 302,000) toward the west and Muzaffarpur (population 185,000) toward the east and also served as a road junction linked to Patna (population 881,000). In addition to its role as a district headquarters and location for the law court and head post office Siwan featured seven colleges, several training institutes, an office of the Life Insurance Corporation of India, and professionals such as dentists and opticians who were located nowhere else in its hinterland. A survey of shopping patterns revealed that the purchase of special products such as tractors, jewelry, clothing and footwear prompted persons from throughout its hinterland to travel to Siwan. Although it supported a cotton-spinning mill, a handloom industry and a number of agro-businesses, Siwan remained a sub-regional headquarters for a predominantly agrarian economy. Its genesis and growth pattern have been rather typical of most such centers that are now entering the ranks of middle cities. The population of Siwan reached 108,000 in 2001, and was projected at 125,000 in 2007.

A different group of small cities owed their growth to a grassroots capitalism that contributed to agglomeration or clustering of related industries and associated services that produce commodities for a national or international market. Within this category we may differentiate between examples where a cluster rested on what Hans Schenk (1997: 308–12) has described as 'an economic structure of poverty', which allowed the exploitation of low-skilled and low-paid labor, and examples where the entrepreneurial assembly of a more highly skilled work force, coordinated with government infrastructure intervention, resulted in a sustainable industrial sector utilizing mid-level technologies.

Sivakasi in Tamil Nadu provides an example of a town that has demonstrated long-term resilience within a 'poverty economy.' Sivakasi's story is intertwined with the saga of a caste group that changed its economic role and social position through a transition to an urban mode of existence. In the early-nineteenth century the Shanar community, later called the Nadars, were a low-ranking caste mostly living in southeast Tirunelveli District, whose standard occupation was 'toddy tapping.' Some of their members began shifting toward commercial occupations, initially specializing in cotton and tobacco, within new trading settlements in the extremely dry areas south of Madurai, where they founded six marketing centers (*pettai*) managed through caste-based street associations and town councils. Sivakasi, already noticeable as a small town in 1821, was initially the most important, with a population that reached 12,000, mostly Nadars, in 1891. By that point it was temporarily losing its prominence to the Nadar town of Virudhunagar, which became a station on the railroad line connecting Madurai to Tuticorin. In 1928, when a rail link was established between Virudhunagar and Sivakasi, all major Nadar councils were maintaining business offices in Madurai as well. Nadars were simultaneously penetrating the wholesale food and grocery business throughout Madras (Hardgrave 1969).

The subsequent transformation of the economic profile in Sivakasi toward an industrial cluster is closely associated with the entrepreneurial activities of three men venerated locally as cultural heroes. The key change occurred in the production of safety matches, which in India were marketed in the form of wooden sticks packaged within small cardboard boxes. During the early-twentieth century it seemed that a multinational corporation with mass-production technology would dominate this market in the form of Swedish Match (founded 1917), which established Western India Match Company (WIMCO) in 1923 and quickly set up factories in Ambernath near Bombay (see Map 19), Calcutta, Madras, Bareilly, and Dhubir in Assam. But already in 1922 two young entrepreneurs from Sivakasi, P. Ayya Nadar (1905–82) and A. Shanmuga Nadar (1903–69), believing that the match industry offered good profits, arranged a sojourn in Calcutta for eight months to learn about the business, before returning to Sivakasi with machines imported from Germany. They established a factory together, but found that mechanized production requiring quality woods was costly. Influenced by M. K. Gandhi's plea for the encouragement of cottage industries, they decided after a year and a half to switch over to hand production utilizing the cheap labor available around town. After initial success, the two entrepreneurs established separate factories in 1926, with Ayya's 'Squirrel' (Anil) brand competing against Shanmuga's 'Crow' (Kaka) brand. Other entrepreneurs in Sivakasi rapidly learned to apply match making techniques to the production of fireworks, which initiated a second growth industry. The labelling for these products originally came from Bombay, but in the 1930s K. S. A. Arunagiri Nadar (1899–1961) started the Nadar Press specializing in litho printing; a change to offset press led to rapid expansion and diversification of a third growth industry. Seven Nadar families with members present on interlocking directorates came to control multiple firms within the matches and fireworks fields, with several additional families important in printing (Hardgrave 1969: 150–1; Hilding 1992; Chandramohan 2005)

The labor-intensive, low-technology production techniques pioneered at Sivakasi and ubiquitous within the 'match belt' located in surrounding sub-districts allowed the cluster of Nadar-dominated companies to compete successfully with more technology-intensive firms like WIMCO. In 1949 the mechanized sector of the match industry produced 20.52 million gross boxes and the 'middle' sector dominated by the match belt produced 6.5 million; by 1981 the mechanized sector had grown to 28 million gross boxes, but the middle sector was producing 60 million and a 'cottage' sector operating as its adjunct was producing 32.4 million boxes (Hilding 1992: 228). Although exposés in the 1980s prompted the factories in Sivakasi to eschew direct employment of children, a survey in 1994 indicated that within the cottage sector, which included many households around Sivakasi headed by unemployed or underemployed agricultural laborers, production of matches at home was an important supplemental income stream that employed perhaps 80,000 children within the age group 6–14 years, with girls outnumbering boys (Moulik and Purushotham 1982; Kothari 1983; Warrier 1985; Government of Tamil Nadu 1994). The utilization of low-paid labor allowed Sivakasi's match works, numbering 67 between 1940 and 1949, to reach 2,020 between 2000 and 2004. By that time the direct employment in the match works in and around Sivakasi totalled about 55,000, in fireworks units 35,000, and in printing units 10,000: with indirect employment generated by these industries estimated at about 149,000 jobs. Women's employment totalled more than 19,000 in factories and 6,000 at home (Xavier 2005). The printing industry, challenged by computerization during the 1990s, upgraded its technology and employed about 50,000 persons in 450 units in 2007. At that point Sivakasi provided 90 percent of India's fireworks, 80 percent of its safety matches, and 60 percent of its offset printing.

The built environment of Sivakasi as it became a town during the early-nineteenth century revolved around an old Shiva temple (to which the Nadars originally were denied access), a Bhadrakali temple on the north side of town, and a Mariamman temple on the east. The early Nadar town council met at the Ammankoyil in the town center (Hardgrave 1969: 111–12). As the city's industrial character took off after Independence a thriving business district took shape and eventually encompassed all of these shrines within a multiple-street pattern fronted by one-to-three story retail establishments, wholesale merchandizers including suppliers to the city's three major industries, and public buildings constructed in part through the philanthropy of local industrialists. The hero-entrepreneurs of Sivakasi played important roles in the city's public life, founding business federations and several colleges for men and women. A. Shanmuga Nadar was Chairman of Sivakasi Municipality 1952–5. P. Ayya Nadar was Chairman of Sivakasi Municipality between 1955 and 1963; during his tenure the government executed the Vaippar-Vembakkottai Drinking Water scheme, involving the construction of a major dam north of the city, which made possible the expansion of industries and population in this drought-prone district (Chandramohan 2005). In the absence of a second, expanded water scheme and given the distributed character of industrial labor (involving, for example, the daily bussing of workers from the surrounding sub-district), Sivakasi reached a population plateau (66,000 in 1991, about 75,000 in 2007) that preserved its character as a small city when most other places in this category continued to experience very rapid demographic expansion.

Let us turn now to small and middle cities growing through the assembly of industrial clusters featuring highly mechanized production within mature sectors and requiring a more highly skilled work force earning higher wages. In most such cases, state-run Industrial Development Corporations or Industrial Infrastructure Corporations played crucial roles in the assembly of land, usually in the form of industrial parks, and in the provision of power, water, and other utilities that were often in short supply outside the parks. The location of such parks rested on decisions by state governments, coordinated with central planning agencies, to strengthen regional clusters within specific industrial sectors while simultaneously distributing employment opportunities to the largest number of districts. We will look briefly at two examples.

The city of Hosur lies in Tamil Nadu very close to its border with Karnataka, about 50 kilometers from Bangalore. In the 1970s its district had some of the lowest development rankings in the entire state; the literacy rate was 29 percent and only 9.4 percent of the population lived in urban areas. Recognizing that Hosur's position near a burgeoning metropolis offered opportunities for the creation of a satellite industrial city, the state government established during the 1970s, through the offices of the State Industries Promotion Corporation of Tamil Nadu (SIPCOT), an industrial complex next to the national highway only 40 kilometers from Bangalore, eventually encompassing over 775 hectares. A separate complex came up on adjacent land under Tamil Nadu's Small Industries Development Corporation (SIDCO). The foundation of a large plant of Ashok Leyland (trucks and buses) in the SIPCOT complex, another large plant nearby of T.V.S Motor Company (motorcycles), and a variety of additional mid-sized factories attracted a skilled workforce to Hosur and strengthened the profile of the Bangalore Metropolitan Region in the automotive and transport sector. A consequence was the growth of many small companies within the state-managed complexes and in Hosur that performed turning and grinding operations or specialized in the production of metal, rubber, and plastic components for larger engineering, automotive and electrical/electronic contractors. The steady multiplication of these small firms contributed to the rapid increase in Hosur's population from 17,000 in 1971 to 42,000 in 1991, 84,000 in 2001, and over 100,000 in 2007. The beneficiaries among the working class: skilled or semi-skilled male immigrants from other urban sites within the state and from other states. Women were almost entirely excluded from the skilled positions and took the lowest-paying jobs in both the formal and informal labor markets; the bulk of the unpaid labor, mostly taking place in the household, remained the sphere of female work. Migration resulted in a large number of all-bachelor housing units and a tight housing market (Heins and Meijer 1990; Leestemaker 1992).

The case of the Pithampur Growth Center offers a number of spatial and organizational similarities to Hosur. Until the 1980s Pithampur was a village located in Dhar District of Madhya Pradesh, about 25 kilometers west-southwest of Indore. In the 1980s the state government elected to create a 1,900-hectare industrial park at Pithampur that would support a central Indian automotive cluster that could become the 'Detroit of India' (a title vociferously and often trumpeted for Pune and Chennai). The park included 122 medium and large-scale industrial units and more than 455 small-scale units. By 2007 the park housed five automotive original equipment manufacturers (Bajaj Tempo, Eicher Motors, Hindustan Motors, Kinetic Motors, and L&T Case), one major tire-producing unit (Bridgestone ACC), and about 30 auto component and ancillary units. The inability of the park to create within only 25 years an ancillary agglomeration of parts and components subcontractors limited the dynamism of the cluster, but the park nonetheless provided employment to approximately 25,000 people (Pithampur Auto Cluster 2007). It drove the growth of Pithampur from 12,000 in 1991 to 68,000 in 2001 and over 100,000 in 2007. It also contributed to the growth of neighbouring Mau (Mhow), which had originated in 1818 as a British cantonment about 8 kilometers southeast of Pithampur, from 75,000 in 1991 to 85,000 in 2001 and about 91,000 in 2007.

The several examples presented here suggest that explanations for the appearance and growth of small and middle cities benefit from an understanding of their regional contexts. From this perspective one may note that a large group of such sites has grown in the immediate vicinity of million cities or megacities, evolving from villages or towns lying adjacent to zones of metropolitan urban expansion. As their populations have become large enough to warrant reclassification as municipalities, some have quickly become engulfed as wards within the city, while others have been able to retain their own cultural, economic and legal identity as components within metropolitan regions – the case of Mumbai provides a number of examples of this latter phenomenon in places such as Thane or Kalyan. Another group of small and middle cities has grown from the galaxy of former towns and sub-district capitals lying 20 to 40 kilometers away from a larger city. These are often conceived as 'counter magnets' to hyper-primacy and serve as hosts for industrial parks in the manner or Hosur or Pithampur. The Indian National Commission on Urbanisation in 1988 identified 329 such towns as 'generators of economic momentum' and discrete population-industrial units. It also began an inquiry into 49 'spatial priority urbanization regions' that exhibited connectivity among poly-nodal concentrations and/or metropolitan galaxies of middle cities. Such an approach introduces the question of the linkages between metropolises, their associated regional clusters of small and medium cities, and the agrarian countryside with its hierarchical patterns of marketing centers.

A series of urban 'corridors' has appeared to connect metropolitan regions and their galaxies but also has come to include fast-growing towns, small cities, and middle cities that lay between metropolises, often as components within continuous or non-continuous sprawl. In Tamil Nadu, for example, the two main urban corridors (1) ran south from Chennai along the coast through Pondicherry past Pudukkottai and (2) ran west from Chennai through Vellore, Salem and Tiruppur to Coimbatore (see Map 18). The latter corridor connected with another that ran through Hosur and then Bangalore, where it intersected a separate link between Bangalore with Mysore. In Andhra Pradesh, Hyderabad stood at the junction of a north-south corridor leading from Adilabad to Hindupur and thence toward Bangalore, and a west-east corridor coming from Sholapur and leading toward Vijayawada-Guntur, where it intersected an east-coast route with Vishakhapatnam as its major node. In Maharasthra, the most impressive corridor ran along India's west coast north from Mumbai through Surat and Vadodara to Ahmedabad. An additional corridor ran from Mumbai to Pune, where it branched into three heading to Aurangabad, Solapur (and then Hyderabad) or Sangli and Kolhapur (and then Belgaum). Another ran from Mumbai through Nasik and Amravati to Nagpur. In Gujarat, where corridors included between 55 and 60 percent of the state's urban population, a subsidiary route ran from Ahmedabad south along the coast through Bhavnagar and another ran west to Rajkot, where it bifurcated into three routes heading to Junagadh, Jamnagar and Gandhidham (Pandya 1999: 108–33; Center for Policy Research 2001).

In 1999 the Government of India implemented the largest transportation infrastructure project since the construction of the railroads in the nineteenth century – a drive to improve 25,000 kilometers of roads lying almost entirely within urban corridors, including the upgrade of national highways (hitherto mostly two-lane roads) to four- or six-lane limited-access highways. The first phase concentrated on the 'Golden Quadrilateral,' a term already used by the railways to describe the route running from Delhi through Kolkata, Chennai, Mumbai, and back to Delhi, and included improvement of connectivity to a number of major ports. The second phase renovated a north-south route from Srinagar through Delhi, Nagpur, Hyderabad, Bangalore, Madurai, and finally Kanyakumari (with a spur through Coimbatore to Kochi), as well as an east-west route from Silchar in Assam through Guwahati, Muzaffarpur, Lucknow, Kanpur, Udaipur, and finally ending on the west coast at Porbandar in Gujarat. Subsequent phases would address the connectivity of state capitals to growth clusters within their metropolitan regions or to major cities within state borders. The project directly connected 17 of the largest cities in India, but would also bring fast road transport to hundreds of towns, small and middle cities already growing within urban corridors (National Highways Authority of India 2007). The comparative advantages enjoyed by cities reached by the project might be as great as those enjoyed by railroad towns 150 years earlier.

Nodes of globalization: The cities of garments and information

The crises and opportunities presented by global markets as South Asian states embraced liberalization affected persons at all levels of the city, but in this section we will turn our attention to cases where the extremely strong advantages offered by cheap South Asian labor led to profound transformations of specific industries and populations. Among the many examples available we may mention briefly Surat (population about 3.1 million in 2007), where a single extended caste group became a player within the world market for cutting and polishing small diamonds. Thousands of workshops in the Varachha Road section of the city, the smallest mere sweatshops, directly employed approximately 150,000 persons and the industry affected perhaps one-third of the city's inhabitants (Engelshoven 1999). But here we are after even bigger changes. We will look more closely at two examples: the ready-made garment industry of Bangladesh (in Dhaka and Chittagong) and the information technology industry of India (in Bangalore and Hyderabad). We will examine the first example from the perspective of its impact on the gendered construction of social space, and the second through its relationship with urban planning.

The ready-made garment (RMG) industry perhaps best exemplified the new international division of labor, providing finished clothing such as T-shirts, pants, and sweaters for export to markets mostly in Europe and North America. The South Asian versions of this 100-percent export-oriented activity began in India in the early 1970s, followed by Sri Lanka and Pakistan in the mid-1970s, and Nepal after 1983. Because clustering around marketing and transportation facilities characterized the industry, it has been primarily an urban phenomenon. In Sri Lanka, most factories and employment existed around Colombo. In Nepal, the Kathmandu Valley was the industry's center. In India, the city of Tiruppur in Tamil Nadu came to produce more than half of all knitwear exports, which in turn constituted about one-third of all RMG exports (Joshi 2002).

The most impressive transformation associated with RMG occurred in Bangladesh. After 1947, when the installed jute factories around Calcutta became unavailable, a jute-processing cluster grew around Chittagong and Dhaka. After the 1971 War of Liberation in Bangladesh, raw and processed jute comprised almost 90 percent of its total exports. Competition from synthetic fibres was steadily replacing jute in international markets, however, creating a bleak export scenario. The import-substitution policies of the post-liberation regime initially delayed the nation's move into export-oriented growth and in 1977–8 there were only nine RMG units generating about US$1 million in earnings. Desh Garments, which began production in Chittagong in 1980, was the first 100 percent export-oriented company in Bangladesh specializing in RMG through a linkage with Daewoo of the Republic of Korea – the latter attempting to circumvent conditions of the Multi-Fibre Agreement (1974–2004) that established country export quotas. The success of Desh prompted members of its management staff to spin off new companies and with support from the national government a new industrial cluster was born. By 1990–91 RMG exports had exceeded in value all other export sectors. In 2002–3 about 3,000 RMG factories in Bangladesh earned 74 percent of total export earnings, generated about US$1.9 billion of value-addition, and contributed 9.5 percent of gross domestic product (Quddus and Rashid 2000; Hoque 2003: 21–154; Siddiqi 2004). The Bangladesh Garment Manufacturers and Exporters Association reported that the total percentage of Bangladesh's exports comprised by RMG stabilized at about 70 percent and their value peaked at US$7.9 billion in 2005–6. The cutthroat international market and the generally slower turnaround required in Bangladeshi conditions meant that its RMG industry thrived only because its labor costs remained among the lowest in the world.

The RMG industry in Bangladesh in 2007 directly employed almost 2 million workers and generated indirect employment for 300,000 in linkage industries supplying fabrics, yarns, accessories, or packaging materials. Dhaka and its immediate vicinity supported at least 80 percent of the job sites. A small group of firms operated as joint ventures with foreign companies based in an export-processing zone, but most firms (including a large number of subcontractors and many firms controlling multiple units) were located within the city or its suburbs. Depending on their size, ranging from 100–200 to thousands of sewing machine, the plants utilized storefronts, warehouses, or old apartment buildings for their shop floors. These plants often had poor ventilation and provided rudimentary facilities for rest periods or medical assistance. Work periods varied according to orders received, but might run 12 hours daily six days a week with overtime intermittent but mandatory. While stimulating the urban real-estate market, RMG firms rarely provided housing for their employees, forcing workers to rent accommodation. Because salaries were low and a substantial minority (e.g. some sewing 'helpers') earned less than the national minimum wage, most workers lived in low-income neighbourhoods and slums. Transportation to the work site was more common in export processing zones, but most employees resided within several kilometers of the factories and walked to work (Hoque 2003: 174).

The global RMG industry displays a pronounced tendency to organize its workforce according to gender, with female workers filling a disproportionate number of the unskilled or semi-skilled jobs typical of garment fabrication. The feminisation of textile labor also typified the Sri Lanka industry and was becoming more pronounced in the Tiruppur cluster, but the relegation of women to about 10 percent of the jobs in Pakistan's textile industry (Joshi 2002: 163) demonstrates that state intervention combined with cultural factors could inhibit this trend. In this context the feminisation of labor in the Bangladesh RMG industry displayed a remarkable contrast to Pakistan and to northern India in general, where the dominant cultural ethos favoured the relegation of female labor to the household.

In Bangladesh approximately 80 percent of the RMG workforce consisted of women, mostly in their late adolescence or their early twenties, and mostly migrants from heavily populated rural areas, whose families had little or no land and no educated adults. On the shop floor, women usually operated or helped with sewing machines, while male workers did ironing or filled managerial posts. Males also constituted a larger percentage of employees within the more technologically complicated knitwear units. The average male worker brought home a larger pay check and females were more likely to earn less than the national minimum wage, although gender disparities were a bit lower within the export processing zones (Wiest et al. 2003: 179–89; Kabeer and Mahmud 2004: 148). Employers targeted the almost completely disorganized female labor force and favoured rural migrants because they were willing to accept the extremely low wages, job insecurity, and poor conditions within the RMG factories. The presence of large numbers of women textile workers was a major factor in altering the urban sex ratios in metropolitan cities, i.e. Dhaka and Chittagong, from 150 in 1961 to 105 in 1993–4. The decline for the age group 15–34 between 1991 and 1996 in slum and squatter settlements was 103 to 65 (Afsar 2003: 74, 77–8; Hoque 2003: 54; Siddiqi 2004: 184–5).

The majority of female garment workers found their jobs through family members, relatives, and acquaintances from their villages or districts and within the city those social circles provided them with assistance in relocation and residence. Most women lived with members of their immediate or extended families or sublet from them, although a minority lived in messes or boarding houses or maintained their own residences. A 1991 survey (Wiest *et al.* 2003: 191–6) found that 79 percent of 212 workers lived in slums or squatter settlements within makeshift shelters of polythene, cardboard, or newspaper, or within thatched huts, typically single-roomed with no sanitation facilities. In a 2001 follow-up survey, 31 out of 50 respondents lived in concrete buildings and 12 lived in tin-shed buildings sharing six rooms with common latrines, bathrooms, and cooking facilities. The earlier female work force had a slightly older age profile and included larger percentages of divorced or widowed women or former domestic servants who had switched to garments. Later migrants were more likely to come from their parents' home directly into garments (Afsar 2003: 67–8; Hoque 2003: 187–205). Because of the long hours and difficult working conditions the average time span spent by women in RMG was about five years. The mostly young, unmarried women were using their jobs to postpone marriage, accumulate a limited savings, contribute to their families back home, and enhance their social value (Afsar 2003: 72; Kabeer and Mahmud 2004: 151–52). Women described their world as a *ferryghat samaj*, or the society of the ferry terminal, a metaphor for the transitory state of their lives (Wiest and Mohiuddin 2003: 202–4).

The women of the Bangladesh garment industry, subject to Eve-teasing in the street and gender-based discrimination and harassment at the workplace (Begum 2002), provide a perspective on the extent to which cultural and economic autonomy was possible or desired within a public life dominated by males. At issue is the interaction between the opportunities made available through factory work and what Naila Kabeer (2000) describes at the 'patriarchal contract,' which ideally provides protection and social support for women while reserving public life and decision-making to men. Kabeer's interviews indicated that for a large minority of the women electing to work in the garment industry patriarchy had failed due to natural disasters, incompetence of male family figures to provide adequate income, or domestic violence. For those women, 'patriarchal risk' had become too great and jobs were a matter of survival; they could not aspire to a renewal of gender subordination at home. For women who remained within a functional patriarchy but who elected garment work to supplement family income, the decision to work outside required negotiations (with spouses, parents, and other relatives) that empowered women to re-define their socially perceived position, within a pattern of gender roles that remained acceptable and unchallenged. In cases where the woman tried to retain her own income the husband might demand it in order to preserve his dominance or, if the husband allowed the woman to retain money, he was expressing his freedom to support his wife even without her contribution. In practice, many women workers were able to negotiate with their husbands concerning the disposition of their earnings and even if they gave most of their salaries to their husbands they were able to retain some for their own use or for their natal families (Ahmed 2004; Ahmed and Bould 2004). In any case, female garment workers showed little inclination to directly challenge ideologies of non-empowerment, remaining focused on marriage and child care along with concerns about self-dignity, honesty, and self-control (Wiest and Mohiuddin 2003: 218–20, 235). The subtle distinctions of class among the workers determined the style of patriarchy they accepted, with concepts of public modesty or personal and family honour retaining their salience in everyday behaviour. Three-quarters of the single women interviewed by Rita Afsar (2003: 73) were waiting for their parents to find suitable husbands for them.

At the other end of the employment spectrum was the phenomenal growth of the information technology outsourcing industry in India, which came to lead the world in this sector. The industry was closely associated with Bangalore, which earned the sobriquet of 'India's Silicon Valley.' As in the case of the diamond or garment industries, the comparative advantages of outsourcing lay in the relatively low costs of labor, but the benefits of information technology jobs flowed primarily to the new middle class who commanded higher education and skills.

Small firms based in Bangalore, including Infosys and Wipro (the latter building on a family business originally specializing in cooking oil during the 1940s) were enjoying success after 1981 in providing computer programmer services to transnational corporations, mostly through 'body shopping' arrangements that sent cheap personnel overseas for on-site consulting. Initial positive results from ventures such as Texas Instruments' installation of a ground station in Bangalore shifted the focus of such programing to sites in India where costs were much lower. Two state interventions then proved beneficial. The first was the establishment by the Government of Karnataka of a 136-hectare campus south of Bangalore along Hosur Road called Electronic (or Electronics) City that was aimed at tenants specializing in high technology (see Map 20). The second was a program of the Indian Department of Electronics called Software Technology Parks of India (STPI), which would provide a ground station and connectivity at 64 kilobits per second to affiliated firms in the private and public sectors. Electronic City's STPI hub went online in 1992, leading an initial cohort including Bhubaneswar, Gandhinagar, Hyderabad, Noida (near Delhi), Pune, and Tiruvanantapuram. The rapid growth of Bangalore's STPI client base and the multiplication of

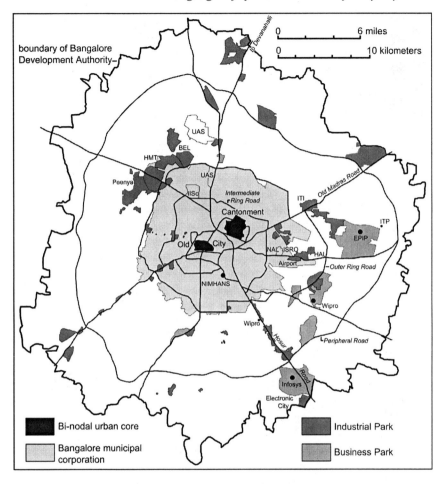

Map 20 Industrial and business parks of Bangalore. Adapted from BDA 2005.

indigenous outsourcing firms as well as local offices of transnational corporations attracted the attention of the Government of Singapore, which arranged with the Government of Karnataka for the construction of an International Technology Park (ITP) by Singapore-based Jurong Town Corporation. Their multi-building, blue-glass-windowed, high-rise complex brought 'international standards' to service-specialty clients needing high-bandwidth telecommunication facilities and guaranteed infrastructure. Its success after 1994 stimulated the development nearby of an Export Promotion Industrial Park (EPIP) that attracted a number of transnational tenants such as General Electric. Such efforts stimulated a classic clustering effect that brought hundreds of companies to Bangalore and employment to perhaps 100,000 by the year 2000. Many newer companies provided backroom processing operations and call centers for transnational clients. The information technology cluster lay mostly in a ring surrounding the eastern half of the city and the old cantonment.

The conflation of information technology and urban planning occurred when the Government of Karnataka's Department of IT and Biotechnology (formed in 1999) visualized an 'IT Corridor' that would connect Electronic City to the International Technology Park within a single project area (Government of Karnataka 2001). Singapore-based Jurong Township Consultants (India) received the contract to prepare planning documents for this corridor. Their final structure plan (Jurong Consultants 2003) traced its lineage to regional concepts used within the United States for places such as Boston's Route 128 phenomenon or North Carolina's Research Triangle, reworked by Kenichi Ohmae for Japan and implemented as the Multimedia Corridor in Malaysia. They moved beyond the model of the industrial park, hitherto dominant in the layouts the public-sector giants or Peenya, and toward the idea of the 'business park' specializing in technology services within a miniaturized green belt specified as 'a showcase environment for IT professionals to live, work, plan, and strike deal.' They also eschewed the original concept of corridor conceived by the state government, which simply linked the locations of extant firms, to encompass an area of 13,700 hectares along the entire eastern periphery of the city, including everything between Hosur Road and Old Madras Road and between the airport and a projected Outer Peripheral Road. Their structure plan called for business park construction in four zones that would provide employment for 773,000 IT professionals, including 15 percent support staff, by 2021. Six residential townships or New Towns would accommodate a population of approximately 936,000, and two regional commercial centers would each serve a population of about 500,000 persons becoming the 'Life Exchange Hub of the entire IT community of Bangalore.' Not content with one corridor, the state government was also mooting the concept of a 'Biotechnology Corridor' running north-south to connect the University of Agricultural Sciences (UAS) and the Indian Institute of Science (IISc) with some versions extending south of the city to include the National Institute of Mental Health and Neuro Sciences (NIMHANS) and projected new businesses within Electronic City. A crucial component in this marketing/planning campaign was a new International Airport coming up north of the city at Devanahalli.

The growth of the information technology community in Hyderabad – a city resembling Bangalore with its bipolar arrangement of old city and cantonment – shows remarkable similarities in chronology and institutional growth. Here also the STPI hub, operational in 1992, tapped the potential of many firms that were coming up to provide outsourcing solutions. The consolidation of Hyderabad's high-technology profile coincided with the establishment of an 'integrated techno-township' or HITEC city that resembled Bangalore's International Technology Park: a 64-hectare site in Kukatpalli Municipal Corporation (population 291,202 in 2001) on the northern edge of Hyderabad Metropolitan Corporation. The showpiece of project's first phase in 1997 was the ten-story Cyber Towers, the heart of a planned township with 500,000 square feet of office space, showrooms, cafeteria, health club, banks, shopping malls, and auditoriums. Early tenants included Microsoft (establishing there its first offshore research facility), Oracle, GE Capital, Hongkong & Shanghai Banking Corporation, and Keane India Ltd. Stage two saw the erection by 2001 of a companion structure named Cyber Gateway with 866,000 square feet of office space, with tenants including Microsoft, GE Capital, Dell, and ICICI Bank. Stage three saw the construction of the adjacent seven-story Cyber Pearl. Additional projects in the vicinity included a 13-hectare development for a 'modern multi-dimensional residential township' at Gachibowli. These projects and nearby middle-class residential layouts were the focus for an information technology workforce that totalled perhaps 75,000 with an additional 10,000 support staff.

The Government of Andhra Pradesh was moving toward a long-range planning document that would highlight the importance of high-technology urbanization and introduce the concept of corridors. In 1999 it commissioned transnational consultants McKinsey & Company to work with a task force of over 100 bureaucrats and experts to produce a document entitled *Andhra Pradesh: Vision 2020*, which clearly showed the influence of the earlier Malaysian corridor. Of the 19 'growth engines' projected by this document, three categories defined as 'knowledge-based' (including information technology, biotechnology and pharmaceuticals) were linked, via examples from the United States and Japan, to accelerated development. The goal was to catch up with Bangalore and to establish 'an information-based society in which IT is a way of life' by promoting the state as a hub for 'world-class' or 'Top 500' companies. In practical terms, *Vision 2020* posited the creation of a Master Plan that would establish a 'significantly expanded version' of HITEC City:

> The Andhra Pradesh Knowledge Corridor will be a large area equipped with the infrastructure required to foster research and develop a new set of IT enabled services, many of which will facilitate the commercialisation of newly-developed technologies. The Knowledge Corridor will foster activity that promotes economic development through the development or exchange of knowledge and technologies. It will have world-class universities that provide easy access to intellectual capital and continually develop knowledge workers. The Knowledge Corridor will provide an investor-friendly environment that not only attracts large corporations to set up their R&D centers here but nurtures entrepreneurship and start-ups…Andhra Pradesh will make a large and pre-emptive strike for the large emerging market for Indian R&D, technology development and remote services by creating India's first comprehensive Knowledge Corridor, combining world class universities, globally competitive and innovative knowledge-based businesses and cutting-edge research centers.
>
> (Government of Andhra Pradesh 1999: 286, 288)

The realization of the Knowledge Corridor, which would grow from the northern suburbs in its early stages, began in 2001 with the establishment by the state government of an organization capturing the slang appellation that was already popular – the Cyberabad Development Authority (spun off from the Hyderabad Urban Development Authority) – which began to prepare a Master Plan for 52 square kilometers around a 'model enclave' including HITEC City. The state next legitimized a biotechnology component for the Corridor by borrowing terminology already used in strategic studies within the United Kingdom and bestowing the name of Genome Valley on an area of approximately 600 square kilometers stretching from the northern to the eastern sides of Hyderabad. The goal here was to claim the title of India's 'biotechnology capital' (*pace* Bangalore). In a move that closely paralleled the planning in Bangalore the Government of Andhra Pradesh decided to construct a new International Airport at Shamshabad, about 21 kilometers south-southwest of the city, within an area of about 459 square kilometers. The proposed Expressway and Outer Ring Road, encircling the metropolitan agglomeration, would connect the airport with Cyberabad on the north/northwest and Genome Galley on the north/northeast. The Knowledge Corridor would grow directly through the international airport with its planned promotion zones and appended high-income residence clusters. In April 2007 the state government brought all these projects within a new Hyderabad Metropolitan Development Authority covering almost 6,300 square kilometers.

Theorization of the new international division of labor, operating at multiple levels of technological sophistication within different economic sectors, creating new hierarchies of global cities, may be one fruitful path toward encompassing the experiences of Dhaka-Chittagong and Bangalore-Hyderabad, which otherwise might appear as a problem of comparing apples with oranges. An alternative (and not contradictory) approach, however, might view these cities' industrial cluster formations against the backdrop of the 'dispersed metropolis' or 'expanded metropolitanized zones of settlement and economic activity,' described by students of Asian urbanization (with a nod toward Indonesia) as a *desakota*, or 'country-city' phenomenon that urbanizes the countryside (Ginsburg 1991). In Bangalore and, to a lesser extent, Hyderabad, earlier master-planning and centralized-planning initiatives that dispersed industrialization to the urban periphery within green belts and concentrated a skilled, educated workforce within science-and-technology nodes created the conditions for an entrepreneurial explosion within the new paradigm of the information society and national strategies for liberalisation. In Chittagong and Dhaka, with their more abbreviated histories of national planning strategy, the mobilization of a large female workforce within a short period was possible through the expansion of transportation and communication facilities, which accompanied the transformation of the countryside from a more strictly agrarian regime into a varied pattern of agriculture, services, and commodity production that provided survival strategies for an impoverished former peasantry.

What is striking about these examples is the variation in the language that has appeared to describe them and its relationship to the built environment, which manifests different levels of class interests. In the Bangladeshi case the language seemed more overtly sociological against a backdrop of muted dissatisfaction with the unorganized character of labor, while the implications for urban planning and housing remained off the table. In the Indian case the concentration on urban planning and 'international standards,' aiming at infrastructure improvements and the real estate market, was in fact no less sociological, but responded to the concerns of a middle class constituency that was finding its voice within a liberalized policy framework.

The cinematic vision

We turn now to a brief consideration of cinema, the pre-eminent medium for the production and transmission of urban popular culture in South Asia. The industry has become not only a major direct and indirect urban employer, but through a massive publicity machine feeding its star system it has moulded the many fan clubs that have served to mobilize the (male) urban poor with important political consequences – particularly in Tamil Nadu, where all Chief Ministers have been closely identified with film. Among the several dozen sectors specializing in regional languages none can compare in scale and influence with the Mumbai film world, which has exerted influence throughout South Asia and beyond through a Hindi-Urdu linguistic format that has proven accessible to audiences everywhere. The almost entirely middle-class directorial and production cadres responsible for generating hundreds of products annually in Mumbai have evolved – partly as a self-conscious marketing strategy and partly because of a mode of production that has separated cinematographic components – a style characterized by relatively long films (2.5 to 3 hours) and the juxtaposition of melodramatic themes, song-and-dance numbers, and action sequences aimed at a mass audience including the urban and rural poor. A small percentage of annual output has subordinated all components to thematic continuity and interests specific to a middle-class audience, and this style of film making has enjoyed growing success as the middle class has achieved greater numerical strength and self-consciousness. Although one may discern traces of the urban imaginary in most Mumbai production, this thematically driven movement offers direct insight into the representation of the urban experience, allowing us, as Ranjani Mazumdar (2007) has shown, to appreciate such films as an 'archive of the city.'

Let us examine some recent contributions by Ram Gopal Varma, who migrated into Mumbai cinema after a stint in the Telugu-language film world. The examples include a crime trilogy written and directed by Varma and directly inspired by Francis Ford Coppola's *Godfather* trilogy, followed by a female revenge drama called *Ek Hasina Thi* ('There Was a Beautiful Girl') directed by Sriram Raghavan and produced by Varma. These films are notable for their almost complete elimination of gestures toward the relationship between the city and the countryside or the relationship between social deviance and nationalist moral discourse that regularly surfaced in earlier Mumbai crime films. The films demonstrate, during the period when Independence makes the transition from lived liminality to historical iconicity, a transition occurring in the representation of the city in South Asia.

In an open letter accompanying the digital videodisk release of *Sarkar* (2005), Varma describes the film as an exploration of power with implications for 'our country, our city, and our neighbourhood.' The plot, which closely parallels that of *The Godfather, Part 1*, follows an important shift in the career of Subhash Nagre, an aging crime boss who has built an underworld empire not through a quest for wealth, but in order to provide justice to a populace victimized by systemic failure in the police and the courts. He inhabits with his extended family an old-style castle-mansion with surrounding garden that has been transformed into a fortress with security personnel bearing automatic weapons, but in fact the security seems almost unnecessary because of the formidable reach of his long-established influence and the loyal support of the populace he has aided over the years. To his constituency he is *Sarkar*, a term for a boss or overlord but also used as a term for government in general. An almost asexual figure, he performs daily worship at his household shrine and moves slowly wrapped in a shawl, speaking rarely while hearing a steady daily litany of woes experienced by petitioners who have been injured by the random violence of the city. His elder son, Vishnu, has used his father's contacts to find a directorial/production role within the Mumbai film industry, but suffers from unresolved Oedipal issues that underlie a coarseness of personality, periodic eruptions of aggression against women, and sudden attacks on those around him. The younger son, Shankar, has just returned from the United States and intends to found a software company with his girlfriend. At this junction a challenge appears in the form of a young gangster based in Dubai, who presents Sarkar with a proposal for gigantic profits through a new smuggling operation that will bring into the country a socially destabilising contraband, the identity of which is left to the viewers' imagination. Sarkar declines the invitation but indicates that he will not allow the Dubai cartel to do it either. This decision sets in motion a coalition of the amoral Dubai entrepreneurs with the police and subordinate leaders of the Mumbai crime world under the intellectual direction of a contemporary Kautilya-like figure posing as a religious mendicant, who suborns the elder son into an assault on the father. Slow to recognize the seriousness of the challenge, Sarkar finds himself suddenly rendered helpless, which forces Shankar to intervene and carry out the fratricidal war needed to save the father. At the end of the film the sacrifice of both sons allows the re-establishment of equilibrium within the parallel moral universe.

In *Company* (2002) the city as built environment appears repeatedly via high-level camera shots of high-rise buildings, which serve as backdrop and goal of the main characters. There are two (anti-) protagonists: Malik, a lieutenant in the gang of the aging and ailing Aslam Ali, and Chandu, a small-time hoodlum who at the beginning is recruited along with five of his cronies to work in Malik's operation. Chandu becomes Malik's right-hand man and joins him when the time comes to eliminate all other lieutenants and force the boss into retirement, appropriating in the process the services of Vilas Pandit, strategist and expert negotiator. As the new power within the Mumbai underworld, known as the Company, the Malik-Chandu combine comes to the attention of Deputy Inspector Virapalli Srinivasan, a former college professor from Kerala. When Srinivasan learns that the two are associating with Mumbai film producers, movie starlets, and politicians, he announces that the police must go after them immediately before they become unassailable. The policeman, who is not averse to dirtying his hands with judicial torture and encounter killings, thus becomes the nemesis and also the analytical observer of the Company. The police manage to force Malik and Chandu into exile amid the luxury high rises of Hong Kong, but the duo retain control of an undamaged business run through cell-phone-mediated telecommunication.

For some time the Company's management team continues to ride high with Malik in business suit making deals in Europe and entering into negotiations with Rahute, a leading politician, who aspires to the position of Home Minister but requires the removal of the incumbent. The Company arranges a suitable road accident for the incumbent minister, but despite meticulous planning Chandu discovers at the last moment that innocent children will be killed. At this crucial juncture, motivated by an impulse of conventional morality instead of the unrelenting quest for profit, Chandu attempts to unilaterally countermand Malik's orders and calls off the hit. Malik must personally intervene to guarantee performance of the contract, as cell phone reports and orders multiply. Chandu flies into a rage. When Pandit-ji comes to mollify him, Chandu believes that this is an attempt to bump him off and he shoots down the only person who can keep the Company together. A bloody civil war erupts within the Company, with the police joining in through targeted murders and, eventually, the cooption of a wounded Chandu. Srinivasan retires to write his memoirs and the viewer is left to ponder the future of a city where politics, real estate, business corporations, and public security are indistinguishable from crime.

Satya (1998), literally 'The Truth,' is chronologically the first of the trilogy, but it pushes to the edge the socio-psychological tensions manifest in the other films in a highly influential contribution to a new *noir* genre in Mumbai cinema. The film begins conventionally with a distant shot of the crowds emerging from Victoria (now Chhatrapati Shivaji) Terminus as the camera slowly zooms in on a single nondescript figure with luggage. This, we will learn, is Satya. Unlike earlier such openings where the viewer will eventually learn that he hails from a smaller city or the countryside, we never learn anything about Satya's past or his motivations for coming to the metropolis. He finds his first accommodation in a small room at the end of a buffalo stable and his first job in a sleazy bar. He is minding his own business when three local punks accost him outside his room and attempt to shake him down for protection money. Satya, who has remained completely impassive throughout the film, initially puts up with their escalating physical abuse until suddenly, without warning or apparent emotion, he strikes like a snake and slashes an assailant across the face. Satya goes back to minding his own business but eventually has a run-in with the *dada* who employs these punks and who finds an opportunity to abuse Satya. Again we witness the initial impassivity and again the sudden violent retaliation. This time the *dada* arranges a jail term for Satya, which enables a fateful meeting with Bhikhu Matre, a crime lieutenant serving a short sentence. Bhikhu takes Satya into his gang and sets him up with a small flat.

In his new role Satya displays an adroitness and cold-bloodedness in advising his new employer through several rounds of gangland murders that elevate Bhikhu to a position just below that of the syndicate boss, Bhau. Meanwhile, Satya has become the friend and then confidant of Vidya, whose declining middle-class family inhabits the flat across the hall in his apartment building. From his solitude, so reminiscent of the main character in *l'Étranger* of Albert Camus, Satya almost emerges to find happiness. But Bhau, who is making a bid for election to the Mumbai Corporation Council, has been putting up with Bhikhu only until the end of the campaign, and when his bid is successful he immediately kills Bhikhu. The police simultaneously take Vidya into custody and grill her about her relationship with Satya, revealing to her the extent of his crimes. Satya moves implacably toward his revenge against Bhau, but is severely wounded and manages only to stagger back to the apartment building where he collapses before Vidya's locked door, begging like an animal for admittance, while she cowers in middle-class horror on the other side at this vision of criminal chaos. The entire exercise in a new existentialism without a semblance of a quest for meaning takes place amid a cinematography that meticulously documents street life and street jobs in the city – a *tour de force* in archival study of daily life.

In *Ek Hasina Thi* we find a cinema of interruption, where the characters encounter rapid changes in their environment ranging from media channel surfing to sudden violence and the imposition of other's wills, while the viewer must process unexpected camera angles particularly during critical action sequences. The main character is Sarika Vartak, a young woman working in a Mumbai travel agency and living alone in her one-bedroom flat. Sophisticated on the surface yet inwardly lonely, she looks for intimacy but is expert in deflecting the unwanted attentions of the men around her. One such is a customer who appears at the office, Karan Singh Rathod, looking for an international plane ticket, who seems to be coming on to her only to experience her quick rejection. Later, as she leaves the office, a street thug snatches her purse and takes off around the corner with it. Coincidentally, Karan is passing by and he runs after the thief, returning after a minute with the purse in hand (But is it a setup?). His gallantry deserves a shared cup of coffee and at a neighbouring shop he goes into his bantering come-on once again; but just as she prepares to enact her defence he receives a cell phone call and must dash off, leaving her perplexed. It is back to normal for Sarika, a round of work, talking to her parents and friends on the phone, doing her nails, and watching television at the flat, until one night after working late she leaves the office and is accosted by three men and a taxi who attempt to abduct her – one of the ultimate middle-class horror fantasies. Suddenly Karan appears again by coincidence and again he saves her. Now, having gained her confidence, he starts hanging around her apartment. Familiarity grows to love and they sleep together, although neither she nor the audience really knows anything certain about him except his claim to be involved in the stock market. Karan asks her to do a favour for him while he is out of town and let one of his friends stay at her apartment for a few hours before catching a plane flight. When the friend shows up with his suitcase he turns out to be a taciturn and shifty fellow who stays only a short while before leaving, promising to retrieve his suitcase. A few hours later, Sarika is watching the news and sees his mug shot along with a story about how he has just died during an abortive assassination attempt against a prominent businessman. Panicky, she is leaving to dispose of his luggage when the police arrive to take her into custody. This begins her transition from innocence to experience.

In the lockup, without bail, Sarika receives the services of Kamalesh Mathur, a lawyer hired by Karan to defend her, who advises her to plead guilty to aiding and abetting with the expectation that the judge will look at her clean record and let her off. Instead she receives a lengthy sentence, and although Karan appears apparently to encourage her to bear her punishment (while continuing to conceal his involvement), a new hardness appears on her face as she turns away. Now she is part of the prison machinery and is defending herself against the aggressions of fellow inmates. Fate takes a turn for the better only after she is taken under the wing of an older inmate who is the widow of a Sarkar-style don; this is the first person in the film with whom Sarika converses only in Hindi instead of the middle-class 'Hinglish' that has dominated so far. When Sarika joins a prison break and escapes, she uses contacts from the older woman to obtain a gun and, with hair cut short, she disappears into the urban jungle. Now it is her turn to take charge, and her first stop is Mathur's apartment. He is found dead the following morning on the roof of a car six floors below, an apparent suicide. Karan receives the news clad in a business suit at a lunch meeting, but attributes the death to some alternative criminal revenge and remains oblivious to the Sarika connection. But we know that she is closing in on him.

The scene shifts to Delhi with footage of the traffic on Chandni Chawk and the Red Fort. Sarika takes an apartment in an older section of the city, she is driving her own car, and obtains a room in a five-star hotel directly across the hall from Karan's room. As she tails him and his new girlfriend while they make the rounds of middle-class shopping and eating areas, she easily blends into the human background in her jeans and chemise. By the evening she has trailed him to a suburban bungalow, sneaks through the garden and up to a first floor window to witness his taking orders (apparently for a contract killing) from the crime boss Sanjiv, who is seated on a bed covered with bundles of money. After Karan leaves the house Sanjiv is found murdered and the money is gone – and her revenge has begun in earnest. Karan still has no idea what is happening as he acrobatically avoids the first hit attempt. He is escaping the second attempt in an upscale retail neighbourhood when he 'accidentally' encounters our heroine who acts as if she is still in love with him. With nowhere else to turn he follows Sarika to her apartment, which allows her to monitor his movements and prolong his agony. There is a moment late in the film when her plans seem to backfire and she lies trussed up with a rope on the apartment floor, badly in need, it seems, of a standard male rescuer, but again she turns the tables on Karan and all her opponents through the precise application of a feigned feminine helplessness. With his life in ruins and her gun to his head, Karan is ready for his final punishment 'far from the city.'

At a number of points during the course of this project, people have asked if it would be possible to present some defining characteristic of the South Asian city or something that one could set forward as its special feature. I have tended to resist this temptation, feeling that the straightforward presentation of the sheer weight and variety of its historical and contemporary expression would allow the reader to decide whether or how to achieve an understanding of its essential qualities. I believe, however, that observing these several cinematic productions at the end of this book may allow us to reach towards a language for what the city is *becoming*. The films gesture toward problems of the city versus the nation, the position of the city as node within global networks, the relationship between gender and domination or responsibility and justice; in these ways they serve as guides for the discussion of the problems in the social sciences that have been the concern of this chapter. As cultural products, however, the films achieve more. Without warranting the subordination of the urban to a unitary meta-narrative – and in practice revelling in the sheer variety and magnitude of urban activity space, these pieces demonstrate through the fates of their characters the ways agency emerges within and because of the contemporary urban experience. Varma's work suggests that, in the same way that a torch is passed from Sarkar to his son or Sarika Vartak transcends gender subordination to achieve control over her life, the city has moved beyond a post-colonial syndrome to provide, unabashedly, accessibility to techno-social self-confidence for those of its inhabitants who understand navigation within it. Such understanding requires the ability to process sudden discontinuities. It demands engagement without rigid commitment to ascribed position such as caste or received moral imperatives of religion or the nation. It generates casualties and is thus monstrous. Satya is a primitive possessor of this understanding in an almost non-human or super-human manner; other characters must learn through the school of hard knocks and the quintessential sequence of the crime/spy story – the chase scene – moving quickly in hitherto unknown or impersonal cityscapes. Exhilarating while informing viewers, these are terrifying experiences that allow the characters to develop focused intentionality. The achievement of the power or knowledge of intentioned socio-spatial navigation within the city and *only* within the city is the special obsession of these films. They suggest the ways in which the individual life-world of the urban experience grows within the crushing mass of institutions, but finds its way within the contemporary South Asian city toward an unexpected subjectivity.

Bibliography

Abraham Meera (1988) *Two Medieval Merchant Guilds of South India.* New Delhi: Manohar.

Abu-Lughod, Janet L. (1989) *Before European Hegemony: The World System A.D. 1250–1350.* New York: Oxford University Press.

Adarkar, Neera, and Meena Menon (2004) *One Hundred Years, One Hundred Voices: The Millworkers of Girangaon: An Oral History.* Calcutta and New Delhi: Seagull Books.

Afsar, Rita (2003) 'Gender, labour market, and demographic change: A case study of women's entry into the formal manufacturing sector in Bangladesh.' In: Brigida Garcia, Richard Anker, and Antonella Pinnelli, (eds.) *Women in the labour market in changing economies: Demographic issues.* Oxford and New York: Oxford University Press. pp. 59–86.

Aghassian, Michel, and Kéram Kévonian (2000) 'Armenian Trade in the Indian Ocean in the Seventeenth and Eighteenth Centuries.' In: Denys Lombard and Jean Aubin, (eds.) *Asian Merchants and Businessmen in the Indian Ocean and the China Sea.* New Delhi: Oxford University Press. pp. 154–77.

Ahmad, Nazimuddin (1971) *Mahasthan: A Preliminary report on Archaeological Excavations.* Karachi: Department of Archaeology and Museums, Ministry of Education and Scientific Research, Government of Pakistan.

Ahmed, Fauzia Erfan (2004) 'The Rise of the Bangladesh Garment Industry: Globalization, Women Workers, and Voice.' *NWSA Journal* 16 (2): 34–45.

Ahmed, S. S., and S. Bould (2004) 'One able daughter is worth 10 illiterate sons: Reframing the patriarchal family.' *Journal of Marriage and the Family* 66 (5): 1332–1341.

Ahmed, Sharif Uddin (1986) *Dacca: A Study in Urban History and Development.* London: Curzon Press; Riverdale MD: The Riverdale Company.

Alam, Muhammad Shafiqul, and Jean François Salles (2001) *France-Bangladesh Joint Venture Excavations at Mahasthangarh: First Interim Report 1993–1999.* Dhaka: Department of Archaeology, Ministry of Cultural Affairs, Government of the People's Republic of Bangladesh.

Alfieri, Bianca Maria, and Federico Borromeo (2000) *Islamic Architecture of the Indian Subcontinent.* London: Laurence King.

Ali, Imran (1988) *The Punjab under Imperialism, 1885–1947.* Princeton: Princeton University Press.

Allchin, F. Raymond (1993) 'The Urban Position of Taxila and its Place in Northwest India-Pakistan.' In Howard Spodek and Doris Meth Srinivasan, (eds.) *Urban Form and Meaning in South Asia: The Shaping of Cities from Prehistoric to Precolonial Times.*

Washington: National Gallery of Art; Hanover and London: University Press of New England. pp. 68–81.

Allchin, F. Raymond (1995) *The Archaeology of Early Historic South Asia: The Emergence of Cities and States*. Cambridge: Cambridge University Press.

Allchin, F. Raymond, and Bridget Allchin (1997) *Origins of a Civilization: The Prehistory and Early Archeology of South Asia*. New Delhi: Viking.

Alter, Joseph S. (1992) *The Wrestler's Body: Identity and Ideology in North India*. Berkeley: University of California Press.

Ansari, Sarah (2005) *Life after Partition: Migration, Community and Strife in Sindh, 1947–1962*. Oxford: Oxford University Press.

Appadurai, Arjun (1995) 'Playing with Modernity: The Decolonization of Cricket.' In: Carol A. Breckenridge, (ed.) *Consuming Modernity: Public Culture in a South Asian World*. Minneapolis: University of Minnesota Press. pp. 23–48.

Arasaratnam, Sinnappah (1986) *Merchants, Companies and Commerce on the Coromandel Coast 1650–1740*. Delhi: Oxford University Press.

Arasaratnam, Sinnappah (1987) 'India and the Indian Ocean in the Seventeenth Century.' In: Ashin Das Gupta and M. N. Pearson, (eds.) *India and the Indian Ocean 1500–1800*. Calcutta: Oxford University Press. pp. 94–130

Arasaratnam, Sinnappah (1989) 'European port settlements in the Coromandel commercial system 1650–1740.' In: Frank Broeze, (ed.). *Brides of the Sea: Port Cities of Asia from the 16ᵗʰ–20ᵗʰ Centuries*. Honolulu: University of Hawaii Press. pp. 75–96

Arasaratnam, Sinnappah (1994) *Maritime India in the Seventeenth Century*. Delhi: Oxford University Press.

Arasaratnam, Sinnappah, and Aniruddha Ray (1994) *Masulipatnam and Cambay: A history of two port-towns 1500–1800*. New Delhi: Munshiram Manoharlal.

Architecture of Manasara (1980) Prasanna Kumar Acharya, tr. repr. New Delhi: Oriental Books Reprint Corporation.

Arnold, David (1993) *Colonizing the Body: State Medicine and Epidemic Disease in Nineteenth-Century India*. Berkeley: University of California Press.

Arora, Shashi (1988) 'The Forms of Urban Organization in the Desert Parts of Rajasthan: A Case Study of Churu (1750–1818 A.D.).' In: Makrand Mehta, (ed.) *Urbanization in Western India: Historical Perspective*. Ahmedabad: Gujarat University. pp. 90–96.

Askari, Syed Hasan, and Qeyamuddin Ahmad, (eds.) (1983) *Comprehensive History of Bihar* 2 (1). Patna: Kashi Prasad Jayaswal Research Institute.

Askari, Syed Hasan, and Qeyamuddin Ahmad, (eds.) (1987) *Comprehensive History of Bihar* 2 (2). Patna: Kashi Prasad Jayaswal Research Institute.

Athar Ali, M. (1986) 'Capital of the Sultans: Delhi during the Thirteenth and Fourteenth Centuries.' In: Robert E. Frykenberg, (ed.) *Delhi through the Ages: Selected Essays in Urban History, Culture, and Society*. Delhi and New York: Oxford University Press. repr. 2001 in *The Delhi Omnibus*. New Delhi: Oxford University Press. pp. 21–31.

Bailey, Greg, and Ian Mabbett (2003) *The Sociology of Early Buddhism*. Cambridge: Cambridge University Press.

Balakrishnan, Deepa (2004) 'Nagore: Harmony in the face of deluge.' *Deccan Herald*, December 30: 9.

Banabhatta (1991) *Kadambari: A classic Sanskrit story of Magical Transformations*. Gwendolyn Layne, tr.. New York and London: Garland Publishing.

Bandaranayake, Senaka (1974) *Sinhalese Monastic Architecture: The Viharas of Anuradhapura*. Studies in South Asian Culture 4. Leiden: E. J. Brill.

Bandaranayake, Senaka (1989) 'Monastery plan and social formation: The spatial organization of the Buddhist monastery complexes of Early and Middle Historical period in Sri Lanka and changing patterns of political power.' In: Daniel Miller, Michael Rowlands and Christopher Tilley, (eds.) *Domination and Resistance*. London and Boston: Unwin Hyman: 179–193.

Bandyopadhyay, Kausik (2005) 'In Search of a Football Ground in Twentieth Century Urban Bengal.' *Soccer and Society* 6 (1): 69–78.

Banerjea, Dhrubajyoti (2005) *European Calcutta: Images and Recollections of a Bygone Era*. New Delhi: UBS Publishers Distributors Pvt. Ltd.

Banerjee, Prajnananda (1987) *Calcutta and its Hinterland: A Study in Economic History of India 1833–1900*. Calcutta: Progressive Publishers

Banerjee-Guha, Swapna (1995) 'Urban Development Process in Bombay: Planning for Whom?' In: Sujata Patel and Alice Thorner, (eds.) *Bombay: Metaphor for Modern India*. Bombay: Oxford University Press. pp. 100–20.

Banga, Indu (1992) 'Karachi and its Hinterland under Colonial Rule.' In: Indu Banga, (ed.) *Ports and Their Hinterlands in India (1700–1950)*. New Delhi: Manohar. pp. 337–58.

Basak, Nandita (2000) *Dynamics of Growth, Regional Perspective: Experience of Five Indian Industrial Towns 1961–1991*. Calcutta: Firma KLM Private Limited.

Basu, Aparna (1986) 'The Foundation and Early History of Delhi University.' In: Robert Frykenberg, (ed.) *Delhi through the Ages: Selected Essays in Urban History, Culture, and Society*. Delhi and New York: Oxford University Press; repr. 2001 in *The Delhi Omnibus*. New Delhi: Oxford University Press. pp. 257–86.

Basu, Susan Neild (1993) 'Madras in 1800: Perceiving the City.' In: Howard Spodek and Doris Meth Srinivasan, (ed.) *Urban Form and Meaning in South Asia: The Shaping of Cities from Prehistoric to Precolonial Times*. Washington: National Gallery of Art; Hanover and London: University Press of New England. pp. 221–40.

Bayly, C. A. (1980) 'The Small Town and Islamic Gentry in North India: The Case of Kara.' In Kenneth Ballhatchet and John Harrison, (eds.) *The City in South Asia: Pre-modern and Modern*. Collected Papers on South Asia 3, Centre of South Asian Studies, School of Oriental and African Studies, University of London. London and Dublin: Curzon Press; Atlantic Highlands NJ: Humanities Press. pp. 20–48.

Bayley, C. A. (1983) *Rulers, Townsmen and Bazaars: North Indian Society in the Age of British Expansion 1770–1870*. New York and Cambridge: Cambridge University Press.

Bayley, C. A. (1986) 'Delhi and Other Cities of North India during the "Twilight." ' In: Robert Frykenberg, (ed.) *Delhi through the Ages: Selected Essays in Urban History, Culture, and Society*. Delhi and New York: Oxford University Press. repr. *The Delhi Omnibus*. New Delhi: Oxford University Press. pp 121–36.

Bayley, C. A. (1996) *Empire and Information: Intelligence gathering and social communication in India, 1780–1870*. Cambridge: Cambridge University Press.

BDA (2005) *Master Plan–2015 Bangalore*, 3; Proposed Land use Maps, BMP and Peripheral Areas. Bangalore: Bangalore Development Authority.

Beall, Samuel, tr. (1884) *Si-yu-ki: Buddhist Records of the Western World*. London Trübner and Company.

Beazley, J. G., and F. H. Puckle (1926) *The Punjab Colony Manual 1*, rev. edn. Lahore: Superintendent, Government Printing, Punjab.

Begley, Vimala, (ed.) (1996) *The Ancient Port of Arikamedu: New Excavations and Researches 1989–1992* 1. Pondichéry: Centre d'Histoire et d'Archéologie, École Française d'Extrême-Orient.

Begley, Vimala, and Richard De Puma, (eds.) (1991) *Rome and India: The Ancient Sea Trade*. Madison: University of Wisconsin Press.

Begum, Nazma (2002) 'Women Workers' Status in Bangladesh: A Case of Garment Workers.' In: Khaleda Salahuddin, Roushan Jahan, and Latifa Akanda, (eds.) *State of Human Rights in Bangladesh: Women's Perspective*. Dhaka: Women for Women. pp. 201–30.

Bhaskaran, Theodore (1996) *The Eye of the Serpent: An Introduction to Tamil Cinema*. Madras: EastWest Books.

Bhaskaran, Theodore (2004) 'Cinema Houses of Chennai.' In: C. S. Lakshmi, (ed.) *The Unhurried City: Writings on Chennai*. New Delhi: Penguin Books India: 75–91.

Bhatia, Sutinder (1991) *Bokaro Steel Plant: Some Economic Aspects*. Bombay: Popular Prakashan.

Bhattacharya, Mohit (1974) *Municipal Government: Problems and Prospects*. Delhi: Research Publications in Social Sciences.

Binford, Mira Reym, Michael Camerini, and Joseph W. Elder (1977) *Wedding of the Goddess*. Madison: Center for South Asian Studies, University of Wisconsin-Madison.

Bisht, Ravindra Singh (1989) 'A New Model of the Harappan Town Planning as Revealed at Dholavira in Kutch: A Surface Study of Its Plan and Architecture.' In: Bhaskar Chatterjee, (ed.) *History and Archaeology*. Delhi: Ramanand Vidhya Bhawan. pp. 397–408.

Blake, Stephen P. (1991) *Shahjahanabad: The Sovereign City in Mughal India, 1639–1739*. Cambridge: Cambridge University Press.

Boardman, Philip (1978) *The Worlds of Patrick Geddes: Biologist, Town Planner, Re-educator, Peace-warrior*. London, Henley and Boston: Routledge and Kegan Paul.

Bombay First (2003) *Vision Mumbai: Transforming Mumbai into a world-class city*. Mumbai: Bombay First, and McKinsey and Company.

Bouchon, Geneviève (2000) 'A Microcosm: Calicut in the Sixteenth Century.' In: Denys Lombard and Jean Aubin, (eds.) *Asian Merchants and Businessmen in the Indian Ocean and the China Sea*. New Delhi: Oxford University Press. pp. 40–49.

Brand, Michael (1991) 'Mughal Ritual in Pre Mughal Cities: The Case of Jahangir in Mandu.' *Environmental Design: Journal of the Islamic Environmental Design Research Centre* 1–2: 8–17.

Brand, Michael, and Glenn D. Lowry, (ed.) (1985) *Fathpur-Sikri: A Sourcebook*. Cambridge, MA: Aga Khan Program for Islamic Architecture at Harvard University and the Massachusetts Institute of Technology.

Brand, Michael, and Glenn D. Lowry, (eds.) (1987) *Fatehpur-Sikri*. Bombay: Marg Publications.

Braudel, Fernand (1972) *The Mediterranean and the Mediterranean World in the Age of Philip II*. Siân Reynolds, tr.. New York: Harper and Row.

Broeze, Frank (1991) 'The External Dynamics of Port City Morphology: Bombay 1815–1914.' In: Indu Banga, (ed.) *Ports and Their Hinterlands in India (1700–1950)*. New Delhi: Manohar. pp. 245–72.

Broeze, F. J. A., K. I. McPherson, and P. D. Reeves (1987) 'Engineering and Empire: The Making of the Modern Indian Ocean Ports.' In: Satish Chandra, (ed.) *The Indian Ocean: Explorations in History, Commerce and Politics*. New Delhi, Newbury Park and London: Sage Publications. pp. 254–301.

Brohier, Richard Leslie (1984) *The Changing Face of Colombo (1505–1972) Covering the Portuguese, Dutch and British Periods*. Colombo: Visidunu Prakashakayo.

Brownlee, David B., and David G. De Long (1991) *Louis I. Kahn: In the Realm of Architecture*. Los Angeles: Museum of Contemporary Art; New York: Rizzoli.

Brush, John E. (1970) 'The Growth of the Presidency Towns.' In: Richard G. Fox, (ed.) *Urban India: Society, Space and Image*. Duke University Program in Comparative Studies on Southern Asia, Monograph and Occasional Papers Series 10. Durham NC: Duke University Press. pp. 91–114.

Buch, Mahesh N. (1987) *Planning the Indian City*. New Delhi: Vikas Publishing House.

Burgess, James (1887) *The Buddhist stupas of Amaravati and Jaggayyapeta in the Krishna district, Madras Presidency, surveyed in 1882, by Jas. Burgess. With translations of the Aśoka inscriptions at Jaugada and Dhauli, by Georg Bühler*. Archaeological Survey of India Reports, New Series, 6. London: Trübner and Company.

Carswell, John (1991) 'The Port of Mantai, Sri Lanka.' In: Vimala Begley and Richard De Puma, (eds.) *Rome and India: The Ancient Sea Trade*. Madison: University of Wisconsin Press. pp. 197–203.

Cashman, Richard (1980) *Patrons, Players and the Crowd: The Phenomenon of Indian Cricket*. New Delhi: Orient Longman.

Centre for Policy Research (2001) *The Future of Urbanisation: Spread and Shape in Selected States*. New Delhi: Centre for Policy Research.

Chakrabarti, Dilip K. (1992) *Ancient Bangladesh, a study of the archaeological sources*. Delhi and New York: Oxford University Press.

Chakrabarti, Dilip K. (1995) *The Archaeology of Ancient Indian Cities*. Delhi: Oxford University Press.

Chakrabarti, Dilip K. (1999) *India: An Archaeological History: Palaeolithic Beginnings to Early Historic Foundations*. New Delhi: Oxford University Press.

Chakrabarti, Dilip K. (2000) 'Mahajanapada States of Early Historic India.' In: Mogens Herman Hansen, (ed.) *A Comparative Study of Thirty City-State Cultures*. Historisk-filosofiske Skrifter 21. Copenhagen: Royal Danish Academy of Sciences and Letters. pp. 375–91.

Chakrabarti, Dilip K. (2004) *Indus Civilization Sites in India: New Discoveries. Marg* 55 (3). Mumbai: Marg Publications.

Chakrabarty, Dipesh (1989) *Rethinking Working-Class History: Bengal 1890–1940*. Princeton: Princeton University Press.

Chakrabarty, Dipesh (2000) *Provincializing Europe: Postcolonial Thought and Historical Difference*. Princeton: Princeton University Press.

Chakravarti, Ranabir (2001) 'Monarch, Merchants and a Matha in Northern Konkan (c. AD 900–1053).' In: Ranabir Chakravarti, (ed.) *Trade in Early India*. New Delhi: Oxford University Press. pp. 257–81.

Chakravarti, Uma (1987) *The Social Dimensions of Early Buddhism*. Delhi: Oxford University Press.

Champakalakshmi, R. (1996) *Trade, Ideology and Urbanization: South India 300 BC to AD 1300*. New Delhi: Oxford University Press.

Champakalakshmi, R. (2001) 'The Medieval South Indian Guilds: Their Role in Trade and Urbanization.' In: Ranabir Chakravarti, (ed.) *Trade in Early India*. New Delhi: Oxford University Press. pp. 326–343.

Chandavarkar, Rajnarayan (1994) *The Origins of Industrial Capitalism in India: Business strategies and the working classes in Bombay, 1900–1940*. Cambridge: Cambridge University Press.

Chandavarkar, Rajnarayan (1998) *Imperial Power and Popular Politics: Class, Resistance and the State in India, c. 1850–1950*. Cambridge: Cambridge University Press.

Chandramohan, D. (2005) 'Thiru. P. Ayya Nadar: The Great Visionary.' *100th Year Celebrations of Shri. P. Ayya Nadar, the Architect of Modern Sivakasi 1905–2005*. Sivakasi: Ayya Nadar Janaki Ammal College. pp. 125–32.

Charvat, Petr (1993) 'External contacts of Sri Lanka in the 1st millennium AD. (Archaeological evidence from Mantai).' *Archiv Orientalni* 61: 13–29.

Chatterjee, Partha (1997) 'The Nation and its Women.' In: Ranajit Guha, (ed.) *A Subaltern Studies Reader, 1986–1995*. Minneapolis: University of Minnesota Press. pp. 240–62.

Chattopadhyay, Swati (2005) *Representing Calcutta: Modernity, nationalism, and the colonial uncanny*. London and New York: Routledge.

Chattopadhyaya, Brajadulal (1994) *The Making of Early Medieval India*. New Delhi: Oxford University Press.

Chattopadhyay, Brajadulal (2003) *Studying Early India: Archaeology, Texts, and Historical Issues*. New Delhi: Permanent Black.

Chaudhuri, Sukanta, (ed.) (1990) *Calcutta: The Living City*. 2 vols. New Delhi: Oxford University Press.

Chaudhury, K. N. (1978) 'Some Reflections on the Town and Country in Mughal India.' *Modern Asian Studies* 12 (1): 77–96.

Chaudhury, K. N. (1985) *Trade and Civilisation in the Indian Ocean: An Economic History from the Rise of Islam to 1750*. Cambridge: Cambridge University Press.

Chenoy, Shama Mitra (1998) *Shahjahanabad: A City of Delhi, 1638–1857*. New Delhi: Munshiram Manoharlal.

Chitalwala, Y. M. (1993) 'Harappan Settlements in the Kutch-Saurashtra Region: Patterns of Distribution and Routes of Communication.' In: Gregory L. Possehl, (ed.) *Harappan Civilization: A Recent Perspective*. 2nd edn. New Delhi, Bombay, and Calcutta: Oxford and IBH. pp. 197–202.

Chopra, Kusum, Atiya Habeeb Kidwai, and Subhash Marcus (2005) 'Urbanization Process in the Undivided Punjab.' In: Reeta Grewal, (ed.) *Five Thousand Years of Urbanization: The Punjab Region*. New Delhi: Manohar; Chandigarh: Institute of Punjab Studies. pp.175–98.

Cidade de Goa: A reconstruction (1994) Panaji: Department of Information and Publicity, Government of Goa.

The Cilappatikaram of Ilanko Atikal: An Epic of South India (1993) R. Parthasarathy, trans. New York: Penguin.

Cimino, Rosa Maria, (ed.) (1994) *Ancient Rome and India: Commercial and Cultural Contacts between the Roman World and India*. New Delhi: Munshiram Manorharlal.

Coccari, Diane M. (1989) 'Protection and Identity: Banaras's Bir Babas as Neighborhood Guardian Deities.' In: Sandria B. Freitag, (ed.) *Culture and Power in Banaras: Community, Performance, and Environment, 1800–1980*. Berkeley: University of California Press. pp. 130–46.

Coningham, Robin (1999) *Anuradhapura: The British-Sri Lankan Excavations at Anuradhapura Salgaha Watta 2*. Vol 1: The Site. BAR International Series 824. Oxford: Archaeopress.

Coningham, R.A.E., and F. R. Allchin (1995) 'The rise of cities in Sri Lanka.' In: F. R. Allchin, (ed.) *The Archaeology of Early Historic South Asia: The Emergence of Cities and States*. Cambridge: University Press. pp. 152–84.

Coomaraswamy, Ananda K. (2002) *Early Indian Architecture: Cities and City-gates*. New Delhi: Munshiram Manoharlal.

Cooper, Ilay, and Barry Dawson (1998) *Traditional Buildings of India*. London: Thames and Hudson.

Corporation of Cochin (2007) 'The Cochin Saga' (http://www.corporationofcochin.org).

Cousens, Henry (1916) *Bijapur and its Architectural Remains*. Archaeological Survey of India, Imperial Series 37. Bombay: Government Central Press.

Crook, Nigel (1993) *India's Industrial Cities: Essays in Economy and Demography*. Delhi: Oxford University Press.

Cunningham, Alexander (1924) *Cunningham's Ancient Geography of India*. Surendranath Majumdar Sastri, (ed.) Calcutta: Chuckervertty, Chatterjee and Company.

Currie, P. M. (1989) *The Shrine and Cult of Mu'in al-din Chishti of Ajmer*. Delhi: Oxford University Press.

Dales, George F. (1965) 'New Investigations at Mohenjo-daro.' *Archaeology* 18 (2): 145–50.

Dani, Ahmad Hasan (1986) *The Historic City of Taxila*. Paris: United Nations Educational, Scientific and Cultural Organization; Tokyo: Centre for East Asian Cultural Studies.

Dar, Saifur Rahman (1993) 'Dating the Monuments of Taxila.' In: Howard Spodek and Doris Meth Srinivasan, (eds.) *Urban Form and Meaning in South Asia: The Shaping of Cities from Prehistoric to Precolonial Times*. Washington: National Gallery of Art; Hanover and London: University Press of New England. pp. 103–122.

Darling, Sir Malcolm (1947) *The Punjab Peasant in Prosperity and Debt*. 4th edn. Oxford: Oxford University Press.

Das, P. K. (2003) 'Slums: The Continuing Struggle for Housing.' In: Sujata Patel and Jim Masselos, (eds.) *Bombay and Mumbai: The City in Transition*. New Delhi: Oxford University Press. pp. 207–34.

Das Gupta, Ashin (1979) *Indian Merchants and the Decline of Surat 1700–1750*. Beiträge zur Südasienforschung, Südasien-Institut, Universität Heidelberg 40. Wiesbaden: Franz Steiner Verlag.

Das Gupta, Ranajit (1994) *Labour and Working Class in Eastern India: Studies in Colonial History*. Calcutta: K. P. Bagchi.

Datta, V. N. (1986) 'Panjabi Refugees and the Urban Development of Greater Delhi.' In: R. E. Frykenberg, (ed.) *Delhi through the Ages: Selected Essays in Urban History, Culture, and Society*. Delhi and New York: Oxford University Press: repr. *The Delhi Omnibus*. New Delhi: Oxford University Press. pp. 287–305.

Davison-Jenkins, Dominic J. (1997) *The Irrigation and Water Supply Systems of Vijayanagara*. New Delhi: Manohar and American Institute of Indian Studies.

Dehejia, Vidya (1972) *Early Buddhist Rock Temples: A Chronological Study*. London: Thames and Hudson.

Deloche, Jean (1993) *Transport and Communications in India Prior to Steam Locomotion. Volume 1: Land Transport*. James Walker, tr. Delhi: Oxford University Press.

Deloche, Jean (1994) *Transport and Communications in India Prior to Steam Locomotion. Volume 2: Water Transport*. James Walker, tr. Delhi: Oxford University Press.

Deloche, Jean (2000) *Senji (Gingi): Ville fortifiée du pays tamoul*. Paris and Pondicherry: École française d'Extrême-Orient and Institut français de Pondichéry.

Deloche, Jean (2004) *Origins of the Urban Development of Pondicherry according to Seventeenth Century Dutch Plans*. Pondicherry: Institut français de Pondichéry.

Deloche, Jean (2005) *Le vieux Pondichéry (1673–1824) revisité d'apres les plans anciens*. Collection indologie 99. Pondicherry: Institut français de Pondichéry and École française d'Extrême-Orient.

Desai, Z. A. (1989) 'The Major Dargahs of Ahmedabad.' In: Christian W. Troll, (ed.) *Muslim Shrines in India: Their Character, History and Significance*. New Delhi: Oxford University Press. pp. 76–97.

De Souza, Teotonio R. (1979) *Medieval Goa: A Socio-economic History*. New Delhi: Concept Publishing Company.

Deyell, John S. (1990) *Living without Silver: The Monetary History of Early Medieval North India*. Delhi: Oxford University Press.

Dhavalikar, M. K. (1993) 'Harappans in Saurashtra: The Mercantile Enterprise as Seen from Recent Excavation of Kuntasi.' In: Gregory L. Possehl, (ed.) *Harappan Civilization: A Recent Perspective*. 2nd edn. New Delhi, Bombay, and Calcutta: Oxford and IBH. pp. 555–568.

Dharmasena, K. (1989) 'Colombo: Gateway and oceanic hub of shipping.' In: Frank Broeze, (ed.) *Brides of the Sea: Port Cities of Asia from the 16th–20th Centuries*. Honolulu: University of Hawaii Press. pp. 152–72.

Dinesh, K. N. (2003) *Structure of Medium Scale Industries in Bhilai*. New Delhi: Northern Book Centre.

Divekar, V. D. (1981) 'Political Factor in the Rise and Decline of Cities in Pre-British India – with special reference to Pune.' In: J. S. Grewal and Indu Banga, (eds.) *Studies in Urban History*. Amritsar: Department of History, Guru Nanak Dev University. pp. 91–106.

D'Monte, Darryl (2002) *Ripping the Fabric: The Decline of Mumbai and its Mills*. New Delhi: Oxford University Press.

Dobbin, Christine (1972) *Urban Leadership in Western India: Politics and Communities in Bombay City 1840–1885*. London: Oxford University Press.

Docker, Edward (1976) *History of Indian Cricket*. Delhi: Macmillan.

Dossal, Mariam (1991) *Imperial Designs and Indian Realities: The Planning of Bombay City, 1845–1875*. Bombay: Oxford University Press.

D'Oyly, Sir Charles (1848) *Views of Calcutta and its Environs*. London: Dickenson and Company.

Doxiades, Konstantinos A. (1968) *Ekistics: An Introduction to the Science of Human Settlements*. New York: Oxford University Press.

Doxiades, Konstantinos A. (1975) *Building Entopia*. New York: W. W. Norton and Company.

Dutta, Maya. (1977) *Jamshedpur: The Growth of the City and its Regions*. Calcutta: The Asiatic Society.

Dwivedi, Sharada, and Rahul Mehrotra (2001) *Bombay: The Cities Within*. Bombay: Eminence Designs Pvt. Ltd.

Dwyer, Rachel, and Divia Patel (2002) *Cinema India: The Visual Culture of Hindi Film*. New Delhi: Oxford University Press.

Eaton, Richard M. (1978) *The Sufis of Bijapur: Social Roles of Sufis in Medieval India*. Princeton: Princeton University Press.

Eaton, Richard M. (1993) *The Rise of Islam and the Bengal Frontier, 1204–1760*. Berkeley: University of California Press.

Eaton, Richard M. (2000) *Essays on Islam and Indian History*. Delhi: Oxford University Press.

Eck, Diana L. (1982) *Banaras: City of Light*. New York: Alfred A. Knopf.

Ehlers, Eckart, and Thomas Krafft (2003) *Shahjahanabad/Old Delhi: Tradition and Colonial Change*. 2nd edn. New Delhi: Manohar.

Engelshoven, Miranda (1999) 'Diamonds and Patels: A report on the diamond industry of Surat.' *Contributions to Indian Sociology* 33 (1 and 2): 353–77.

Erdosy, George (1988) *Urbanisation in Early Historic India*. BAR International Series 430. Oxford: B.A.R.

Erdosy, George (1995) 'City states of North India and Pakistan at the time of the Buddha.' In: F. R. Allchin, (ed.) *The Archaeology of Early Historic South Asia: The Emergence of Cities and States*. Cambridge: Cambridge University Press. pp. 99–122.

Evenson, Norma (1966) *Chandigarh*. Berkeley and Los Angeles: University of California Press.

Evenson, Norma (1989) *The Indian Metropolis: A View Toward the West*. New Haven and London: Yale University Press.

Farid, Gholam Sharfuddin (2001) *Picture Postcards from Calcutta 1895–1980*. Kolkata: Mehmood Imran.

Feldhaus, Anne (2003) *Connected Places: Region, Pilgrimage, and Geographical Imagination in India*. New York: Palgrave Macmillan.

Fernandes, Leela (1997) *Producing Workers: The Politics of Gender, Class, and Culture in the Calcutta Jute Mills*. Philadelphia: University of Pennsylvania Press.

Fernandes, Leela (2006) *India's New Middle Class: Democratic Politics in an Era of Economic Reform*. Minneapolis and London: University of Minnesota Press.

Fick, Richard (1920) *The social organisation in North-East India in Buddha's time*. Calcutta: University of Calcutta.

Fiser, Ivo (2001) 'The Problem of the *Setthi* in Buddhist Jatakas.' In: Ranabir Chakravarti, (ed.) *Trade in Early India*. New Delhi: Oxford University Press. pp. 166–98.

Forster, William (1998) *England's Quest of Eastern Trade*. London and New York: Routledge.

Fox, Richard G. (1970) 'Rurban Settlements and Rajput "Clans" in Northern India.' In: Richard G. Fox, (ed.) *Urban India: Society, Space and Image*. Duke University Program in Comparative Studies on Southern Asia, Monograph and Occasional Papers Series 10. Durham NC: Duke University Press. pp. 167–85.

Francfort, Henri-Paul (1985) *Prospections archéologiques au nord-ouest de l'Inde: Rapport préliminaire 1983–1984*. Paris: Éditions Recherche sur les Civilisations.

Francis, Peter (2002) *Asia's Maritime Bead Trade 300 B.C. to the Present*. Honolulu: University of Hawai'i Press.

Friedman, John, and Goetz Wolff (1982) 'World City Formation: An Agenda for Research and Action.' *International Journal for Urban and Regional Research* 6 (3): 209–44.

Fritz, John M., George Michell, and M. S. Nagaraja Rao (1984) *Where Kings and Gods Meet: The Royal Centre at Vijayanagara, India*. Tucson: University of Arizona Press.

Gadre, Pramod B. (1986) *Cultural Archaeology of Ahmadnagar during Nizam Shahi Period (1494–1632)*. Delhi: B. R. Publishing Corporation.

Gangar, Amrit (1995) 'Films from the City of Dreams.' In Sujata Patel and Alice Thorner, ed. B*ombay: Mosaic of Modern Culture*. Bombay: Oxford University Press: 210–24.

Ganger, Amrit (2003) 'Tinseltown: From Studios to Industry.' In: Sujata Patel and Jim Masselos, (ed.) *Bombay and Mumbai: The City in Transition*. New Delhi: Oxford University Press. pp. 267–300.

Gast, Klaus-Peter (1998) *Louis I. Kahn: The Idea of Order*. Michael Robinson, tr. Basel and Boston: Kirkhaüser.

Gauba, Anand (1988) *Amritsar: A Study in Urban History (1840–1947)*. Jalandhar: ABS Publications.

Ghosh, Amitav (1992) *In an Antique Land: History in the Guise of a Traveler's Tale*. London: Granta Books.

Gibb, H. A. R. (1971) *Ibn Battuta: Travels in Asia and Africa, 1325–1354*. Cambridge: Cambridge University Press and Hakluyt Society.

Gillion, Kenneth L. (1968) *Ahmedabad: A Study in Indian Urban History*. Berkeley and Los Angeles: University of California Press.

Ginsburg, Norton (1991) 'Extended Metropolitan Regions in Asia: A New Spatial Paradigm.' In: Norton Ginsburg, Bruce Koppel and T. G. McGee, (eds.) *The Extended*

Metropolis: Settlement Transition in Asia. Honolulu: University of Hawaii Press. pp. 27–46.

Gokhale, Balkrishna Govind (1979) *Surat in the Seventeenth Century: A Study in Urban History of pre-modern India.* Scandinavian Institute of Asian Studies Monograph Series 28. London and Malmo: Curzon Press.

Gokhale, Balkrishna Govind (1988) *Poona In the Eighteenth Century: An Urban History.* Delhi: Oxford University Press.

Gommans, Jos J. L., and Dirk H.A. Kolff (2001) *Warfare and Weaponry in South Asia 1000–1800.* New Delhi: Oxford University Press.

Gooptu, Nandini (2001) *The Politics of the Urban Poor in early Twentieth-Century India.* Cambridge: Cambridge University Press.

Gordon, Stewart (1988a) 'Burhanpur: Entrepot and hinterland, 1650–1750.' *Indian Economic and Social History Review* 25 (4): 425–42.

Gordon, Stewart (1998b) *Jute and Empire: The Calcutta Jute Wallahs and the Landscapes of Empire.* Manchester and New York: Manchester University Press.

Goswami, Omkar (1992) 'Sahibs, Babus and Banias: Changes in Industrial Control in Eastern India, 1918–50.' In: Rajat Kanta Ray, (ed.) *Entrepreneurship and Industry in India, 1800–1947.* Delhi and New York: Oxford University Press. pp. 228–59.

Government of Andhra Pradesh (1999) *Andhra Pradesh: Vision 2020.* Hyderabad: Government of Andhra Pradesh.

Government of India (2005) *National Maritime Development Programme.* New Delhi: Ministry of Shipping, Road Transport and Highways, Department of Shipping.

Government of Karnataka (2001) *The Bangalore Road Show.* Bangalore: Department of IT and Biotechnology.

Government of Maharashtra (2004) *Transforming Mumbai into a World-Class City: First report of the Chief Minister's Task Force.* Mumbai: Government of Maharashtra.

Government of Nepal (2002) *Nepal Demographic and Health Survey 2001.* Kathmandu: Family Health Division, Department of Health Services, Ministry of Health; Kathmandu: New Era; Calverton MD: ORC Macro.

Government of Pakistan (2006) *Pakistan Statistical Year Book 2006.* Islamabad: Ministry of Economic Affairs and Statistics, Statistics Division, Federal Bureau of Statistics.

Government of Tamil Nadu (1994) *Report on Survey of Child Labour in the Match Belt: Tamil Nadu.* Madras: Department of Social Welfare.

Grewal, J. S. (1975) *In the By-Lanes of History: Some Persian Documents from a Punjab Town.* Simla: Indian Institute of Advanced Study.

Grewal, J. S. (1981) 'Ramdaspur to Amritsar: From a Town to a City.' In: J. S. Grewal and Indu Banga, (eds.) *Studies in Urban History.* Amritsar: Department of History, Guru Nanak Dev University. pp. 115–22.

Grewal, J. S. (1984) 'Business Communities of Punjab." In: Dwijendra Tripathi, (ed.) *Business Communities of India: A Historical Perspective.* New Delhi: Manohar. pp. 209–24.

Grewal, J. S., and Veena Sachdeva (2005) 'Urbanization in the Mughal Province of Lahore (c. 1550–1850).' In: Reeta Grewal, (ed.) *Five Thousand Years of Urbanization: The Punjab Region.* New Delhi: Manohar; Chandigarh: Institute of Punjab Studies. pp. 107–27.

Grewal, Reeta (1997) 'Urban Revolution under Colonial Rule.' In: Indu Banga, (ed.) *Five Punjabi Centuries: Polity, Economy, Society and Culture, c. 1500–1990.* New Delhi: Manohar. pp. 438–54.

Guha, Amalendu (1984) 'More about the Parsi Sheths: Their Roots, Entrepreneurship, and Comprador Role, 1650–1918.' In: Dwijendra Tripathi, (ed.) *Business Communities of India: A Historical Perspective*. New Delhi: Manohar. pp. 109–50.

Guha, Ramachandra (2002) *A Corner of a Foreign Field: The Indian History of a British Sport*. London: Picador.

Guha, Sumit (1996) 'Potentates, Traders and Peasants: Western India, c. 1700–1870.' In: Burton Stein and Sanjay Subrahmanyam, (eds.) *Institutions and Economic Change in South Asia*. Delhi: Oxford University Press. pp. 71–84.

Gumperz, Ellen McDonald (2001) 'City-Hinterland Relations and the Development of a Regional Elite in Nineteenth-Century Bombay.' In: Ian J. Kerr, (ed) *Railways in Modern India*. New Delhi: Oxford University Press. pp. 97–126.

Gunawaradana, R. A. H. L. (1989) 'Anuradhapura: Ritual, Power and Resistance in a Precolonial South Asian City.' In: Daniel Miller, Michael Rowlands and Christopher Tilley, (eds.) *Domination and Resistance*. London and Boston: Unwin Hyman. pp. 155–78.

Gupta, Ishwar Prakash (1986) *Urban Glimpses of Mughal India: Agra, the Imperial Capital (16th and 17th Centuries)*. Delhi: Discovery Publishing House.

Gupta, Narayani (1981) *Delhi between Two Empires 1803–1931: Society, Government and Urban Growth*. New Delhi: Oxford University Press; repr. 2001 *The Delhi Omnibus*. New Delhi: Oxford University Press.

Gupta, Narayani (1986) 'Delhi and its Hinterland: The Nineteenth and early Twentieth Centuries.' In: Robert Frykenberg, (ed.) *Delhi through the Ages: Selected Essays in Urban History, Culture, and Society*. Delhi and New York: Oxford University Press; repr. 2001 *The Delhi Omnibus*. New Delhi: Oxford University Press. pp. 137–56.

Gupta, Narayani (1991) 'Urbanism in South India: Eighteenth–Nineteenth Centuries.' In: Indu Banga, (ed.) *The City in India History: Urban Demography, Society, and Politics*. New Delhi: Manohar; Columbia MO: South Asia Publications. pp. 121–47.

Gupta, Samita (1993) 'Theory and practice of town planning in Calcutta, 1817–1912: An appraisal.' *Indian Economic and Social History Review* 30 (1): 29–55.

Gupte, R. S. (1967) *The Art and Architecture of Aihole*. Bombay: D. B. Taraporevala Sons and Company.

Gutschow, Niels (1982) *Stadtraum und Ritual der newarischen Städte im Kathmandu-Tal: Eine architekturanthropologische Untersuchung*. Stuttgart: Verlag W. Kohlhammer.

Gutschow, Niels, and Ganesh Man Basukala (1987) 'The Navadurga of Bhaktapur – Spatial Implications of an Urban Ritual.' In: Niels Gutschow and Axel Michaels, (eds.) *Heritage of the Kathmandu Valley*. Sankt Augustin: VGH Wissenschaftsverlag. pp. 135–66.

Gutschow, Niels, and Bernhard Kölver (1975) *Ordered Space, Concepts and Functions in a Town of Nepal*. Wiesbaden: Kommisssionsverlag Franz Steiner.

Habib, Irfan (1982a) *An Atlas of the Mughal Empire*. Delhi: Oxford University Press.

Habib, Irfan (1982b) 'Population.' In: Tapan Raychaudhuri and Irfan Habib, (eds.) *The Cambridge Economic History of India. Vol. 1: c.1200–c. 1750*. Cambridge: Cambridge University Press. pp. 163–71.

Haider, Saraswati (2000) 'Migrant Women and Urban Experience in a Squatter Settlement.' In: Véronique Dupont, Emma Tarlo, and Denis Vidal, (eds.) *Delhi: Urban Space and Human Destinies*. New Delhi: Manohar, Centre de Sciences Humaines, and Institut de Recherche pour le Développement. pp. 29–50.

Hall, Kenneth R. (1980) *Trade and Statecraft in the Age of the Colas*. New Delhi: Abhinav Publications.

Hambly, Gavin R. G. (1982) 'Mughal India.' In: Tapan Raychaudhuri and Irfan Habib, (eds.) *The Cambridge Economic History of India Vol. 1: c.1200—c.1750.* Cambridge: Cambridge University Press. pp. 434–51.

Hansen, Kathryn (2002) 'Parsi Theatre and the City: Locations, patrons, audiences.' In: *Sarai Reader 2: The Cities of Everyday Life.* New Delhi: Centre for the Study of Developing Societies and Society for Old and New Media. pp. 40–49.

Hansen, Thomas Blom (2001) *Wages of Violence: Naming and Identity in Postcolonial Bombay.* Princeton and Oxford: Princeton University Press.

Hardgrave, Robert L., Jr. (1969) *The Nadars of Tamilnad: The Political Culture of a Community in Change.* Berkeley and Los Angeles: University of California Press.

Hardgrove, Anne (2004) *Community and Public Culture: The Marwaris in Calcutta.* New Delhi: Oxford University Press.

Harrigan, Patrick (1998) *Kataragama: The Mystery Shrine.* Chennai: Institute of Asian Studies.

Harris, Nigel (1978) *Economic Development, Cities and Planning: The Case of Bombay.* Bombay, Oxford and London: Oxford University Press.

Hart, Henry H. (1950) *Sea Road to the Indies.* New York: Macmillan.

Hasan, Arif. (2002) *Understanding Karachi: Planning and Reform for the Future.* 2nd edn. Karachi: City Press.

Hasan, Arif, and Masooma Mohib (2003) 'The Case of Karachi, Pakistan.' *Understanding Slums: Case Studies for the Global Report on Human Settlements 2003.* Development Planning Unit, UN-Habitat (http://www.ucl.ac.uk/dpu-projects/Global_Report).

Hazareesingh, Sandip (2001) 'Colonial Modernism and the flawed paradigms of urban renewal: Uneven development in Bombay, 1900–1925.' *Urban History* 28 (2): 235–55.

Hebalkar, Sharad (2001) *Ancient Indian Ports with Special Reference to Maharashtra.* New Delhi: Munshiram Manoharlal.

Heins, J. J. F., and E. N. Meijer (1990) 'Population movements to a growth-pole: the case of Hosur, Tamil Nadu.' *Third World Planning Review* 12 (3): 231–47.

Heitzman, James (1980) 'Early Buddhism, Trade, and Empire.' In: Kenneth A. R. Kennedy and Gregory L. Possehl, (eds.) *Studies in Archaeology and Paleoanthropology of South Asia.* New Delhi: Oxford IBH. pp. 121–37.

Heitzman, James (1997) *Gifts of Power: Lordship in an Early Indian State.* New Delhi: Oxford University Press.

Heitzman, James (2001a) 'Urbanization in Southern India, 900–1900.' In: S. Rajagopal, (ed.) *Kaveri: Studies in Epigraphy, Archaeology and History.* Chennai: Panpattu Veliyiittakam. pp. 299–330.

Heitzman, James (2001b) 'Urbanization and Political Economy in Early South India: Kanchipuram during the Chola Period.' In: Kenneth R. Hall, (ed.) *Structure and Society in Early South India: Essays in Honour of Noboru Karashima.* Delhi: Oxford University Press. pp. 117–156.

Heitzman, James (2004) *Network City: Planning the Information Society in Bangalore.* New Delhi: Oxford University Press.

Heitzman, James (2008) 'The Urban Context of Early Buddhist Monuments in South Asia.' In: Akira Shimada and Jason Hawkes, (eds.) *Buddhist Stūpas in South Asia: Recent Archaeological, Art-Historical, and Historical Perspectives.* New Delhi: Oxford University Press.

Heitzman, James, and S. Rajagopal (2004) 'Urban Geography and Land Measurement in the Twelfth Century: The Case of Kanchipuram.' *Indian Economic and Social History Review,* 41 (3): 237–68.

Heitzman, James, and Smriti Srinivas (2005) 'Warrior Goddess versus Bipedal Cow: Sport, Space, Performance and Planning in an Indian City.' In: James Mills, (ed.) *Subaltern Sports: Politics and Sport in South Asia*. London: Anthem Press. pp. 139–71.

Herbert, John (1982) 'The Karachi Development Programme: 1967–1985: An Interim Appraisal.' In: John L. Taylor and David G. Williams, (eds). *Urban Planning Practice in Developing Countries*. Oxford: Pergamon Press. pp. 77–122.

Hilding, Per (1992) *Technology in a Controlled Economy: The Match Industry in India*. Richmond, Surrey: Curzon Press and Nordic Institute of Asian Studies.

Hill, Kenneth, W. Seltzer, J. Leaning, S. J. Malik, and S. S. Russel. (2006) 'The Demographic Impact of Partition: Bengal in 1947.' *Working Paper 06–08*. Cambridge: Weatherford Center for International Affairs, Harvard University.

Hoque, Serajul (2003) *Global Trade Liberalization: Impact on the Readymade Garments Industry in Bangladesh*. Frankfurt am Main: Peter Lang.

Hosagrahar, Jyoti (2005) *Indigenous Modernities: Negotiating Architecture and Urbanism*. London and New York: Routledge.

Hoskote, Ranjit (2007) 'Versions of a Postcolonial Metropolis: Competing Discourses on Bombay's Image.' In: Klaus Segbers, (ed.) *The Making of Global City Regions: Johannesburg, Mumbai/Bombay, São Paulo, and Shanghai*. Baltimore: Johns Hopkins University Press. pp. 258–78.

Hourani, George F. (1995) *Arab Seafaring in the Indian Ocean in Ancient and Medieval Times*, rev. edn. Princeton: Princeton University Press.

Husain, A. B. M., (eds.) (1997) *Gawr-Lakhnawti*. A Survey of Historical Monuments and Sites in Bangladesh SHMSB 002. Dhaka: Asiatic Society of Bangladesh.

Hutt, Antony (1988) *Goa: A Traveller's Historical and Architectural Guide*. Buckhurst Hill, Essex: Scorpion Publishing Limited.

Irving, Robert Grant (1981) *Indian Summer: Lutyens, Baker, and Imperial Delhi*. New Haven and London: Yale University Press.

Islam, M. S. (1980) 'Life in the Mufassal Towns of Nineteenth-Century Bengal.' In: Kenneth Ballhatchet and John Harrison, (eds.) *The City in South Asia: Pre-modern and Modern*. Collected Papers on South Asia 3, Centre of South Asian Studies, School of Oriental and African Studies, University of London. London and Dublin: Curzon Press; Atlantic Highlands NJ: Humanities Press. pp. 224–56.

Jacquemin, Alain R. A. (1999) *Urban Development and New Towns in the Third World: Lessons from the New Bombay Experience*. Aldershot: Ashgate.

Jain, Kailash Chand (1972) *Ancient Cities and Towns of Rajasthan: A Study of Culture and Civilization*. Delhi: Motilal Banarsidass

Jain, L. C. (1998) *The City of Hope: The Faridabad Story*. New Delhi: Concept Publishing.

Jain, V. K. (1990) *Trade and Traders in Western India (AD 1000–1300)*. New Delhi: Munshiram Manoharlal.

Jansen, Michael (1978) 'City Planning in the Harappa Culture.' In: Dalu Jones and George Michell, (eds.) *Art and Archaeology Research Papers 14*. London: AARP. pp. 69–74.

Jansen, Michael (1993) *Mohenjo-Daro: City of Wells and Drains. Water Splendour 4500 Years Ago*. Bergisch Gladback: Frontinus Society Publications.

Jarrige, Catherine, Jean François Jarrige, Richard H. Meadow, and Gonzague Quivron, (eds.) (1995) *Mehrgarh: Field Reports 1974–1985 from Neolithic times to the Indus Civilization*. Karachi: Department of Culture and Tourism, Government of Sindh, Pakistan.

Johnson, William A. (1966) *The Steel Industry of India*. Cambridge MA: Harvard University Press.

Jones, Stephanie (1992) *Merchants of the Raj: British Managing Agency Houses in Calcutta Yesterday and Today.* Houndmills and London: Macmillan.

Joshi, Gopal, (ed.) (2002) *Garment industry in South Asia: Rags or riches? Competitiveness, productivity and job quality in the post-MFA environment.* New Delhi: South Asia Multidisciplinary Advisory Team, International Labour Organization.

Joshi, Rajendra (1988) 'Naya Shahar (Beawar): The Emergence of a Colonial Town.' In: Makrand Mehta, (ed.) *Urbanization in Western India: Historical Perspective.* Ahmedabad: Gujarat University. pp. 109–29.

Joshi, S. K. (1985) *Defence Architecture in Early Karnataka.* Delhi: Sundeep Prakashan.

Juergensmeyer, Mark (1991) *Radhasoami reality: The Logic of a Modern Faith.* Princeton: Princeton University Press.

Jurong Consultants (2003) *IT Corridor Bangalore, India: Structure Plan Final Report.* Bangalore: Jurong Township Consultants (India) Pvt. Ltd.

Kabeer, Naila (2000) *The Power to Choose: Bangladeshi Women and Labour Market Decisions in London and Dhaka.* London and New York: Verso.

Kabeer, Naila, and Simeen Mahmud (2004) 'Rags, Riches and Women Workers: Export-oriented Garment Manufacturing in Bangladesh.' In: Marilyn Carr, (ed.) *Chains of Fortune: Linking Women Producers and Workers with Global Markets.* London: Commonwealth Secretariat.

Kalia, Ravi (1994) *Bhubaneswar: From a Temple Town to a Capital City.* Carbondale and Edwardsville: Southern Illinois University Press; Delhi: Oxford University Press.

Kalia, Ravi (1999) *Chandigarh: The Making of an Indian City.* 2nd rev. edn. New Delhi: Oxford University Press.

Kalia, Ravi (2004) *Gandhinagar: Building National Identity in Postcolonial India.* Columbia SC: University of South Carolina Press; New Delhi: Oxford University Press.

Kamerkar, Mani (1988) 'Thana: A Study of Urban Development as a Hinterland of Bombay (1800–1900).' In: Makrand Mehta, (ed.) *Urbanization in Western India: Historical Perspective.* Ahmedabad: Gujarat University. pp. 233–44.

Kanwar, Pamela (1990) *Imperial Simla: The Political Culture of the Raj.* Delhi: Oxford University Press.

Karachi under the Raj 1843–1947 (2004) 4 vols. Karachi: Pakistan Herald Publications.

Karim, Abdul (1964) *Dacca: The Mughal Capital.* Dacca: Asiatic Society of Pakistan.

Kaul, H. K., (ed.) (1985) *Historic Delhi: An Anthology.* New Delhi: Oxford University Press.

Kautilya (1992) *The Arthasastra.* L. N. Rangarajan, (ed.), tr. New Delhi: Penguin Books.

Kautilya's Arthasastra (1915) R. Shamashastri, tr. Mysore: Mysore Printing and Publishing House.

Kennedy, Dane (1996) *The Magic Mountains: Hill stations and the British Raj.* Berkeley: University of California Press.

Kenoyer, Jonathan Mark (1998) *Ancient Cities of the Indus Valley Civilization.* Karachi: Oxford University Press and American Institute of Pakistan Studies.

Kenoyer, Jonathan Mark (1991) 'The Indus Valley Tradition of Pakistan and Western India.' *Journal of World Prehistory* 5 (4): 331–85.

Kenyon, Kathleen M. (1970) *Archaeology in the Holy Land.* 3rd Edn. New York: Praeger.

Kerr, Ian J., (ed.) (2001) *Railways in Modern India.* New Delhi: Oxford University Press.

Kervran, Monique (1999) 'Multiple Ports at the Mouth of the River Indus: Barbarike, Deb, Daybul, Lahori Bandar, Diul Sinde.' In: Himanshu Prabha Ray, (ed.) *Archaeology of Seafaring: The Indian Ocean in the Ancient Period.* Delhi: Pragati Publications. pp. 70–153.

Kidambi, Prashant (2004) 'An infection of locality: Plague, pythogenesis and the poor in Bombay, c. 1896–1905.' *Urban History* 31 (2): 249–67.

Kidwai, Atiya Habeeb (1989) 'Port cities in a national system of ports and cities: A geographical analysis of India in the twentieth century.' In: Frank Broeze, (ed.) *Brides of the Sea: Port Cities of Asia in the 16ᵗʰ–20ᵗʰ Centuries*. Honolulu: University of Hawaii Press. pp. 207–22.

Kidwai, Atiya Habeeb (1991) 'Urban Atrophy in Colonial India: Some Demographic Indicators.' In: Indu Banga, (ed.) *The City in Indian History: Urban Demography, Society, and Politics*. New Delhi: Manohar; Columbia MO: South Asia Publications. pp. 149–71.

King, Anthony D. (1976) *Colonial Urban Development: Culture, Social Power, and Environment*. London and Boston: Routledge and Kegan Paul.

King, Anthony D. (1995) *The Bungalow: The Production of a Global Culture*. 2ⁿᵈ edn. Oxford and New York: Oxford University Press.

Kippen, James (1997) 'The Musical Evolution of Lucknow.' In: Violette Graff, (ed.) *Lucknow: Memories of a City*. New Delhi: Oxford University Press. pp. 181–95.

Kirkpatrick, Joanna (2003) *Transports of Delight: The Riksha Arts of Bangladesh*. Bloomington and Indianapolis: Indiana University Press.

Kling, Blair B. (1992) 'The Origin of the Managing Agency System in India.' In: Ray, Rajat, (ed.) *Entrepreneurship and Industry in India, 1800–1947*. Delhi and New York: Oxford University Press. pp. 83–98.

Koenigsberger, Otto H. (1952) 'New Towns in India.' *Town Planning Review* 23 (2): 95–132.

Kosambi, Meera (1985) 'Commerce, Conquest and the Colonial City: Role of Locational Factors in the Rise of Bombay.' *Economic and Political Weekly* 20 (1): 32–37.

Kosambi, Meera (1986) *Bombay in Transition: The Growth and Social Ecology of a Colonial City, 1880–1980*. Stockholm: Almqvist & Wiksell International.

Kosambi, Meera (1988) 'Indigenous and Colonial Development in Western Maharashtra.' In: D. W. Attwood, M. Israel, and N. K. Wagle, (eds.) *City, Countryside and Society in Maharashtra*. Toronto: Centre for South Asian Studies, University of Toronto. pp. 1–34.

Kothari, Smitu (1983) 'There's Blood on Those Matchsticks.' *Economic and Political Weekly* (July 2): 1191–1202.

Krishna Murthy, K. (1977) *Nagarjunakonda: A Cultural Study*. Delhi: Concept Publishing Company.

Kulke, Hermann (1995) 'The Early and the Imperial Kingdom: A Processural Model of Integrative State Formation in Early Medieval India.' In: Hermann Kulke, (ed.) *The State in India 1000–1700*. Delhi: Oxford University Press. pp. 233–62.

Kulke, Hermann, and Dietmar Rothermund (1986) *A History of India*. Totowa, NJ: Barnes and Noble.

Kumar, Nita (1988) *The Artisans of Banaras: Popular Culture and Identity, 1880–1986*. Princeton: Princeton University Press.

Kumar, Radha (1989) 'Family and factory: Women in the Bombay cotton textile industry, 1919–1939.' In: J. Krishnamurty, (ed.) *Women in Colonial India: Essays on Survival, Work and the State*. Delhi: Oxford University Press. pp. 133–62.

Kumar, Sunil (2002) *The Present in Delhi's Pasts*. New Delhi: Three Essays Press.

Kumar, Suresh (1986) *Social Mobility in Industrializing Society*. Jaipur: Rawat Publications.

Kundu, Nitai (2003) 'The Case of Kolkata, India.' *Understanding Slums: Case Studies for the Global Report on Human Settlements 2003*. Development Planning Unit, UN-Habitat (http://www.ucl.ac.uk/dpu-projects/Global_Report).

Lafont, Jean-Marie (2001) *Chitra: Cities and Monuments of Eighteenth-Century India from French Archives*. New Delhi: Oxford University Press.

Lal, B. B. (2002) 'Historicity of the Mahabharata and the Ramayana: What has Archaeology to Say in the Matter?' In: S. Settar and Ravi Korisettar, (eds.) *Indian Archaeology in Retrospect 4: Archaeology and Historiography: History, Theory and Method*. Manohar: Indian Council of Historical Research. pp. 29–70

Lal, Makkhan (1984) *Settlement history and rise of civilization in Ganga-Yamuna doab, from 1500 B.C. to 300 A.D.* Delhi: B.R. Publishing Corporation.

Lang, Jon, Madhavi Desai, and Miki Desai. 1997. *Architecture and Independence: The Search for Identity – India 1880 to 1980.* Delhi: Oxford University Press.

Lannoy, Richard (1999) *Benares Seen from Within*. Seattle: University of Washington Press.

Lari, Yasmeen, and Mihail D. Lari (1996) *The Dual City: Karachi During the Raj*. Karachi: Heritage Foundation and Oxford University Press.

Leestemaker, Joanne Heyink (1992) 'Women at the labor markets of Hosur.' In: J. J. F. Heins, E. N. Meijer, and K. W. Kuipers, (eds.) *Factories and Families: A Study of a Growth Pole in South India*. New Delhi: Manohar. pp. 71–88.

Leichty, Mark (2003) *Suitably Modern: Making Middle-Class Culture in a New Consumer Society*. Princeton and Oxford: Princeton University Press.

Leonard, John G. (1973) 'Urban Government Under the Raj: A Case Study of Municipal Administration in Nineteenth-Century South India.' *Modern Asian Studies* 7 (2): 227–51.

Levathes, Louise (1994) *When China Ruled the Seas: The Treasure Fleet of the Dragon Throne 1405–1433*. New York: Simon and Schuster.

Levy, Robert I. (1987) 'How the Navadurga Protect Bhaktapur: The effective meanings of a symbolic enactment.' In: Niels Gutschow and Axel Michaels, (eds.) *Heritage of the Kathmandu Valley*. Sankt Augustin: VGH Wissenschaftsverlag. pp. 105–34.

Levy, Robert I. (1990) *Mesocosm: Hinduism and the Organization of a Traditional Newar City in Nepal*. Berkeley: University of California Press.

Lewandowski, Susan J. (1977) 'Changing Form and Function in the Ceremonial and the Colonial Port City in India: An Historical Analysis of Madurai and Madras.' *Modern Asian Studies* 11 (1): 183–212.

Liscombe, Rhodri Windsor (2006) 'In-dependence: Otto Koenigsberger and modernist urban resettlement in India.' *Planning Perspectives* 21: 157–78.

Liu, Xinru (1988) *Ancient India and Ancient China: Trade and Religious Exchanges AD 1–600*. Delhi: Oxford University Press.

Llewellyn-Jones, Rosie (1985) *A Fatal Friendship: The Nawabs, the British and the City of Lucknow*. New Delhi: Oxford University Press; repr. 2001 *The Lucknow Omnibus*. New Delhi: Oxford University Press.

Llewellyn-Jones, Rosie (2006) (ed.) *Lucknow: City of Illusion*. New York: Alkazi Collection of Photography; Munich: Prestel.

Losty, J. P. (1990) *Calcutta, City of Palaces: A Survey of the City in the Days of the East India Company 1690–1858*. London: British Library and Arnold Publishers.

Lutgendorf, Philip (1991) *The Life of a Text: Performing the* Ramcaritmanas *of Tulsidas*. Berkeley: University of California Press.

Mackay, Ernest J. H. (1938) *Further Excavations at Mohenjodaro: Being an official account of Archaeological Excavations at Mohenjo-daro carried out by the Government of India between the years 1927 and 1931*. 2 vols. New Delhi: Government of India.

Malville, John McKim (2001) 'Cosmic Landscape and Urban Layout.' In: John M. Fritz and George Michell, (eds.) *New Light on Hampi: Recent Research at Vijayanagara*. Mumbai: Marg Publications. pp. 112–25.

Maria, Sajida Iqbal, and Muhammad Imran (2006) 'Planning of Islamabad and Rawalpindi: What Went Wrong?' 42nd ISoCaRP Congress, Istanbul, Turkey.

Markovits, Claude (2000) *The Global World of Indian Merchants*. Cambridge: Cambridge University Press.

Marshall, P. J. (1985) 'Eighteenth-century Calcutta.' In: Robert Ross and Gerard J. Telcamp, (eds.) *Colonial Cities: Essays on Urbanism in a Colonial Context*. Leiden: Martinus Nijhoff. pp. 87–104.

Marshall, Sir John (1915) 'Excavations at Bhita.' *Archaeological Survey of India Annual Report* 1911–12: 29–94.

Marshall, Sir John (1931) *Mohenjo-daro and the Indus Civilization*. 3 vols. London: Arthur Probsthain.

Marshall, Sir John (1951) *Taxila: An Illustrated Account of Archaeological Excavations*. 3 vols. Cambridge: University Press.

Masselos, Jim (1991) 'Appropriating urban space: social constructs of Bombay in the time of the Raj.' *South Asia* 14 (1): 33–65.

Masselos, Jim (1992) 'Changing Definitions of Bombay: City State to Capital City.' In: Indu Banga, (ed.) Ports *and Their Hinterlands in India (1700–1950)*. New Delhi: Manohar. pp. 273–316.

McCrindle, John Watson (1877) *Ancient India, as described by Megasthenes and Arrian; being a translation of the fragments of the Indika of Megasthenes collected by Dr. Schwanbeck, and of the first part of the Indika of Arrian*. Calcutta and London: Thacker, Spink and Company; repr. New Delhi: Today & Tomorrow's Printers & Publishers.

McGuire, John (1983) *The Making of a Colonial Mind: A Quantitative Study of the Bhadralok in Calcuta, 1857–1885*. Canberra: Australian National University.

Mazumdar, Ranjani (2007) *Bombay Cinema: An Archive of the City*. Minneapolis: University of Minnesota Press.

MCGB (1964) *Report on the Development Plan for Greater Bombay*. Bombay: Municipal Corporation of Greater Bombay Development Plan Committee; Government Central Press.

Meher, Rajkishor (2003) 'The social and ecological effects of industrialisation in a tribal region: The case of the Rourkela Steel Plant.' *Contributions to Indian Sociology* 37 (3): 429–457.

Mehta, R. N. (1987) 'Ahmedabad: A Topographical, Toponymical and Archaeological Perspective.' In: B. M. Pande and B. D. Chattopadhyaya, (eds.) *Archaeology and History: Essays in Memory of Shri A. Ghosh*. Delhi: Agam Kala Prakashan. pp. 363–74.

Mellaart, James (1967) *Çatal Hüyük: A Neolithic Town in Anatolia*. London: Thames and Hudson.

Menon, Meena (2007) 'Rs. 9,000-crore "slum-free" Dharavi Redevelopment Project runs into roadblock.' *The Hindu*, 6 June.

Metcalf, Thomas R. (1989) *An Imperial Vision: Indian Architecture and Britain's Raj*. New Delhi: Oxford University Press.

Michell, George (1977) *The Hindu Temple: An introduction to its meaning and forms*. Bombay: B. I. Publications; London: Paul Elek.

Michell, George, and Richard Eaton (1992) *Firuzabad: Palace City of the Deccan*. Oxford and New York: Oxford University Press.

Michell, George, and Bharath Ramamrutham (1993) *Temple Towns of Tamil Nadu*. Bombay: Marg Publications.

Michell, George, and Mark Zebrowski (1999) *Architecture and Art of the Deccan Sultanates.* New Cambridge History of India 1: 7. Cambridge: Cambridge University Press.

Mines, Mattison (1994) *Public Faces, Private Voices: Community and Individuality in South India.* Berkeley: University of California Press.

Mitra, Debala (1971) *Buddhist Monuments.* Calcutta: Sahitya Samsad.

MMRDA (1999) *Regional Plan for Mumbai Metropolitan Region 1996–2011.* Mumbai: Mumbai Metropolitan Region Development Authority.

Mohsin, K. M. (1980) 'Murshidabad in the Eighteenth Century.' In: Kenneth Ballhatchet and John Harrison, (eds.) (1980). *The City in South Asia: Pre-modern and Modern.* Collected Papers on South Asia 3. Centre of South Asian Studies, School of Oriental and African Studies, University of London. London and Dublin: Curzon Press; Atlantic Highlands NJ: Humanities Press. pp. 69–87.

Mohsin, M. (1964) *Chittaranjan: A study in urban sociology.* Bombay: Popular Prakashan.

Mokashi, D. B. (1987) *Palkhi: An Indian Pilgrimage.* Philip C. Engblom, tr. Albany: State University of New York Press.

Momin, M. (1991) 'Urbanisation in the Brahmaputra Valley circa A.D. 600–1200.' In: Jai Prakash Singh and Gautam Sengupta, (eds.) *Archaeology of North-Eastern India.* New Delhi: Vikas Publishing House. pp. 260–79.

Moosvi, Shireen (1987) *The Economy of the Mughal Empire c.1595: A Statistical Study.* Delhi: Oxford University Press.

Morris, Morris D. (1983) 'The Growth of Large-Scale Industry to 1947.' In Dharma Kumar, (ed.) *The Cambridge Economic History of India.* Vol. 2: c.1757–c.1970. Cambridge: Cambridge University Press. pp. 553–676.

Morrison, Kathleen D. (1995) *Fields of Victory: Vijayanagara and the Course of Intensification.* Berkeley: Archaeological Research Facility, University of California.

Moulik, T. K., and P. Purushotham (1982) 'The Match Industry in Sivakasi: A Case Study of Technology, Working Conditions and Self-Employment.' *Economic and Political Weekly, Review of Management* (May): 43–53.

Mughal, Mohammad Rafique (1992) 'Early Muslim Cities in Sindh and Patterns of International Trade.' *Islamic Studies* 31 (2): 267–86.

Mughal, Mohammad Rafique (1997) *Ancient Cholistan: Archaeology and Architecture.* Rawalpindi, Lahore, and Karachi: Ferozsons Private Limited.

Mukherjee, S. (2002) 'Urbanization and Migration in India: A Different Scene.' In: H. S. Geyer, (ed.) *International Handbook of Urban Systems: Studies of Urbanization and Migration in Advanced and Developing Countries.* Cheltenham and Northampton MA: Edward Elgar. pp. 525–59.

Mukhopadhyay, Tapati (2001) *Shanghai and Mumbai: Sustainability of Development in a Globalizing World.* New Delhi: Samskriti.

Murcott, Susan (1992) *The First Buddhist Women.* Berkeley: Parallax Press.

Murphy, Rhoads (1997) 'Colombo and the Re-making of Ceylon: A Prototype of Colonial Asian Port Cities.' In: Frank Broeze, (ed.) *Gateways of Asia: Port Cities of Asia in the $13^{th}-20^{th}$ Centuries.* London and New York: Kegan Paul International. pp. 191–210.

Naim, C. M., and Carla Petievich (1997) 'Urdu in Lucknow / Lucknow in Urdu.' In: Violette Graff, (ed.) *Lucknow: Memories of a City.* New Delhi: Oxford University Press. pp. 165–80.

Nair, Janaki (2005) *The Promise of the Metropolis: Bangalore's Twentieth Century.* New Delhi: Oxford University Press.

Nandy, Ashis (1983) *The Intimate Enemy: Loss and Recovery of Self Under Colonialism*. Delhi: Oxford University Press.

Naqvi, Hamida Khatoon (1972) *Urbanisation and Urban Centres under the Great Mughals 1556–1707*. Simla: Indian Institute of Advanced Study

Naqvi, Hamida Khatoon (1974) *Mughal Hindustan: Cities and Industries 1556–1803*. 2nd edn. Karachi: National Book Foundation.

Naqvi, Hamida Khatoon (1986) *Agricultural, Industrial and Urban Dynamism under the Sultans of Delhi 1206–1555*. New Delhi: Munshiram Manoharlal.

National Highways Authority of India (2007) http://www.nhai.org.

Nazir Akbarabadi (1984) 'The Vile World Carnival: A Shahr-Ashob.' Shamsur Rahman Faruqi and Frances W. Pritchett, tr. *Annual of Urdu Studies* 4: 25–35 (http://www.columbia.edu/itc/ mealac/pritchett/00fwp/published/txt_nazir_carnival. html).

Neild, Susan M. (1979) 'Colonial Urbanism: The Development of Madras City in the Eighteenth and Nineteenth Centuries.' *Modern Asian Studies* 13 (2): 217–46.

Nijman, Jan (2006) 'Mumbai's Mysterious Middle Class.' *International Journal of Urban and Regional Research* 30 (4): 758–75.

Nilsson, Sten (1973) *The New Capitals of India, Pakistan and Bangladesh*. Scandinavian Institute of Asian Studies Monograph 12. London: Curzon Press.

Oldenburg, Veena Talwar (1984) *The Making of Colonial Lucknow 1856–1877*. repr. *The Lucknow Omnibus*. New Delhi: Oxford University Press.

Orr, Leslie (2000) *Donors, Devotees, and Daughters of God: Temple Women in Medieval Tamilnadu*. New York and Oxford: Oxford University Press.

Pandya, D. G. (1999) *Pattern of Urban Settlements in Gujarat*. Ahmedabad: Karnavati Publications.

Panini, M. N. (1978) 'Networks and styles: Industrial entrepreneurs in Faridabad.' In: Satish Saberwal, (ed.) *Process and Institution in Urban India: Sociological Studies*. New Delhi: Vikas Publishing House. pp. 91–115.

Parasher, Aloka (1991) 'Social Structure and Economy of Settlements in the Central Deccan (200 B.C–A.D. 200).' In: Indu Banga, (ed.) *The City in Indian History: Urban Demography, Society, and Politics*. Columbia, MO: South Asia Publications; New Delhi: Manohar. pp. 19–46.

Parasher, Aloka (1992) 'Nature of society and civilisation in early Deccan.' *Indian Economic and Social History Review* 29 (4): 437–77.

Pearson, M. N. (1976) *Merchants and Rulers in Gujarat: The Response to the Portuguese in the Sixteenth Century*. Berkeley: University of California Press.

Pearson, M. N. (1987a) 'India and the Indian Ocean in the Sixteenth Century.' In: Ashin Das Gupta and M. N. Pearson, (eds.) *India and the Indian Ocean 1500–1800*. Calcutta: Oxford University Press. pp. 71–93.

Pearson, M. N. (1987b) *The Portuguese in India*. New Cambridge History of India 1.1. Cambridge: Cambridge University Press.

Pearson, M. N. (2003) *The Indian Ocean*. London and New York: Routledge.

Perera, Nihal (1999) *Decolonizing Ceylon: Colonialism, Nationalism, and the Politics of Space in Sri Lanka*. New Delhi: Oxford University Press.

Perlin, Frank (1993) *'The Invisible City: Monetary, Administrative and Popular Infrastructures in Asia and Europe, 1500–1900.'* Aldershot, Hampshire, and Brookfield VT: Variorum.

Pethe, Vasant P. (1988) 'Factors in Demographic-economic Evolution of a City of Maharashtra: A Case Study of Sholapur City.' In: Makrand Mehta, (ed.)

Urbanization in Western India: Historical Perspective. Ahmedabad: Gujarat University. pp. 337–51.

Petievich, Carla R. (1990) 'Poetry of the Declining Mughals: The *Shahr Ashob*.' *Journal of South Asian* Literature 25 (1): 99–110.

Pinney, Christopher (2004) *'Photos of the Gods': The Printed Image and Political Struggle in India*. London: Reaktion Books.

Pithampur Auto Cluster (2007) http://222.pautocluster.com.

Possehl, Gregory L., (ed.) (1999) *Indus Age: The Beginnings*. Philadelphia: University of Pennsylvania Press.

Possehl, Gregory L. (2002) *The Indus Civilization: A Contemporary Perspective*. Walnut Creek CA: AltaMira Press.

Prakash, Om (1998) *European commercial enterprise in pre-colonial India*. New Cambridge History of India 2.5. Cambridge: Cambridge University Press.

Prakash, Vikramaditya (2002) *Chandigarh's Le Corbusier: The Struggle for Modernity in Postcolonial India*. Seattle and London: University of Washington Press.

Prasad, Kameshwar (1984) *Cities, Crafts and Commerce under the Kusanas*. Delhi: Agam Kala Prakashan.

Prasad, Om Prakash (1989) *Decay and Revival of Urban Centres in Medieval South India (c.A.D. 600–1200)*. New Delhi: Commonwealth Publishers.

Punwani, Jyoti (2003) ' "My Area, Your Area": How Riots Changed the City.' In: Sujata Patel and Jim Masselos, (eds.) *Bombay and Mumbai: The City in Transition*. New Delhi: Oxford University Press. pp. 235–64.

Qadeer, Mohammad A. (1983) *Lahore: Urban Development in the Third World*. Lahore: Vanguard Books.

Quddus, Munir, and Salim Rashid (2000) *Entrepreneurs and Economic Development: The Remarkable Story of Garment Exports from Bangladesh*. Dhaka: University Press Limited.

Quraeshi, Samina (1988) *Lahore: The City Within*. Singapore: Concept Media.

Rajadhyaksha, Ashish, and Paul Willemen (1994) *Encyclopaedia of Indian Cinema*. New Delhi: Oxford University Press.

Rajan, K. (1996) 'Early Maritime Activities of the Tamils.' In: Himanshu Prabha Ray and Jean-François Salles, (eds.) *Tradition and Archaeology: Early Maritime Contacts in the Indian Ocean*. New Delhi: Manohar. pp. 97–108.

Rajasekhara, S. (1985) *Early Chalukya Art at Aihole*. New Delhi: Vikas Publishing House.

Ramachandran, R. (1989) *Urbanization and Urban Systems in India*. New Delhi: Oxford University Press.

Ramachandran, Sudha (2005) 'China's Pearl in Pakistan's Waters.' *Asia Times Online*, March 4.

Ramaswamy, Sumathi (2004) *The Lost Land of Lemuria: Fabulous Geographies, Catastrophic Histories*. Berkeley, Los Angeles and London: University of California Press.

Ramaswamy, Vijaya (1993) 'Craft Work & Wages in Medieval Tamilnadu (based on inscriptions from the 8th to 13th century).' In: Narayani Gupta, (ed.) *Craftsmen and Merchants: Essays in South Indian Urbanism*. Chandigarh: Urban History Association of India. pp. 27–42.

Rao, Purnachandra, (ed.) (1989) 'Special Report on Hyderabad City.' In: *Census of India 1981*, part X-E, Series 2, Andhra Pradesh. Hyderabad: Controller of Publications.

Rau, Wilhelm (1973) *The Meaning of pur in Vedic Literature*. Abhandlungen der Marburger Gelehrten Gesellschaft 1. Munich: Wilhelm Fink Verlag.

Raval, R. L. (1988) 'Growth of Port Mandvi (Kutch) as an Urban Centre (1750–1850).' In: Makrand Mehta, (ed.) *Urbanization in Western India: Historical Perspective*. Ahmedabad: Gujarat University. pp. 97–108.

Ray, Haraprasad (1987) 'China and the "Western Ocean" in the Fifteenth Century.' In: Satish Chandra, ed. *The Indian Ocean: Explorations in History, Commerce and Politics*. New Delhi, Newbury Park and London: Sage Publications. pp. 109–24.

Ray, Himanshu Prabha (1986) *Monastery and Guild: Commerce under the Satavahanas*. Delhi: Oxford University Press.

Ray, Himanshu Prabha (1995) 'Trade and Contacts.' In: Romila Thapar, (ed.) *Recent Prespectives of Early Indian History*. Bombay: Popular Prakashan. pp. 142–75.

Ray, Pranabranjan (1974) 'Urbanization in Colonial Situation: Serampore.' In: M. S. A. Rao, (ed.) *Urban Sociology in India: Reader and Source Book*. New Delhi: Orient Longman. pp. 115–49.

Ray, Rajat Kanta (1979) *Urban Roots of Indian Nationalism: Pressure Groups and Conflict of Interests in Calcutta City Politics, 1875–1939*. New Delhi: Vikas.

Ray, Rajat Kanta (1984) 'The Bazar: Indigenous Sector of the Indian Economy.' In: Dwijendra Tripathi, (ed.) *Business Communities of India: A Historical Perspective*. New Delhi: Manohar. pp. 241–68.

Ray, Rajat Kanta (1992) 'Calcutta or Alinagar: Contending Conceptions in the Mughal-English Confrontation of 1756–1757.' In: Indu Banga, (ed.) *Ports and Their Hinterlands in India (1700–1950)*. New Delhi: Manohar. pp. 45–61.

Ray, Rajat Kanta (1995) 'Asian Capital in the Age of European Domination: The Rise of the Bazaar, 1800–1914.' *Modern Asian Studies* 29 (3): 449–554.

Rehman, Abdul, and James L. Wescoat, Jr. (1993) *Pivot of the Punjab: The Historical Geography of Medieval Gujrat*. Lahore: Dost Associates Publishers.

Richards, John F. (1975) *Mughal Administration in Golconda*. Oxford: Clarendon Press.

Richards, John F. (1993) *The Mughal Empire*. New Cambridge History of India, 1.5. Cambridge and New York: Cambridge University Press.

Ring, Laura A. (2006) *Zenana: Everyday Peace in a Karachi Apartment Building*. Bloomington and Indianapolis: University of Indiana Press.

Roberts, Michael (1989) 'The two faces of the port city: Colombo in modern times.' In: Frank Broeze, (ed.) *Brides of the Sea: Port Cities of Asia from the 16th–20th Centuries*. Honolulu: University of Hawaii Press. pp. 173–87.

Robson, David (2002) *Geoffrey Bawa: The Complete Works*. London: Thames and Hudson.

Rossa, Walter (1997) Indo-Portuguese Cities: A contribution to the study of Portuguese urbanism in the Western Hindustan. Lisbon: Commisão Nacional para as Comemorações dos Descobrimentos Portugueses.

Rotzer, Klaus (1984) 'Bijapur: Alimentation en eau d'une ville Musalmane du Dekkan auxXVIe-XVIIe siècles.' *Bulletin de l'École Française d'Extrême-Orient* 73: 125–96.

Roy, U. N. (2000) 'Problem of Urban Decline in the Gupta Age (c. A.D. 300–600): A Fresh Investigation.' In: S. C. Bhattacharya, V. D. Misra, J. N. Pandey, and J. N. Pal, (eds.) *Peeping through the Past: Prof. G. R. Sharma Memorial Volume*. Allahabad: Department of Ancient History, Culture & Archaeology, University of Allahabad. pp. 213–34.

Sachdev, Vibhuti, and Giles Tillotson (2002) *Building Jaipur: The Making of an Indian City*. London: Reaktion Books.

Sahai, Jugendra (1980) *Urban Complex of an Industrial City*. Allahabad: Chugh Publications.

Saheb, S. A. A. (1998) 'A "Festival of Flags": Hindu-Muslim devotion and the sacralising of localism at the shrine of Nagore-e-Sharif in Tamil Nadu.' In: Pnina Werbner and Helene Basu, (eds.) *Embodying Charisma: Modernity, locality and the performance of emotion in Sufi cults*. London and New York: Routledge. pp. 55–76.

Sarao, K. T. S. (1990) *Urban Centres and Urbanisation as reflected in the Pali Vinaya and Sutta Pitakas*. Delhi: Vidyanidhi.

Sarin, Madhu (1982) *Urban Planning in the Third World: The Chandigarh Experience*. London: Mansell Publishing Limited.

Sarkar, H. (1987) 'Emergence of Urban Centres in Early Historical Andhradesa.' In: B. M. Pande and B. D. Chattopadhyaya, (eds.) *Archaeology and History*. Delhi: Agam Kala Prakashan. pp. 631–42.

Sarkar, H., and Misra, B. N. (1972) *Nagarjunakonda*. New Delhi: Archaeological Survey of India.

Sarkar, Sumit (1997) *Writing Social History*. Delhi: Oxford University Press.

Sarkar, Sumit (2002) *Beyond Nationalist Frames: Relocating Postmodernism, Hindutva, History*. Delhi: Permanent Black.

Sassen, Saskia (1991) *The Global City: New York, London, Tokyo*. Princeton: Princeton University Press.

Sato, Masanori (1997) 'The Formative process of Towns and Market Towns/Villages in south-eastern Rajasthan, 1650–1850 A.D.' In: Masanori Sato and B. L. Bhadani, *Economy and Polity of Rajasthan: Study of Kota and Marwar (17th–19th centuries)*. Jaipur: Publication Scheme. pp. 57–86.

Schenk, Hans (1997) 'Alleppey: From a Port without a City to a City without a Port.' In: Frank Broeze, (ed.) *Gateways of Asia: Port Cities of Asia in the 13th–20th Centuries*. London and New York: Kegan Paul International. pp. 294–317.

Schnepel, Burkhard (2002) *The Jungle Kings: Ethnohistorical Aspects of Politics and Ritual in Orissa*. New Delhi: Manohar.

Selvadurai, Shyam (1999) *Cinnamon Gardens*. New York: Hyperion.

Sen, Samita (1999) *Women and Labour in Late Colonial India: The Bengal Jute Industry*. Cambridge: Cambridge University Press.

Seneviratna, Anuradha (1994) *Ancient Anuradhapura: The Monastic City*. Colombo: Archaeological Survey Department.

Sengupta, Gautam (1996) 'Archaeology of Coastal Bengal.' In: Himanshu Prabha Ray and Jean-François Salles, (eds.) *Tradition and Archaeology: Early Maritime Contacts in the Indian Ocean*. New Delhi: Manohar. pp. 115–27.

Sewell, Robert (1962) *A Forgotten Empire: Vijayanagara*. Repr. New Delhi: National Book Trust.

Seymour, Susan, (ed.) (1980) *The Transformation of a Sacred Town: Bhubaneswar, India*. Boulder CO: Westview Press.

Shaffer, Jim G. (1993) 'Reurbanization: The Eastern Punjab and Beyond.' In: Howard Spodek and Doris Meth Srinivasan, (eds.) *Urban Form and Meaning in South Asia: The Shaping of Cities from Prehistoric to Precolonial Times*. Washington DC: National Gallery of Art. pp. 53–67.

Shanmugam, P. (2000) 'A City in Transition: Early Medieval Kanchipuram.' In: K. Damodaran, (ed.) *Tamilnadu: Archaeological Perspective*. Chennai: Department of Archaeology, Government of Tamilnadu. pp. 8–33.

Sharar, Abdul Halim (2001) *Lucknow: The Last Phase of an Oriental Culture*. Tr. E. S. Harcourt and Fakhir Hussain. London: Elek. repr. *The Lucknow Omnibus*. New Delhi: Oxford University Press.

Sharma, G. D. (1984) 'The Marwaris: Economic Foundations of an Indian Capitalist Class.'
In: Dwijendra Tripathi, (ed.) *Business Communities of India: A Historical Perspective.*
New Delhi: Manohar. pp. 185–207.

Sharma, G. R. (1969) *The Excavations at Kausambi 1957–59.* Delhi: Manager of
Publications.

Sharma, Kalpana (2000) *Rediscovering Dharavi: Stories from Asia's Largest Slum.*
New Delhi: Penguin Books.

Sharma, Ram Sharan (1965) *Indian Feudalism: c. 300–1200.* Calcutta: University of
Calcutta.

Sharma, Ram Sharan (1987) *Urban Decay in India (c. A.D. 300–c. 1000).* New Delhi:
Munshiram Manoharlal.

Sharma, Ram Sharan (2001) *Early Medieval Indian Society: A Study in Feudalisation.*
Hyderabad: Orient Longman.

Sharma, Sunil (2004) 'The City of Beauties in Indo-Persian Poetic Landscape.' *Comparative
Studies of South Asia, Africa and the Middle East* 24 (2): 73–81.

Shaw, Annapurna (2004) *The Making of Navi Mumbai.* New Delhi: Orient Longman.

Shokoohy, Mehrdad, and Natalie H. Shokoohy (1994) 'Tughluqabad, the earliest surviving
town of the Delhi sultanate.' *Bulletin of the School of Oriental and African Studies* 57 (3):
516–50.

Siddiqi, Hafiz G. A. (2004) *The Readymade Garment Industry of Bangladesh.* Dhaka:
University Press Limited.

Siddiqui, Iqtidar Husain (1989) 'The Early Chishti Dargahs.' In: Christian W. Troll, (ed.)
Muslim Shrines in India: Their Character, History and Significance. New Delhi: Oxford
University Press. pp. 1–23.

Sidhu, S. S. (1983) *The Steel Industry of India: Problems and Perspective.* New Delhi:
Vikas Publishing House.

'Singapore Port remains world's busiest by shipping tonnage' (2006) *Asian Economic
Times*, January 17

Singh, M. P. (1985) *Town, Market, Mint and Port in the Mughal Empire (1556–1707).*
New Delhi: Adam Publishers and Distributors.

Singh, R. L. (1955) *Banaras: A Study in Urban Geography.* Banaras: Nand Kishore and
Brothers.

Singh, Rana P. B., (ed.) (1993) *Banaras (Varanasi): Cosmic Order, Sacred City, Hindu
Traditions.* Varanasi: Tara Book Agency

Singh, S. N. (1990) *Planning and Development of An Industrial Town* (A Study of Kanpur).
New Delhi: Mittal Publications.

Singh, Upinder (1999) *Ancient Delhi.* New Delhi: Oxford University Press.

Singh, Upinder (2004) 'Cults and shrines in early historical Mathura (c. 200 BC–AD 200).'
World Archaeology 36 (3): 378–98.

Sinha, Pradip (1978) *Calcutta in Urban History.* Calcutta: Firma KLM Private
Limited.

Sinha, Sutapa (2002) 'Archaeology of the Medieval City of Gaur.' In: Gautam Sengupta and
Sheena Panja, (eds.) *Archaeology of Eastern India: New perspectives.* Kolkata: Centre
for Archaeological Studies and Training, Eastern India. pp. 331–62.

Sivaramakrishnan, K. C. (1982) 'Durgapur: Case Study of an Indian Steel Town.'
In: John L. Taylor and David G. Williams, (eds.) *Urban Planning Practice in Developing
Countries.* Oxford: Pergamon Press. pp. 144–59.

Slusser, Mary Shepherd (1982) *Nepal Mandala: A Cultural Study of the Kathmandu Valley.*
2 vols. Princeton: Princeton University Press.

Smith, Monica L. (2006) 'The Archaeology of South Asian Cities.' *Journal of Archaeological Research* 14: 97–142.

Sreemani, Soumitra (1994) *Anatomy of a Colonial Town: Calcutta, 1756–1794.* Calcutta: Firma KLM Private Limited.

Srinivas, Smriti (2001) *Landscapes of Urban Memory: The Sacred and the Civic in India's High-Tech City.* Minneapolis: University of Minnesota Press.

Srinivas, Smriti (2008) *In the Presence of Sai Baba: Body, City and Memory in a Global Religious Movement.* Boston and Leiden: Brill; Hyderabad: Orient Longman.

Srinivasan, Doris Meth, (ed.) (1989) *Mathura: The Cultural Heritage.* New Delhi: American Institute of Indian Studies.

Srinivasan, N. R. (1988) *Ripples: Socio economic impact of Bhilai.* Bhilai: Bhilai Steel Plant, Steel Authority of India Limited.

Stein, Burton (1980) *Peasant State and Society in Medieval South India.* Delhi and New York: Oxford University Press.

Study Group for Greater Bombay (1959) *Reports of the Panels Appointed by the Study Group for Greater Bombay.* Bombay: Government Central Press.

Subrahmanyam, Sanjay (1990a) *The Political Economy of Commerce: Southern India 1500–1650.* Cambridge: Cambridge University Press.

Subrahmanyam, Sanjay (1990b) *Improvising Empire: Portuguese Trade and Settlement in the Bay of Bengal 1500–1700.* Delhi: Oxford University Press.

Subrahmanyam, Sanjay (1993) 'The Port City of Masulipatnam, 1550–1750: A Bird's Eye View.' In: Narayani Gupta, (ed.) *Craftsmen and Merchants: Essays in South Indian Urbanism.* Chandigarh: Urban History Association of India. pp. 47–74.

Subramanian, Lakshmi (1996) *Indigenous Capital and Imperial Expansion: Bombay, Surat, and the West Coast.* New Delhi: Oxford University Press.

Talbot, Ian (2006) *Divided Cities: Partition and Its Aftermath in Lahore and Amritsar, 1947–1957.* Karachi: Oxford University Press.

Tampoe, Moira (1989) *Maritime Trade between China and the West: An Archaeological Study of the Ceramics from Siraf (Persian Gulf), 8th to 15th centuries A.D.* BAR International Series 555. Oxford: B.A.R.

Tan, Tai Yong, and Gyanesh Kudaisya (2000) *The Aftermath of Partition in South Asia.* London and New York: Routledge.

Tanabe, Akio (1999) 'Kingship, Community and Commerce in Late Pre-Colonial Khurda.' In: Noboru Karashima, (ed.) *Kingship in Indian History.* New Delhi: Manohar: 195–236.

Thakur, Raj Nath (1985) *Micro-regional Central Place System in India (A Case Study of the Siwan Region).* New Delhi: Inter-India Publications.

Thakur, Vijay Kumar (1981) *Urbanisation in Ancient India.* New Delhi: Abhinav Publications.

Thakur, Vijay Kumar (2000) 'Urban Centers in Early Medieval Bengal: An Archaeological Perspective.' In: S. C. Bhattacharya, V. D. Misra, J. N. Pandey, and J. N. Pal, (eds.) *Peeping through the Past: Prof. G. R. Sharma Memorial Volume.* Allahabad: Department of Ancient History, Culture & Archaeology, University of Allahabad. pp. 270–78.

Thakur, Vijay Kumar, and Kalpana Jha (1994) 'Towns and Trade in the *Samaraichchakaha*: Text and Context.' In: N. N. Bhattacharyya, (ed.) *Jainism and Prakrit in Ancient and Medieval India.* New Delhi: Manohar. pp. 295–324.

Thakur, Renu (1994) 'Urban hierarchies, typologies and classification in early medieval India: c. 750–1200.' *Urban History* 21 (1): 61–76.

Thankappan Nair, P. (1989) *Calcutta in the 19th century: Company's days.* Calcutta: Firma KLM.

Thapar, Romila (1984) *From lineage to state: Social formations in the mid-first millennium B.C. in the Ganga Valley*. Bombay: Oxford University Press.

Thapar, Romila (1997) 'Early Mediterranean Contacts with India: An Overview.' In: F. De Romanis and A. Tchernia, (eds.) *Crossings: Early Mediterranean Contacts with India*. New Delhi: Manohar. pp. 11–40.

Thapar, Romila (2002) *The Penguin History of Early India: From the Origins to AD 1300*. New Delhi: Penguin Books.

Thorner, Daniel (2001) 'The Pattern of Railway Development in India.' In: Ian J. Kerr, (ed.) *Railways in Modern India*. New Delhi: Oxford University Press. pp. 80–96.

Tillotson, G. H. R. (1987) *The Rajput Palaces: The Development of an Architectural Style, 1450–1750*. New Haven and London: Yale University Press.

Tillotson, Sarah (1994) *Indian Mansions: A Social History of the Haveli*. Cambridge: Oleander Press.

Timberg, Thomas A. (1978) *The Marwaris: From Traders to Industrialists*. New Delhi: Vikas Publishing House.

Tinker, Hugh (1954) *The Foundations of Local Self-Government in India, Pakistan and Burma*. London: University of London, the Athlone Press.

Tosi, Maurizio (1991) 'The Indus Civilization beyond the Indian Subcontinent.' In: Michael Jansen, Maire Mulloy and Gunter Urban, (eds.) *Forgotten Cities on the Indus: Early Civilization in Pakistan from the 8th to the 2nd Millennium BC*. Mainz: Verlag Philipp von Zabern. pp. 11–128.

Turner, Paula J. (1989) *Roman Coins from India*. London: Royal Numismatic Society.

Tyrwhitt, Jaqueline, (ed.) (1947) *Patrick Geddes in India*. London: Lund Humphries.

Umar, Muhammad (2001) *Urban Culture in Northern India during the Eighteenth Century*. New Delhi: Munshiram Manoharlal.

UN-Habitat (2003) *Slums of the World: The face of urban poverty in the new millennium?* Nairobi: United Nations Human Settlements Programme.

UN-Habitat (2005) *Financing Human Shelter: Global Report on Human Settlements 2005*. London: Earthscan; Nairobi: United Nations Human Settlements Programme.

UN-Habitat (2006) *State of the World's Cities Report 2006/7*. London: Earthscan; Nairobi: United Nations Human Settlements Programme.

UNICEF (2006) *The State of the World's Children 2007*. New York: United Nations Children's Fund.

United Nations (2005) *World Urbanization Prospects: The 2005 Revision*. New York: United Nations Department of Economic and Social Affairs, Population Division.

Van Wersch, H. (1992) *The Bombay Textile Strike, 1982–83*. Delhi: Oxford University Press.

Varady, Robert G. (2001) 'Modern Agents of Change.' In: Ian J. Kerr, (ed.) *Railways in Modern India*. New Delhi: Oxford University Press. pp. 257–61.

Vatsyayana Mallanaga (2002) *Kamasutra*. Wendy Doniger and Sudhir Kakar, tr. Oxford: Oxford University Press.

Verghese, Anila (2004) 'Deities, cults and kings at Vijayanagara.' *World Archaeology* 36 (3): 416–31.

Verma, H. C. (1986) *Dynamics of Urban Life in Pre-Mughal India*. New Delhi: Munshiram Manoharlal.

Verma, H. S. (1985) *Bombay, New Bombay and Metropolitan Region: Growth Process and Planning Lessons*. New Delhi: Concept Publishers.

Vincent, Rose, (ed.) (1992) *Pondichéry, 1674–1761: L'échec d'un rêve d'empire*. Série Memoires 24. Paris: Éditions Autrement.

Visaria, Leela, and Pravin Visaria (1983) 'Population 1757–1947.' In: Dharma Kumar and Tapan Raychaudhuri,(eds.) *The Cambridge Economic History of India* 2. Cambridge: Cambridge University Press.

Volwahsen, Andreas (2002) *Imperial Delhi: The British Capital of the Indian Empire.* Munich, Berlin, London and New York: Prestel.

Vora, Rajendra, and Suhas Palshikar (2003) 'Politics of Locality, Community, and Marginalization.' In: Sujata Patel and Jim Masselos, (eds.) *Bombay and Mumbai: The City in Transition.* New Delhi: Oxford University Press. pp. 161–82.

Wagle, Narendra K. (1995) *Society at the Time of the Buddha.* 2nd rev. edn. Bombay: Popular Prakashan.

Wagoner, Phillip B. (1993) *Tidings of the King: A Translation and Ethnohistorical Analysis of the Rayavacakamu.* Honolulu: University of Hawaii Press.

Wagoner, Phillip B. (1996) 'From "Pampa's Crossing" to "The Place of Lord Virupaksha:" Architecture, Cult, and Patronage at Hampi before the Founding of Vijayanagara.' In: D. Devaraj and C. S. Pahl, (eds.) *Vijayanagara: Progress of Research 1989–91.* Mysore: Directorate of Archaeology and Museums. pp. 141–74.

Wagoner, Phillip B. (2001) 'Architecture and Royal Authority under the Early Sangamas.' In: John M. Fritz and George Michell, (eds.) *New Light on Hampi: Recent Research at Vijayanagara.* Mumbai: Marg Publications. pp. 12–23

Walcott, Susan M., and James Heitzman (2006) 'High Technology Clusters in India and China: Divergent Paths.' *Indian Journal of Economics and Business*, Special Issue on India and China: 113–30.

Wallerstein, Immannuel (1974) *The Modern World System.* New York: Academic Press.

Wallerstein, Immannuel (2004) *World-system Analysis: An Introduction.* Durham: Duke University Press.

Warriar, E. K. (1985) *The Match Industry in Sivakasi, Sattur: Towards Removal of Child Labour. Report of a study presented to the Ministry of Labour, Government of India.* Madras: Madras Institute of Development Studies.

Waseem, Mohammad (1990) 'Urban Growth and Political Change at the Local Level: The Case of Faisabad City, 1947–75.' In: Akbar S. Ahmed, (ed.) *Pakistan: The Social Sciences' Perspective.* Karachi: Oxford University Press. pp. 207–28.

Watt, Carey Anthony (2005) *Serving the Nation: Cultures of Service, Association, and Citizenship.* New Delhi: Oxford University Press.

Watters, Thomas (1904–5) *On Yuan Chwang's Travels in India, 629–645 A.D.* 2 vols. London: Royal Asiatic Society.

Weber, Steven A., and William R. Belcher, ed. (2003) *Indus Ethnobiology: New Perspectives from the Field.* Lanham: Lexington Books.

Weisshaar, H. J., H. Roth, and W. Wijeyapala, (eds.) (2001) *Ancient Ruhuna: Sri Lankan-German Archaeological Project in the Southern Province* 1. Kommission fur Allgemeine und Vergleichende Archäologie des Deutschen Archäologischen Instituts, Bonn, Materialien zur Allgemeinen und Vergleichenden Archäologie 58. Mainz am Rhein: Verlag Philipp von Zabern.

Wiest, Raymond, and Helal Mohiuddin (2003) 'Shifting Social Relations and Cultural Change in the Livelihood Strategies of Women Garment Workers of Bangladesh.' In: Matiur Rahman, ed. *Globalisation, Environmental Crisis and Social Change in Bangladesh.* Dhaka: The University Press Limited. pp. 209–243.

Wiest, Raymond, Amana Khatun, and Helal Mohiuddin (2003) 'Workplace, Residence and Relationships among Garment Workers in the Globalising Export Economy of

Bangladesh.' In: Matiur Rahman, (ed.) *Globalisation, Environmental Crisis and Social Change in Bangladesh*. Dhaka: The University Press Limited. pp. 165–208.

Wheatley, Paul (1971) *The Pivot of the Four Quarters: A Preliminary Enquiry into the Origins and Character of the Ancient Chinese City*. Chicago: Aldine Publishing Company.

Wheeler, Sir Mortimer (1968) *The Indus Civilization*. 3rd edn. Cambridge: Cambridge University Press.

Whitehouse, David (1996) 'Sasanian maritime activity.' In: Julian Reade, (ed.) *The Indian Ocean in Antiquity*. London and New York: Kegan Paul International and The British Museum.

Winius, George D., and Marcus P. M. Wink (1991) *The Merchant-Warrior Pacified: The VOC (The Dutch East India Company) and its Changing Political Economy in India*. Delhi: Oxford University Press.

Wink, André (1990) *Al-Hind: The Making of the Indo-Islamic World 1: Early Medieval India and the Expansion of Islam, 7th–11th Centuries*. Leiden: E. J. Brill.

World Bank (2005) *World Development Report 2006: Equity and Development*. New York: World Bank and Oxford University Press.

World Gazetter (2007) http://www.worldgazetteer.com.

Xavier, A. Joseph, and G. Yogeswaran (2005) 'Thiru. P. Ayya Nadar: A Forerunner.' *100th Year Celebrations of Shri. P. Ayya Nadar, the Architect of Modern Sivakasi 1905–2005*. Sivakasi: Ayya Nadar Janaki Ammal College. pp. 177–80.

Yadava, B. N. S. (2001) 'Chivalry and Warfare.' In: Jos J. L. Gommans and Dirk H. A. Kolff, (ed.) *Warfare and Weaponry in South Asia 1000–1800*. New Delhi: Oxford University Press. pp. 66–98.

Yalland, Zoe (1987) *Traders and Nabobs: The British in Cawnpore 1765–1857*. Wilton, Salisbury, Wiltshire: Michael Russel.

Yang, Anand (1998) *Bazaar India: Markets, Society, and the Colonial State in Bihar*. Berkeley: University of California Press.

Index